CW00347623

The
Economist
Guide

ITALY

The
Economist
Guide

ITALY

Hutchinson

Published in Great Britain by
Hutchinson Business Books Limited
An imprint of Century Hutchinson
Limited
20 Vauxhall Bridge Road, London
SW1V 2SA

The publishers welcome corrections
and suggestions from business
travellers; please write to
The Editor,
The Economist Guides,
Axe and Bottle Court,
70 Newcomen Street,
LONDON SE1 1YT

Series Editor Stephen Brough
Assistant Series Editor Brigid Avison
Editors Jane Carroll (*overview*); Moira
Johnston (*travel*)
Designer Alistair Plumb
Editorial Assistants Mary Pickles,
Bettina Whilems
Design Assistant Alison Donovan
Production Controller Shona Burns
Indexer Fiona Barr

Contributors *Overview* George
Armstrong, John Earle, Antonio
Manca Graziadei, James Hansen,
David Lane, Nial McGinley, Martin
Rhodes, Clare Royce; *travel* Frances
Roxburgh, Paul Holberton, Susie
Boulton

Acknowledgements and thanks are
also due to Burton Anderson, Niccolo
Caderni, Patricia Carruthers, Elido
Fazi, Georgina Gordon-Ham,
Massimo Mondani and Tony Robbins

First published in Great Britain 1990

**British Library Cataloguing in
Publication Data**

Italy.- (The Economist guides).
1. Italy - Visitors' guides
914.5'04928

ISBN 0-09-174342-7

Maps and diagrams by Oxford
Illustrators, Oxford, England
Typeset by Tradespools, Frome,
England
Printed in Italy by Arnoldo
Mondadori, Verona

Contents

Glossary

azioni shares

BNL Banca Nazionale del Lavoro

Borsa Stock Exchange

bustarella (literally, small envelope) a "backhander"

CAP Common Agricultural Policy of the EC

clientelismo political patronage

Comecon Council for Mutual Economic Assistance, the Communist bloc economic and trade cooperation organization

Confindustria Confederazione Generale dell'Industria Italiana, the Italian employers' organization

DC Democrazia Cristiana, the Christian Democrat party

Democristiani The Christian Democrats

EC European Community. The European Economic Community (EEC) came into being on January 1 1958. Its aim was to create a Common Market and to harmonize members' economic policies. Members are Belgium, Denmark, France, Greece, Ireland, Italy, Luxembourg, the Netherlands, Portugal, Spain, the UK and West Germany. The EEC, Euratom and the European Coal and Steel Community are increasingly being regarded as a single entity, referred to as the EC

EFIM Ente Partecipazioni e Finanziamento Industria Manifatturiera. State-owned agency which controls numerous companies, mostly in the industrial sector

EMS European Monetary System which came into force in March 1979; its aim is to create monetary stability in Europe through an exchange rate mechanism which allows member currencies a fluctuation margin against a central rate

ENEL Ente Nazionale per l'Energia Elettrica, the state-owned company responsible for generating and distributing electricity

ENI Ente Nazionale Idrocarburi, the state-owned energy corporation which controls many companies, not all in the energy sector

GDP Gross Domestic Product. The best measure of a country's economic performance, GDP is the total value of a country's annual output of goods and services. Normally valued at market prices, it can be calculated at factor cost, by subtracting indirect taxes and adding subsidies

GNP Gross National Product. A country's GDP plus residents' income from investments abroad minus income accruing to nonresidents from investments in the country

ICE Istituto Nazionale per il Commercio Estero, the national institute for foreign trade

"Il novantadue" "Ninety-two," referring to 1992, the date when, in theory, the single European market is to be established

IRI Istituto per la Ricostruzione Industriale, the state-owned agency which controls numerous public-sector banking and industrial enterprises including some which have been partially privatized

IVA Imposta sul Valore Aggiunto, value-added tax

lottizzazione the process by which senior posts in public-sector bodies traditionally are shared out among the political parties

Mezzogiorno literally "midday," the South of Italy, also known as *Italia meridionale*

NATO North Atlantic Treaty Organisation, founded in 1949 as an international collective defence organization linking a group of European states with USA and Canada. France withdrew from NATO's military structure in 1966

NIC Newly Industrializing Countries

OECD Organisation for Economic Cooperation and Development

OPEC Organization of Petroleum Exporting Countries

sindacati trade unions

soci members, partners

SpA Società per Azioni

TIR International Road Transport Convention

Verdi members of the Green Party

Using the guide

The Economist Guide to Italy is an encyclopedia of business and travel information. If in doubt about where to look for specific information, consult either the Contents list or the Index.

City guides

Cities are dealt with region by region. The guides to the main cities follow a standard format, as follows: information and advice on arriving, getting around, city areas, hotels, restaurants, bars, entertainment, shopping, sightseeing, sports and fitness, and a directory of local business and other facilities such as secretarial and translation agencies, couriers, hospitals with emergency departments, and florists. There is also a map of the city centre locating recommended hotels, restaurants and other important addresses.

Other cities in each region are covered in less detail, concentrating on the main commercial and industrial activities, hotels, restaurants, opportunities for relaxation and the most useful information sources.

Abbreviations

Credit and charge cards AE American Express; DC Diners Club; EC Eurocard only; MC MasterCard (Access, Eurocard); V Visa (Barclaycard). ***Figures*** Millions are abbreviated to m; billions (meaning one thousand million) to bn.

Publisher's note

Although *The Economist Guide to Italy* is intended first and foremost to provide practical information for business people travelling in Italy, the general information will also be helpful to anyone doing business with Italy, wherever and however that business may be conducted.

Price bands

Price bands are denoted by symbols (see below). These correspond approximately to the following actual prices at the time of going to press. (Although the actual prices will inevitably go up, the relative price category is likely to remain the same.)

Hotels
(one person occupying a standard room, including service and tax)

L	up to L90,000
L/	L90,000–130,000
L//	L130,000–170,000
L///	L170,000–220,000
L////	L220,000–300,000
L/////	over L300,000

Restaurants
(typical meal, including half a bottle of house wine, coffee and service)

L	up to L30,000
L/	L30–50,000
L//	L50–70,000
L///	L70–90,000
L////	L90–110,000
L/////	over L110,000

INTRODUCTION

Postwar Italy is a success story. Defeated, humiliated and demoralized in 1945, it has built, forty years later, one of the strongest economies in the world. The Christian Democrat party has led in all elections and consequently has been in all of the nearly 50 governments since World War II. At first it headed broadly based coalitions which included the Communists, but the latter were ejected in the cold war atmosphere of 1947 and have remained in opposition ever since, apart from a brief period of cooperation in the 1970s. The Christian Democrats looked leftwards again in 1963, when they admitted the Socialists into the coalition under the *centro-sinistra* (centre-left) formula; they had paved the way the year before by nationalizing electricity. In more recent years the Christian Democrats have twice ceded the post of prime minister to smaller allies – to the Republican Giovanni Spadolini in 1981–82 and to the Socialist Bettino Craxi in 1983–87 – but they have always retained key ministries. Several individual Christian Democrats have repeatedly been in government. Though the party is open to charges of manipulation and corruption it has provided underlying continuity and stability, strong enough to withstand the terrorist attacks of the 1970s.

In the late 1980s, for the first time since World War II the Christian Democrats faced a serious challenge from their aggressive ally, Craxi's Socialists, who are also a threat to the Communists. Still the second party in numbers of votes, the Communists have been rudderless since the severance of their ties with Moscow and the death in 1984 of their leader Enrico Berlinguer.

Economic achievement

The economy has progressed under this political set-up – many would say in spite of it. Three periods can be distinguished. First came Marshall Aid and the postwar reconstruction of a devastated economy – the "Italian miracle" – running into the 1960s. A more stormy period followed, spanning the social and industrial unrest of the late 1960s, the two oil shocks in the 1970s – which pushed inflation up to 20% in 1980 – and recession in the early 1980s. A subsequent strong recovery has been fed by falls in the dollar and in oil prices, and inflation has been kept in check, though at the price of persisting high unemployment. In 1987 the Italians claimed that in GDP they had overtaken Britain and were not far behind France – but it has to be said that included in this calculation was an estimated amount representing Italy's large black economy.

Unbalanced and uneven

It is debatable whether the country is well prepared to meet the dismantling by 1992 of barriers between EC countries. Firstly, the economy is unbalanced; the entrepreneurial spirit and the material wealth are found mainly in the North, while much of the South has remained backward, in spite of a massive injection of funds. Secondly, the pattern of economic activity is uneven. There is a handful of dynamic, large private firms, often family owned, and operating throughout the world. The very large public sector ranges from the profitability of oil conglomerate ENI to years of accumulated losses in the steel sector. Similarly, the cooperative movement, one of the most extensive in Europe, ranges from a few aggressive and successful concerns to others struggling for survival. But the backbone of the economy is made up of thousands of small private firms: energetic, flexible, quick in initiative, but still unsophisticated financially and inexperienced internationally.

Tackling the problems

The services on which these firms have to rely are often inadequate and, when provided by the state, are in many cases disgraceful. There are more than a thousand banks; 600 of these are village savings banks of only local importance, and the whole banking network is still too fragmented for the needs of the economy. Some leading public-sector banks are having to be restructured and partially privatized in order to operate more competitively. Since the world depression of the 1930s the Bank of Italy has been given strict powers of control over the banking system. In recent years it has been loosening its controls, to encourage rationalization, modernization and greater competition before 1992. But memories of collapses such as that of the Sindona banks in 1974 and of Calvi's Banco Ambrosiano in 1982 are a deterrent against going too far too fast. Although many financial services are still underdeveloped, unit trusts (mutual funds), which were started only in the mid-1980s, have surged ahead. These have been able to tap a personal savings rate which as a proportion of income is second only to Japan's.

Public services such as posts and telecommunications, social welfare, and the administration of justice often seem to have scarcely moved into the twentieth century. Equally inefficient is the taxation system, which permits widespread evasion among all except salary- and wage-earners. A lack of overall policy is all too evident over issues such as the protection of the environment, and national and local transport services.

Of prime concern is uncontrolled government spending, the highest among major western countries. Successive governments have promised to contain the chronic budget deficit and to reduce their borrowing requirement, but the day when this, as a percentage of GDP, will fall to a single figure is not in sight.

There are signs that politicians have begun to take public finances more seriously, after repeated warnings by the central bank and by private industry. Unfortunately, governments come and go but bureaucrats remain. The public administration is in four tiers: central government, regions (introduced since World War II), provinces and *comuni*, or local authorities. It behaves like an army entrenched against change. But changes will have to be effected, and a huge backlog of legislation cleared, if Italy is to prepare itself for the single European market. Nevertheless, most Italian businesses are looking forward to *il novantadue* with optimism. Italy is at its best when having to adapt to rapid change.

The Economic Scene

Natural resources

Italy's rapid rate of postwar growth has been achieved despite its lack of natural resources. The most serious deficiencies are in fuels: although Italy has some natural gas, it is almost wholly dependent on imports for supplies of oil and coal. Its range of other minerals is varied but thinly spread. Very little of the land, apart from the Po valley and a few much smaller areas, is suited to agriculture. Moreover, an unevenly developed and often highly inefficient farming system is ill-adapted to Italy's food requirements, which have to be met by large imports of cereals, meat and dairy produce.

Agriculture

Farm production now accounts for a much smaller proportion of GDP than in the past, down from about 25% in the 1950s to just over 4% today. The number of people engaged in the sector has also declined, from over 40% of the workforce 30 years ago to about 10% at present, although this is still much larger than in France or West Germany. Italy is far from self-sufficient in food, which shows an annual trade deficit of about L8,000bn.

A fragmented structure The mass exodus from agriculture – the result of migration to better-paid industrial jobs both at home and abroad and, to a lesser extent, of mechanization – has not been accompanied by much change in the average size of farms. In the 1930s there were some 9m farmers working 4.2m holdings. By the 1980s, there were only 2m farmers on 3.3m holdings, but the size of the average farm had grown only slightly over the 50-year period, to 7.2ha/17.8 acres, compared with 15ha/37 acres in Germany and 32ha/79 acres in France.

Italian farming is dominated by small one-man operations. About three-quarters of all holdings involve part-time labour. The polarization of the system between a small number of large commercial farms and a large number of small farms (which are often under-capitalized and inefficient) lies at the root of the sector's problems.

Land reform after World War II was intended to break up the old feudal estates and redistribute the land. In the centre of the country, ownership was in the hands of a small number of landlords, and farmworkers were locked into an exploitative system of sharecropping (*mezzadria*). In the South, a feudal relationship between landlord and tenant survived on the large estates or *latifundia*. In response to unrest and numerous violent incidents in the early 1950s, some 700,000ha/1,730,000 acres of land were parcelled out, creating a dense network of small private holdings. But although ownership was reformed, the sector as a whole remained inefficient. Productivity improved and incomes increased in some parts, but many of the new farms were too small to be viable. Some of the worst problems were in the South and in Sicily where reform was obstructed by the Mafia.

The CAP The EC's Common Agricultural Policy (CAP) has hardly helped since it has been shaped primarily for producers of milk, meat and cereals in northern Europe, not for the farmers of fruit, olives and vines in the south. The EC's funds for modernization have been blocked or misused by an inefficient and easily corrupted bureaucracy. Paradoxically, Italy has been a net contributor to the CAP, helping to subsidize the surplus production of well-off farmers in West Germany, France, the Netherlands and the UK.

Production Geography and climate have favoured the North: apart from the *"Tavoliere"* (checker-board) wheat-growing area in Apulia, the South has no equivalent of the fertile, well-irrigated Po plain with its high yields of wheat (including the hard durum varieties for pasta production), maize and, increasingly, barley. Rice is a specialized crop, exported in large quantities. The most valuable forms of livestock – cattle and pigs – are also farmed in the North, with sheep and goats more numerous in the South. Vines for wine are grown throughout the country, while olives are produced mainly in the centre and the South. An interesting feature of tree crops is that they are frequently grown alongside field crops in a system known as *coltura promiscua*. Citrus fruits are found in the South, and Sicily accounts for about 60% of all produce. Deciduous fruits (peaches, pears, plums, apricots, cherries and nectarines) are grown primarily in Campania and Emilia-Romagna.

Forestry
Forest covers more than 6m ha/15m acres of land but the wood produced is of low commercial value apart from the quality timber found in the Italian Alps (accounting for a quarter of forested area and more than a third of production). The Alpine chestnut and pine are used mainly for construction. Chestnut forests are found also in the northern Apennines and Calabria.

Fishing
Despite Italy's long coastline, fishing is not particularly important. Apart from the Adriatic (which provides more than half of the total catch), the Italian seaboard is not very suitable for fishing because of the limited continental shelf. To compensate, much fish for the Italian market is caught by Mediterranean and Atlantic fleets. However, tuna and sole from the northern Adriatic command high prices, and the seas around Sicily are a profitable source of tuna, anchovies and sardines.

Energy
Italy has to import most of its energy needs, including 96% of its oil and 92% of its coal. However, it has been able to develop production of indigenous natural gas to the point where this provides some 9% of total energy consumption.

The main gas fields are in the Po plain and the Po delta and offshore in the Adriatic, and there have been further finds in the South. Oil fields have been discovered and developed in the Po plain, Calabria and Sicily, but these have not lived up to their earlier promise. Coal is mined in Sardinia and Valle d'Aosta but deposits are meagre. Rivers in the Alps and Apennines provide hydroelectric power, but this energy source was already fully exploited by the late 1950s and production has stagnated since then. Geothermal sources at Lardarello in Tuscany generate a small amount of electricity.

Non-fuel minerals
Metallic and non-metallic minerals are found in varied but far from abundant quantities. Although iron ore, bauxite, antimony and sulphur are all extracted, the only minerals of consequence are mercury (of which Italy is among the leading world producers), lead, zinc, pyrites, salt and asbestos. The regions with the main deposits of non-fuel minerals are Sardinia, Tuscany, Sicily and Trentino-Alto Adige. The workable bauxite reserves are in Abruzzo, Campania and Apulia.

Chalks and clays are widespread and commercially useful, as are deposits of asphaltic and bituminous rocks. Marble and building stone are very important; the most famous is the white marble from Carrara, used by generations of Italian sculptors, but there is also white marble from Val d'Ossola, red marble from Verona, black from Varenna and orange from Siena.

Mineral and thermal waters are found in significant amounts in many regions throughout the peninsula.

Human resources

The past 40 years have seen Italy transformed. With 53% of Italians in towns of over 20,000 people, it is now a highly urbanized society. There have been huge shifts of population from the country to the city and from the South to the centre and the North. In the process, the traits of a traditional society are disappearing, but disparities remain between a prosperous North and a poorer, less modernized, Mezzogiorno.

Population growth and density

Italy has always been a populous country. At the end of the 18th century it had 18m people, compared with France's 27m (in a larger, more fertile country) and Britain's 10m. Its present population is 57.3m, and this would have been much larger but for the 9m who have permanently emigrated. Density of population is high. Italy had reached almost 90 people per sq km/233 per sq mile in the 1860s, when the country was unified. By the 1980s, this had more than doubled to 190/492, with the most heavily populated parts in the North.

Growth pattern Demographic trends in Italy are now those of a modern industrial nation. A high rate of growth in the past (an estimated 6.7% a year in the late 19th and early 20th centuries) has dropped dramatically since World War II, down to about 0.2% in the 1980s. Changing views on women, the church and the family have wrought a minor revolution. The birth rate has fallen sharply from 30 per thousand population in the 1920s to just under 10 today. A law permitting abortion was approved by parliament in the late 1970s and a referendum endorsed this decision in 1981. Contraception, though opposed by the church, is accepted by most people. The extended family is increasingly rare, at least in the urbanized regions, and there are now only three people in the average household, down from four in the 1950s. Single-person households, once a rarity, now make up a fifth of the total.

As elsewhere in Europe, the population is ageing: about one-fifth of all Italians are now over 60.

Internal migration

Italy is still two countries, in economic, social and cultural terms: the South's population is poorer, younger and more fertile than that of the North, and its overall and infant mortality rates are still higher. Poverty and lack of employment in the South have spurred migration, and some 3m people have drifted north since World War II, with the peak years of movement in the 1950s and 1960s. Towns like Genoa, Milan, Turin and Bologna grew rapidly from this influx. The original migrants were poor and unskilled, forming an insecure urban under-class, but a second wave of migrants in the 1970s was younger and better educated, seeking more highly qualified jobs.

Returning migrants Since the 1970s the trend has slowed and there has been considerable return migration. Large numbers of workers have also returned from abroad. In the early 1970s almost a million Italians were working in West Germany, Switzerland and France, but rising unemployment levels in the host countries have forced many to return home, helping to swell the unemployment figures in the South.

Immigration

No one knows precisely how many immigrants Italy has. The official figure is around 400,000 but the real total is probably near 1.4m if it includes illegal Third World immigrants whose existence goes largely unrecorded. Most of these come from the Philippines, Tunisia, Ethiopia, Egypt and Cape Verde and their illegal status makes them vulnerable to exploitation. Tunisians generally work in agriculture and fishing in Sicily, and Filipinos are often found working as housemaids in middle-class city homes.

Urbanization

Italy's towns and cities grew fastest in the 1950s. In 1951 only 22 cities had more than 100,000 people; there were 36 by 1964 and 50 by 1983. The three largest cities (excluding suburbs) are Rome (3m), Milan (1.7m) and Naples (1.2m). Italy's metropolitan areas have continued to grow in the 1970s and 1980s, though at a much slower rate than before. Their growth is due to the spread of new suburbs, because the population of city centres has been contracting. Some cities in the South, including Naples and Catania, have become smaller, despite higher birth rates and lower migration to the North, because overcrowding and high housing costs have encouraged people to move to commuter towns and villages.

The workforce

In 1987, the total workforce numbered some 23.7m, of whom 2.83m (12%) were unemployed. The proportion of economically active people has always been low in Italy, and fell from 60% in the 1860s to just over 33% in the 1970s. This fall can be explained by a continuing cultural antipathy to women in work, and declining numbers of the very young and the elderly in the workforce. Since the 1970s the proportion has climbed slowly to its present level of just over 40% (compared with almost 44% in France), though there are wide regional disparities. Women represent just over a third of those in work.

Uneven unemployment

Unemployment is very unevenly spread among the sexes, age groups and regions. For example, of the 2.83m unemployed in 1987, 73% were in the 14–29 age group. The rate of unemployment was higher for women (19.6%) than for men (8.1%); for the under-30s, male and female, it was 26%. By contrast, only 2% of men over 30 living in the centre and North were unemployed.

The structure of employment In the decade from the late 1970s, the number working in agriculture fell by a third to 10.7% of the total, while those working in services increased from 46% to almost 57%. Industrial employment, meanwhile, has fallen from 38% to 32%. However, regional disparities are wide and in many parts of the South a third of the workforce is still in agriculture, compared with only 4% in Lombardy in the North.

The black economy The size of the unofficial economy means that it is difficult to produce a true picture of the workforce. Italy's black economy has been estimated at 20–30% of GNP. At least 2.5m workers are involved, mostly in the service sectors. Women and the elderly form the majority, with a growing proportion of illegal immigrants.

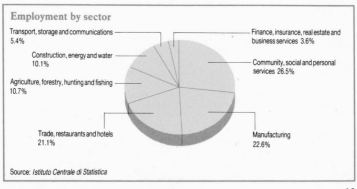

Employment by sector

Transport, storage and communications 5.4%

Construction, energy and water 10.1%

Agriculture, forestry, hunting and fishing 10.7%

Trade, restaurants and hotels 21.1%

Finance, insurance, real estate and business services 3.6%

Community, social and personal services 26.5%

Manufacturing 22.6%

Source: *Istituto Centrale di Statistica*

International trade

Italy is one of the world's most dynamic exporting nations. It needs to be, for its dependency on imported energy and raw materials is high, second only to that of Japan. However, some worrying trends emerged in the late 1980s. Export success in the past was in low- and medium-technology products – precisely those in which Italy now faces growing competition. At home, Italians have developed a taste for expensive foreign products, particularly cars and high-tech consumer goods. The result is a widening deficit in trade.

The deficit

Italy's visible trade has usually shown a deficit, mainly because of huge imports of energy and food products. The deficit climbed to over L18,000bn in 1984 and 1985 but weaker oil prices subsequently helped correct the balance. Nevertheless, the late 1980s have seen the trade gap widen again.

Export problems Italian products are becoming less competitive on foreign markets because of rising wage costs at home, the export offensive of Japan, South Korea and Taiwan, and exchange rate variations. The result has been a slide in Italy's share of international trade: while worldwide exports grew by about 6% between 1986 and 1987, Italy's grew by only 3%, although in 1988 they showed a recovery.

Key exports

Italy's exports are dominated by manufactured goods but high-tech products account for a smaller proportion of the total than in similar trading nations such as the UK and France. Its strengths lie in medium- and low-tech areas: industrial and office machinery (almost a quarter of all exports in 1986), automobiles and transport equipment, textiles, clothing, footwear and chemicals.

In some sectors, Italy dominates the Western European market. Fiat, which constantly vies with Audi/vw for first place in the car exporters' league, had the largest share of the market in 1987, accounting for more than 14% of cars sold. Despite growing competition from the Far East, the Italians still supply nearly 40% of white goods and a third of all domestic appliances.

Competition threat Exporters of textiles, clothing, machinery and transport equipment have been hit by a host of problems, including the growing challenge from low-cost Far Eastern and NIC producers. The creation of a single European market in 1992 is viewed with some apprehension. At present a number of products, including South Korean and Taiwanese shoes and Japanese cars, have restricted access to the Italian market despite free circulation in most other EC countries. It is unlikely that this kind of protection will continue.

The export promotion agency, Istituto Nazionale per il Commercio Estero (ICE), provides comprehensive data on foreign markets to help companies identify emerging opportunities. There have been calls for reform of Italy's poorly coordinated export policies and the ministries of trade and foreign affairs are now collaborating more closely.

Key imports

Since 1986, imports of both investment and consumer goods have been growing fast to meet increased demand, with a big surge in industrial production, and wages outpacing the annual inflation rate. Imports climbed by 5% in 1986 and 10% in 1987, and this trend looks set to continue, though at a slower pace, into the 1990s. Fuels, food (mainly meat and dairy products) and agricultural goods (animal feeds in particular) are the largest items on the import bill.

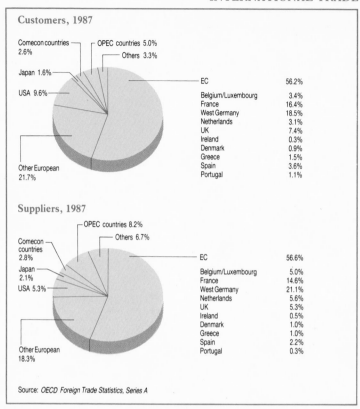

Customers, 1987

Comecon countries 2.6%
OPEC countries 5.0%
Others 3.3%
Japan 1.6%
USA 9.6%
Other European 21.7%

EC	56.2%
Belgium/Luxembourg	3.4%
France	16.4%
West Germany	18.5%
Netherlands	3.1%
UK	7.4%
Ireland	0.3%
Denmark	0.9%
Greece	1.5%
Spain	3.6%
Portugal	1.1%

Suppliers, 1987

OPEC countries 8.2%
Others 6.7%
Comecon countries 2.8%
Japan 2.1%
USA 5.3%
Other European 18.3%

EC	56.6%
Belgium/Luxembourg	5.0%
France	14.6%
West Germany	21.1%
Netherlands	5.6%
UK	5.3%
Ireland	0.5%
Denmark	1.0%
Greece	1.0%
Spain	2.2%
Portugal	0.3%

Source: *OECD Foreign Trade Statistics, Series A*

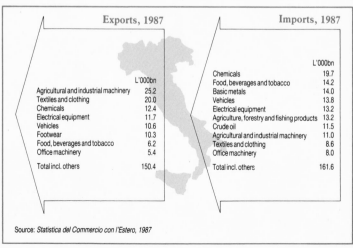

Exports, 1987

	L'000bn
Agricultural and industrial machinery	25.2
Textiles and clothing	20.0
Chemicals	12.4
Electrical equipment	11.7
Vehicles	10.6
Footwear	10.3
Food, beverages and tobacco	6.2
Office machinery	5.4
Total incl. others	150.4

Imports, 1987

	L'000bn
Chemicals	19.7
Food, beverages and tobacco	14.2
Basic metals	14.0
Vehicles	13.8
Electrical equipment	13.2
Agriculture, forestry and fishing products	13.2
Crude oil	11.5
Agricultural and industrial machinery	11.0
Textiles and clothing	8.6
Office machinery	8.0
Total incl. others	161.6

Source: *Statistica del Commercio con l'Estero, 1987*

The nation's finances

While Italians have been congratulating themselves about *il sorpasso* – Italy's overtaking of Britain, according to some calculations, to become the world's fifth-largest industrial power – economists and politicians have been less sanguine about Italy's other achievement: one of the highest debt-to-GNP ratios (93%) in the OECD. Tackling this and the large and growing budget deficit (about 12% of GDP in the late 1980s) is one of the government's most urgent tasks, but a culture of public-sector profligacy and a long tradition of tax evasion also make it the most difficult.

The budget

In principle, government spending has built-in fiscal rigour: the constitution specifies that new laws can be passed only if their financing can be assured. However, the annual Finance Act, which sets out public spending targets, can be passed before specific measures for achieving these targets are devised. Moreover, during its passage, amendments made by parliament (often under the influence of special-interest lobbies) can boost expenditure far beyond the treasury's original estimates. A great deal of spending escapes the government's control in any case, since about half of all expenditure is disbursed by quasi-independent health authorities and by the various levels of local government. Central government has little option

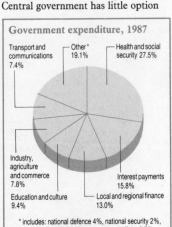

Government expenditure, 1987

Transport and communications 7.4%

Other* 19.1%

Health and social security 27.5%

Industry, agriculture and commerce 7.8%

Interest payments 15.8%

Education and culture 9.4%

Local and regional finance 13.0%

* includes: national defence 4%, national security 2%, housing 1.3%, international affairs 2.7%

Source: *Bank of Italy Annual Report 1988*

but to bail them out when they overspend, as they generally do.

Revenue Public spending leapt from 35% of GDP in the early 1970s to about 60% in the late 1980s: again, one of the highest ratios in the OECD. The government had to increase the tax burden, which rose from 33% of GDP in 1975 to 47% in 1985. This was higher than the EC average of just over 44% and well above that of the USA and Japan (both around 30% of GDP). By 1988 the proportion had been reduced to about 40%. Corporation tax is low by international standards and, despite reforms in recent years, the self-employed are still often able to evade the tax net. In 1984, some 50% of income tax and 26% of Imposta sul Valore Aggiunto (IVA – value-added tax) were successfully evaded but legislation passed in 1985 aimed to clamp down heavily on the self-employed in particular. Overall, however, income tax as a percentage of GDP (13% in 1986) is about the EC average; indirect taxes, at just over 9%, are below the average. Social security contributions are the most important single source of revenue (about 35%). Direct taxes provide about 33% and indirect taxes 24%.

Expenditure Some of the pressures pushing up spending are those common to nearly all Western countries. In particular, it is becoming increasingly expensive to support the growing number of older people: women can draw retirement pensions from the age of 55 and men from 60 (but it has been proposed to raise the minimum age to 65 for both). Other pressures are political and peculiar to the Italian system. A third of all pensions are invalidity pensions, which are notoriously open to abuse. Lack of central control over health service spending has allowed this to grow rapidly; it currently accounts for 12% of public expenditure. The public sector wage bill in recent years has been growing by about 11% a year (much faster than inflation).

Tackling the deficit The deficit has been increasing by 23% a year since 1981. Interest payments accounted for 70% of the deficit in 1987. However, thanks to the high level of personal savings (23% of disposable income, or 19% of GDP in 1987), the government has been able to borrow from the public and keep its foreign debt to only about 3% of the total.

The government led by Ciriaco De Mita, which came to power in April 1988, pledged itself to cut public spending, to make central and local government bodies more accountable and to reform the budgetary process so that fewer cost-raising amendments can be introduced after the budget has been approved.

Easing exchange controls

Until the mid-1980s, the export and import of currency was strictly controlled. But in the last few years the flow of funds across frontiers has been considerably eased, notably by the elimination of a 25% non-interest-bearing deposit on foreign direct and portfolio investments and fewer restrictions on currency imports and exports. Controls are due to be removed completely to conform with

EC plans for the single European market.

Managing the lira The lira is given greater freedom to diverge from the European Monetary System (EMS) central rate than other member currencies – by up to 6% compared with 2.25% – but the Bank of Italy's policy is to keep its movement within a narrower band. In 1988 the lira was diverging by about 3%.

Balance of payments

The persistent deficit on current account can be blamed on Italy's chronic visible trade deficit. There is normally a surplus on invisibles, the main contribution coming from tourism. Although more Italians are travelling abroad, their spending continues to be outstripped by revenue from the large influx of foreign tourists, and net earnings under this head are usually at least L10,000bn. Emigrants' remittances, though less important than in earlier decades, still provide a useful L3,500bn a year. Net outgoings on investment income remain high, and a new feature of the current account is that there are net government transfers out of Italy, reflecting higher spending on development aid.

The outflow of capital has increased in the late 1980s, following the relaxation of exchange controls and the international expansion of Italian companies. Capital inflows in the late 1980s have also been healthy, however, attracted by high returns on Italian government securities and by new equity investment opportunities.

Balance of payments (L'000bn)	1983	1984	1985	1986	1987
Exports of goods (fob)	103.6	120.4	138.5	134.4	140.8
Imports of goods (cif)	112.8	138.8	157.2	139.1	148.9
Visible balance	-9.2	-18.4	-18.7	-4.7	-8.1
Invisible balance	9.9	11.1	11.9	3.4	5.0
Current account balance	0.7	-7.3	-6.8	-1.3	-3.1

Source: *Bank of Italy Annual Report 1987*

The Industrial Scene

Industry and investment

Italy's "economic miracle" in the two decades following the end of World War II was spectacular partly because it started from a small industrial base. The 1970s brought stagnation in large-scale industry: the two oil price shocks and serious labour unrest were prime causes of damage to output. Small firms continued to flourish and proliferate, however, and by the 1980s industry had begun to show healthy improvement as a result not only of lower oil prices and tamed unions, but also of the innate abilities of Italian entrepreneurs, engineers and designers: inventiveness and quickness to adapt to changing circumstances.

Structure of industry

Apart from a handful of big names, small- and medium-sized companies dominate the private sector, and are backed up by numerous specialized trade associations which protect their interests and lobby parliament on their behalf.

Large public sector The state plays a very large and complex role in industry, but the trend in the 1980s has been to reduce its role through partial privatization (see *Government and business*).

North–South gap Industry, particularly the more dynamic sectors, is concentrated in the North and centre, but government aid after 1950 led to new industries being set up in the underdeveloped South, the Mezzogiorno.

Government policy

There is no overall government strategy or coordinated policy for industry, apart from that relating to the Mezzogiorno. The Ministry of Industry is very small and lacks the necessary resources and expertise to provide companies with advice and assistance. There have been several attempts, not always very successful, to aid entire industrial sectors or to bail out specific firms. Since the early 1980s there have been incentives for companies to introduce automation and new technology.

R&D Italy lags behind in technological innovation, and although government investment in R&D has risen to 1.45% of GNP, from less than 1% in the late 1970s, it is still below the EC average of 1.8%.

Investment

Gross fixed investment in 1987 was 19.8% of GDP, compared with 23.8% in 1981. The late 1980s brought a new surge in investment, however, with companies' purchase of machinery rising by 10% in both 1987 and 1988.

Stock market In the late 1970s and early 1980s a number of medium-sized firms sought a listing on the Milan Borsa, bringing with them thousands of small savers venturing for the first time into the equity markets. Initial enthusiasm was followed by burnt fingers, during the long bear run in the 18 months preceding the October 1987 international crash.

New sources of finance Italy's emerging merchant banking sector is likely to help industry to expand, develop and diversify during the 1990s, and venture capital, also a new feature, will assist small businesses in particular (see *Financial markets*).

Foreign investment in Italy, which levelled off during the 1970s, has been rising again in the 1980s, although it is mostly through the acquisition of existing local firms and is still relatively small compared with that in most other EC countries. There has been a shift to the service sector, which now receives about two-thirds of new investment.

Vehicles

For the first two decades of the postwar period the reputation of Italy's automobile industry abroad was based mainly on sports cars made by independent makers Alfa Romeo, Ferrari, Lamborghini, Lancia and Maserati. Fiat's acquisition of Lancia and a controlling stake in Ferrari shook up the industry. The process of concentration was virtually completed when Fiat bought troubled Alfa Romeo from state holding corporation IRI at the end of 1986, giving it a trio of famous badges. With Maserati and its associate Innocenti in difficulty, and Lamborghini out of the race, Fiat *is* the Italian automobile industry.

The Italian market

Registration of Italian cars reached a record 2m in 1988 and put Italy in fourth place among European markets, after West Germany, France and the UK.

Tax penalties for big cars Long-standing fiscal factors have had a big effect on the structure of the market. Large cars incur top rates of IVA (value-added tax) and are hit by progressive annual licence charges. The differential favouring small cars has helped these to take a dominant share of the market. About three-quarters of Italian sales are in the small car segments.

Diesel incentive Diesel (derv) is taxed at considerably lower rates than gasoline (in mid-1988, 61% of the price at the pump compared with 78%) which, in spite of higher annual licence costs for diesel-engined cars, has encouraged the use of diesel engines even in small cars.

Slow-rising sun Penetration of the Italian market by the Japanese has been slight. Since the mid-1950s a bilateral agreement (sought by the Japanese) has restricted direct imports of Japanese cars into Italy to 2,550 annually. However, the advent of the single European market should, in theory, open the door to large numbers of Japanese cars made in countries such as the UK.

Fiat

The Turin company ran into serious difficulties in the 1970s when its cars had a poor reputation and it was hit by labour unrest and massive debts.

The turning point was in 1980 when Fiat won a confrontation with the trade unions and laid off more than 20,000 workers. Job cuts have continued, lowering the automobile work force from 141,000 in 1981 to 99,000 at the end of 1986 (a figure lifted to 130,000 at year-end 1987 by the acquisition of Alfa Romeo). Fiat has also invested heavily in factory automation systems.

Market leadership Fiat has captured market share through an extensive programme of model renewal and greater attention to quality. In 1987 Alfa Romeo's contribution allowed the Fiat group to claim European market leadership with a 14.3% share.

Indices of industrial production (1980 = 100; average per day)	
	1987
General	103.1
Energy, gas and water	107.9
Basic food products	110.1
Textiles	104.3
Clothing	91.4
Footwear	77.0
Machinery	84.8
Electrical and electronic equipment	125.9
Automotive products	100.9
Metal construction materials	79.3
Chemicals	113.5
Office machinery and data processing	274.0

Source: *Bollettino Mensile di Statistica*

19

Model renewal The Lancia Delta's European Car of the Year Award in 1980 proved a breakthrough. This success was repeated in 1983 by the highly successful Fiat Uno. Fiat is now aiming to shift the emphasis to larger cars, which offer bigger margins. The Alfa Romeo 164 was launched at the end of 1987 and the Tipo, launched in 1988, is Fiat's attempt to win command of the segment long dominated by Volkswagen's Golf (Rabbit).

International growth Fiat depends on its dominant position in the home market (57%), and its production is almost entirely in Italy. The company has to decide whether it evolves as a pan-European group or expands through joint ventures, as it has done quite actively with Ford (trucks) and Peugeot-Citröen (light commercial vehicles), and in Turkey and the Eastern bloc.

Mechanical engineering

After playing a key role in Italy's postwar boom, the mechanical engineering sector experienced a difficult period in the early 1980s. Industry leaders blamed this on the lack of government support, an over-valued lira and a slow-down in international trade. However, in the latter part of the decade output picked up, thanks to companies' creativity in design and their ability to respond quickly to shifts in demand.

Small is beautiful

Engineering is still considered by many Italians to be *the* profession, and it is strongly emphasized by the universities. The sector is Italy's biggest employer but, like much of Italian industry, mechanical engineering production is made up of small to medium-sized firms, typically with fewer than 500 employees, which farm out large quantities of production work to small suppliers, exploiting the Italian tradition of craftsmanship. As a result, Italian firms have been more adaptable to radical changes in demand and better able to provide a specialist service for smaller customers than their larger competitors.

In many cases, a particular industry is concentrated in one region, exploiting a network of local contacts and facilities. Examples are hand tools in Laveno, north of Milan, and farm equipment in Reggio Emilia.

Exports continue to account for a large part of total sales as firms drive to broaden their market geographically for their engineering products. In 1987, the sector achieved a 5% increase and accounted for one-third of total Italian exports. However, a worrying 20% jump in imports meant that there was almost a trade deficit in engineering goods, something unheard of in decades.

Textile machinery

Concentrated mainly in the northern regions of Piedmont, Lombardy and Veneto, the textile machine industry has produced double-figure growth in most years since the end of World War II. Exports made up around 60% of sales in 1987. Over one-third of exports have gone in recent years to other EC countries, just under 30% to Asia, and about 10% each to North America and Eastern Europe.

The industry's 400 or so companies have adapted to changing demands, for example for synthetics in the 1970s and more recently for natural fibres, allowing Italy to maintain its strong international position, joint third with Japan.

A typically successful firm is Lombardy-based Protti, specializing in cotton tubing and cashmere machinery. Protti prides itself on its professional after-sales service and its introduction of modern electronics to guarantee higher output quality. It employs only 300, but its annual sales are worth about L30bn.

Machine tools

One of the best performers has been the machine tools industry which ranks as the world's fifth largest, with a 7% share of the global market. Export sales grew by 7% in 1987, following a sparkling performance a year earlier. By stressing technological quality and enhancing production flexibility, Italy's 400 machine tools producers have been able to protect their world ranking.

Robotics

Italy's impressive drive into robotics began in the early 1970s, when several large companies began to combine expertise in machine tools and in electronic control. Among these are Olivetti Controllo Numerico, which has branched into assembly robots and metering and flow systems, Mandelli, a major machining centre manufacturer, and Fiat's robot-making specialist Comau.

At present, about 50 companies – nearly all in the northern regions of Piedmont, Lombardy and Emilia-Romagna – produce robots. Total industry sales in 1987 were L220bn. The machine tools industry association, UCIMU, chastises the government for its lack of any special incentive for such a key high-tech sector, although there is a centre for national research in Rome.

Comau

Consorzio Macchine Utensili (Machine Tools Consortium) accounts for about 30% of industry revenue. It was created by Fiat in 1973, originally to equip the VAZ plant in Togliattigrad in the USSR. Comau is one of the world's most important suppliers of production systems, with sales of L905bn in 1987, although sales to companies within the Fiat group accounted for a majority of total revenue.

By the early 1980s, Comau was already established as a leading world supplier of transfer lines for the automobile industry. Since then, it has deliberately attempted to diversify its customer base, designing flexible manufacturing systems for plants in various sectors. One example is the advanced storage system for packages of different sizes, using robotized lifts and conveyors, built for Benetton's plant in Treviso.

Electronics and electrical engineering

Performance by Italy's electronics and electrical engineering industry weakened during the mid-1980s. Peaking in 1983, the trade surplus started to decline and in 1987, for the first time, the industry returned a trade deficit.

Main sectors

The strongest sector in export terms is electrical consumer goods, which in 1987 recorded a L3,454bn surplus of sales over domestic demand and accounted for 21% of total production. The largest manufacturing sector is electronic equipment and systems for business and industry (36% of production); nevertheless, the value of imports is considerably greater than that of exports of these goods. The sector with the biggest trade deficit is electronic consumer goods; in the late 1980s domestic output covered only about 45% of demand.

Italian market About 40% of Italian demand is for electronic equipment and systems for business and industry. The other main sectors are plant for electricity generation and distribution (about 12% of demand), electrical consumer goods (10%) and electronic consumer goods (8%).

Electronics

Components Italy became a leading player in European electronics when in 1987 state-owned SGS (part of the state holding corporation IRI) merged with the microelectronics activities of France's Thomson-CSF. Judged by 1987 sales the 50–50 joint venture ranked second in Europe to Philips/Signetics and 13th in the world. Losses amounted to $203m on sales of $863m in the venture's first year; but, following reorganization, SGS-Thomson expected to break even in 1988. The company's three main sites in Italy, two near Milan and the third in Sicily, have both production and advanced R&D facilities.

Telecommunications At the end of 1987 the government approved a ten-year National Telecommunications Plan which aims to upgrade Italy's much-criticized system to the level of other major European countries.

During the mid-1980s state-owned Italtel, whose strengths are in public switching and user systems, sought a partner. It seemed to have found one in the Fiat subsidiary Telettra whose strong area is transmission systems. Though Telettra is only half the size of Italtel, the proposed Telit joint venture foresaw equal stakes for Fiat and IRI. After two years of negotiations the Telit venture was acrimoniously abandoned at the end of 1987. Recognizing the need for working on a larger scale and in preparation for the single European market, both companies were seeking cross-border agreements when going their separate ways in 1988.

Computers *Informatica* is the biggest part of the sector manufacturing electronic equipment and systems for business and industry. Demand has increased rapidly over recent years, the market rising by 13.2% to L5,917bn in 1987. But national production, facing tough foreign competition, has lost ground in the late 1980s. Olivetti is Europe's leading computer maker, and its sharply reduced deliveries of PCs have probably affected overall Italian figures. Their launch of a new range at the end of 1987 could strengthen national performance.

Consumer goods Since the 1960s Italian performance in large domestic appliances, such as refrigerators, washing machines and dishwashers, has been strong (see *White goods*). There has been less success with small household appliances, where French and West German manufacturers do well and, notwithstanding attempts to build a national consumer electronics industry, foreign penetration has been on a large scale in "brown goods" (televisions, radios and hi-fi). Imports take 70% of the market overall, a figure which rises to nearly 100% in the case of videorecorders.

Avionics Italy developed substantial capability during the 1970s and 1980s, achieving total sales of L3,033bn in 1987. Foreign sales, however, have been badly affected by softness in export markets and by the weak dollar. Exports were slightly less than one-third of total sales in 1987, compared with 43% in the previous year. The principal national company is Selenia, an IRI subsidiary, which manufactures civil radar and space systems as well as being a major defence contractor.

Electrical power plant

The crisis that began in the early 1980s has worsened in the late 1980s. Electricity corporation ENEL's difficulty in implementing its construction programme is the reason why Italian engineering companies, led by state-owned Ansaldo and private-sector Tosi, have been operating at only about 50% of capacity. Ansaldo has been successful in selling power station plant to China and other developing countries, but tough conditions in the world market prevent this from being an easy alternative to sales at home. Gruppo Industrie Elettriche is very active abroad.

ANIE

Associazione Nazionale Industrie Elettrotecniche ed Elettroniche is Italy's association of electrical and electronics engineering companies. It has a membership of 628 firms.

White goods

The white goods sector generates a substantial surplus for Italy's external trading account, with export sales running at more than four times imports. Italian manufacturers clearly dominate Europe in the production of large appliances, a position achieved through competitive prices, flair for design and their ability to adapt quickly.

Market share

Italy represents only 15% of the total European market for white goods, excluding microwave ovens, but its share of manufacturing is 39%, more than one and a half times larger than that of its closest competitor, West Germany. Estimates put the total European market at 36m units in 1987. Exports in this sector are predominantly large appliances, and there is a consistent trade surplus of about L3,400bn. This contrasts with a deficit in small household appliances – toasters, irons, food processors, electrical tools – which make up the bulk of imported electrical consumer goods.

Leading names

Three Italian names appear among those leading the manufacture of white goods in Europe: Zanussi, Merloni and Candy.

Zanussi, the biggest, with annual sales of over 4m units, also sells under brand names such as Rex, Castor and Zoppas. About 70% of sales are generated in export markets. The company is part of Sweden's Electrolux, which acquired control from the Zanussi family in 1984 after the Italian firm ran into financial difficulties.

Merloni Until it bought Indesit from the official receiver in late 1987, Merloni Elettrodomestici sold only under the Ariston label. As a result of the takeover Merloni now has a 20% share of the domestic market (up from 16%). More importantly, it has increased its share of the export market. Indesit has always been stronger abroad, with foreign sales absorbing about 70% of production; the UK takes 40% of the company's exports. The Merloni group now lies second to Zanussi in Italy and third in Europe (with a 10% share) since the acquisition of Indesit, after Electrolux-Zanussi-Thorn (23%) and Philips-Bauknecht (12%). Part of Merloni's success is due to its policy of operating smallish plants which foster good industrial relations.

Centres of production

Zanussi Elettrodomestici employs about 9,000 workers at its six Italian factories. Its principal production plant is in the northeast at Porcia, and the second largest plant is at Susegana in the adjoining province. Merloni's production is centred on three medium-sized plants in the Marches region. The total work force at its five Italian plants is about 2,000. Before it went into receivership, Indesit had about 6,000 workers at its two plants near Turin and three plants at Caserta near Naples. About 1,400 jobs were saved with Merloni's acquisition operation.

Looking to the future

Increased demand for white goods in most of Europe is unlikely, but there is potential for growth in Spain, Portugal and Greece. This underlies Merloni's manufacturing presence at Setúbal in Portugal and Zanussi's plants in Spain, at Alcalà de Henares and Logroño. In Northern Europe the market is largely limited to replacement machines.

High levels of investment have raised production capacity, and the rise in prices of domestic appliances has failed to keep pace with inflation, a sign that surplus capacity exists. This problem for Italian producers is aggravated by low-cost imports from Comecon countries into some export markets.

Food and drink

Pasta and pizza, now familiar all over the industrialized world, reflect the simple origins of a cuisine evolved by a once poor people. Italians nevertheless pay great attention to food, although they are conservative, not to say nationalistic, in their taste. However, deeply ingrained habits are yielding to acceptance of industrially prepared food and even, to a limited extent, to fast and convenience foods. Change offers a variety of opportunities for commercial and industrial rationalization, which have been slower than in other developed countries.

Eating habits

Although there are wide regional variations, Italian cuisine is based on the Mediterranean diet of pasta, fresh vegetables and fruit, olive oil and herbs. In poorer households in particular, shopping is still done daily, for immediate consumption.

Resistance to frozen foods Italians are still suspicious of frozen foods, just as they are of anything in a tin. They prefer to buy several days' old "fresh" fish rather than the frozen article processed immediately on a mid-Atlantic factory ship.

A changing society These habits are however being eroded by the changes that have followed industrialization: smaller families; more people living alone; more women at work; urbanization; increasing adoption of the northern European working day, with its short lunch break. This has all encouraged, on the one hand, the industrialized preparation of packaged and convenience foods and, on the other, eating away from home, whether in restaurant or work-place canteen. Change is more visible in the North than in the economically less-developed South.

Fast foods are a growth area, resisted however by the existing trade. McDonalds was unable to open its first franchise, in Rome, until 1986. By 1988 it had four (Bolzano, Bologna, two in Rome) with a fifth planned in Verona, but none in Milan, where, however, indigenous hamburger chains are common.

Health foods Wholefoods and vegetarian foods began to make an appearance in the late 1960s but have never really caught on; interest has focused more on low-calorie "slimming" foods.

The food industry

Food processing is the third largest industrial sector after the mechanical engineering and textile industries, with annual sales of more than L120,000bn. But the industry is backward and fragmented, lacking capital resources and management skills, and with scarcely any links with agricultural suppliers. The majority of businesses are family owned, with 10–20 employees, and there is only a handful of really big groups.

The big companies Top domestic groups include Ferruzzi (cereals, oils, sugar), state-owned SME, Barilla (pasta and biscuits), Galbani (dairy products and groceries), Ferrero (confectionery), Parmalat (dairy products), Lavazza (coffee) and Bertolini (spices).

The IRI food sector holding company is SME, with brand names such as Cirio, Bertolli and De Rica in preserved foods, and Motta, Alemagna and Pavesi in confectionery, bakery goods and ice cream, together with retailing (GS supermarkets) and autostrada catering. The government barred a sale of SME to Carlo De Benedetti at a time when he already owned Buitoni-Perugina and IRI has said that it will not be privatized.

The multinationals have made substantial inroads, in a series of acquisitions which looks set to continue. Nestlé, which had already bought up the dairy products firm

Invernizzi, in 1988 took control of Buitoni-Perugina (pasta, biscuits, confectionery, olive oil) from the De Benedetti empire, which itself had acquired the Perugia-based group in 1985.

Other prominent multinationals are Kraft (which owns Locatelli – dairy products), General Foods (Negroni – salami), Nabisco (Saiwa – biscuits), Heinz (Plasmon – baby foods) and Unilever (Algida, Eldorado and Toseroni ice cream brands, Dante olive oil).

Retailing

The cooperative movement is the retailing leader, with 1987 sales of over L5,000bn. Then follow Standa Euromercato (sold by Ferruzzi in 1988 to Silvio Berlusconi, private TV magnate) and SMA, with La Rinascente, Despar, Esselunga, GS Supermercati and PAM.

Despar is part of an international association of individual retailers; the supermarkets are named Eurospar. The cooperative movement has promoted a similar association called CONAD.

Small is powerful Small shops numbered 315,000 in 1988, down from 407,000 in 1971. The small shopkeepers have a strong Christian Democrat lobby in parliament and try to delay the grant of new permits for supermarkets. Supermarkets number fewer than 3,000 and account for only about 13% of food sales, but they are spreading, and even hypermarkets and discount stores are appearing, often set up with advice from French groups. (See *Importing, exporting and distribution*.)

Alcoholic drinks

Wine Italy is the world's largest producer of wine and is a contributor to the European wine lake. About 7.6bn litres/2bn US gals a year are produced but only about 60% of that is drunk. Consumption per head has fallen in the last ten years from 112 litres to 71; young people prefer soft drinks and beer.

The industry spans large, sometimes multibeverage corporations; bottling firms, not always dedicated to quality; individual estate owners, jealous of their reputations; down to smaller growers, many of them linked to one of the big cooperative movements, either the left-wing Lega or the Catholic Confederazione (see *Power in business*).

Promoting quality The response to overproduction is, on the EC level, to support distillation into alcohol and reduction of vineyards, and, on the national level, to promote standards and quality. The alcoholic strength and volume must be stated on the label – a law that, it is claimed, puts Italy ahead of rival producing countries. The DOC (Denominazione di Origine Controllata) mark, inspired by the French AOC, should at least guarantee a reasonable table wine. Six wines qualify for the highest mark, DOCG (Denominazione di Origine Controllata e Garantita): Brunello di Montalcino, Vino Nobile di Montepulciano and Chianti, all from Tuscany; Barolo and Barbaresco, from Piedmont; and, controversially, Albana di Romagna.

Exports Only 120m litres/32m US gals a year are sold abroad, much of it to Western Europe. Bulk sales of southern wine, high in alcohol but low in quality, used to have a market in France for blending purposes, until demonstrating French growers emptied tanker-loads into the sea. In 1986 the methanol scare – limited to a handful of minor producers – slashed exports by 37.5% in volume, but they recovered subsequently.

Export promotion concentrates on quality wines, particularly to the USA, together with some special lines, such as sparkling red Lambrusco wine.

Domestic liquors, such as vermouth, brandy and grappa, have given ground on the home market to whisky, now ubiquitous; but varieties of *amaro*, a postprandial herb-based drink, have been holding their own.

Energy

Italy depends on imports to satisfy 80% of its energy requirements. This, and heavy reliance on oil as a primary source, make the country hostage to changes in international energy markets, although since 1985 it has benefited from the slump in oil prices and the fall of the dollar. In 1987 oil accounted for nearly 59% of total energy consumption. Demand forecasts and government policy are set out in the National Energy Plan, which aims to reduce dependence on imports both by energy savings and by diversification of primary sources.

National Energy Plan

Italy's politicians responded to the second oil shock at the end of the 1970s by approving a national energy plan (PEN) in 1981. The objectives of this and of a revised plan in 1985 were the reduction of import dependence and the diversification of energy sources. Central to both PENs was a programme for constructing nuclear and coal-fired electricity power stations. A new PEN announced in 1988, covering the period to the year 2000, effectively abandoned the nuclear option as a result of political and public pressure.

Primary sources Imported oil provides more than half of energy needs, imported natural gas 12%, imported coal 9%, domestic natural gas 9%, and hydropower and geothermal power together 6%.

Forecasts On present trends, primary energy consumption is forecast to rise to 180m tonnes of oil equivalent (TOE) a year by the end of the century, but proposed energy savings would cut this to 170mTOE. Imports should fall from 81% in the late 1980s to 76%.

Nuclear politics

The Chernobyl incident brought radioactive clouds to Italian skies and gave a boost to the country's anti-nuclear lobby. During summer 1986 Italy's "Greens" and left-of-centre parties collected signatures to support referenda on separate energy issues. Held in November 1987, the three referenda revealed an overwhelming anti-nuclear majority. Italy's toehold in nuclear technology consisted only of two small 1960s stations and a larger station which started commercial operation in 1981. The results from the ballot box led to the permanent closure of the small Magnox nuclear station at Latina and the suspension of electricity production at Trino, southeast of Turin, and at Caorso, south of Milan. The 75%-completed Montalto di Castro nuclear station will be converted to other fuels and work has been halted on another nuclear station planned for Trino.

Electricity

The state electricity corporation, Ente Nazionale per l'Energia Elettrica (ENEL), has warned that the country faces a serious risk of power cuts in the 1990s if new plant is not built. In the early 1970s less than 25% of total energy consumption was electricity; by the late 1980s it had risen to nearly 33% and its share is expected to grow by more than one-third during the 1990s. ENEL forecasts that electricity demand in the year 2000 will be 315 terawatt-hours (twh) compared with 210twh in 1987.

Capacity ENEL's existing generating capacity amounts to 43,000MW; the corporation wants to be able to call on 56,600MW by 1995 and 65,400MW by the end of the century. The possibilities for adding further hydro capacity are now limited and geothermal power and solar energy can offer only marginal contributions, so ENEL needs to build conventional fuel-burning stations to meet the growing demand for electricity.

Imports ENEL has set itself the task of reducing electricity imports to zero.

In 1987 purchases of electricity from neighbouring countries, mainly France, amounted to 23twh. This satisfied 11% of total electricity demand.

Coal ENEL's plans focus on a programme of construction of new coal-fired plant and the conversion of oil-burning stations to coal. The corporation forecasts that production from coal-fired plant will be 137twh at the end of the century, compared with 28twh in 1987. But the programme has suffered delays because of local concern about pollution.

Gas In 1987 imported gas satisfied 61% of total demand of 38bn cubic metres (BCM), compared with 52% of 27BCM ten years earlier. Long-term contracts with the USSR, Algeria and the Netherlands will make a total of 30BCM available in the 1990s. Italy's dependence on imports will then probably be about 65%.

Pipelines The Transmed pipeline carries Algerian gas across Tunisia under the Sicily Channel into Italy. The pipeline carrying Soviet gas from the Czechoslovakian border across Austria and into the northeast has recently been doubled at a cost of L1,100bn.

Indigenous natural gas is the energy source with which Italy is most richly endowed. Postwar finds in the Po Valley have been followed by discoveries of much larger gas fields off the Adriatic coast. Proven reserves amount to about 270BCM which would last about 18 years at the current rate of extraction. However, substantial availability of imported gas has caused the state hydrocarbons holding corporation Ente Nazionale Idrocarburi (ENI) to cut its national resources programme. This originally aimed at lifting indigenous gas production from the 1987 level of 15BCM to 18BCM in the 1990s. The increase will probably be only 1BCM.

Oil ENI's national resources programme also concerns oil. Italy's proven oil reserves amount to only about 95m tonnes, barely more than Italy's total annual oil consumption in the late 1980s.

---

1 tonne = 1.1025 US tons.

Clothing and footwear

Italian design flair is most visible in clothes and footwear. Milan's fashion collections attract wide attention and many Italians claim that the city has now overtaken Paris as the world's fashion capital. But in addition to excellent styling, the clothes and shoes industries benefit from a high level of manufacturing flexibility: Italian firms' ability to respond quickly to shifts in market requirements gives them a sharp competitive edge.

Clothing

Italian fashion names have won recognition at home and abroad. Top stylists include Giorgio Armani, Gianni Versace, Valentino, Krizia, Gianfranco Ferrè, Missoni and Biaggiotti. These display their latest creations at the fashion show Milano Collezioni. Florence also has several major fashion events, including Pitti Uomo (men's clothes), Pitti Bimbo (children's clothes), Pitti Lingerie, Pitti Trend (new-wave fashion for young men and women) and Pitti Filati (yarns for clothing). Rome's shows are also important.

Leisure wear High fashion is not the only area in which the Italian clothing industry excels. Firms have profited from the boom in sports and leisure clothes during the 1970s and 1980s. Leaders in this large and growing sector include Benetton, Stefanel, Fila and Ellesse.

Textiles A thriving textile industry annually provides some 45,000 tonnes/49,600 US tons of silk, 250,000 tonnes/275,600 US tons of cotton fabric and 175,000 tonnes/ 192,900 US tons of woollen fabric.

Footwear

Italy produces about 465m pairs of shoes a year, many of which go to export markets.

Famous names At the top end of the market Salvatore Ferragamo is regarded as Italy's leading shoemaker, though Gucci also enjoys a strong reputation, particularly in the USA and Japan. Di Varese also sells to the upper segment of the market but is less exclusive.

Sports shoes sales, after several years of growth, have turned down under the effect of fierce competition, though Italy retains clear world supremacy in making ski boots.

Employment

Clothing firms with more than 20 workers provide jobs for a total of about 170,000. In the textiles sector, the silk industry employs nearly 13,000, the wool industry 110,000 and the cotton industry 61,000. About 153,000 work in Italy's knitwear industry, producing socks, underwear and other knitted garments. More than 120,000 are employed in footwear manufacture.

Increasing efforts by the authorities to combat tax evasion are hitting the extensive black economy which involves many small family firms engaged in outwork.

Production centres

The textiles, clothing and footwear industries are widely spread. Como is the silk capital; top-quality woollens are made around Biella near Turin; Prato, near Florence, is the centre for regenerated woollens; several major clothing manufacturers are located in the northeast.

Varese, northwest of Milan, Vigevano near Pavia and the central Adriatic provinces in the Marches and Abruzzo regions are centres of footwear production.

Exports

Italians give considerable attention to their appearance and spend a great deal on clothes and shoes. Helped by these discerning and high-spending consumers at home, the industries have been able to build a strong position in export markets.

However, Italian producers, particularly those manufacturing low- and mid-priced clothing and footwear, are under threat from countries in the Far East and South America where labour costs are low.

The clothing industry has been described as the "cutting edge" of Italian exports. Italian clothing makers achieved total sales of L13,350bn in 1987, of which L5,540bn came from foreign customers. The value of imports was little more than one quarter of exports, thereby allowing the industry to make a substantial surplus contribution to the balance of payments. However, imports have been growing much faster than exports: in 1988 they rose by 14.5%, while exports grew by only 1.6%.

Slightly less than 40% of export sales are in men's outer clothing while women's outer clothing accounts for a little more. Other EC countries provide Italy with its biggest outlets, particularly West Germany, which takes nearly 27% of exports. The second largest individual market is the USA, taking about 13%, followed closely by France. Spain is seen as a promising new market for Italy's top fashion houses.

Footwear exports Signs of weakening in the appeal of the "Made in Italy" label are causing concern. Nevertheless, footwear continues to be a bigger contributor than clothing to the revenue side of the country's trading account. In 1987 the industry exported footwear worth L6,820bn, covering imports more than 13 times. As with clothing, the largest export market is West Germany (sales of L1,700bn in 1987), followed by the USA and France, with just over L1,000bn each.

Chemicals

The Italian chemical industry has had a poor reputation on several counts. Politics are ever-present in a sector where the state holding corporation ENI is a protagonist with its subsidiary EniChem and where until the early 1980s the state was Montedison's largest shareholder. An increasing trade deficit implies that efforts to create an efficient Italian chemicals industry through political intervention and huge investment subsidies have been unsuccessful. The industry has also failed to win friends among environmentalists and the communities where plant is located. Incidents at Montedison's Massa and Cengio plants in 1988 and action over EniChem's Manfredonia plant suggest that the warning of the Seveso dioxyn disaster was not fully heeded.

Products

Petroleum products Large-scale investment made Italy the refinery of Europe until the advent of super-tankers and new capacity in the Gulf. In the late 1980s it was clear that there were too many refineries and that primary distillation capacity of about 125m tonnes/138m US tons exceeded requirements by about 30m tonnes/33 US tons.

Primary and secondary chemicals During the 1980s there has been a widening of the trade gap in primary and secondary chemicals. Between 1982 and 1987 the deficit doubled to L6,456bn; one-half of this derived from trade with West Germany. Italy was a net importer of all principal primary chemicals in 1987, the deficit being particularly large in resins and plastic materials. The low technological content of Italian products is partly responsible for the large deficit in secondary chemicals.

Synthetic fibres In contrast to primary and secondary chemicals, fibres achieve a trade surplus overall – L214bn in 1987. Strong products in the sector are acrylic, polyamidic and polypropylene fibres, whose export contributions substantially outweigh deficits in cellulose and polyester. Montefibre, a Montedison subsidiary, is Italy's main producer of synthetic fibres and one of Europe's largest.

Pharmaceuticals Italy's pharmaceuticals industry employed nearly 65,000 people at the end of 1987, a year in which sales of its limited product range totalled L10,934bn and the industry deficit was only L687bn. Montedison leads the national industry through Farmitalia Carlo Erba, a subsidiary of the Erbamont sub-holding. Erbamont is a world leader in anti-cancer chemotherapeutic agents, including Andriamycin, Farlutal and Pharmorubicin.

Notwithstanding the complaints against the state pricing system for drugs, Italy's large market (the world's fifth largest and growing rapidly) has attracted most major foreign manufacturers. The large number with plants just south of Rome (attracted by proximity to the capital and regional incentives) include Wellcome, Fisons (which bought Rome-based Italchimici in 1988), Wyeth, Dow-Lepetit, Abbott, Pfizer and Bristol.

Problems

Constant political intervention has not benefited national chemicals companies. They allocate insufficient resources to R&D to permit the development of innovative, high added-value products. This is partly due to low profits, or losses; but it also reflects the smaller size of Italian companies compared with their international competitors. However, the merger of EniChem's chemicals operations with part of Montedison's has put the new joint venture, Enimont, eighth in the world behind Ciba and ahead of Rhône-Poulenc.

Defence

In the 1970s and early 1980s oil-rich Middle Eastern and African states bought from Italy not only because its equipment was price competitive but also because it represented an alternative to the two super-powers and to former colonial nations Britain and France. Conditions in the late 1980s became far less buoyant, but Italy had used the good years to reduce the gap which separated its armaments makers from Europe's leaders.

Public and private

Holding corporations (IRI and EFIM) have substantial interests in defence work. Major projects for the government are usually awarded to subsidiary companies within the state holding system, but opportunities exist for the private sector. Fiat has an aero-engine subsidiary which works extensively on defence contracts. Its Telettra telecommunications and Snia-BPD missile propulsion subsidiaries are also active in military work. Defence business accounts for at least 10% of the Fiat group's sales, though this is not clear from the company's accounts.

Foreign presence US defence manufacturers, including Litton and Irvin, have Italian subsidiaries. Britain has a good foothold in Italy's military electronics industry with Marconi Italiana (part of GEC), Elettronica (Plessey has a 49% stake) and Elmer (Ferranti-ISC).

Sea

The fat years of building warships for export ended in 1984. State-owned Fincantieri delivered 10 frigates and 13 corvettes to foreign navies between 1978 and 1984. It also built six corvettes and four frigates for Iraq, later encountering embargo obstacles. *The Navy's* large building programme has meant that Fincantieri's yards have not been idle. They delivered three corvettes and amphibious transport in 1987, and were contracted to supply two Animoso class super-destroyers, four Minerva class corvettes and two Sauro class submarines.

Land

Italy's most spectacular and talked-about success is the pistol. In 1985 Beretta's 9 calibre Parabellum was declared the victor in a competition to re-equip the US Army with side-arms. At the other end of the scale, through EFIM subsidiary Oto Melara, Italy has built a considerable reputation for big guns. In collaboration with Fiat's Iveco truck subsidiary, Oto Melara is working on a second-generation tank and a new armoured car.

Air

Aeritalia, an IRI subsidiary, is the Italian partner on the Tornado project, holding a 12.4% stake. The company also has a 21% stake in the European Fighter Aircraft (EFA) and is the lead partner with Brazil's Embraer in the AMX light fighter bomber project.

Helicopters EFIM subsidiary Agusta enjoys good standing in the rotary-wing sector. It has high expectations of the EH101 helicopter, being built in collaboration with the UK's Westland. It is also working on the NH90 land transport and anti-submarine helicopter and Tonal, a multi-role combat helicopter.

Missiles and electronics

State-owned Selenia is Italy's leader in radar and command and control systems. It also makes missiles, as does Oto Melara. Italy's missile armoury includes Otomat (Oto Melara, seaborne surface-to-surface), Albatros (Selenia, seaborne surface-to-air) and Spada (Selenia, land-based surface-to-air).

Selenia and Elettronica are both heavily involved in military aviation electronics, and Aeritalia and Agusta are boosting their avionics systems capability.

Insurance

Italy's insurance business originated in Trieste. The city's role until 1918 as the Austro-Hungarian empire's main port, coupled with the central European business mentality of its inhabitants, bred an attitude to insurance lacking in more happy-go-lucky parts of Italy itself. In the 1980s the market throughout Italy has expanded rapidly, with industrial insurance likely to be a strong growth area in the 1990s.

The companies

About 225 companies (165 Italian, the rest foreign-controlled) operate in a market with premiums totalling L23,000bn (1987), including L5,000bn in the life sector. Six groups specialize in reinsurance, and another 30 or so insurance companies include it in their business.

Assicurazioni Generali of Trieste is the biggest company in the non-life sector while the state-owned INA (Istituto Nazionale Assicurazioni) dominates life assurance. Overall, Generali and its main life subsidiary Alleanza take first place, with premium income in Italy in 1987 of L2,788bn, ahead of INA and its associate Assitalia (Le Assicurazioni d'Italia), with premiums of L2,617bn. It is Europe's third largest insurance group, and the world's second largest in terms of market capitalization. Generali's largest single shareholders are merchant banks Mediobanca and Lazards Frères. Gruppo Generali (parent company, affiliates and subsidiaries) comprises 54 insurance companies. Its foreign subsidiaries include Northern Star Insurance in Britain, Deutscher Lloyd in West Germany and Union Suisse in Switzerland.

Second in Italy's non-life league, SAI (Società Assicuratrice Industriale), was once owned by Fiat and is now part of the Ligresti industrial group.

The fast-growing Unipol of Bologna (120th in terms of non-life premium income in 1972, sixth in 1987), owned by the left-wing Lega cooperative movement, has broken with tradition by floating shares on the Milan bourse. (See *Power in business.*)

Foreign companies hold a very large share of Italy's insurance market, either directly or through controlling interests in local firms: 27.8% in 1988, compared with 10% in Britain and 8% in France. Zürich Insurance is the leading foreign firm. Riunione Adriatica di Sicurtà (RAS), which moved some years ago from Trieste to Milan, is now owned by West Germany's Allianz. Lloyd Adriatico, based in Trieste, passed under the control of Swiss Re in 1988.

Investment Companies follow conservative policies, though the law allows broad scope for the investment of assets. In recent years about a third has been held in government fixed-interest securities, at least a quarter in property, and a little more and a little less than 10% respectively in bonds and equities. Firms are increasingly moving into a wider range of financial services.

The market

While non-life sectors have been expanding annually at 14–15%, life assurance increased by about 35% in both 1986 and 1987. Although it may be difficult to maintain the pace, this and other forms of personal insurance have benefited from cracks in the wide-ranging but malfunctioning national system of social insurance. In the life sector, however, companies are restricted by a requirement to reinsure a percentage of new business (30% in the first five years, less thereafter) with INA.

Outlook Motor vehicle insurance is one of the less promising sectors, as third-party premium levels are fixed by the government. Industrial insurance, however, is a growth area. Italy's myriad small businesses are beginning to be hungry for insurance and other financial services.

Advertising and PR

A turnaround in the public perception of publicity and the astonishing growth of private TV stations have wrought major changes in Italian advertising since the 1970s. Growing appreciation by young people, high consumer spending and more polished presentation have all helped to make advertising one of Italy's fastest growing industries since the 1970s. Prospects appear bright, despite the failure to expand internationally. The PR sector, though still in its infancy compared with that of many other Western countries, is beginning to gain a foothold, and commercial sponsorship, particularly of sport and TV programmes, is much used by large industrial firms and banks.

Advertising

Almost every year since 1980, growth in spending on advertising has been in double figures. Annual billings from TV commercials rose from about L188bn in 1979 to L3,500bn in 1988 and they account for more than half of all spending on advertising.
Newspapers and magazines have about 35% of the market. The major areas of advertising spending are food products, cars, drinks and clothes, in that order. Banks and financial institutions, keen to reach middle-class investors, and the state, increasingly anxious to provide information, have been major new sources of revenue.

There has been a sharp change in public opinion on advertising, especially among the young. Gone are the days of the 1970s when radicals regarded it as merely a capitalist tool. A Milan cinema even presents, once a year, an all-night show consisting entirely of commercials from many countries. Home-grown advertising, however, is still in many cases quaint or unsophisticated, lacking in wit and characterized by ham acting and much reliance on the use of attractive actresses.

Direct marketing has been far less successful than advertising, hampered by Italy's appalling postal service and out-of-date telephone system. However, toll-free telephone numbers (*numeri verdi*: "green" numbers) are gradually coming into use.

Crossing frontiers One weakness has been the industry's inability to market itself internationally. However, this may be changing: Publitalia, Berlusconi's advertising management company, in 1988 won an exclusive contract to supply advertising from the West to Soviet viewers. It also supplies the Yugoslav station Capodistria, which specializes in live sports.

Control The Grande Giuria di Pubblicità (Grand Jury of Advertising), made up of agencies, TV stations, publishers and major spenders, decides on most questions of taste or morals.

TV predominates More than 1,000 privately owned stations have been set up and as many as 30 are available in large cities. This explosion has been the key to a huge increase in TV advertising. The dominant figure is Silvio Berlusconi, who owns the three main private channels – Italia Uno, Rete Quattro and Canale Cinque – which together account for over 40% of all TV revenues. His Publitalia also supplies the other private stations with advertising. (See *Power in business*.)

At present, private stations can use up to 18 minutes an hour for advertising, though this falls to 13 minutes at prime time. The state-owned RAI is allowed few advertising breaks in shows.

Agencies McCann-Erickson and Young & Rubicam are the largest advertising agencies in Italy. Two Italian firms, Armando Testa and Mac Communicazione Integrata, are third and fourth, while J. Walter

Thompson and Saatchi & Saatchi come fifth and sixth respectively. These six alone account for about 25% of the market. No Italian agency is quoted on the Milan Borsa. Few European firms have taken over Italian agencies, with the exception of France's Belier group, which now ranks in Italy's top ten.

PR

Public relations (the English term is used) is expanding rapidly but it was a late starter in Italy and is still fairly small-scale and unsophisticated. There is much more emphasis on cocktail parties than, for example, clear-headed explanations of a company's financial position or strategy. However, several universities, including Bocconi in Milan, now offer courses in PR which aim to turn out a new breed of professional.

Firms The sector comprises hundreds of small- to medium-sized companies catering to just a few specialized clients. Most are located in Milan and Rome and they concentrate on a limited number of sectors: fashion, beauty products, TV and financial services in particular. The handful of large firms includes Maveglia and SCR.

Major international firms with offices in Italy include Burson-Marsteller and Hill & Knowlton. Among those which have bought out local concerns are Ogilvy & Mather (Sintonia) and D'Arcy Masius Benton & Bowles (Seci).

Sponsorship

The majority of commercial sponsors are large firms or banks and in most cases they go for a high level of media exposure rather than prestige. Sole sponsorship is the norm. Annual spending in the late 1980s was about L900bn (excluding the sponsoring of TV programmes). There have been calls to amend the tax laws to allow relief on sponsorship spending.

Sport dominates the scene, largely because of the guaranteed exposure on TV. Both national and local stations devote a large part of their programming to sport, and particularly to soccer. Players have company names emblazoned on their jerseys. Italian soccer teams are the playthings of the wealthy individuals who own them, but they are partly financed by commercial sponsors: Gianni Agnelli's Juventus is sponsored by domestic appliance manufacturer Ariston; Silvio Berlusconi's AC Milan by a textile firm, Mediolanum; Roma by pasta maker Barilla; and Napoli by the UK-based confectionery group Mars. Basketball teams take the names of their sponsors, who often change annually, so that what was Tracer Milano one year became Philips Milano the next.

Savings banks, which are required by law to devote a certain percentage of their earnings to public service activities, are prominent in cultural sponsorship. Cassa di Risparmio di Firenze is sole sponsor of Florence's international music festival, Maggio Musicale.

Fiat and Olivetti are also big spenders on sponsorship of the arts, which get much less media coverage than sport but which carry greater prestige. Usually they set up and manage a project rather than just provide the finance. Fiat's flagship is Palazzo Grassi in Venice, which it bought in 1984 and turned into a highly successful museum with changing exhibitions.

Literary events are sponsored by fashion designer Krizia, who regularly brings distinguished foreign writers to Milan to give talks or take part in discussions.

Many TV programmes are sponsored, both on the state-owned RAI and on Berlusconi's independent channels. Mass popular appeal is favoured rather than high culture. The Standa supermarket chain, for example, presents variety shows. Berlusconi's ownership of Standa and other potential programme sponsors, together with his TV empire and involvement in the advertising business, put him in an extraordinarily dominant position.

Leading private companies

The table of Italy's 3,500 largest companies published each year by the weekly business magazine *Il Mondo* highlights the important role of the public sector in the country's industry and commerce. State-owned companies held four of the top five places in 1987, with the electricity corporation ENEL in first place (see *Government and business*). Fiat's automobile division was ranked second. Its industrial vehicles division Iveco was among the top ten, which also included two companies owned by Esso and two by IBM.

Fiat

Italy's largest private-sector group has made considerable progress since the critical 1970s, and is often cited as the best example of national industrial recovery. In 1981 the group was barely breaking even; in 1987 profits were L2,373bn. Best known as an automobile maker, the Turin company owns Lancia, Ferrari and, since the beginning of 1987, Alfa Romeo. Extensive model renewal helped Fiat Auto to sales of more than 2m cars in 1987 and cars accounted for 58% of group sales. Trucks and buses provided a further 17%. The Fiat group embraces related industries such as tractors, steel, vehicle components, factory automation (Comau) and lubricants. Wider diversification involves the Agnelli group in civil engineering (Impresit), aviation, defence and fibres (Snia-BPD), telecommunications (Telettra) and newspaper publishing (Turin's daily newspaper *La Stampa*).

Montedison-Ferruzzi

The conglomerate which resulted from Ferruzzi's takeover of Montedison at the end of 1987 is Italy's second largest private-sector group. The controversial takeover was followed by complex corporate restructuring and financial manoeuvring in 1988. Montedison had four segments before being taken over; chemicals, energy, pharmaceuticals and services. Reorganization stripped out services, including Rome's daily newspaper *Il Messaggero*, the Standa retail chain, the Fondiaria insurance company and

real estate interests. Montedison remained the parent company for its industrial activities, under the control of Ferruzzi Agricola Finanziaria, an industrial sub-holding of Ferruzzi Finanziaria. Montedison controls the US Himont corporation (the world's largest polypropylene producer), and owns Ausimont (specialty chemicals) and Erbamont (pharmaceuticals). Substantial agro-industry operations are controlled by Ferruzzi Agricola Finanziaria, including the French Béghin-Say sugar company and US Central Soya. Ferruzzi group has European leadership in sugar, starch and edible oils/proteins. Ferruzzi Finanziaria directly controls Montedison's former services segment and subsidiaries in agriculture/ livestock, trading, storage and cement.

Olivetti

No Italian industrial company enjoys such a high reputation as Olivetti for stylish products. It became the first European company to exhibit products and graphic work at New York's Museum of Modern Art, where the Lexikon 80, Lettera 22 and Valentine typewriters are on permanent display. However, good design was not enough and in the 1970s the company ran into serious difficulties. Carlo De Benedetti, now a star business figure, became Olivetti's CEO in 1978 and imposed large-scale labour reductions and strategic product diversification. In 1989 he increased his shareholding from 19% to over 40%; this was the result of AT&T of the USA swapping its stake for one in De Benedetti's holding company CIR. In 1978 office products (typewriters, copiers, calculators and furniture) generated 50% of sales revenue. Olivetti's switch to computers and office automation cut the contribution of office products to 17% in 1987 and it became Europe's top office automation company. R&D activities and investment in fixed assets absorbed 13% of net revenues in 1987 when the company launched the LSX 3000 line of minicomputers. Internationalization is at the heart of Olivetti's strategy. It acquired control of Britain's Acorn Computers in 1985 and West Germany's Triumph Adler the following year. Numerous cross-border acquisitions and joint ventures aim at obtaining innovative products and raising distribution capacity. In 1988/89 Olivetti was restructured into three separate companies: Olivetti Systems and Networks (data processing), Olivetti Office (mainly typewriters) and Olivetti Information Services (information technology).

Pirelli

Pirelli is known not only for its products but for stylish calendars and the graceful Milan skyscraper, built as its headquarters. In the 1970s an abortive union was forged with Britain's Dunlop. Unlike Dunlop, Pirelli has since enjoyed better fortune. Its principal activity is tyre manufacturing (it ranks fifth in the world) which generated about 44% of sales in 1987. Cables for power transmission, telecommunications and windings accounted for 39%. Two-thirds of sales are in Europe. North American sales are less than one-tenth of the total. In 1988 Pirelli was outbid by Bridgestone in the battle for Firestone, but succeeded in acquiring Armstrong Tire.

At home a major corporate reorganization announced in 1988 was designed to eliminate the complex structure involving Swiss and Italian industrial holding companies and a Swiss management company.

Benetton

Benetton began in 1965 to produce colourful woollen and cotton garments aimed at the growing youth and leisure markets. It started its retail chain at Belluno in 1968; a year later it opened its first foreign outlet, in Paris. Within ten years of the first opening, Benetton shops numbered about 1,000. At the end of 1987 about 4,000 retail outlets were selling Benetton clothing through concession agreements. Exports account for about two-thirds of sales. The company uses two other trade names, 012 and Sisley, and has diversified into cosmetics and made brand agreements with Polaroid for sunglasses and Bulova for watches. Though its shares are quoted, Benetton remains a family company run by three brothers and one sister. Luciano, born in 1935 and the oldest, is chief executive, with responsibility for defining strategy and directing market policy. Styling and design fall to Giuliana, while Gilberto runs the financial side and Carlo manages production and foreign operations.

Fininvest

Silvio Berlusconi's Fininvest group is one of the recent stars in Italy's business firmament. With the acquisition of the Standa retail chain from Ferruzzi group in 1988, Fininvest became Italy's third largest private-sector group. Its starting point was construction. After undertaking real estate developments around Milan in the 1960s and 1970s, Berlusconi focused on the service sector. Through RTI, his group controls Italy's largest private television networks (Canale 5, Italia Uno and Rete 4). Fininvest also controls an advertising subsidiary, publishing activities and AC Milan football club. In the 1980s the company diversified extensively into financial services: a network of 2,100 salesmen (Programma Italia) sells insurance, real estate bonds and mutual funds. The group is wholly owned by the Berlusconi family.

The Political Scene

The government of the nation

Italy was unified as a nation under a monarchy in 1870 but, in the aftermath of the disastrous years of Fascist rule and World War II, the Italians voted in a referendum in 1946 in favour of a republic. The vote was 12.7m for a republic and 10.7m for maintaining the king, with the more impoverished South solidly monarchist. A provisional head of state was named while a constitutional assembly, representing all parties, prepared the republic's new constitution which went into effect in January 1948. Italy's first parliament was elected four months later.

The constitution

The Italian constitution, as it appears on paper, has been called the best or one of the best in modern times. However, in general it has not been regarded as the supreme law, but rather a catalogue of ideals. The existing laws that governed everyday affairs at all levels could not in any case have been ignored or replaced overnight. Even today the majority of laws are those codified under the Fascists' 22-year regime. More than 40 years later, parliament still has not bothered to cancel some anti-democratic laws.

The president

The president is head of state and his role is almost identical to that once held by the king. His official residence is Rome's former royal palace, the Quirinale, which had been the pope's official residence until 1870. Several presidents have chosen to live in their own homes and use the Quirinale as their office.

The president is elected by parliament in a secret ballot for a seven-year term. In one such election, the MPs had to vote 23 times before a candidate had the necessary two-thirds majority.

He is more than a figurehead, having greater power than, say, the British sovereign. He nominates the prime minister (president of the council of ministers – Consiglio dei Ministri), after consulting all political party leaders, and he may, as happened in July 1987, nominate someone not on any party's shortlist. He appoints ministers, on the recommendation of the prime minister. The president is also commander of the armed forces.

All laws passed by parliament must be signed by the president. Both Francesco Cossiga, the Christian Democrat who was elected to the post in 1985, and his Socialist predecessor, Sandro Pertini, have withheld their signatures from public finance bills when the necessary funds were not available. The president is guarantor of the constitution and also can play an active role as mediator in political crises, expressing an opinion or making a recommendation in the form of a message to parliament. Both Pertini and Cossiga enhanced their office's prestige by "expressing concern" in public over serious shortcomings in the state's duties towards its citizens.

There is no vice-president. If the president is out of the country, or incapacitated, the president of the senate becomes acting head of state.

Parliament

Parliament is elected every five years. Since 1972, parliament has been prematurely dissolved by the president five times, at the request of the majority of party leaders. Early elections were sought when the coalition government's internecine feuds had become too serious and when one or more of the parties thought they would make a better showing in new elections. No general election since 1972 has drastically altered the division of seats.

Two houses Parliament's two houses – the senate (Senato) and the chamber of deputies (Camera dei Deputati) – have the powers to make laws and to indicate the direction the government should take. The Camera has 630 members, who must be aged at least 25; the Senato has 315 elected members and 7 nominated life members. Senators must be at least 40. There is no upper or lower house: the most glaring flaw in the parliamentary system is that the constitution gives them identical functions and powers.

Elections for both Camera and Senato take place at least every five years. All citizens over the age of 18 can vote in elections to the Camera, and those over 25 can vote for the Senato. The constitution describes voting as a civic duty rather than a right. Elections are by proportional representation and a party that has gained, say, 20% of the national vote for the Camera will occupy that percentage of the Camera's seats. There is no lower limit on the share of votes required in order to gain a seat, which means that Italy's numerous small parties all play a significant role.

Deputies are returned from 32 multi-member constituencies, senators from single-member constituencies based on the regions, each of which (except the two smallest) must have at least seven senators.

Legislation The duplication of functions means that a bill must pass both houses without amendments. When amendments are proposed, the bill must be sent back for redrafting by the house where it originated. This shuttle continues until a single text emerges.

In an average year, 4,000 government and private members' bills are presented. Those that do get through parliament usually take years to do so. For any cabinet to function in recent years, the prime minister has been obliged to resort to laws by executive decree. These must be ratified by parliament within 60 days – otherwise they lapse – but they are given priority.

The secret ballot, which allowed members to vote against their party's line, perhaps against their own constituents' wishes, was abolished, except for certain cases, in October 1988, following lengthy and heated debate. The secret vote had allowed all manner of Machiavellian intrigue and repeatedly brought about the collapse of governments: by this date Italy had had 48 administrations in about 40 years.

Referenda The constitution provides for a referendum to be held on the abrogation of laws passed by parliament if at least 500,000 signatures are collected. Enabling legislation was not passed until 1970 but referenda have been held on several issues, including divorce, increased police powers to combat terrorism and organized crime, and nuclear power.

Decentralized government

Since 1970 Italy's 20 regions have had considerable autonomy. Five which were already in existence have greater autonomy than the rest: Sicily, Sardinia, Valle d'Aosta (which has a mainly French-speaking population), Trentino–Aldo Adige (South Tyrol, with a large German-speaking population) and Friuli-Venezia Giulia. Each region has a legislative council (Consiglio Regionale) which is elected by universal suffrage every five years. Power is devolved to the regions in numerous important areas, including health, education, police and public works, but they depend on Rome for revenue as they cannot levy taxes.

The provincial authorities lost most of their functions when the regions were created but they still have some responsibilities, such as local roads. Of much greater importance are the elected local authorities which run Italy's 8,000 *comuni*, a classification covering cities, towns and villages.

The reins of power

At the national level, political power is held not by parliament but by the political parties. All decisions ultimately are party decisions, from the nomination of coalition cabinet members to the appointment of candidates for all important public-sector offices, forming a substratum of power known as the *sottogoverno*. Political patronage (*clientelismo*) is widespread: the street-sweeper and the managing director of the opera house may well have got their jobs because of a *raccomandazione* from a political party. Parties theoretically are not allowed to accept donations from companies or from trade unions. In an effort to stem corruption, the parties voted in the 1970s that the treasury should grant them subsidies based on their percentage of the national vote. However, tales of back-door contributions continue to appear regularly in the national press.

Cabinet posts

Apart from a few rare exceptions, all cabinet ministers are chosen by the parties. Almost all Italian postwar governments have been coalitions, and the distribution of cabinet posts involves much haggling. The most important posts are those held by the ministers of foreign affairs, the interior and the treasury, followed by defence, public works and, gaining in importance, foreign trade.

Foreign affairs Italy is now very active in affairs affecting countries of the Mediterranean basin and in East–West relations; it also plays an important behind-the-scenes role in the Middle East.

Home affairs The interior minister is responsible for law and order. The State Police are under his command, as is domestic counter-espionage which sometimes in the past has included spying on rival politicans.

The treasury acts with the central bank to determine monetary policy and has the task of finding ways to finance Italy's chronic budget deficit. The minister holds the important post of chairman of the interministerial committee for credit and savings, the body which regulates the banking sector.

Key personalities

Bettino Craxi, who became Socialist Party leader in 1976, is the most "modern" of the leaders and is dedicated to power. In the early 1980s he broke a record by staying in office as prime minister for almost four years. Under his influence, the venerable Socialist Party emblem was stripped of its hammer and sickle and now flaunts a large red carnation. He is the most interesting politico of his generation (he was born in Milan in 1934) but he does not always inspire complete trust.

Achille Occhetto In 1988 the Communists chose a new leader, Achille Occhetto, (born in Turin in 1936) to do what a new broom is expected to do. Like Craxi, Occhetto is from a well-off family; also like him, he did not take a university degree – a rare thing in Italy's political world – and instead jumped straight into party politics.

Ciriaco De Mita became leader of the Christian Democrat party (the DC) in 1982 and was re-elected in 1986, thanks to his skill in managing the often tense relations between the party's various factions. He became prime minister in 1988. Before leading the party he was relatively little known, although he had held ministerial posts. His strong Southern accent (he was born in 1928 in Avellino but educated at the Catholic University of Milan) and the fact that he does not seem comfortable in the limelight place him slightly apart from most political leaders, but he is admired for his sharp intellect.

Giovanni Spadolini, former Republican Party leader, was elected president of the senate in 1987. Six years earlier he had become the first prime minister from a party other than the DC, yet he had entered politics only in 1972, at the age of 47. Before that he was a professor of history in his native Florence, editor of the Bologna daily *Il Resto del Carlino* and then from 1968 to 1972 of *Corriere della Sera* in Milan. He has written numerous books and essays and his demeanour remains that of a distinguised professor.

Giulio Andreotti, who became prime minister for the sixth time in July 1989, has long been one of the most powerful men in government, and one of his many nicknames is "Machiavelli".

Civil service

Italy inherited its civil service system from Napoleon but, unlike France, has no special school to train the officials. There is a shortage of highly trained, top-calibre people in the civil service, which is also weighed down by antiquated structures and procedures (the central bank is a notable exception). A programme of modernization was set in motion in 1988 with the appointment of Antonio Maccanico as minister for institutional reform. He is not an elected deputy but a highly respected civil servant, former head of the president's office and latterly chairman of Mediobanca.

A feature of the civil service is that a large proportion of its staff is from the South, perhaps illustrating the popular assumption that, while Northerners like money, Southerners like power.

The church

The church in Italy is separate from the state. The Lateran Pacts (treaty and concordat) signed with the Fascist government in 1929 established the Vatican City as an independent state,

but it was not until 1984 that relations between the Holy See and the Republic were formalized, in a new concordat. Under this agreement, the Catholic religion ceased to be Italy's official religion. But the Vatican, the Italian church and the state are inextricably linked in many ways. One is the Vatican's real property holdings, particularly in Rome and the surrounding area. Another is the fact that the pope is also bishop of Rome and primate of the Roman Catholic church in Italy.

From time to time, the pope is accused of interfering in Italian domestic affairs, and in the early days of the Republic the Italian bishops were explicitly campaigning for the DC, even though there was no direct link between church and party. That activity is on the wane, as is church attendance.

Declining power The church suffered two shattering defeats in 1974 and 1981: the referenda which gave public approval for the legalization of divorce and of abortion. These demonstrated the decline of its power to influence public opinion and individual choice.

Lay organizations Nevertheless the church is still deeply involved in education and in charitable works, and the wide range of thriving lay organizations provides it with a valuable channel for indirect influence. One of these is the powerful Comunione e Liberazione (CL), whose political wing, Movimento Popolare, strives to prod the DC back on to a straight and narrow Catholic path.

The Mafia

The existence of the Mafia can make normal business life difficult in much of Sicily. Calabria and the Naples area are affected, to a lesser extent, by the activities of the 'Ndrangheta and the Camorra respectively. The Mafia has always supported the DC – partly because this is the party which, as dominant coalition partner, has controlled the award of most big government contracts.

Party politics

Political observers everywhere watched the new Italian Republic's first national election in 1948 with keen interest and, in some quarters, trepidation. Many thought that the Communist-Socialist joint ballot might win the majority. The result instead gave 48% to the Vatican- and USA-backed Christian Democrats (Democristiani or DC), while the combined vote for the Partito Comunista Italiano (PCI) and the Partito Socialista Italiano (PSI) was only 31%. In each general election until 1979, the DC's vote was eroded, while the Communists gradually gained ground. However, the latter's upward trend seemed to have been definitively broken in the 1987 elections.

Coalition government

For more than 40 years the DC has been the largest party and the PCI the second largest. The PCI remains the major opposition party, and the largest Communist party in Western Europe. Since the smaller parties have not been willing to join the Communists in the national government, the DC has been able to dominate more than 40 successive coalition governments. That is known as political stability, Italian-style. Recent coalitions have required five parties' support just to get off the drawing-board. Sustained harmony is difficult as each party tends to act as a prima donna – "without me there'll be no opera."

At the 1987 general election for the chamber of deputies the DC won 34.3% of the votes, the PCI 26.6%, PSI 14.3%, Movimento Sociale Italiano (MSI) 5.9% and Partito Repubblicano Italiano (PRI) 3.7%.

Democrazia Cristiana

The DC's exponents have always ranged from non-aligned left to ultra-right, but the party's electorate can be defined as centre-right: people who want to be protected from change and, in particular, those who fear the Communists. The Italian press still refers to the DC as the "Catholic party," although there are no formal links with the Church.

A large section of the DC opposed party leader Aldo Moro in the 1970s when he was labouring to bring the Communists into the government. His efforts were cut short in 1978 when he was murdered by the extreme-left Red Brigade terrorists, who aimed to wreck all moves towards national conciliation.

Factions The DC is an amalgamation of clearly defined factions, each with its own private suite of offices in Rome and its own house journal.

Power Being in the centre of power for over 40 years has laid the DC more open to charges of corruption than other parties. Another privilege is control, through political appointments to key posts, of major public-sector industries and banks.

Partito Comunista Italiano

The PCI's 1.5m card-carrying members remain constant, thanks to the party's efficient management, among other factors. Its popularity reached a peak in the 1970s when its charismatic and widely respected leader Enrico Berlinguer was promoting the "historic compromise." Under this, the PCI agreed not to vote against the government, in return for regular and detailed consultations. The Communists ended this arrangement in 1979, because the DC was taking a harder line against them. In the 1987 general election the party lost 1m votes, with younger voters defecting to the Socialists, Radicals or Greens. Another cause was the uninspired leadership of Alessandro Natta, who became party boss in 1985 after the sudden death of Berlinguer. Natta's ill-health led in 1988 to his replacement by Achille Occhetto.

Communist strongholds The PCI has been more successful in gaining power at local government level – except in the South where, despite poverty and high unemployment, the voters have not been swayed towards any left-wing party. Paradoxically, the PCI vote is stronger in such beacons of culture and wealth as Bologna, Florence, Ravenna, Milan and Turin which share distrust of Rome's central powers and a tradition of anti-clericalism. Also, the North in general suffered much more during the Nazi occupation, which converted many people to Marxism. Wherever the PCI is strong, in villages or large cities, local administration is likely to be better. Political corruption within the PCI is relatively rare and suspected persons are rapidly expelled from the party.

Not Moscow's servant The PCI supported Moscow's invasion of Hungary in 1957, but not the 1968 invasion of Czechoslovakia, and firmly condemned the Soviets' Afghanistan adventure. No knowledgeable person today could say that the PCI is Moscow's servant. All evidence points towards its total autonomy.

Partito Socialista Italiano

The PSI and PCI were twinned by choice until 1963 when, with an alleged consenting nod from Washington, the PSI was admitted into the first centre-left cabinet. As a result the PSI lost votes in the next election. The big change came after 1976, under the leadership of Bettino Craxi. In 1983 he became Italy's first Socialist prime minister, a post he held for nearly four years. The party's share of the national vote has continued to rise, at national and local elections.

The smaller parties

Neo-fascists The only party which might be called extremist is the neo-fascist Movimento Sociale Italiano (MSI). In the 1970s its share reached nearly 10%. It still has a fairly strong following in Southern cities (it is the

second largest party in Naples), and among the Italian-speaking minority in parts of Trentino–Alto Adige (aligned against the region's German-speakers and their Südtiroler Volkspartei). However, in general its support is on the wane, as elderly one-time *fascisti* die off.

The Partito Repubblicano Italiano is an influential "common sense" centre party, strong in the North, with a history dating back to Mazzini. It has about 20 deputies in the chamber.

The Partito Socialista Democratico Italiano is a 1947 spin-off from the PSI and, as the latter party has grown in strength and credibility, has lost its raison d'être, although it is still represented in parliament as a party in its own right.

The Partito Liberale Italiano is a party of the centre-right with roots in the 19th century and a strong anti-clerical tradition. Its supporters are mainly people from the business world or the *alta borghesia* (upper middle class) who fear the rise of the Communists but who are opposed to the church's influence, or find aspects of DC politics unacceptable.

The Partito Radicale has lobbied, against great odds and with remarkable success, in favour of civil rights legislation. There is a strong intellectual component in its membership but it seems to have become increasingly eccentric, particularly in its choice of unconventional parliamentary candidates, the most publicized being the *"pornodiva"* Cicciolina.

Greens The newest and fastest-growing party is that of the Lista Verde, which made its maiden appearance as a national party in 1987, when it won 2.5% of the votes, campaigning on an anti-nuclear, environmentalist ticket. The *Verdi* ("greens") have 13 deputies in the chamber.

Democrazia Proletaria, with eight deputies, is all that is left of the lively political activity to the left of the Communists which flourished in the 1960s and early 1970s.

National security

Italy's armed forces total about 386,000 men, of whom nearly 258,000 are conscripts. There are no women in military service. There are three separate national police forces, whose functions sometimes overlap. Defence spending represents about 2.7% of GDP.

The armed forces

The army's strength is about 265,000, the air force's 73,000 and the navy's 48,000. The navy was once the most highly regarded service, partly because of its admirable wartime record, but the air force, with its high-tech image, is now a more popular choice with conscripts (who can choose their uniform only if they volunteer before their call-up papers arrive). The army is held in less esteem, with the exception of two very prestigious corps in which there is often a family tradition of service: the commando-type *Bersaglieri* and the mountain-based *Alpini*.

Conscription in theory affects all young men of 18 and over, who must do 12 months' service (18 months' in the navy), but this can be postponed until the completion of university studies. Some manage to avoid conscription altogether by prolonging their studies, or taking long sojourns abroad. It is widely believed that the better off, and those from families able to pull strings, are the most successful at exploiting the various let-out clauses, such as those based on supposed medical grounds, from flat-footedness upwards.

The police

The three national police forces and the local police (*vigili urbani*) are separate from each other but the demarcation of their responsibilities is in many cases blurred.

Polizia di Stato The State Police (still often called by their former name, *Pubblica Sicurezza*) have a paramilitary structure and are supervised by the Interior Ministry. They operate mainly in urban areas, although they have motorcycle patrols out on the highways, and they are responsible for public order. Founded in Fascist times, the force has a reputation for toughness and is the most disliked of the internal security forces. Its political section, SISDE (Servizio per l'Informazione e la Sicurezza Democratica), carries out intelligence work. Enrolment is about 83,300, of whom 6% are women.

The Carabinieri, numbering about 90,000 men, come under the jurisdiction of the Defence Ministry and have distinguished themselves for bravery in wartime. Their splendid red and black uniforms with cocked hats are a legacy of their early-19th-century origins in Piedmont. Although they do have public order responsibilities, their main functions are less localized than those of the State Police. Tracking down art thieves is one of their jobs, and they have helicopter and other mechanized units. Espionage and counter-espionage are also part of their business, through their special branch, SISMI (Servizio per l'Informazione e la Sicurezza Militare). Although the *Carabinieri*, a large proportion of whom are Southerners, are the butt of many popular jokes, it is to them that most ordinary people turn for help, rather than to the State Police.

The Guardia di Finanza, also a paramilitary force and also founded in Piedmont, in the late 18th century, has 49,000 men and is supervised by the Finance Ministry. It mans the *dogana* (customs) and investigates tax fraud, corruption and other financial malpractices.

Vigili urbani are the local police, responsible for traffic control in particular and answerable to the local council. They can make arrests for petty crime, but in cases of more serious offences they call in the State Police or the *Carabinieri*.

International alignments

Italy is a steadfast member of the Western Alliance and a committed believer in European unity. Italians are enthusiastic internationalists and it is fitting that the treaty which established the European Economic Community was signed in Rome. More than 80% of the Italian electorate turn out to vote for their Euro-MPs. Italy is also a conscientious member of the UN and has on occasion provided military personnel for UN peacekeeping missions.

Defence commitments

There can be no more unquestioning NATO partner than Italy. The government has been almost unswerving in its trust in the Pentagon, even when faced with vociferous opposition in parliament and in the public squares: riots greeted the arrival of the first US forces at Italian NATO bases in 1950. NATO's South European Command has its headquarters in Naples. Following Spain's announcement that it no longer wanted the American F-16 aircraft based on its territory, the Italian government in mid-1988 agreed to NATO's request to accommodate the fighter-bombers, and allocated them a base at Crotone in Calabria.

This was part of the Italians' 40-year-old balancing act, which requires them to be loyal to Washington while simultaneously holding hands (and doing business) with all the Islamic states which once were a part of the Roman Empire. Italy's self-appointed role as a bridge between Europe and North Africa and the Middle East has led sometimes to soured relations with Israel.

Economic relationships

The EC Italy's enthusiasm for European unity has its roots in the struggle for its own unification. It is also a reaction to the bombastic nationalism of Fascism. Moreover, being part of a new and united Europe was seen in the aftermath of World War II as a means of repairing the terrible moral and economic damage the country had suffered. Italy worked harder than any other member to drag Britain into the EC,

partly motivated by a fear of being crushed between France and West Germany: it wanted the UK as an ally. Despite its enthusiasm for the ideals of the EC, Italy often drags its feet in implementing directives. For example, it did not get around to introducing value-added tax (IVA) until at least 18 months after Britain had joined. Also, in most years Italy fails to use the CAP fund set aside for its farmers. Until the arrival of Greece as an EC member, Italy held the "club's" record for the number of times it had been delinquent in observing EC rules.

Aid to the Third World

Italy was a latecomer to the list of major international aid donors. Until the early 1980s its aid to the Third World was almost entirely restricted to humanitarian assistance. It has caught up rapidly to become one of the leading donors in terms of sums allocated. The aid budget, which in 1980 was 0.17% of GNP, by 1988 had reached 0.4%, a larger proportion than Canada's or the UK's, although still below the UN target of 0.7%.

About two-thirds of the aid is bilateral and, of this, about 80% is tied to the procurement of Italian goods and services. The emphasis is on a small number of sub-Saharan African countries, mainly Somalia, Ethiopia, Mozambique and Tanzania, with smaller amounts going to Latin America, North Africa and Lebanon. In 1987 Italy spent L3,200bn on aid, nearly half as grants and food aid. In terms of quality of aid, Italy may score fewer points than its high spending suggests, because of a lack of experience in aid projects.

The Business Scene

Government and business

State involvement is widespread in Italian industry and finance. The public sector not only controls strategic services such as rail and air transport, telecommunications, and power generation and distribution, it also owns, or has a controlling interest in, shipping lines, shops, restaurants, hotels and tourist villages, and it makes glass, aluminium, chemicals and even olive oil and ice cream. The public presence is particularly strong in banking: 75% of the sector is publicly controlled. The distribution of jobs to political appointees, a process known as *lottizzazione*, is a well-rooted feature of Italian life.

State holding system

The state holding system is based on the Istituto per la Ricostruzione Industriale (IRI) and on two other holding corporations, Ente Nazionale Idrocarburi (ENI) and Ente Partecipazioni e Finanziamento Manifatturiera (EFIM). The three holding corporations are overseen by the Ministero delle Partecipazioni Statali (Ministry of State Investments), which also serves as the institutional reference point for the Ente Autonomo Gestione Cinema (EAGC), which controls the large Cinecittà film studios in Rome.

Decision-making in the state holding system is two-tiered: political and managerial. At a political level the government appoints the chairman and boards of directors of IRI, ENI and EFIM and approves their strategic guidelines. The chairmanship of IRI falls to candidates preferred by the Christian Democrats. Following a fierce political struggle at the start of the 1980s, the Socialists have claimed the right to place their man at the top of ENI. The political colour of EFIM's chairmanship used to be Social Democrat but is now uncertain.

Managerial autonomy? Companies within the state holding system are organized as joint stock companies and are regulated by private company law. Their management contracts, labour relations and financial operations are similar to those of private sector companies. The holding corporations claim that there is a high degree of managerial autonomy in their subsidiaries. However, they ensure that subsidiaries adhere to plans acceptable at a political level.

IRI

The biggest of the three holding corporations, IRI employs about 420,000 people in widely differing sectors. The corporation was established in 1933 to deal with the collapse of a large part of the Italian banking system. It bailed out major banks, keeping control of them and taking over their portfolios of shareholdings in industrial companies (see *Banks and other financial institutions*).

In recent years the results from IRI's banks have mitigated the heavy losses returned by other subsidiaries and even allowed a return to profit in 1986. In 1987, despite losses of L126bn in IRI's industrial sector, there was an overall profit of L190bn.

Steel Biggest of IRI's loss-makers and largest in terms of employment, the steel company Finsider has been the centre of controversy. Proposed rationalization centres on much-needed capacity cuts, which would reduce the work force by about one-third from the 84,500 employed in 1987; but the large steelworks at Naples and Taranto are in depressed areas of high unemployment, and state companies do not usually dismiss workers.

Finmeccanica is the sub-holding that controls subsidiaries in mechanical engineering, such as power and transport engineers Ansaldo and the aerospace company Aeritalia. It also controlled Alfa Romeo before the automobile maker was sold off. This was an important contributor to the large losses suffered by Finmeccanica.

Other industrial sub-holdings The interests of IRI also embrace leading electronics and telecommunications companies, including Selenia, Elsag and Italtel. Its sub-holding Fincantieri owns shipyards, another loss-making sector.

Ships and ice cream A highly diversified conglomerate, IRI controls the national radio and television organization RAI, the national airline Alitalia, shipping lines (including Lloyd Triestino and Italia), and the state telecommunications body STET, which in turn owns the national telephone system SIP. It also owns construction firm Italstat (which owns a large part of the autostrada network) and civil engineering firms Condotte and Italstrade, and the SME food, retail distribution and catering group. Through SME the state owns the country's leading olive oil brand Bertolli and the Motta/Alemagna confectionery and ice cream brands.

ENI

Twenty years younger than IRI and employing about 130,000, ENI was established with the object of operating in all phases of the oil industry. The corporation quickly became international, particularly through the oil exploration and development company Agip and its refining and distribution sister Agip Petroli.

Energy remains the core of ENI's activities. In addition to Agip's oil and gas reserves, ENI has access to coal through Agip Carbone, which is involved in trading and is also an operator in South Africa, Australia and Venezuela. The corporation's subsidiary Snam is responsible for gas imports and for gas transport and distribution. Snam also operates ENI's oil tanker fleet. (See *Energy*.)

Engineering There are important ENI subsidiaries in the mechanical engineering plant and service sectors. Snamprogetti provides engineering for refineries and for fertilizer and chemicals plant. Saipem drills wells and lays pipelines. Nuovo Pignone makes pumps, compressors and other items of plant and equipment for the oil, petrochemicals and electricity industries; it also makes textile machinery, as does Savio, another ENI subsidiary.

Chemicals are the third main area of ENI's activities. EniChem heads a sector containing numerous companies with production ranging from base chemicals and polymers to diversified chemicals such as synthetic fibres, artificial rubber, fertilizers and detergent intermediates. EniChem and the private company Montedison formed a joint venture, Enimont, in 1988 (see *Chemicals*).

Other ENI activities include substantial minerals operations producing not only zinc, lead, copper and their derivatives but also ceramic tiles. An ENI sub-holding controls a chain of hotels and tourist complexes. Another controls the daily newspaper, *Il Giorno*, and a news agency.

EFIM

The smallest of the state holding corporations, with about 37,000 employees, EFIM was established in 1962.

Defence is a sector in which EFIM has several major subsidiaries. Oto Melara, one of Italy's best-known defence engineering companies, is controlled by Finanziaria Ernesto Breda, an EFIM sub-holding. Finanziaria Aviofer Breda, another sub-holding, controls the helicopter maker Agusta. (See *Defence*.)

From buses to baking foil Both Ernesto Breda and Aviofer Breda have interests outside the defence sector. Subsidiary companies make forgings, pumps for power stations, buses and rolling stock for railways. Two other sub-holdings give EFIM a dominating national presence in aluminium and glass production. In the case of aluminium EFIM has a vertically integrated operation, from smelting to the production of foil for household use.

Privatization

There is little support for the selling off of state-owned companies. The political right treats the top jobs in public sector industries as rewards for faithful party service. The same is also true of the left, even though it may be camouflaged by a screen of political principle.

Full privatization has been infrequent. The main instances were IRI's controversial disposal of Alfa Romeo to Fiat (at the end of 1986), ENI's sale of its Lanerossi textile group to Gruppo Marzotto in 1987 and EFIM's withdrawal from the food industry.

The proposed sale of IRI's SME food group to CIR, Carlo De Benedetti's main holding company, encountered serious opposition and a court decision in spring 1988 left SME under IRI's control (see *Power in business*).

Banks In disposing of its unstrategic subsidiaries, IRI's Banco di Roma sold Banco Centro Sud to Citicorp and Banca Tamai di Spilimbergo to Banca Popolare di Verona.

A smaller share There was a series of gradual partial privatizations before the 1987 stock market collapse. IRI reduced its stakes in the three national-interest banks (see *Banks and other financial institutions*) and in other quoted companies – Alitalia, Aeritalia, the telephone corporation SIP and Cementir, its cement subsidiary. At the end of 1988 the stake held by IRI's three banks in Mediobanca, Italy's most important investment bank, was reduced from about 55% to 25%. ENI sold minority stakes in some of its subsidiaries, in particular Saipem and Nuovo Pignone. This process of diluting the holding corporations' stake in their subsidiaries is described by ENI's chairman as "collecting cash

without losing control." In future, joint ventures with private-sector companies will probably be the preferred way to reduce or keep in check the state's role in Italian business.

The Mezzogiorno

The state holding corporations are expected to help the development of the country's poorer South by directing part of their investment towards the regions of the Mezzogiorno. EFIM in particular has a high concentration of operations there.

Special help Established at the beginning of the 1950s, the Cassa per il Mezzogiorno, the development fund for the South, started with infrastructure projects to take water and electricity to Southerners and to reduce their isolation by improving road and rail communications.

Incentives to private business followed, aimed at encouraging new factories and jobs. Since the 1960s the government has offered capital grants, soft loans, tax breaks and reduced social security charges to industries setting up new plants or expanding existing activities in the South (see *The business framework*).

New structure The Cassa was wound up in 1985 and replaced the following year by a new institutional structure for boosting development in the South and for allocating funds. The new scheme is aimed at encouraging individual and cooperative enterprise. The authorities of Italy's southern regions now have the responsibility for proposing and approving projects. However, their lack of relevant expertise meant that most of the funds remained untapped more than two years after the new system began. A total of L120,000bn was allocated for the nine years 1986–94. A central department in Rome examines technical feasibility and a new agency, Agenzia per la Promozione dello Sviluppo del Mezzogiorno, administers the financing aspects, including relations with the EC.

Power in business

In a country where connections and recommendations continue to be widely regarded as the surest way to make progress, and where organized crime grips large areas, it is not surprising that the nature and exercise of power in Italian business should have particular characteristics and connotations. Extremely close links between business and politics are fostered by a system in which the state controls large sections of industry and finance. But not only are there fraternities of political families: Italian business is also heavily based on real family ties. (See *Leading private companies.*)

Dynasties

Giovanni (Gianni) Agnelli, Fiat's chairman, has often been described as the uncrowned king of Italy. His "kingdom" comprises 20–25% of the total capitalization of the Italian stock market. The dynasty was founded by the present chairman's grandfather, who established the Turin automobile company in 1899. The group has spread widely into newspaper publishing, bioengineering, construction, telecommunications, defence and finance. The Agnelli family maintains tight control through a stake amounting to about 40%.

Ala nobile The Agnellis, led by Gianni with the support of his brother Umberto, rule the *ala nobile* (noble wing) or *salotto buono* (best drawing room) of Italian business. Leading princes at court are Leopoldo Pirelli (the tyre and cables magnate) and Luigi Orlando (head of the SMI/LMI/ GIM copper and metals group).

Mutual defence The *ala nobile* has a structure which aims to protect its members against the attacks or infiltration of outsiders. Gemina, the Agnelli/Fiat investment company, and Mediobanca, the merchant bank, are key nodes in a complex network of cross-holdings between family-controlled corporations. Significant cross-holdings exist between Gemina, Mediobanca, SMI/LMI/GIM, Pirelli and other leading industrial and financial groups.

Keeping it in the family The arrival of new generations of family members leads to fragmentation of ownership and the risk of weaker control. The

aristocrats of Italian capitalism are taking steps to avoid dilution of individual family interests. Fiat led the way in 1987 when a partnership, known as Giovanni Agnelli and Company, was established into which the Agnellis have locked their controlling shareholdings in the Fiat Group. The Agnellis' move was copied by other leading families.

New condottieri

Three names feature among the newcomers whose increasing importance during the 1980s poses a challenge to the power of the establishment. They all have great flair and all, like Agnelli, provide colourful copy for Italy's press.

Carlo De Benedetti, Olivetti's chief executive who had a brief spell as Fiat's managing director in 1976, has been in the vanguard. He doubled his stake in Olivetti to about 40% in 1989, and has extensive interests outside this group. Through his investment companies COFIDE and CIR, De Benedetti has insurance and banking interests. His group has been diversifying also into food, car components and communications. European expansion in the mid-1980s brought him significant stakes in Yves Saint Laurent, the French car components firm Valeo and Société Générale de Belgique, although he failed in a bid to secure control of the Belgian conglomerate.

Raul Gardini is a newer character on Italy's business stage. From relative obscurity at Ravenna's Ferruzzi agro-industry group, Gardini sprang to public notice during the mid-1980s with a series of international operations in agriculture: the successful takeovers of Central Soya and Béghin-Say and the failed bid for British Sugar Corporation. At home the costly and spectacular takeover of the Montedison chemicals group, completed in 1987, was followed by rationalization and asset stripping to reduce debt.

Silvio Berlusconi caught the spotlight of public attention after winning leadership in private television. Having found a loophole which allowed him to break the state-owned RAI's television monopoly, he has built up the world's fourth largest private network, and claims nearly 45% of the national audience. Berlusconi started out in the 1960s with real estate development, later expanding into construction (with a major housing scheme, known as Milano 2000), advertising, insurance, financial services, publishing and cinemas. He is something of a popular hero, particularly in his home city, where he owns AC Milan football club. His empire, which is wholly family controlled, grew still further with the acquisition in 1988 of the Standa supermarket chain from Gardini's Ferruzzi-Montedison group.

Supporting players

There is no shortage of support for the main protagonists in Italian business. Cesare Romiti, Agnelli's right hand and steel glove as managing director of Fiat, was regarded as a strong potential candidate for the chairmanship of the industrialists' confederation Confindustria in 1988. But he decided to stay at Fiat and the job went to Sergio Pininfarina, a less astringent character.

Pininfarina succeeded Luigi Lucchini, the Brescia steel magnate who stamped his four-year period as the industrialists' leader with an aggressive brand of uncompromising capitalism. Lucchini, a lesser member of the *ala nobile*, had taken over from

Vittorio Merloni, who has been successful with the family domestic appliances firm Ariston. Neither Merloni nor Luciano Benetton, founder of the clothing chain, has a place in the *ala nobile*.

Confindustria

The Confederazione Generale dell'Industria Italiana operates from headquarters in Rome but has a capillary organization throughout Italy, with regional, provincial and sectoral groups. Confindustria has a respected research department and provides a strong voice for Italy's private sector industrialists. The presidency, held in the 1970s by Gianni Agnelli and former Bank of Italy governor Guido Carli, is generally regarded as prestigious.

Agricultural lobby

In keeping with the national character, Italy's large farming community counts its forces on a family basis. The Confederazione Nazionale Coltivatori Diretti, generally abbreviated to Coldiretti, represents most of the country's agricultural self-employed. It measures its membership in family units, of which there are about one million.

The organization claims to be strong everywhere, though the backward Mezzogiorno at one extreme and the traditional northeast and northwest corners at the other end of the peninsula, are strongholds.

Political colour Firm allegiance to the Christian Democrat party has always been the line followed by the farmers' main representative body. After the 1987 elections, the Coldiretti were able to claim parliamentary representation of 18 deputies and 8 senators, all Christian Democrats. Southern deputy Arcangelo Lobianco has led the legislature's agricultural chorus since 1980 when he became Coldiretti chairman. There is little difficulty in winning the ear of the minister of agriculture, whose nomination in coalition governments

belongs to the Christian Democrats.
Campaigning lobby Under Lobianco
the Coldiretti launched three major
campaigns in the early 1980s.
"Vertenza Europa" was directed
against the EC Common Agricultural
Policy, which Italian farmers see as
favouring North European rather than
Mediterranean produce. The
"Vertenza Agricoltura" aimed at
reviving the productive and social role
of Italian agriculture. It engendered
the third campaign, *"Progetto Aquila,"*
which seeks to challenge
multinationals' strength in the food
industry. The Coldiretti are present in
food through Federconsorzi, a
grouping of about 3,500 agricultural
consortia, which controls the Polenghi
Lombardi food group and has a stake
in Italy's largest private sector bank,
Banca Nazionale dell'Agricoltura.

The Cooperatives

Italy's cooperative movement operates
in many areas: agriculture, fishing,
housing, construction, retailing,
industry, banking and finance.
Altogether there are more than
100,000 cooperatives. About one half
are housing ventures which are able to
facilitate home purchase because of
the fiscal advantages which they enjoy
and because of their status as non-
profit-making bodies. As well as
buying their homes through a
cooperative, Italians can choose to
bank with a cooperative bank: *banche
popolari* and *casse rurali* are
cooperatives (see *Banks and other
financial institutions*).
Political affiliations Left-wing Lega
Nazionale Cooperative e Mutue is the
best-known grouping. At the other
end of the political spectrum,
Confederazione Cooperative Italiane –
Conf-cooperative – is the Catholic/
Christian Democrat association to
which almost all *casse rurali* are tied.
It is particularly strong in the North
(Lombardy, Alto Adige and Veneto).
Associazione Generale Cooperative
Italiane (AGCI) is the youngest of the
three main cooperative groups, and its
ambitions of building a strong centrist

(Republican and Social Democrat)
grouping seem unrealistic.
The Lega The predominantly
Communist Lega is the oldest
(founded 1886) Italian cooperative
association. Construction cooperatives
such as CMC Ravenna and CMB Carpi
have helped to spread the name,
working on major projects throughout
Italy and abroad, especially in
developing countries. Both Ravenna
and Carpi are in the Emilia Romagna
region, a Communist and Lega
stronghold.
Agriculture and retail distribution are
important. The Lega's 1,350 shops,
employing about 20,000 staff, have
become increasingly significant in
Italy's retail sector, particularly food.
Financial services In spite of its
political colour, the left-wing
cooperative movement has been giving
growing attention to financial services.
A Lega affiliate controls the stock
market-quoted insurance company
Unipol which, with the Lega's retail
associations, launched a merchant
bank (Finec) in 1987 (see *Insurance*).
A retail bank (Banec) was established
later that year in Bologna, the Lega's
capital.
Future Italy's cooperative movement
claims to be a middle road between
capitalism and state ownership. But it
failed to grasp the opportunities
offered by the crises in state- and
private-sector industry during the
1970s and early 1980s. Though in
many respects an "insider," the
movement continues to remain
outside the circle of real power.

Multinationals

The multinationals are clearly
outsiders yet they have had a
considerable impact on Italian
business. Corporations such as
Unilever, IBM and Procter & Gamble
are well entrenched with substantial
manufacturing and marketing
operations. These and other
multinational companies have served
as schools for teaching modern
management techniques to a new
breed of manager.

Italy's family companies have drawn heavily on the human resources of the multinationals to recruit their financial, production and marketing technocrats. They have absorbed the skills of treasury and management, cost accounting, production control, and product, sales and advertising strategy. But Italian business, while borrowing the outward forms of international (particularly American) corporate procedures, still retains an essentially Latin, family-centred power structure.

Business and politics

The state enjoys a wide presence in industry and finance through its holding corporations (IRI, ENI and EFIM) and through the government's responsibility – though often indirect – for appointing the senior members of the boards of the country's main banks and the savings banks. This has led to hard political negotiation over the allocation of top jobs. (See *Government and business*.)

Party links Even where the state is not directly involved, some private sector business people are generally believed to enjoy ties with parties. Lucchini, Merloni and Calisto Tanzi (of dairy product group Parmalat) are linked to the Christian Democrats, Nicola Trussardi (fashion) and Berlusconi to the Socialists.

Many scandals during the 1970s and 1980s revealed the symbiosis between business and politics. The crashes of Michele Sindona's Banca Privata Italiana and Roberto Calvi's Banco Ambrosiano, the collapses of the SIR and Liquigas chemical companies and the failures of construction companies (notably Caltagirone), as well as disclosures regarding the illegal masonic lodge P2 (Propaganda Due), showed a murky side to the business/politics relationship. Even apart from these highly publicized affairs, it is felt that relations between business and the state, whether represented by politicians or civil servants, still fall short on ethical standards. Paying the "*bustarella*" for contracts, the

installation of utilities or speeding up bureaucratic procedures is regarded as the norm, especially at local government level.

Anti-trust

There was increasing discussion during the late 1980s about the need for anti-trust legislation and for tougher rules to regulate stock market dealings, given that Italy will have to align itself with the rest of the EC as 1992 approaches.

Media control Particular concern has been registered over the weighty role which Fiat plays in the economy overall, and not least in its control of two of Italy's three largest daily newspapers (*La Stampa* and *Corriere della Sera*). De Benedetti has substantial interests in the Mondadori publishing house, which in 1989 gained a majority shareholding in Italy's best-selling and most respected daily, *La Repubblica*, and Berlusconi controls *Il Giornale*. A plan to prevent individuals or business groups from controlling both newspapers and TV channels, the "zero option," was broadly agreed by politicians during 1988, but legislation was still far off.

The financial world Italy's major groups have diversified into the financial sector. De Benedetti (control of Latina), Agnelli (Toro), Gardini (Fondiaria) and Berlusconi (Mediolanum) all have insurance interests. Both Agnelli and Berlusconi are involved in mutual funds.

Following its partial privatization, most main players have stakes in merchant bank Mediobanca (see *Banks and other financial institutions*). Way beyond retirement age, former chairman Enrico Cuccia continued in the 1980s to exercise power at Mediobanca to protect the interests of the *ala nobile*. In retail banking De Benedetti has a stake in Credito Romagnolo while Agnelli, through Gemina, held a stake of nearly 13% in Nuovo Banco Ambrosiano in 1988. The central bank is anxious to limit the intrusion of Italy's industrial groups into the banking world.

The business framework

In some respects the Italian business world differs notably from that of most other European countries. Fiat and Olivetti are far from being typical Italian enterprises. Most business units are very small, difficult to identify either as competitors or as potential partners; they also work within or close to Italy's black economy, thus gaining a competitive edge over foreign companies paying their taxes and employees' social security contributions. The state is both an important customer and a daunting competitor. State-owned industrial companies employ some 600,000 people and all are protected in some way from private – and particularly from foreign – competition. Nearly all private companies are wholly owned by, or at any rate controlled by, families; the number of Italian citizens investing directly on the stock exchange is tiny, though growing. Italians save nearly 23% of their incomes – more than any other Europeans – but they prefer to put their money in government paper (which is lightly taxed), houses and, to a certain extent, mutual funds.

Società per Azioni (SpA)

The most common business structure in Italy is a kind of joint stock company, the Società per Azioni (SpA), of which there are nearly 50,000. SpAs are the only type of company that can be quoted on the Borsa (stock exchange), but only about 150 are listed and most SpAs are private companies. The SpA has been the form preferred not only by private Italian industry but also by foreign multinationals for their subsidiaries and by state-owned enterprises. The latter are usually SpAs whose shares are held directly or indirectly by the state.

Regulations An SpA must have at least two shareholders, three statutory auditors and a minimum capital of L200m. Capital increases or bond issues of more than L2bn must be authorized by the treasury. There are no restrictions on the number or nationality of the directors (*amministratori*), who must prepare annually a balance sheet and a report on the company's activities.

Liabilities of the directors and statutory auditors are defined by the 1942 Civil Code (Codice Civile) as amended by later legislation. The Civil Code also lays down the form and content of the annual financial statement. Companies quoted on the Borsa must also present an interim half-year report, as well as a balance sheet, to its regulatory body, the Commissione Nazionale per le Società e la Borsa (Consob), meeting more stringent and up-to-date requirements. Multinationals usually also prepare accounts in the form adopted by the parent company. (See *Accountancy*.)

A copy of the Civil Code accounts must be lodged with the Court of Chancery (Cancelleria del Tribunale) within whose jurisdiction the company's registered offices are located, where it is open to inspection. These Chancery-held accounts are the only available source of information on the activities of many Italian companies. In mid-1988 Law No. 291 introduced important changes in the annual registration tax payable by SpAs, which now varies from L9m for SpAs with a registered capital (*capitale sociale*) of less than L500m or less to L120m on those with a capital of L10bn or more.

Società a Responsabilità Limitata (SRL)

Until mid-1988, smaller industrial companies and most legal, financial and other service companies were organized under the other important legal form, the *Società a Responsabilità*

Limitata (SRL). Law No. 291 differentiated sharply between the annual taxes on the registration of SpAs and SRLs and simplified the legal procedures relating to the latter. As a consequence, nearly 1,500 companies, including some as large and well-known as Fiat-owned Alfa Romeo, changed their juridical status to that of SRL in the first six months after the law became effective.

Simpler rules SRLs differ from SpAs in that they cannot embody their capital (L20m minimum) in negotiable certificates and therefore cannot be listed on the Borsa. Legal procedures, particularly after Law No. 291, are simpler than those regarding SpAs. Transfers of shareholdings must be registered in the capital stock register (Libro dei Soci) but can be made before a notary; general meetings can be called by registered letter instead of by publication in the Official Gazette, as is required for SpAs. The annual registration tax is a flat L2.5m.

Branch company

A branch company (*filiale*) may be registered by a foreign company, although the SpA or SRL structure is generally preferred. Registration requires presentation of the deeds of incorporation (*statuto*) and of a power of attorney certified by a notary and by the Italian consulate in the home country. Uncertainties about the tax treatment of dividends is one reason why the branch structure has not been popular with foreign investors. If the company's branch is considered to be a "permanent establishment," dividends are deemed to pass through the branch and are taxable.

Partnership

Various kinds of partnership exist in Italy, but none of them is much favoured by foreign investors.

SNC (Società in Nome Collettivo) is a general or unlimited partnership in which all partners are jointly and severally liable without limitation for partnership obligations.

SAS (Società in Accomandita Semplice) In this case, liability is limited to the extent of the original capital investment for limited partners, but is joint, several and unlimited for general partners. An SAS may not issue bonds, nor may its capital be represented by shares.

SApA (Società in Accomandita per Azioni) This is similar to an SAS but its capital is represented by shares and it may issue bonds.

Sole traders and simple partnerships are responsible for their operations to the extent of the traders' business assets and personal property.

Setting up a company

All persons or entities engaging in any form of business activity in Italy must be registered with the local chamber of commerce (*camera di commercio*).

The procedures for setting up a company are regulated by the 1986 law embodying the Second EC Directive. For an SpA, the founders must sign the articles of incorporation (*statuto*) and subscribe all or part of the share capital before a notary public. The articles must be deposited with the chancery of the relevant local court (Cancelleria del Tribunale) within 30 days. The company may not start its activities, except under the directors' personal liability, until the court has given its consent (*nulla osta*). During this period – which may be as short as 15 days but is often longer – at least 30% of the initial capital is held frozen in an interest-bearing deposit account with a bank.

Foreign investment

Services sector Foreign investment in the services sector is usually made by buying into an existing firm, at a price which must be recognized as "suitable" (*congruo*) by the Stockbrokers' Committee (Comitato degli Agenti di Borsa). Other foreign investment in this sector is subject to the same regulations as investment made by Italian companies.

In manufacturing, foreign investment used to be regulated by legislation passed in 1956, at a time when Italy was both capital-starved and anxious to tie its economy firmly to the West. For multinationals it was an open door: joint ventures were not obligatory, and unlimited repatriation of profits was allowed.

These provisions are continued in the new rules set out in the Testo Unico which came into force on January 1 1989 and completed the sweeping liberalization of Italy's exchange controls initiated in 1988. The Testo Unico has two basic premises: that foreign investment activities do not threaten Italy's balance of payments, and that all such activities are permitted unless explicitly forbidden.

Competition law

Italy still has hardly any independent anti-trust provisions, though, as a member of the EC, it is bound by those of the Treaty of Rome outlawing interference with free competition between member states.
An anti-trust bill presented to Parliament early in 1988 would extend the EC anti-trust provisions to activities within Italy. It outlaws agreements which would limit free competition by, for example, fixing sales or purchase prices, limiting or regulating production, sharing markets or materials, and similar abuses of positions of market dominance. A special supervisory authority would be set up with a monitoring and advisory role. The bill, although government-sponsored, is unlikely to have a rapid passage through Parliament.

Mergers and acquisitions

Italy has as yet no specific regulations dealing with mergers and acquisitions. In the opinion of some experts, any supervision would in the end be political and open to corrupt practices. Nevertheless, a non-government bill proposed in 1988 that mergers and acquisitions leading to the formation of a group with a total annual turnover of more than L500bn

and/or a market share greater than 50% should be notified to the supervisory authority proposed by the anti-trust bill.

Corporate taxation

About one-tenth of tax revenue is provided by the two corporation taxes IRPEG and ILOR and one-sixth by the value-added tax (IVA).
IRPEG (Imposta sul Reddito delle Persone Giuridiche) is levied (at a rate of 36% in early 1989) on the worldwide income (including income from government securities) less expenses of resident companies and branches of foreign companies. Permissible deductions include interest and documented royalty payments, ILOR and INVIM (see below), certain indirect taxes and Italy's heavy stamp duties (these last yield the Finance Ministry almost as much as does IRPEG itself).
Dividends distributed in Italy are subject to IRPEG, as well as to a 10% withholding tax, but dividend recipients may claim a tax credit equivalent to the IRPEG payment. Dividends paid abroad are subject to IRPEG plus a 32.4% withholding tax, unless the latter is reduced by tax treaty.
Depreciation allowances are on a straight-line historic cost basis; the amortization period depends on the nature of the assets, and varies from 30 years for buildings to 2 years for some tools and equipment. All research expenditure can be deducted, either as it is incurred or over five years. New rules for accelerated depreciation introduced in 1988 allow for a maximum of 75% of expenditure on investment, expansion and modernization to be deducted in the first three years. Occasionally, inflation forces the government to allow a revaluation of assets.
ILOR (Imposta Locale sui Redditi) is not really a local income tax as understood elsewhere, since it is paid at the same 16.2% rate throughout Italy. Most of the rules concerning its payment are the same as for IRPEG,

except that losses cannot be carried forward and dividends from resident and nonresident corporations are ILOR-exempt.

IVA The average standard rate of value-added tax (Imposta sul Valore Aggiunto) in early 1989 was 19%, with rates of 2% on basic foodstuffs, 9% on non-basic foods, textiles and some raw materials, and 38% on luxuries. The 1989 budget proposals included some increases in IVA. Exports are IVA-exempt and imports are taxed, post duty, at the same rates as domestic products.

Other taxes Italy has no real capital taxes, and capital gains taxes are restricted to a tax on the increase in the value of real estate, Imposta sull'Incremento di Valore degli Immobili (INVIM), paid at rates varying from 3% to 30%. Gains from the sale of capital assets are taxable as income unless set aside for reinvestment. A tax on the office premises of all businesses and professional people, payable to the local authority, was introduced in June 1989. Interest on government securities is subject to a withholding tax of 12.5% and that on bank deposits and current accounts to one of 30%. In both cases, the interest is considered as income for corporation tax purposes. Taxes on royalties and fees paid abroad are usually regulated by tax treaty.

Incentives for investment

These have long been available in the poorer South of Italy – the Mezzogiorno – and are now regulated by Law No. 64 of 1986. An important innovation of the new law is that it includes help to the services sector. Some sectors (including oil, basic petrochemicals, synthetic fibres and nonferrous metals) are not eligible for incentives. The law divides the various areas of southern Italy into three annually reviewed categories: category A includes the very poor areas (such as central Sicily), B the medium poor (such as Naples) and C the not-so-poor (for example, the area

just south of Rome). The level of assistance is graded so that the biggest incentives are allocated to the poorest areas and also to those industries regarded as priority sectors: those that are import-saving, export-oriented or high-tech.

A generous package Incentives include cash grants and soft loans, a ten-year holiday from IRPEG and, for reinvested profits, from ILOR, rebates on IVA and some relief from Italy's high social security contributions.

Public agencies and state-owned companies must reserve 30% of their total budget expenditure for purchasing from companies located in the Mezzogiorno. This ruling has never been respected to the letter, but some firms selling products with a large potential market in the state sector, such as telephones or defence equipment, have found it worthwhile to site their factories in the South. The state-owned Finanziaria Meridionale (FIME) will provide up to 49% of the equity for joint ventures in the South, and its subsidiary, FIME Leasing, will lease land, buildings and plant for 5–10 years.

This incentives package is one of the most generous to be found anywhere in Europe, and it covers an area containing nearly one-third of the Italian population. Not surprisingly it has run foul of the EC and help will be phased out in some areas (eg just south of Rome, and the Adriatic Marches) between 1991 and 1993. It is possible that some incentives, including those regarding social security contributions and IVA, will have to be withdrawn altogether from the Mezzogiorno package.

Detailed information on the assistance available can be obtained from the Associazione Bancaria Italiana (ABI), Piazza del Gesù 19, 00186 Rome.

Other areas Limited help is also available for investment in some, mainly mountainous, areas of northern Italy. Trieste can provide some soft loans and capital grants.

Employment

Until the 1980s, Italian workers had a reputation for militancy and for disruptive and costly strike action, while employers complained that the labour market was over-regulated, responsible in part for the growth of unregulated employment in the informal, black economy.

Times have changed, however. The unions suffered a major defeat in the 1980 Fiat strike, when 40,000 white-collar workers marched in protest at continued industrial action by militant shop-floor trade unionists. Since then, they have been on the defensive. Weakened by internal conflict, declining membership and a shift in industrial power towards management, the once strong and united unions are now just shadows of their former selves. They have conceded ground on flexibility (the relaxation of controls on recruitment, dismissals and work contracts) and have been forced to accept reforms of Italy's system of wage-indexation, the *scala mobile*. The threat now is of unofficial rank-and-file strike action, which the major unions are unable to control.

Labour unions

The unions, having been weak and fragmented, grew dramatically in power after the so-called "Hot Autumn" strikes in 1969. The Workers' Charter (*Statuto dei Lavoratori*), or Law 300, of 1970 was a response to the growing militancy of the unions, and it met most of their demands. In particular, it legalized organization in the workplace – previously there had been no automatic right to this – and it laid the foundation for a highly regulated system of labour relations.

Union power was further strengthened in 1972 when the three major confederations of unions formally decided to sink some of their political differences in the cause of presenting a united front. In particular, they agreed that union leaders should not also hold political party posts.

Union membership rose from 29% of the work force in 1969 to more than 50% in the late 1970s. By the late 1980s it had fallen to 35–40%.

The major confederations are the Communist-dominated Confederazione generale italiana del lavoro (CGIL), with about 4.5m members, the Christian Democrat Confederazione italiana dei sindacati lavoratori (CISL) with 2.9m and the centre-Socialist Unione italiana del lavoro (UIL) with 1.3m. Not all these members are in the active labour force and if retired and other non-working members are discounted, the figures are reduced to, respectively, 3.2m, 2.4m and 1.2m.

Independent unions There are many independent unions (*sindacati autonomi*), not affiliated to any of the three major confederations. They are especially strong in the public sector – education, the health service and transport – and are notorious for their wild-cat strikes and disregard of the conventions established between management and the larger unions.

The Cobas Since 1987, new groups have emerged which are not officially unions at all, but loosely organized rank-and-file committees (*comitati di base*) known as the *Cobas*. These have no links with political parties, are often organized on an *ad hoc* basis, and are almost exclusively in the public sector. They have outflanked the major unions in the public sector wage disputes and pose a major threat to industrial relations peace and wage stability. Their militant posture poses a threat to the larger, more moderate unions which have been attempting to present themselves as reasonable and reliable partners in bargaining while seeing their former strength ebbing.

Employees' rights and representation
An extensive system of worker
protection and rights was established
by the Workers' Charter of 1970,
backed by the bargaining strength of
the unions. The Charter applies to
firms with more than 15 workers and
to agricultural enterprises with more
than five. It gives workers'
representatives extensive rights to
information and consultation.

Representation Generally, workers
are represented by a works council
(*consiglio di fabbrica*) whose activities
may range from simply voicing
workers' grievances and demands to
monitoring the company's investment
strategies and production plans.

The right to strike is guaranteed by
Article 40 of the 1948 Italian
Constitution and reinforced by the
1970 Charter. Since wild-cat and
sympathy strikes are not illegal,
industrial action tends to be used as a
first rather than last resort, although it
is usually sporadic and short-lived,
because the unions have meagre strike
funds. Nevertheless, in the worst
strike year on record – 1969 – 300m
man-hours were lost in disputes.

A voluntary strike code was agreed in
1980 by the three major
confederations and the number of lost
man-hours dropped to 130m in 1982
and to only 32m in 1987. In 1986 the
government reached an agreement
with the unions whereby any union
breaking the code (which stipulates a
ten-day warning for strike action)
would be barred from the bargaining
table. However, the smaller and less
moderate unions are not bound by the
code. Since 1987, *Cobas* have caused
chaos in schools and in rail, air and
maritime transport with wild-cat
strikes and a refusal to acknowledge
any codes of procedure.

Recruitment Traditionally unions and
the government have regulated
recruitment through the system of
collocamento numerico, or numerical
hiring, whereby employers are
required to hire workers on a "first-
come, first-served" basis from lists at
local employment offices. This has
applied only to firms with more than
35 workers and all but the biggest
firms have been able to evade the
rules to a great extent. Under 1984
legislation aimed at deregulating the
labour market, only 50% of new
employees have to be recruited under
this system. Employers must also fill
15% of their jobs from among
disabled people and the victims of
terrorism. However, there is no
legislation to combat employers'
discrimination against women.

Dismissals Employers covered by the
Workers' Charter must show "just
cause" for firing workers; unjustified
dismissals can lead to heavy fines and
compulsory reinstatement. Firms may
lay off workers by applying to the
government's wage guarantee fund
(Cassa Integrazione Guadagni) which
is funded by employers' contributions
and pays the employees up to 90% of
their former salaries, in principle for a
limited period. In practice the wage
fund's payments have often been
prolonged indefinitely, virtually
becoming unemployment benefit. The
basic state unemployment benefit
until recently was only about L800 a
day. Since 1987 it has been increased
to 15% of previous pay and was due to
be raised to 20% from 1990.

Working hours The statutory
maximum working week is 48 hours,
although the average for both blue-
and white-collar workers is about 40.
In some sectors, collective agreements
specify fewer hours, as in banking,
where the working week is 36 hours
and 40 minutes. Shorter working
hours have also been introduced
under company agreements. So-called
"solidarity contracts" have reduced
working time in certain firms so as to
share out work and cushion the effects
of restructuring.

Wage bargaining and productivity
Traditionally, bargaining has been
split between three tiers – the
national, industrial and firm or plant
levels – but in the 1980s there has
been a significant shift in bargaining
to the company level. This shift

coincides with the collapse of union unity in 1984 over national negotiations on the *scala mobile*, Italy's system of wage indexation. *The scala mobile* Managed by the unions and employers together, this system links wage increases to a price index calculated from a selection of basic goods. Until 1985 a negotiated proportion of pay automatically rose in line with the cost-of-living index. The proportion varied between 64% and 90%.

Controversy over the system's inflationary consequences blocked wage bargaining in the early 1980s. By 1984 there was a deep split among the unions on the indexation issue. The government eventually introduced new regulations, ratified by a national referendum in 1985, under which wages up to a certain level (which at the end of 1987 was fixed at L629,055 a month) are fully index-linked; above that, only 25% of pay is index-linked. *Labour costs* increased slightly faster than inflation (by 1.5 percentage points) between 1980 and 1983, but slowed down (to 0.7 points more) between 1983 and 1986. The main problem is in the public sector where salaries have been increasing since the early 1980s by 11–12% a year and where efficiency is low. Since 1983, wage differentials have been increasing and there is a growing trend for employers to introduce merit and bonus payments and to link pay to performance.

Workers' participation
The German concept of co-management has never been accepted in Italy. Employers have viewed such proposals with horror, fearing an intolerable interference in their affairs. Trade unions, meanwhile, consider co-management little better than class collaboration. But recently there have been signs of a growing interest in profit-sharing schemes and in employee stock options, although these clearly aim simply to extend the corporate culture to the workforce rather than involve it in decisions.

In the public sector limited attempts to involve the unions in decisions have been made in the state holding companies IRI, ENI and EFIM. The IRI agreement (the *protocollo IRI*) on "joint management" has increased workers' rights to information and participation, in return for a strike code. So far, however, real participation has been minimal and the strike code frequently broken.

Managers and executives
Middle managers and senior white-collar employees (known in Italy as *quadri*) have been struggling for years to attain a similar professional status to that of senior managers (*dirigenti*). As it is they have been stuck in a no-man's land between the latter and lower-level employees in terms of negotiations on pay, benefits and conditions.

Several organizations lobby government and employers on their behalf: the Confederquadri and Unionquadri (with some 70,000 members each) and Italquadri (with about 9,000). Only the first aspires to the role of a fully-fledged trade union (managers are generally hostile to the idea of union membership) but they all share an aim, to defend the professional status of managers and combat any attempts to flatten out wage differentials.
Senior managers (the *dirigenti*) are not covered by the statutory rules governing other workers but have their own highly preferential system of agreements. Their interests are represented and advanced by the FNDAI (Federazione Nazionale Dirigenti Aziende Industriali) which claims a membership of 95,000. Most are employed under contracts which afford a high degree of protection against dismissal (employers can incur enormous fines for "unjustly" firing a manager) and a system of pay increments linked to age rather than merit. In the late 1980s, senior managers earned on average some L113m a year, of which about 10% was in the form of bonuses.

Banks and other financial institutions

Italy's banking system claims to include both the world's oldest operational bank, the Monte dei Paschi di Siena (founded in the 15th century), and the largest savings bank, the Cassa di Risparmio delle Provincie Lombarde (Cariplo). Four factors characterize Italian banking. First, the system is highly fragmented with more than 1,100 different credit institutions operating – although 250 of them account for 90% of banking activity. Second, the system is dominated, directly or indirectly, by the public sector, which controls about three-quarters of banking activity. Third, the system has been largely closed and protected from outside competition. Fourth, Italian banks suffer from cumbersome bureaucracy: efficiency, modernization and the provision of services fall short of market demands.

Retail banking system

Retail banks are classified according to a rather arcane system of categories, but the borders between these are somewhat blurred. Within each category there is great variation in the size of banks and also of their geographical spread: while some operate at national level, most are regional or even local. The permutations of these three characteristics – category, size and territory – produces a confusing array of institutions.

Types of retail bank

Istituto di credito di diritto pubblico: public law bank
Banca di interesse nazionale: national-interest bank
Cassa di risparmio: savings bank
Monte di credito su pegno: savings bank originating from pawn operations
Banca popolare cooperativa: people's cooperative bank
Cassa rurale e artigiana: rural and artisans' bank
Banca di credito ordinario: ordinary credit bank

Public law banks This category comprises six large publicly owned banks, including the country's biggest bank in terms of deposits, the Banca Nazionale del Lavoro (BNL), which was established early in the Fascist era. The others are Istituto Bancario San Paolo di Torino, Monte dei Paschi di Siena, Banco di Napoli, Banco di Sicilia and Banco di Sardegna. With the exception of the last named, all are among Italy's ten largest banks. Although the public law banks operate nationally and have branches in the major cities, their countrywide coverage is far from complete and regional ties or connections with cities of origin remain important. Three-quarters of the ordinary share capital of the BNL is owned by the treasury; the rest is held by savings banks and public bodies. Non-voting savings shares in the BNL are quoted on the Milan stock market and so are those issued by Banco di Napoli and Banco di Sardegna. The Monte dei Paschi di Siena and Istituto Bancario San Paolo di Torino are foundations without share capital.

National-interest banks The state holding corporation IRI (see *Government and business*) has a majority stake in the three national-interest banks, which are joint stock corporations whose ordinary shares are quoted on the Milan stock exchange. Banca Commerciale Italiana, Credito Italiano and Banco di Roma have about 400 branches each and are among the ten largest Italian banks, but do not provide balanced national coverage. Banca Commerciale

Italiana is strongest in Lombardy, Credito Italiano is also most strong in the North and Banco di Roma in the centre.

Savings banks Including the nine *monti di credito su pegno*, small foundations dating back to the 15th and 16th centuries, there are about 85 banks in this category, holding more than one-quarter of total deposits in the banking system. In most cases, savings banks operations are limited to provincial branch networks, but Cariplo is a regional bank and even has footholds outside Lombardy, with over 400 branches in various parts of Italy. Savings banks were the first to operate a collaborative cashpoint network and were Italy's pioneers in automated funds transfer.

People's cooperative banks There are more than 130 banks in this category, holding about one-sixth of total deposits in the banking system. Largest is Banca Popolare di Novara which serves many Italian regions, with nearly 400 branches, but most banks of this type are local affairs. Investors are *soci* (partners) and each has one vote. Shares in the largest people's cooperative banks are traded on the unlisted securities market.

Other categories There are more than 720 rural and artisans' banks, only one of which has more than 10 branches – most have only one or two. Most of the 116 "ordinary" banks are very small but the category includes several larger banks: among these are Banca Nazionale dell'Agricoltura, Banca Toscana (controlled by Monte dei Paschi di Siena), Istituto Bancario Italiano (controlled by Cariplo) and Banco di Chiavari e della Riviera Ligure (controlled by Banca Commerciale Italiana), Credito Romagnolo and Nuovo Banco Ambrosiano.

Foreign banks

There are about 35 foreign banks, most of which operate from Milan, though some also have branches in Rome. Two foreign institutions have acquired local banks in recent years: Citibank owns Banco Centro Sud and Deutsche Bank owns Banca d'America e d'Italia.

Banking association

Associazione Bancaria Italiana (ABI) represents all categories of bank. It operates as a pressure group and lobby, speaking for the banking system to the monetary authorities and the political world. The ABI also undertakes research, publishes a monthly journal, and coordinates the work of the interbank automation organization, Società per l'Automazione Bancaria SIA.

Central bank and regulation

The Bank of Italy – Banca d'Italia – is the central bank. It has its headquarters in Rome and a network of provincial offices. The bank enjoys an excellent reputation for efficiency, integrity and independence from political influences. It is run by career bankers, most of whom have worked their way up through the bank, or have worked in international organizations such as the IMF. The procedure by which senior officials are appointed is such that no single political party can gain control of the bank.

Supervision The Bank of Italy's *Vigilanza* is responsible for overseeing the country's banking system. It inspects books and analyses banks' reports to identify the credit system's weaker or anomalous members.

Default Bad loans reached 8.4% of total lending at the end of 1987. Two central bureaus help in controlling default.

Centrale dei Rischi The Bank of Italy oversees lending through this central risks bureau, which gathers information on bank loans to firms as well as on certain other bank operations.

Centrale dei Bilanci A central accounts bureau was established in 1983, with the participation of the Bank of Italy and major banks. It gathers and analyses the annual financial statements of 30,000 Italian companies. Its aim is to assist banks to improve their quality of lending.

Capital ratios the Comitato Interministeriale per il Credito e il Risparmio (CICR), the interministerial committee for credit and savings, which is headed by the treasury minister, regulates the capitalization of Italian banks. It issued a ruling in December 1986 which states that all facilities (including guarantees) extended by Italian banks, by both domestic and foreign branches, must not exceed 12.5 times capital resources. Advances made by Italian branches must not exceed 22.5 times capital resources. Banks are allowed until June 1991 to bring their ratios to the required levels.

Bank appointments Public ownership of most of Italy's banking system has led to politicization of bank appointments. There is frequently a struggle between the political parties who share out between them appointments to the boards of public law banks, savings banks and some medium- and long-term special credit institutions. The Christian Democrats still control the most important appointments – to the posts of chairman and managing director – in the majority of cases. However, the BNL is in the hands of the Socialists, who have been fighting hard for a bigger piece of the cake, and are aiming at Cariplo in particular. Appointments are made by CICR.

Medium- and long-term banking

The Banking Act of 1936, still in force, though with some modifications, forbade banks to hold stakes in industrial and commercial firms. It also drew distinctions between short-term lending and lending over medium and long term. Prior to the introduction in March 1988 of liberalization measures, Italy's retail banks, with the exception of savings banks, could engage only in short-term lending.

Loans to business Credit institutions providing firms with longer-term finance include Centrobanca, controlled by the *banche popolari*, Interbanca, controlled by the "ordinary" banks, and Efibanca, 31% owned by BNL. Isveimer (Istituto per lo Sviluppo Economico dell'Italia Meridionale) is a specialist institution offering medium-term lending at subsidized and market interest rates to firms operating on the mainland of Southern Italy.

Regional credit There are 15 regional medium-term credit institutions (*mediocredito regionali*). These lend to industry, particularly to medium and small firms, for financing exports the purchase of new plant.

Merchant banking During the mid-1980s a lively debate on merchant banking led to a relaxation in February 1987 of the 1936 Banking Act. The Bank of Italy subsequently provided detailed regulatory framework, permitting three areas of activity: consultancy and assistance in investment funding and corporate development (mergers and acquisitions); management of corporate financing operations (loans and risk capital); and investment in shares and bonds.

Conditions Spread of portfolio risk must be ensured and to this end no single investment is allowed to exceed 20% of assets. Shareholdings must be minority and temporary, with the merchant banks excluded from involvement in management of the companies in which they invest. The Bank of Italy set the minimum share capital at L50bn.

Istituto Mobiliare Italiano (IMI) is Italy's largest financial conglomerate. This state-owned institution operates in many sectors including corporate finance and investment banking.

Mediobanca With its holdings and cross-investments, this institution has had a key role in Italian finance since its establishment immediately after World War II. Until early 1988, IRI's three national-interest banks owned a majority shareholding in Mediobanca. Partial privatization reduced their combined stake to 25% (see *Government and business*).

Others in merchant banking Large retail banks have become involved in merchant banking. BNL already had an independent industrial credit operation (Sezione Speciale per il Credito Industriale) and used this to establish Finanziaria Italiana di Partecipazioni (FIP), an investment bank with minority holdings in industrial companies. Credito Italiano has a domestic merchant bank (Fincor Merchant Credit) and another in the UK (Credito Italiano International). Istituto Bancario San Paolo di Torino has a stake in London merchant bankers Hambros and at home it has established Sanpaolo Finance.

Mortgage lending A total of 21 Italian institutions are permitted to supply mortgage loans for property purchase; these are regulated by rules governing medium- and long-term lending. Until 1988, Italy's retail banks were, in general, excluded from making long-term loans for house purchase.

Payments system

The Bank of Italy in 1987 published a "White Book" which was critical of the country's payments system. The study found that cash payments are still preferred by most Italians. This is partly because cash transactions are easier to hide from the tax authorities. Payment by cheque has failed to find favour also because of banks' value dating conditions (involving back-dated debiting of the drawer's account and delayed crediting of the payee's account), and the length of time

needed for cheque operations. There is no centralized clearing system for all banks, and clearance can take up to 29 days.

Credit cards Payment by credit card has been very slow to develop in Italy. *Carta Si* is a national bank credit card system established in 1985 by ABI, 16 major banks and four central institutions representing different categories of bank. Run by Servizi Interbancari (from which it gets its name) it ties in with 90% of the national banking system. It absorbed *Eurocard Italiana* (owned by Credito Italiano and a group of savings banks) and *Comites* (Banca Commerciale Italiano's credit card) and has agreements with *Visa/Barclaycard* and *MasterCard/Eurocard/Access*. Nevertheless, *Carta Si* had distributed fewer than 1m cards by the end of 1988 and had signed contracts with only 80,000 points of sale. Its competitor, *Bankamericard/Visa*, owned by Banca d'America e d'Italia, had more than 1m cards in use in 1988.

The Top Ten Banks	Assets, end 1987 $'000m
Banca Nazionale del Lavoro	96.1
Istituto Bancario San Paolo	73.1
Monte dei Paschi di Siena	67.2*
Banca Commerciale Italiana	62.5
Banco di Napoli	59.3
Banco di Roma	56.4
Cariplo	53.9
Credito Italiano	50.4
Banco di Sicilia	31.1
Istituto Mobiliare	23.8**

* unconsolidated figures
** at March 31 1987

Source: *The Banker*

Financial markets

Italy's stock markets earned a murky reputation in the 1960s and 1970s, with the Milan exchange considered as little more than a gambling casino. During the 1985–86 boom it seemed that Milan's market might become an important investment centre. These hopes have not been realized and Milan's market remains under-developed, under-regulated and best left to insiders. The small investor and outsider should at any rate take care.

Borsa valori di Milano

Dealing Milan's stock market, established in 1808, operates under the auspices of the city's chamber of commerce. There were 124 authorized stockbrokers (*agenti di cambio*) at the beginning of 1988, with a total of 461 representatives permitted to work on Milan's dealing floor. An executive committee of eight brokers (*Comitato Direttivo degli Agenti di Cambio*) oversees activities and acts as a pressure group.

The Borsa operates a call auction system for setting prices. However, the authorities believe that 70% of dealing takes place outside the exchange, thereby distorting the pricing system. Dealing is either against cash or on account, settlement being made at the end of the exchange's monthly account period. A deposit is required for dealing on account.

Size The number of listed shares at the end of 1987 was 339, of which 219 were ordinary shares (*azioni*). There were also 15 preference shares and 105 non-voting savings shares (*azioni di risparmio*). In addition, 1,280 fixed-interest bonds (*obbligazioni*) were traded on the Milan market. The number of companies whose shares were quoted was 204, with a further 20 suspended. One year earlier there had been 184 plus 18 suspended.

Leading shares Fiat ordinary shares are the most widely traded on Italian stock markets, accounting for about one-eighth of total trading volume. Assicurazioni Generali and Montedison shares have each accounted for about one-tenth of volume over recent years. Olivetti and insurance companies RAS and SAI are also focal points of investor interest.

Performance

Indices The market's performance is usually measured by five general indices. Most frequently used are the MIB historical index (*MIB storico*), whose 1,000 base was set at the start of 1975, and the MIB current index which is reset at 1,000 at the beginning of each year. Sectoral indices are kept by the Banca Commerciale Italiana (Comit) and Banca Nazionale del Lavoro (BNL).

Collapse The Milan market had turned down before the international crash in October 1987. The boom in Italian equities started ahead of other markets and Milan peaked in May 1986 when the MIB historical index reached 13,804. It had already lost more than one-quarter when the crash occurred. The index bottomed at 7,375 in November 1987 and during 1988 there was a certain revival.

Capitalization of companies listed on Milan's Borsa at the end of 1987 amounted to L140,721bn, which was about one-quarter lower than a year earlier. That Milan enjoyed a major boom is underlined by the fourfold increase in the market's capitalization over the four-year period 1983 to 1987.

New listings Analysts consider that there are several hundred candidates ripe for quotation, even though market conditions deterred applications for quotation in the second half of 1987 and in 1988. Family companies have traditionally shied away from stock market listing, though attitudes have started to change with new generations of managers and the need for risk capital. Among those which have taken the plunge is domestic appliance maker Merloni Elettrodomestici.

Other markets

Official stock markets operate in nine other cities, including Rome, Turin, Genoa and Naples, but fewer securities are quoted on these exchanges and their total trading volume is less than one-tenth that of Milan.

An unlisted securities market, mercato ristretto, exists on which stocks which do not have official quotation are traded. Dealing is most active in Milan where about 40 stocks change hands. *Mercati ristretti* operate in Rome and some other cities with official markets but the choice of securities is very small. More than one-third of the stocks quoted on Milan's USM are people's cooperative banks (*banche popolari*) whose statutes prevent full listing. For many other companies, the USM is seen as a stepping-stone to quotation on the main board.

Regulation

Consob (Commissione Nazionale per le Società e la Borsa) is Italy's companies and stock exchange commission. It was established in 1974 under legislation which introduced substantial changes in regulating stock markets. Consob oversees stock market activities and has power to suspend shares and to require companies to supply information.

Requirements for quotation include: minimum paid-up share capital of L500m; accounts showing profits in the two preceding financial years; freely transferable shares with unrestricted dividend rights; wide distribution of shares with at least 25% available to the public.

Reform In 1985 Consob suggested a new system based on computerized continuous trading. Two years later it published a wide-ranging document, "Blueprint for the Reform of the Securities Market." This covered regulation of insider trading, takeover bids, price manipulation, interest-bearing securities, unlisted securities, market participants and their regulation. The authorities want to implement changes before 1992.

Monte Titoli, Italy's central clearing and share custody system, started operating in 1981. It was created with the support of the Bank of Italy, which continues to be a shareholder. Consob's proposals for reform envisage a central role for Monte Titoli in the organization and functioning of the market. This would involve the company in the allotment process for share issues and public offers. During 1987 the nominal value of shares held by Monte Titoli increased three-fold and at year-end the company was the depository for shares amounting to 30% of the total nominal quoted value.

Nonresidents investing during the boom on the Milan market were discouraged by difficulties in settlement, which Monte Titoli should now help to overcome. There are no restrictions on portfolio investment but if share certificates remain in Italy, they should be deposited with an Italian agent bank. Dividends are subject to withholding tax, taxation being regulated by bilateral agreements.

Mutual funds

The first domestic mutual funds (unit trusts) were launched only in 1981. Consob shares a supervisory role with the central bank. The funds grew large in 1986 on the back of the stock market boom. By the end of that year their total assets stood at L65,077bn, but they had shrunk to L59,449bn at year-end 1987. At the end of 1987 management companies were running a total of 72 funds, mostly income and balanced income/equity funds.

Banks and insurance companies have been protagonists in this new form of saving, in which interesting alliances have been forged. Primegest links Fiat Group, Monte dei Paschi di Siena and Merrill Lynch. Hambros is tied to Eurofond (a subsidiary of Istituto Bancario San Paolo di Torino) and Chase Manhattan to Berlusconi's Fininvest.

Accountancy

The principles of modern accountancy are said to have been born in the Renaissance city states of Florence and Venice. However, it is only in recent years that many businesses have installed management accounting and treasury control systems. Nevertheless, there is evidence that Italian skills for innovative accounting have not been lost. The many firms operating in the black economy have considerable expertise in keeping at least two sets of books.

Audit

Italian joint stock companies are required to appoint boards of statutory auditors (*collegi sindacali*). Limited liability companies with share capital greater than L100m also have statutory auditors (*sindaci*). (See *Business framework*.) These have a limited role. They report to the shareholders that financial statements are drawn up according to legal requirements and undertake certain limited aspects of management control. They do not perform audits as known in US or UK business and indeed are unable to do so. *Sindaci* are present at meetings of boards of directors and are not independent. Statutory auditors must not be confused with independent auditors. *Independent audit* is recent in Italy, introduced only in 1975 under Presidential Decree DPR 136. This lays down that the financial statements of companies whose shares are quoted on Italian stock markets should be subject to audit by external auditors (*revisori*). A timetable was established for implementation, with separate, staggered deadlines set for different sectors of the economy.

Under DPR 136, audit firms must check that accounting records are properly kept, ensure that the balance sheet and the profit and loss account agree with the books, and that asset valuation complies with Civil Code principles. The audit firm's report, opinion and notes must be recorded in a book kept at the company's head office. This record must also show procedures and checks undertaken during the audit and the names of the audit team.

Approved firms The companies and stock exchange commission, Consob, keeps a roll of approved firms, the Albo Speciale delle Società di Revisione, on which firms must be registered if they wish to practise in Italy.

The majority of partners or directors in audit firms must be accountants registered with Italy's professional bodies and have at least five years' audit experience. Foreign professional qualifications, however, may be accepted by Consob. Foreign audit firms may also obtain registration on Consob's roll and be authorised to work in Italy.

Areas of work Audit firms must confine their activities to audit work and accounting-oriented advice to management. Tax and general management consultancy and executive search are forbidden. These limitations have led audit firms to set up separate consultancy firms. Nevertheless Consob believed that the requirement for independence was not always being met and consultancy became a major issue of friction between the firms and the authorities in the mid-1980s.

The profession

Dottori commercialisti These are accountants who are graduates in economics and commerce and have passed relevant professional examinations. International companies usually refer to them in English as commercial practitioners. A national council (Consiglio Nazionale dei Dottori Commercialisti) lays down standards and has a supervisory role. Most *commercialisti* practise as independent accountants and company tax and finance advisers. Audit firms encourage their staff to qualify as *dottori comercialisti*. *Ragionieri* have a diploma from technical high school. Some *ragionieri* are effectively only book-keepers but the best have professional skills to match those of graduates. *Revisori ufficiali dei conti* are accounts auditors who enjoy the status of public officers. The boards of statutory auditors of large corporations are required to have a *revisore ufficiale dei conti* as chairman. *Assirevi*, the Associazione Italiana Revisori Contabili, is the association of audit firms. Members must be registered on Consob's roll. One of its functions is to formulate fee scales.

Accounting principles

The Consiglio Nazionale dei Dottori Commercialisti in the late 1980s has been defining accounting principles and audit standards (*principi contabili* and *principi di revisione*).

Accounting principles had been agreed in eight areas by August 1988, including those concerning stocks, fixed assets, accounts payable, accounts receivable, securities, shareholdings and consolidation.

Audit standards agreed include ethical standards, internal control, and a series of technical standards for stocks, depreciation, accruals, reserves and other areas of auditing activity. *Audit certification reports* must confirm that the financial statements are prepared in accordance with correct accounting principles. Where those issued by the Consiglio Nazionale dei Dottori Commercialisti are incomplete, Italian audit firms refer to the standards issued by the International Accounting Standards Committee (IASC).

Firms

More than 20 firms are authorized to undertake independent audit in Italy. The international "Big Eight" are all present and mergers of small Italian firms with big internationals include

Toris with Price Waterhouse and Compagnia Europea di Revisione ed Organizzazione with Peat Marwick Mitchell (now KPMG).

The "Big Eight" hold approximately 90% of the market for audit services and all have extensive office networks in Italy. Local audit firms have to struggle to win business. Italian companies have preferred to engage international firms because these offer prestige signatures which are recognized worldwide and because large firms provide guarantees on quality, staff and organizational structure.

Leaders Arthur Andersen, the first international firm to "Italianize," is recognized as the leader, probably holding about 20% of the market. Its Italian client list includes Fiat, Benetton and Olivetti. In the late 1980s Arthur Andersen was earning annual fees of L4.1bn from auditing parts of the Fiat group, whose total annual audit expenses amount to L11.3bn. The big international firms which were slow to replace their US and British partners and managers with Italians lost market share to firms which "Italianized" earliest.

Mergers in late 1989 between some of the "Big Eight" were evidence of a growing concentration of accountancy work in a few very big firms.

Prospects

The voluntary use of independent audit represents about two-thirds of all audit work in Italy and this will continue to be the growth area, until Italy enacts the EC Fourth Directive on company accounts. Italian companies are increasingly aware of the need for openness in their accounting procedures and of the inadequacies of Civil Code accounts.

The appointment of an audit firm can be renewed only twice following the first three-year appointment. Significant changes are in sight at the end of the 1980s as companies are compelled to change their auditors.

The law

Italy's legal system is based on Roman law and its Napoleonic codification, modified by the Fascist codification of the 1930s and 1940s and the copious legislation of the following republican years. At its apex is the Constitutional Court which has the power, frequently used, to abrogate laws it considers unconstitutional, thereby exercising a *de facto* legislative (and political) function. Decisions of all other courts are not binding but carry authority in relation to the importance of the court. Legal commentaries by academics and lawyers also play a part in influencing court decisions. It is a system that requires the reconciliation of conflicting legal rules which have been set out at different times and with different aims, and creates plenty of work for lawyers but a lot of uncertainty for their clients.

The courts

There are four principal types of court: criminal, civil, administrative and tax. In all four divisions there are three levels of judgment: a first instance (eg Pretura Civile, Tribunale Civile, Tribunale Amministrativo Regionale), a second instance (eg Tribunale Civile, Corte d'Appello Civile, Consiglio di Stato), and final appeal, but only on points of law, heard by the Corte di Cassazione, which also resolves conflicts of jurisdiction.

The judiciary Judges are not drawn from the ranks of lawyers; they have a separate career structure. Most start hearing cases when they are around 30, after leaving university and passing a special state examination, and the main criterion for promotion is the number of years spent in the profession. Judges are independent, in the sense that they do not depend directly on any of the branches of the State. They elect part of their own Council (Consiglio Superiore della Magistratura) which has disciplinary and advisory functions; some members of the Council are appointed by the President of the Republic who, as President of the Council, guarantees its independence. Despite this, the judiciary plays a part in political life, with judges not infrequently initiating or being used as weapons in policy battles. However, the judiciary reflects a very wide range of political ideas and interests, and a reasonable degree of impartiality may be counted upon.

Litigation

Civil litigation is adversarial. Parties must claim what they want and prove what they claim. The procedure is supposed to be largely oral, but in fact is based largely on written briefs; direct questioning of witnesses by counsel is not permitted.

Litigation is lengthy, with long gaps between hearings; on average it takes 2–3 years for each instance of a case to be concluded. Court costs and lawyers' fees are normally paid by the losing party, but the courts have discretion to require the successful party to contribute. Awards of costs tend to be low, usually covering only a fraction of the actual costs, which partly explains why there is such a large amount of litigation.

The profession

The titles by which lawyers are known reflect the number of years they have been in practice, though there are special exams that can be taken to speed the ascent up the title tree.

Procuratori are newly qualified lawyers who, having completed two years' apprenticeship and passed the state examination, are allowed to appear only in courts within the district of the local Court of Appeal. There are 26 Courts of Appeal.

Avvocati After six years in practice a *procuratore* becomes *avvocato*, able to appear in courts throughout Italy and charge higher fees.

Avvocati cassazionisti are those lawyers who, after eight years as *avvocati*, are allowed to appear before the Court of Cassation.

Notai are public officers who have the exclusive power to certify and authenticate contracts and other unilateral acts such as donations and wills. Some contracts, such as the transfer of real property, obtain validity vis-à-vis third parties only when they are certified and authenticated by a notary.

Commercialisti belong to a separate profession and undergo a different training from lawyers. They do all the work connected with tax matters (see *Accountancy*).

Numbers There are about 50,000 lawyers in Italy (7,000 in Rome, 4,300 in Milan), 5,200 *notai* and 15,000 *commercialisti*.

Professional bars The Consigli dell'Ordine, of which there are 159, are organized and elected locally. However, there are national rules which govern ethics and fees and forbid all forms of publicity. Disbarment is the ultimate sanction held by local bars over their members. The Consiglio Nazionale Forense, the advisory national bar, also acts as an appeal court on disciplinary decisions of the local bars.

Fees

There is a fixed scale of fees for litigation; contingent fees are not allowed. For non-litigation matters, the maximum fee which can be charged by law is 5% of the value of the matter (contract, settlement etc). However, among the "international" law firms it is usual for fees to be calculated on a time basis, ranging from about L30,000 per hour for young clerks to L300,000 per hour for experienced lawyers. Many firms charge corporate and private clients different hourly rates and vary their charges according to the degree of technical difficulty or the risks and liability to which the firm is exposed.

Statements of fees are usually accompanied by a more or less detailed breakdown of work done.

Choosing a firm

If the firm you use at home cannot help, a useful starting point is the reference guide *Martindale and Hubbell*.

"International" firms There are roughly 50 firms in Italy that deal with international legal transactions or local matters involving non-nationals. Their size ranges from a minimum of two or three partners with the same number of legal assistants and/or associates to a maximum of 10 partners with about 20 legal assistants and/or associates. However, only one firm in Italy is this big, and only about 15 have more than five partners. Some of these firms also have part-time associates, usually academics who provide specialist advice.

"Specialist" firms usually comprise one experienced specialist lawyer, employing two or three legal assistants. These firms sometimes work together with bigger firms when their special skills are needed.

Traditional roles and the future

The legal profession in Italy is very fragmented. The majority of lawyers still practise on their own or in small family firms, and the bigger firms suffer from rapid turnover of personnel. This is mainly due to the resistance of Italians in general, and Italian lawyers in particular, to the idea of partnerships, where the *esprit de corps* of the firm prevails upon the individual's ego and ambition. In many firms there is an assumption that sooner or later one or more partners will break away and set up their own firm, taking clients with them. With the increasing demand that 1992 liberalization will bring for sizable firms offering a wide range of legal expertise, Italian lawyers may find themselves under threat from the big foreign firms who will be only too happy to provide that kind of service.

Importing, exporting and distribution

Italy's is an open economy, though less so than West Germany's or the UK's. It is very dependent on foreign trade, and both exports and imports amount to about 18% of GDP (see *International trade*). Problems affecting trade with Italy include long credit terms and payment delays but mostly they derive from deficiencies in public services, especially the notoriously inefficient postal and telephone systems, and slow customs procedures. Important factors to be considered include the relatively undeveloped distribution network, and the marked regional differences – particularly between North and South – in business methods and consumer preferences.

Tariffs and taxes

Imports from other EC countries – which represent about 56% of the total – are free of duty, but all imports, from any source, are liable to IVA (value-added tax). Changes in IVA rates are being implemented to bring them into line with those levied elsewhere in the EC, but because of their inflationary impact the government has been dragging its feet in carrying them out. The tax is remitted on exports.

Non-EC imports Tariffs on imports from non-EC countries are regulated by the EC's Common Customs Tariff (CCT) except in the case of products regulated by the Common Agricultural Policy (CAP).

There are annually renewed quotas on imports from Comecon countries, China and Vietnam. Most goods originating outside the Communist bloc can be imported without restrictions, without licences and without the country of origin being specified, with the exception of Japanese cars (see *Vehicles*). Information on mandatory and voluntary trade standards in Italy can be obtained from Ente Nazionale Italiano di Unificazione, Piazza Diaz 2, 20123 Milan.

Customs

There are customs points at the ports and in many other towns. The most important ports are Genoa and Naples, the most important internal customs are at Milan, Turin, Verona, Bologna and Rome.

Procedures are being simplified, particularly in the case of EC imports, and clearance times are falling: three or four days is still usual, but two days is becoming more common.

Samples without commercial value generally may be imported duty-free; the procedure for other samples is complicated and best put in the hands of an Italian freight forwarder.

Trieste has a free trade zone, as have, in theory, Genoa, Naples and Venice. These last three have never been activated, however, and are not recognized by the EC. At Trieste, goods may be held in the free port for an indefinite period without duty being payable. Payment of frontier charges (*oneri di confine*) can be delayed for six months, although interest is payable.

Identifying opportunities

The first approach to the Italian market is usually made via ministries and the Italian embassy in the home country, but there is no substitute for a visit.

Fairs A preliminary feel of the market is best acquired by visiting one or more of the many specialized trade fairs (list from Istituto Nazionale per il Commercio Estero, Via Liszt 2, 00144 Rome). They are a good place for identifying agents as well as potential customers and competitors. Reserve everything, including your hotel, well in advance. Beware of small regional fairs, often organized for and by local politicians.

Where to sell Where to enter the

market depends on the product line. For example, Milan is the first choice for consumer goods, since incomes in Lombardy are nearly 50% above the national average and customers are more open to new products. Rome may be a more appropriate target for high-tech products, however. This is partly because this is still a rapidly growing sector in the region and also because of the presence of big potential clients: the ministries (very important in Italy's highly centralized system of government), organizations such as the Consiglio Nazionale delle Ricerche (National Research Council), and the state holding corporations' vast network of subsidiaries (see *Government and business*).

Selling to the government Success in selling to products bought only by governments or their agencies usually requires a manufacturing base in Italy, preferably in the South. Direct contact with government purchasers is best put into the hands of Italian professionals: the laws, regulations and practices are complicated; moreover, "backhanders" may be necessary. The employment of the appropriate "consultant" is one way of channelling sweeteners into the appropriate pockets.

Adapting to the market

Letters, sales literature and servicing instructions should be in good Italian: get translations checked by a suitably qualified person with Italian as their mother tongue. Weights, measures and packaging must be in metric sizes. Foreign origin need not be shown on labels; however, in some cases it can be a plus point on the Italian market.

Standards Numerous legal and trade requirements and standards must be observed in making or marketing products in Italy. This is particularly true of foodstuffs – where Italian requirements are, on paper, the stiffest in Europe – and also pharmaceuticals. However, as various EC harmonization measures come into force, standards will be governed by

European regulations. For some products, licences are also required.

Selling methods

How to sell depends on the product, the market and the size of intended commitment. The local partner, whether representative, agent or licensee, must be chosen with great care and a long-term relationship should be the objective: Italians, once they have established a business relationship, prefer to continue dealing with the same person year after year.

Local distributors Raw materials, semi-finished and capital goods are often sold through brokers and commission agents. Foreign companies, even including some with manufacturing bases in Italy, usually entrust the selling of consumer goods to Italian distributors, though they may retain other aspects of marketing such as advertising.

It must be noted that a "distributor" in Italy would generally be called an agent elsewhere. The reason for avoiding the word "agent" in letters or documents – even though it is used in speech – is that agency arrangements are regulated by the Italian Civil Code and this, written at a time when an agent was often in a subordinate position with regard to a contracting company, specifies not only that an agent must have exclusive distribution rights in his territory but also that he has the right to a severance payment based on sales during the period of the contract.

An impelling reason for trusting distribution to others is that it is difficult for foreign companies, inevitably under the jealous scrutiny of Italian competitors, to compete successfully in an area where the widely practised evasion of social security, severance and tax obligations can give indigenous firms an edge over law-abiding foreigners.

More than one needed Although in some cases one distributor can be responsible for the whole country, and even the whole Mediterranean area, usually two or even three distributors – covering Northern, central and Southern Italy respectively – are needed. This is because the areas are not only a long way apart, they also have very different income levels and consumer buying habits.

Rights and responsibilities

Competent distributors will usually insist on exclusive rights in their territories and, often, that close competitors be excluded from the allocation of other territories. There are no restrictions in Italy (unlike in the EC as a whole) on the granting of exclusive distribution rights.

In general the distributor takes delivery of the goods at the point of customs and organizes sales. He or she assumes all risks and responsibilities, including the payment of taxes and the sorting out of legal difficulties.

Payments For most commodities, payments are made after either 90 days, six months or a year, and are generally not billed in lire; preferred currencies are Deutschmarks, Swiss Francs and ECUs. This means that the exchange risk is borne by the distributor – often no small consideration for the exporting company. Some articles (including automobiles) are in many cases handled under a form of leasing.

Distributors make their own arrangements (usually rolled-over bank credit) for financing deals with slow payers, a difficult problem in Italy. In general, the bigger the client, state or private, the longer the payment delay.

Representatives Consumer products – even some produced by multinationals with plants in Italy – are often put into the hands of commercial representatives. In effect, representatives buy the product at the point of customs (or the factory gate) and resell it, thus taking on the exchange risk, which is limited in the case of other EMS currencies.

Licensing agreements with Italian firms are common, but the details are rarely made known. They are not subject to any particular regulation, though transfers of royalties and fees abroad are subject to those on foreign investment which came into force on January 1st 1989.

Franchising can pose legal difficulties, since the franchising relationship, in Italian law, falls uneasily between that of the agent and that of the licensee. Nevertheless, it does seem peculiarly suited to the Italian distributive system because it allows spirited entrepreneurs easy access to the tax- and social-security-free world of the small shopkeeper (see below). Italian companies use it increasingly, particularly in the clothing and shoes sectors. As with all innovations, it is less common in the South.

Patents and trademarks

A patent (brevetto) can take about five years to register, but temporary protection is available once the claim has been filed. The Ufficio Centrale Brevetti at the Ministry of Industry issues patents, which are usually for a period of 20 years. Novelty, though required by law, in practice is rarely established through examination, and patents are rarely contested since the burden of proving nullity rests exclusively with the challenger.

The patentability of computer software has been much discussed, with disagreement over whether patent law or copyright law should apply. Several bills have been drafted on this matter, but they are likely to be overtaken by a proposed EC directive, whereby computer software would be covered by copyright. Italy is a party to the International Agreement on the Protection of Industrial Property (Paris Convention) and to the 1973 Munich European Convention on patents.

Trademarks are also issued by the Ufficio Centrale Brevetti. The granting of a trademark can take several years, but protection is available from the time the application has been filed. A trademark is also protected on the basis of its prior use, and protection may be lost if it is not used for three years. Italy is a party to the 1891 Madrid Agreement on the international registration of trademarks.

Product liability

Product liability in Italy is regulated by Presidential Decree No. 224 of May 1988 which implemented EC Directive No. 85/374. The decree makes the producer liable for damage caused by a defect in the product. Previously consumers had found it difficult to get any redress in the courts. The basic test is that the product must be as safe as can be expected in relation to its reasonably foreseeable use. The instructions supplied with it are taken into account, as is its intended end-user. More stringent criteria apply to products designed for children.

If the judge thinks it "likely" that a product defect is responsible for the alleged damage, the producer can be required to advance the cost of a technical investigation.

Distribution

Transportation into Italy The transport of Europe-sourced goods is commonly by TIR, which is usually quicker and cheaper than rail transport. There is always the risk, however, of disgruntled officials taking industrial action which halts customs clearance at road frontiers. Airports are increasingly congested and have a very bad strike record. Genoa is the largest port, with all types of warehousing and other facilities. Livorno is the biggest container-handling port.

Freight forwarders All the major Italian freight forwarders – Gondrand, Bolliger and Merzario are three of the biggest – have offices or agents in all the European capitals, and their own bonded and unbonded warehouses at all major customs points.

Distribution within Italy is usually by road, since the railways are slow and, with the exception of the Milan–Rome stretch, getting slower. There are

good toll highways (autostrade) down the spine of Italy, the Adriatic coast and almost all of the west coast. There are also many east–west links, but driving on the most important one, the Turin–Venice autostrada, can be horrific, particularly on the Turin–Milan section.

Retailing

Retailing is still mainly in the hands of nearly 1m small shopkeepers, nearly half of whom sell food. There is a limited number of wholesalers, and small shopkeepers increasingly are purchasing from cash-and-carry chains such as Metro. The cooperatives are also prominent in retailing (see *Power in business*).

There are fewer than 3,000 department stores and supermarkets, and these account for well under 10% of retail sales. This situation is very slowly changing, with the expansion of supermarket chains and the appearance of a few hypermarkets (see *Food and drink*). The main department stores are La Rinascente, Coin and Standa.

Licences Each retailer is licensed to sell a small range of products and these licences can be bought, sold and inherited. Supermarkets, with their wide range of goods, need many licences to open up. Numerous permits from many different bodies are also required.

Small is stronger So far, the political will to simplify this system, unfavourable to big firms, has not been forthcoming: small shopkeepers have considerable political clout, particularly in the leading Christian Democrat party. Their survival is also helped by the Italian habit of daily food-shopping and by economic factors: though their margins are high, their credit terms are easy; they can offer "discounts" (in other words, they do not charge value-added tax to known customers); and they often opt out of paying the heavy social security contributions which add nearly 50% to supermarket wage bills.

Business Awareness

Italian business activity is highly personalized. Companies are owned by individuals and families rather than by anonymous masses of shareholders, and long-standing business relationships are greatly valued. Personalities are more important than job-titles, so outsiders should take care to find out where real power lies within a company.

Doing business in Italy can be frustrating, mainly because of bureaucratic delays and obstacles, but there are plenty of opportunities for those prepared to learn the rules.

Business attitudes

For most Italians, work is a necessity rather than a passion. It is poor form to admit to "ambition" – somewhat akin to "greed" in Italian eyes. Lifelong employment with the same firm is still the norm, particularly in the state sector and in large organizations, and promotions tend to be tied more to seniority than to merit.

North v South There is some truth in the cliché of a hardworking North and an unproductive South – though in fairness, the difference is due more to the poor organization and scarce resources of the South than to a greater degree of laziness.

There is a significant division between the generally over-manned and under-organized state sector and the private sector, which works both more and better. It follows that public-sector organizations located in the South work at even slower speeds than those in the North, while, at the other extreme, the pace in the private and productive North would at times make a Japanese auto-worker blanche.

No corporate control A company's concern with the private lives of its executives is minimal by, say, German or American standards. The practice of taking into consideration the spouse's personality and social activities when deciding an important promotion for an employee would cause puzzlement and rage in Italy. What an executive does in out-of-office hours is entirely his or her affair. Homosexuality, for instance, is a private concern and not a question for the company. Security checks are unheard of and unacceptable.

Formality still prevails in Italian offices and, in general, subordinates are not on first-name terms with their bosses.

Working hours and holidays

In Southern Italy, the working day in private firms begins at about 9am and runs until roughly 1pm. The long lunch break lasts until 4 or so. It is common for offices in the South to be open until 7 or even as late as 9.

This kind of daily schedule was once the rule throughout Italy, but the "nine-to-five" routine began to move into the North 20 years ago and slips farther south each year. Offices in Milan, Turin and other northern cities now keep standard international hours and northern lunches tend to be a grab-a-sandwich affair unless there is entertaining to be done. Firms with more than 20 employees must provide some kind of canteen.

Public sector offices follow a different timetable, which usually runs from 8am to 2pm, although there are regional variations. If you need to contact a senior bureaucrat in a ministry, call between 10 and 1. In the afternoon, everyone goes home – or, in many cases, they go moonlighting on a second job.

Saturday Although until the 1970s it was common for Italian offices to open half a day on Saturday, this is now rarely done and you are pushing your luck to attempt to interest an

Italian in your business affairs over the weekend unless the question is genuinely urgent or you are on very familiar terms.

Home is sacrosanct It is still possible in Italy to maintain a rigid separation between private and working life. Italians are proud of this. The home is a sanctuary and it is considered very poor form to take work home either over the weekend or in the evenings. Italian business people with catching up to do will stay late in the office or go in on Saturday if necessary; they will *not* spread paper over the kitchen table and will not even happily take a telephone call at home.

Public holidays in Italy are fewer than in most Latin countries and the tendency is for even more saints' days to drop off the calendar. However, the business traveller should be warned that every Italian city celebrates the feast of its patron saint as a legal holiday. Milan, for instance, closes for the festival of St Ambrose, though no other part of Italy does. Rome celebrates the festival of Saints Peter and Paul. (See *Holidays* in **Planning and Reference**).

Bridging the gap There is also the risk of hitting a *ponte* (bridge), the day or two separating a holiday from a weekend. The *ponte* tends to become part of the holiday, creating a long weekend ideal for a major outing. Many businesses, although officially open, virtually grind to a halt.

Vacations Italy follows the southern European practice of closing down for August. People start disappearing from offices in the second half of July and the late-returners may well not show up again until mid-September.

No business travel should be planned to Italy within this period unless specific appointments have been made. Even then, a key colleague who must be consulted will always turn out to be on holiday. As a result, important decisions are rarely taken in this period. Something similar happens around Christmas. Decisions are avoided from Christmas Eve to Epiphany (Jan 6th).

Corporate hierarchies

At the top, titles are relatively easy to interpret. The chairman of the board of directors is the *presidente del consiglio d'amministrazione*. However, the *presidente* is not usually the chief executive officer. That is normally the *amministratore delegato*, the "managing director," though many Italian firms muddy the waters by having more than one.

Board members are *amministratori* or *consiglieri*, whereas *direttori* are the equivalent of managers or vice-presidents.

Decision makers

Beyond the handful of easily understood corporate titles, there is a problem. Italians tend to believe that authority travels with individuals rather than with positions or titles. This means that organizational charts are often a joke. Foreign business people are frequently puzzled by the need, when an important decision has to be taken, to consult a colleague with no apparent involvement in the matter in hand.

To make matters worse, private-sector firms in Italy are *all* run by their owners, though in varying ways. The Anglo-Saxon "public company," with broadly diluted ownership and the final say in the hands of professional managers, does not exist in Italy. Therefore, the last word on important issues is very often with people who may not even have a formal corporate title, especially when one or more layers of holding company separates ownership from management.

It is often even considered inappropriate for managers to own voting stock in the company which employs them. This is official policy in Italy's largest private company, Fiat.

Hidden hierarchies Italian corporations are shot through with informal horizontal chains of command. Called a *cordata* (literally, a team of mountain climbers on the same rope), in many cases these are the groups which actually call the tune.

This very modern idea of parallel channels is essentially feudal in concept, based on various levels of personal, reciprocal fealty. The prestige of a *cordata* is shared by all its members, the group moving up and down in power in a wavelike fashion all across the company according to the changes in status of its leading members.

The *cordata* mechanism escapes formal analysis and is impenetrable to outsiders, which means it is more than usually necessary to have a reliable contact with solid inside knowledge when dealing with a large Italian firm.

Managerial types

There are only two kinds of senior corporate manager in Italy: traditional and Americanized. The watershed between these two groups is the spreadsheet. The first group would not touch a spreadsheet analysis of anything with a ten-foot pole. The second would barely order lunch without it.

The traditional Italian manager is a well-educated humanist with a built-in abhorrence of anything technical. Technical, except at academic levels, is "grubby." His view of management is exquisitely political, based entirely on dealing with individuals and on maintaining working equilibria among them. He travels with very small quantities of paper and is above all a skilful negotiator.

The Americanized manager has an MBA. He is strongly influenced by the techniques of marketing, whatever his actual responsibilities. He has a white board on the wall of his office and uses it continually. He believes that while the sum is greater than its parts, only the parts are controllable. He is at times a dangerously rigid negotiator, but is far better at the detailed work necessary for an operational agreement. This type of manager is still in the minority but is gaining in both numbers and influence.

Indicators of rank

As in many other countries, large potted plants, original prints on the wall, a couch, a large desk and so on are rough indicators of rank. Good-looking secretaries, on the other hand, generally are not, other than in glamorous businesses such as advertising. The secretary's language skills are a better clue to the boss's importance.

Parking arrangements, especially reserved parking in a large city, are often a reliable indicator, but foreign business travellers will rarely have a chance to see their host's private automobile since high-ranking executives will send a driver to meet a visitor.

Executive dining rooms and washrooms exist but are not widely used in Italy. In smaller cities going home for lunch still distinguishes management (*dirigenti*) from clerical and shop-floor employees (*impegnati* and *operai*), who eat cheaply in the company cafeteria. However, in some large companies top management rubs shoulders with the workers in the same canteen.

Women in business

There are hardly any women at the decision-making levels of Italian business. One of the very few areas where there are women in management is the obvious one of fashion. They are slightly more prominent in the professions but are still rare in engineering and similar sectors. At Olivetti, for example, only 3% of the engineers are women.

The lack of women in managerial positions is in some ways a surprise because Italian social legislation rather favours women in the work place with, for example, very generous maternity benefits and a national network of nearly free day-care centres. There is also a reasonably large pool of well-educated female candidates. However, there is no legislation to ensure equal opportunities in employment for men and women.

Foreign businesswomen

Businesswomen arriving from other countries are taken seriously and even treated with a certain bemused respect. Italian business is sophisticated enough to know very well that its nearly male-only world is no longer the international rule.

However, a women who is travelling with male colleagues will have to make explicitly clear that she is not simply along for the ride as a secretary. Ideally, she should travel with a male very obviously her junior and avoid moving about in large groups where her role will be much more difficult for observers to define.

Most Italian men still treat women with a certain amount of gallantry, though without condescension – opening doors for them, for example – and such gestures should be accepted gracefully.

Hands-on encounters The days of bottom-pinching harassment of foreign women in the streets are largely past, but here, too, the distinction between the northern and southern halves of the country comes into play: any female visitor with the poor sense to climb on to a crowded Naples bus in, say, tight shorts is likely to find that pinching has been replaced by the *mano morta*, the "dead hand" casually propped against some part of the body.

Doing business

A preference for "dealing with someone you know" pervades all Italian business. Personal contact, even if it is nothing more than a handshake at a trade fair, transforms a stranger into someone who will at least be listened to.

Getting to know you Advantage should be taken, therefore, of every possible opportunity to make the social acquaintance of Italians with whom business might be done at some date. Business should not be discussed at social occasions, however. Even asking someone what he or she does for a living can be seen as coming on too strong, though it is probably acceptable from a foreigner.

The temptation to hand out business cards at parties and gallery openings, between acts at the theatre, and on other social or semi-social occasions must be resisted. The trick is to ask each person in the group about the others present. This is not only perfectly acceptable, it provides a ready-made source of conversation.

Before telephoning The cold telephone call is perhaps even less appreciated in Italy than it is in most other countries. Italians like to have their calls pre-announced. Write first, or send a telex or a fax. Then call to talk about the message. Italians want to know who you are before they talk. A piece of paper creates the illusion that you are a known quantity.

Meetings

On entering a business meeting, it is important to shake hands with every person in the room. Then, after everyone has sat down, you should be prepared to follow up by exchanging business cards with anyone you don't know.

The person leading the meeting will be at the head of the table. Though likely, it is not necessarily the case that he or she will be the most senior person present; a number two may be delegated to run the meeting so that if the chief is called out, this will not disrupt the proceedings.

Although practice varies between companies, Italians generally do not consider the formal meeting an appropriate way to decide significant matters. Big, sit-down meetings typically are held not so much to reach decisions as to ratify them and communicate them to other levels. Major decisions are usually taken behind the scenes.

Languages In large Italian companies, it is quite common to hold business meetings in English if any non-Italian is present. At smaller firms, it may be necessary to make sure in advance that an English speaker will be present. French, although spoken by many well-educated managers of the older generation, is now rarely used as a commercial language in Italy.

Negotiation

Negotiating is an art in Italy: to the Italian way of thinking, the key management art. Enormous care and study are dedicated to any negotiation – and the more important the subject in hand, the less that background preparation will show.

Studied nonchalance is often the style; any display of urgency is considered to weaken one's bargaining position. Dramatically "changing the cards on the table" – for example, when an agreement seems near, suddenly bringing in a broad set of new demands – is another often-used technique.

The unexpected closing of the meeting is another ploy. They are, however, only pretending that the whole thing is of minor importance to them. Just when the visitor is finally resigned to letting the whole thing slip away, the agreement can come together with amazing speed.

The result is that negotiating an important agreement in Italy can be the emotional equivalent of a roller-coaster ride. It is essential to stay calm; keeping the visitor rattled and uncertain is part of the game.

Agreements It must always be remembered that the Italian concept of a "contract" does not grow out of the Anglo-Saxon legal tradition, which sees the formal document outlining the agreement as merely a secondary instrument, compared with the real contract – the understanding between two parties.

Generally speaking, Italians consider that the document itself is the contract. This means that an attempt to establish the "intentions" in the mind of contracting parties is of very limited importance. What holds is the text of the agreement, right down to the last comma or semi-colon.

Communications

There is a certain tendency in Italy not to take telephone messages as seriously as written communications. Consequently, it can often be difficult to get someone to return your call. The solution is to send a fax message. Fax, though widely used in Italy, is still something of a novelty and as a result carries with it a useful sense of urgency.

The Italian telephone system does not function well, so what in another country would be improbable stories of attempted but unsuccessful calls ought to be given some credence. Curiously, it can be more difficult to place a call within Italy than to call out of the country.

Although telex is widely used, the long waiting times and the numerous bureaucratic difficulties in getting a hook-up are such that many companies simply do without.

Many large companies do not attempt to use the Italian postal service for anything more important than mailing catalogues. For local deliveries, they use either company drivers or private "pony express" (Italians employ this English expression) delivery services for even routine communication. Between cities, or with other countries, private couriers are often used for urgent correspondence: this is the only means of ensuring overnight delivery.

Electronic mail barely exists and is not a usual channel for business communication.

Hospitality

Hospitality has an essential ceremonial role in Italian business activities. There is no way to escape from it and trying to do so would only give offence, even if your host would clearly rather be at home in front of the TV. However, it is not usual for work as such to be conducted while sitting at the table – especially the polishing of detail leading to an operating agreement. The working breakfast is almost unknown.

Hospitality in Italy means dining, and entertaining is almost invariably done in restaurants. It is very unusual to be taken, say, to the opera or a sporting event, unless there is a genuine friendship between host and visitor. Dining is a serious business. Substantial quantities of prestige can be won or lost at the table.

Who pays? Although a mild attempt to pay is not out of place the third or fourth time you are invited out by your Italian host, do not expect to win arguments about who picks up *il conto*.

On the other hand, when you are doing the inviting, you *must* win. Insist. It's a game, and the rules are very clear to your guest. Paying wins prestige and Italians will occasionally go as far as to slip a waiter a hefty tip beforehand to make certain you do not get the check.

The rules do not usually apply to women business visitors, who will find it almost impossible to win.

Where to go It is usually wise to leave the choice of restaurant to your guest, even if you can recommend an excellent one. Italians have strong opinions about restaurants. If you choose one that your guest does not especially esteem, he will over-praise it after the meal and think less of you. Moreover, if you let him choose, he will certainly take you somewhere really good. It is a matter of honour.

Who comes? Business dining in Italy usually involves only a very small group. A large table-full of people is almost a guarantee of poor service in a country where ordering is generally the result of a drawn-out negotiation with the waiter.

If you are travelling with your spouse, then he or she is included if the invitation is to dinner rather than lunch. Do not, though, expect to meet your host's spouse unless he or she is thoroughly internationalized.

When you are returning hospitality, consult your Italian contact before inviting his or her colleagues. Social or semi-social relationships often do not parallel those in the office and you risk creating an uncomfortable evening if you guess incorrectly about rank.

Nuances A dinner invitation carries, unsurprisingly, greater weight than one to lunch. It is a substantial mark of respect. The one-to-one invitation too is more significant than one which embraces two negotiating teams.

Do not expect to be invited to your host's home. If you are, be slightly startled. It is a mark of extraordinary intimacy and, unless you feel that that is appropriate, worry that he is trying to sell you London Bridge. The only exceptions are Top People, and those managers with a very long American experience, more accustomed to entertaining business guests at home.

Etiquette

Italian etiquette is more about behaving with dignity and thoughtfulness than about following rigid rules of formality.

Greetings

Hands are shaken both on meeting and on taking leave. Shake hands with everyone present if that is possible. This goes for both men and women. A man should not attempt to *kiss* a woman's hand unless he does this very naturally indeed.

Note that cheek kissing, sometimes employed by female friends, does *not* involve actual kissing. The cheeks rub, first one then the other, and a soft lip-smacking sound is made near the ear.

Close male friends may embrace while pounding one another on the back, but they do not make kissing sounds.

Titles

Personal titles in Italy are as important as job titles are relatively unimportant. *Dottore* is the most common and, unless actually borne by a medical doctor, simply means that its bearer is a university graduate. You will never offend an Italian by calling him Dottore. When in doubt, use it. The female version is Dottoressa, but is less widely used in speech than Dottore.

The other personal titles in current

use are *Ingegnere*, engineer; *Avvocato*, lawyer; and *Architetto*, architect. These are used in all forms of address, spoken and written, and reflect the holder's prestige, not just their professional qualification. Like *Dottore*, they are normally used on their own, without surname attached. *Professore* crops up surprisingly often; many professors hold part-time university posts and pursue parallel careers in business or politics.

Ragioniere, bookkeeper, and *Geometra*, something like surveyor, are rather less prestigious titles in common use. *Signore* (or *Signor* plus surname) is plain "Mister," but perfectly polite. *Signora* (with or without surname) is used nowadays for all women, married or single, except the very young; *Signorina* is normally restricted to those in their early 20s or younger.

A *Cavaliere del Lavoro* is someone who has received a form of knighthood from the Italian government for services to business. The title of *Commendatore* is a rather more weighty honour. Noble titles, though they still exist in Italy, are generally ignored in business circles.

Cards

Business cards are appreciated, especially since an Italian would not consider it polite to ask a foreigner to spell out his or her otherwise incomprehensible name.

Italian business cards tend to black-and-white sobriety and, as a curious general rule, are uninformative in proportion to the importance of their bearer – the more he or she matters, the less the card says.

Dress

There is no real risk of dressing too formally, but some risk of being too informal. Italians dress with care, associating sloppiness with poverty rather than with a devil-may-care "creative" lifestyle.

Both the Italians and their climate make a clear distinction between summer and winter clothing and so

should visitors. This means wool in the winter and cotton or silk in the summer. There is a third season as well - the *mezza stagione*, "half season" – where clothing is of an intermediate weight for spring and autumn wear.

To make the right impression, the male business visitor should go for a well-cut suit, conservative in style and sober in colour. A fashionable sports jacket and grey worsted trousers would also be appropriate. Avoid dazzling shirts or ties. The visiting business woman should dress expensively, remembering that good clothes are a badge of success in Italy, but she should go for the quietly elegant look rather than anything either revealing or conspicuous.

Gifts

Business visits at senior managerial level often involve ritual gift-giving. The gift should be luxurious but without evident commercial value. Many Italian firms privately publish glossy, top-quality illustrated books for this purpose. Coffee-table books, though hard to carry around, are a safe choice for foreign visitors as well. Consumables – liquors, gastronomic delicacies from the visitor's country, such as single malt whisky, good Cognac, smoked salmon – may also be appropriate.

Small luxury items like lighters, travel alarm clocks and pen sets must be prestige goods. Italians are rather snobbish about this class of merchandise and will barely wait till you are out of the room to turn the item over and see where it was made and by whom. Asia still means "cheap" to Italians, so it is wise to avoid gifts bearing "made in Korea" or similar labels.

Conversation

There are no particular taboos in polite conversation, though it is worth noting that Italians do not tell dirty jokes in the company of people they do not know well; nor do they appreciate people who do. It is best to avoid World War II topics.

As always, let your Italian host criticize his own country and political parties and do *not* agree too enthusiastically. Interest shown in local art and architecture, food, wine and scenery always goes down well.

Drink and tobacco

With the exception of cab drivers, no one in Italy cares if you smoke, even if they don't themselves or have recently stopped. Many Italians are unaware of the strong anti-smoking sentiments held by a growing number of Britons and Americans.

Be more careful about that other vice, drink. You rarely see public drunkenness in Italy, and even tipsiness is considered a sign of a weak character. Most Italian women drink very little. Forget before-dinner cocktails, even if offered, and accept a glass of dry vermouth instead. Those who don't drink at all will not be pressed; in Italy it is much easier to refuse alcohol than to refuse food, and the excuse "Doctor's orders" is accepted without question.

Never, *ever*, allow yourself to get drunk. It is unforgivably bad form.

Business media

There is no truly national newspaper although a few major dailies have considerable circulation outside their own region: *La Stampa* (published in Turin), *Corriere della Sera* (Milan) and *La Repubblica* (Rome and Milan editions). All the newspapers contain a large proportion of weighty, analytical articles, and there are no popular tabloids such as those in the UK.

Business dailies

There are, for all practical purposes, only two significant business dailies in Italy; *Il Sole/24 Ore*, which is owned by the Italian Confederation of Industrialists (Confindustria), and *Italia Oggi*, acquired in 1988 by the Ferruzzi group.

The first is read by every Italian business person of any significance. Until recently, it had the largest

circulation of any European business paper, but it has now been overtaken by the *Financial Times*, with which it shares the distinction of being printed on pink paper.

Some people read *Italia Oggi* in addition to *Il Sole*, because it is an alternative voice to that of Confindustria. It gives more space to financial and stock market news than *Il Sole*, but the paper, founded in 1968, has yet to find a solid readership base.

General dailies

Business coverage by the general dailies is poor and often too closely linked to ownership and/or editorial policies.

All the major dailies are linked to big industrial names. *La Stampa* and *Corriere della Sera* belong to the Agnelli group. *Il Messaggero* belongs to Montedison, and so to the Ferruzzi group. The country's largest daily, *La Repubblica*, is 64% owned by the De Benedetti group, though a tough editor keeps it substantially independent.

Other major papers have direct links to state-owned companies or to political parties. *Il Giorno* is owned by the state hydrocarbons corporation ENI, *Il Popolo, Avanti!* and *L'Unità* are the organs of, respectively, the Christian Democrat, Socialist and Communist parties.

Regional dailies

There are several regional newspapers whose names are well known and which are influential within their home territory, but are scarcely read outside, such as *Il Resto del Carlino* (Bologna), *La Nazione* (Florence), *Il Tempo* (Rome) and *Il Mattino* (Naples). *Il Giornale* (Milan) does circulate throughout the North, however, and *Il Messaggero* (Rome) has some nationwide circulation.

Business periodicals

The most important business weekly is *Il Mondo*, published by Rizzoli and so somewhat under the sway of the

Agnelli group and Fiat. It is news-oriented, but likes to slip in some rather heavy editorial comment. Its reporters will quote you accurately and murder you with context.

There are several glossy publications, including *Capital*, related to the German magazine with a similar name, and *Class*. They purport to discuss business issues, but appeal principally to salaried employees preparing themselves to become rich and powerful. They are nearly worthless as a source of business news or analysis.

Though their field of interest is very specialized, two strictly financial weeklies deserve a mention here: *Lettera Finanziaria* and *Milano Finanza*. Both are widely read, but for different reasons: the first is authoritative, the second is interesting.

Special-interest periodicals

Italy has a very wide range of trade magazines but they are generally poor and their influence is limited even within their chosen field. The practice of trading editorial space for advertising purchases limits their utility to readers and undermines credibility in general.

General periodicals

Italy's news weeklies, *L'Espresso* and *Panorama*, have a *Time/Newsweek* format; however, they are not really news magazines in the American sense, but rather magazines of opinion. Their coverage of business matters is at best superficial and often mildly dangerous since they typically employ news items to make a point rather than to inform. Nevertheless, Italian business makes use of them.

Foreign-language publications

The European edition of the *Financial Times* has the largest circulation in Italy of any foreign daily. Following far behind are *The Wall Street Journal* and *International Herald Tribune*. *The Economist* is the most widely read foreign business periodical.

Television

The state-owned Radiotelevisione Italiana (RAI) has three TV networks, each with a distinct political identity: Christian Democrat, Socialist (plus the smaller lay parties) and Communist respectively for Channels 1, 2 and 3. There are also three private networks, all owned by the Berlusconi industrial group, which do not yet have a news operation as such.

The only business coverage on television is provided by a programme on RAI's Channel 1 every afternoon at 2.30, and the emphasis is on financial and stock market information.

Cultural Awareness

A historical perspective

Italy has the most densely chronicled history of any country in Western Europe. The Etruscans, Greeks and Romans, the papacy, dukedoms and city states, the Spanish, Austrian and French rulers, all gave way eventually to the unification of the Italian peninsula and its islands only in 1870. "We have created Italy," said Massimo D'Azeglio, one of the prime movers of unification, "now we must create Italians."

Rise of the comuni Following the fall of the Roman Empire, Italy was repeatedly invaded from the north. The Germanic Holy Roman Empire and the Papacy vied for power in the peninsula from the late 10th century, a struggle which allowed the most prosperous cities to turn themselves into self-governing *comuni* of which the most powerful were Venice, and Milan and Florence. Sicily and much of the South were conquered by the Normans in the 11th century and later passed to the house of Anjou, then that of Aragon.

Renaissance The rise of rich merchant families, lavish patrons of the arts, helped Italy and particularly Florence to become the centre of Europe's cultural and artistic rebirth from the late 14th century to the early 16th. Families such as the Este of Ferrara, Gonzaga of Mantua, Visconti of Milan and Medici of Florence, took control of their *comuni*, transforming them into *signorie*. Only Venice remained a republic.

Foreign domination Rivalries and constant wars between the *signorie*, together with the financial collapse of many banking families, ruined by the effects of European wars, opened the way for invaders. From the early 16th century all Italy, apart from Venice and the Papal States, came under the rule of either Spanish or French dynasties. Austria became the dominant power in the north, through dynastic succession, in the 18th century. Napoleon later invaded, attacking the Austrians and setting up republics in their place, but proclaimed himself King of Italy in

1805. After his regime's collapse, the pre-Napoleonic situation was restored, but the seeds of a nationalist movement had been sown.

Risorgimento Secret societies were formed and there were insurrections in many parts of Italy. Piedmont assumed the leadership, at first through the political activities of Mazzini and Cavour, then also through its monarchy. The King of Piedmont and Sardinia with French help went to war against the Austrians, driving them out of all areas but Venice by 1860. Garibaldi liberated Sicily and Naples the following year, Venice was taken in 1866 and when Rome and the Papal States fell to Italian forces in 1870 unification, under the House of Savoy, was complete.

United Italy The South remained extremely poor; millions emigrated to the Americas. In World War I Italy fought with Britain and France against Germany.

Fascism Economic crisis and violent social disturbances followed the war. Benito Mussolini, previously a socialist leader, formed the Fasci di Combattimento in 1919. The party gained a parliamentary majority in 1924 and two years later Mussolini assumed dictatorial powers. Although the Fascists' programme of economic reforms and land reclamation initially helped many of the poorest people, the regime's harshness and ineptitude had resulted in widespread disillusionment by the outbreak of World War II, in which Italy fought on Germany's side. Following Mussolini's downfall in 1943, Italy signed an armistice with the Allies. Mussolini was executed by partisans in 1945. The country became a republic the following year.

Postwar revival There was rapid economic expansion in the next two decades. The South remained poor, however. Large numbers of Southerners emigrated to northern Europe and the Italian North. A period of strikes and social unrest began in 1968, sparked off by student demonstrations. Economic problems and right- and left-wing terrorist activities overshadowed the 1970s, but in the 1980s Italy entered a period of social stability and joined the ranks of the world's most buoyant economies.

Key dates

753BC Rome founded by Romulus, according to legend.
509BC Roman Republic founded.
60BC First triumvirate formed by Pompey, Crassus and Julius Caesar.
44BC Caesar declared Dictator for life but assassinated same year.
30BC Egypt annexed by Augustus. Roman Empire begins.
AD64 St Peter arrives in Rome, according to tradition.
306 Constantine proclaimed emperor and seven years later gives legal status to Christianity.
330 Constantine moves capital of the Roman Empire to Constantinople. Rome's slow decline begins.
476 Last emperor deposed after invasions by Goths and Vandals.
476–1305 Italy ruled successively by Ostrogoths and Lombards. Growth of independent city states.
c1300 Dante Alighieri starts his *Divine Comedy*, the first major work in the Florentine vernacular, which eventually becomes the basis for the Italian language.
1815–70 The period of the Risorgimento, the movement for Italian independence and unification.
1859 Austrians expelled from Lombardy, with help of Napoleon III.
1860 Garibaldi and his "Thousand" liberate Sicily and Naples.
1861 Victor Emmanuel II of Sardinia

and constitutional monarch of Piedmont proclaimed king of Italy; Turin declared first Italian capital.
1870 Italian troops capture Rome, which is declared Italy's capital.
1915–18 Italy fights on Allied side in World War I. Alto Adige and Trieste become Italian territory.
1918–22 Great political and social unrest; strikes paralyse industry and services.
1919 Benito Mussolini founds Fascist movement.
1922 Fascists march on Rome. Mussolini named prime minister.
1929 The Lateran pacts signed with Pope Pius XI, recognizing sovereignty of Vatican City.
1935 Italy invades Abyssinia.
1936 Rome-Berlin Axis formed.
1939 Italy invades Albania.
1940 Italy enters World War II.
1943 Allies land in Sicily. Mussolini ousted from power. New government declares war on Germany, whose forces occupy much of Italy.
1944 Rome liberated by Allies.
1946 King abdicates. His son, Umberto, reigns for only one month.
1946 Abolition of the monarchy.
1947 New constitution promulgated.
1948 New constitution comes into force. First postwar election; Christian Democrat party under Alcide de Gasperi wins overall majority.
1951 Italy is founder member of the European Coal and Steel Community.
1957 Italy is a founder member of the EEC and of Euratom.
1963 "Opening to the left" begins: Christian Democrats invite Socialists into government for first time.
1976–79 "Historic compromise;" Communist leader Enrico Berlinguer agrees not to oppose government, in return for a voice in policy-making.
1981 Scandal of secret masonic lodge "P2," allegedly linked with criminal and right-wing extremist circles; many prominent figures implicated.
1982 Collapse of Banco Ambrosiano.
1987 *Il sorpasso*: Italy claims to have overtaken Britain to become the world's fifth largest economy.

Beliefs, attitudes and lifestyles

The Italian outlook on life is partly the product of a history that has seen constant warring between factions and many changes of ruler. This has bred a certain cynicism toward authority, and an ability to survive in difficult circumstances. It has also reinforced the instinct to look after the needs of self and family first of all; a sense of social responsibility comes far down the list of Italian attributes. Appearances are all-important, not only in the sense of smart clothes, but in the idea of *bella figura*: making a good impression matters deeply.

National identity

Even 120 years after Italy's unification as a nation, "the Italians" do not really exist. Regional differences are very marked and, in particular, the North and the South are like different countries. Regional dialects are still widely spoken among family and friends.

Regional sentiment A 1986 study found that 62% of Italians had difficulty in feeling that they belonged to a national collective group. When a Sicilian or a Piedmontese goes abroad the passport and the bearer may say "Italian" but the true homeland will be proclaimed with pride. Excessive attachment to one's native town or village is called *campanilismo* – from *campanile*, the parish church belltower.

National pride Italians are most proud to accept their national label when Italy does well in an international sports competition, such as soccer's World Cup, when an Italian wins the Nobel Prize (even if as a member of a Harvard faculty), or when they see a Ferrari go by. However, an opinion poll has shown that the majority of Italians consider Italy the best country to live in – meaning, presumably, the part they themselves live in.

Attitudes

Money Italians are Europe's most serious savers, and the first investment is likely to be a house or apartment: putting one's money "in bricks" is considered wise. Treasury bonds account for 40% of personal investments; the stock market has always been viewed with suspicion.

Wealth fascinates Italians. The popular illustrated weeklies are full of articles describing the lifestyle of super-rich industrialists and film stars. The country's economic prosperity is relatively new and there is an ever-present fear of poverty just around the corner, a horror of having to wear shabby clothes or stay in second-rate hotels. Nevertheless, materialism is outweighed by an appreciation of the good things of life that are free.

Politics Even in a land of paradoxes, where anarchy lies waiting around every corner, where the bureaucratic apparatus is not only inefficient but weighted heavily against the individual, and where politicians are rated by their ability to make a *raccomandazione* which results in someone getting a job as a postman or a company being awarded a multimillion dollar government contract, nearly 90% of the Italians vote almost every year in municipal, provincial, regional or national elections. About 80% also vote in the frequent referenda.

In theory, voting is compulsory because the constitution cites it as a civic duty. This is not enforced but political parties put pressure on their supporters to turn out at elections and, particularly in villages, failure to vote is noted by the neighbours. Italians are highly politicized: newspapers are full of lengthy articles on current parliamentary intrigues and personalities, and politics are a constant topic of conversation. Political allegiances are almost always known to friends, colleagues and neighbours. Even so, Italians' attitude towards their elected representatives, particularly those sent to parliament, is often cynical.

Religion Cynicism also pervades the popular view of the church. Priests, like politicians, are part of life, but not essential, and they are certainly not superior creatures. There are, of course, large numbers of devout people, but a strong vein of anti-clericalism persists from the days when the church had immense power and when priests frequently interfered in the private affairs of individuals. The sentiment is also a legacy of the 19th century when the papacy was a major obstacle to the struggle for Italian unification.

However, most Italians take a pragmatic line. Although church-going has fallen sharply, about 80% of babies are still baptized and 70% of (first) marriages are in church. This may be partly to please parents and grandparents but many Italians, even of the younger generation, still go to Mass at least at Christmas and Easter. Catholicism remains a weighty presence in the nation's conscience and, of course, in its cultural heritage.

Young people who are practising Catholics tend to join one of the various lay groups, many of which are involved in community work (see *The reins of power*).

Attitudes towards non-Catholic religions are tolerant. There are about 200,000 Protestants. The Waldensian Church, founded in the 12th century, was never recognized by Rome. It is the largest of the Protestant churches and the majority of its adherents are in Piedmont. Evangelical groups such as Jehovah's Witnesses and Seventh Day Adventists have made many converts. The Jewish population numbers fewer than 40,000.

Issues The Italians tend to suddenly wake up to key issues and pursue them with vigour. The enviroment is the latest hot issue: nuclear power is now in effect finished as a result of referenda; sea pollution is of great concern; and the debate on hunting has cut across all political and social divides.

Social classes Italians are less class-conscious than most Europeans. Social discrimination against southerners living in the North is almost always based on the educational levels of both parties; very rarely is it of a rabid nature. Snobbishness tends to be limited to the way people dress, for example, or the quality of their furniture, their china, the pictures on their walls.

Foreigners Italians are remarkably free from stereotyping prejudices. There have been some unpleasant patches, but the Jewish communities in Italy have fared well. Families who had never knowingly seen a Jew opened their homes to them during the Nazi occupation, as did many convents and monasteries. There are said to be about 1.2m Africans and Asians now in Italy, and about half of them work illegally or semi-legally, mainly in menial jobs. The only blacks who are resented – mainly by shopkeepers – are those who have been brought to Italy, mostly from Senegal, by Italians who make them sell on the streets and beaches "native handicrafts" manufactured in southern Italy or South Korea. Other foreigners, on the whole, are genuinely liked by most Italians, except perhaps by some of those who must cater to "package" tourists.

Authority The government minister, the boss and the mayor are treated with great respect, even deference, as a matter of course. However, this is a courteous ritual and involves a personal relationship, however distant. The abstract idea of authority is one which Italians love to ridicule. Breaking petty rules is a matter of amusement, and of honour. An authoritarian manner is greatly resented. Memories of Fascist rule are still present, which is one reason for the general dislike of the State Police, a force which was created in that period.

Authority also took a tumble with

the student revolt of 1968 which radically changed attitudes of a whole generation.

Heroes People worthy of respect are those in the arts, skilled craftsmen, captains of industry and (honest) wine-makers.

Law and order

The number of known crimes in 1987 was 2.2m, an increase of 11% over two years. More than half were thefts and, of these cases, only 3% resulted in a conviction. The prison population is usually between 32,000 and 37,000, about half of whom are on remand or waiting for their appeals to be heard. Every citizen has a *certificato penale*, a blank certificate on which criminal offences are recorded. The document must be produced, for example, with applications for civil service jobs.

Despite a stepped-up government campaign, with a series of mass trials of hundreds of *mafiosi*, and despite the courageous stand taken by a number of magistrates and other officials in Sicily, the Mafia's grip seems to be as tight as ever.

Drugs It was not until the late 1960s that the Sicilian Mafia began to exploit the Italian drug market, mainly in the prosperous North. Today anti-drug police dogs can be seen patrolling the grounds of Italy's secondary schools, and drug-related crimes are common.

The family

Family ties, like church ties, have significantly loosened in the last 40 years. However, families still stick together: 30% of people under the age of 34 live with their parents. Few single young people leave home to live on their own, although this is a growing trend in large cities, particularly in the North.

The large family, where a dozen children was considered desirable and a good investment, is a thing of the past. Italy's birth rate is now about 10 per thousand population and, together with West Germany's, is the lowest in the world.

Marriage and divorce Since 1970 it has been possible to obtain a divorce in Italy. Many Italian couples had already formed second families and initially there was a small stampede to qualify for a divorce. Today the divorce rate is one of the lowest in Europe. The Christian Democrats promoted a referendum aimed at abolishing the new divorce law, but 59% of the Italians voted to keep it.

Sex and morality

The defeat over the divorce issue might have been a lesson to the Christian Democrats but, a few years later, they called another referendum to abolish the new law permitting legal abortions in certain cases. There was a 68% vote to keep the abortion option.

In 1968, Pope Paul VI, going against his advisers, ruled in his Encyclical *Humanae Vitae* that the relatively new contraceptive pill was immoral and forbidden to Catholics. Most Italians had not heard of the pill until the resulting uproar in the international press. The news, though negative, was instructive.

At about this time, the once sacred precepts on relations between young men and women were steadily being relaxed. In the cities, at least, cohabitation prior to marriage became both common and chic, although only in certain sections of society and not in the South. The "Gay Lib" movement was also set in motion.

Women

Italian women won the right to vote in 1946. Women had been active in the Resistance during the Nazi occupation, and several were nominated as candidates in the Republic's first general election by the Communist Party (PCI), which has continued to nominate more women for public office than the other major parties. The Radical Party (PRI) has also put many women in parliament and lobbied for women's rights. Almost a half of the Green Party's deputies are women.

In the last 20 years the number of women in parliament's two houses has risen from 28 to 88. The president of the chamber of deputies is a woman: the Communist Nilde Iotti. The Christian Democrat Tina Anselmi was the first woman to occupy an important cabinet post (as minister of labour in 1976), though she is best known for her dogged but level-headed chairing of a commission investigating the subversive freemasons' lodge, P2, in the early 1980s. Susanna Agnelli, granddaughter of Fiat's founder, was appointed under-secretary of state for foreign affairs in 1983.

Violence A bill passed in 1988 aims to eliminate loopholes in the anti-rape laws and to make any form of sexual violence, including verbal harassment at work, a more serious offence.

Employment Although women are not excluded by law from any job (except for the armed forces), there is no equal opportunities legislation and there is considerable discrimination against women. Women make up 41.3% of the workforce (see *Employment*).

Married women have gained many basic rights only since the late 1960s. Before then, adultery by a wife was a criminal offence; she had few rights over her children and none over the property she brought to the marriage.

Young single women have won a great deal of social and sexual freedom, though they are still more accountable to their parents than are their brothers, or their Northern European counterparts.

Feminism began to emerge at the end of the 1960s but has had a relatively low profile. Italian feminists have generally concentrated on a limited number of issues, and have campaigned less forcefully on employment opportunities than on, for example, rape.

The home

When the mercantile class emerged in the 15th century, it built its homes like small fortresses, with different generations occupying different floors and a shop at street level for the family business. The Italian home today is still a kind of fortress. Non-family visitors, particularly foreigners, in most cases will be invited for coffee at a café or dinner in a restaurant.

Italians prefer to own rather than rent their homes and more than 60% of homes are owner-occupied. However, most young couples have to start off with a rented apartment: loans for house purchase are normally granted for only 60% of the property's value, must be repaid – usually at high interest rates – in 10–15 years, and are quite difficult to obtain. Since there is a shortage of rented accommodation, many young people start off married life under their parents' roof. A recent innovation are housing cooperatives, whereby a group of people get a joint loan and build their own apartment block.

Quality of life

A survey in the late 1980s ranked the 95 provincial capitals according to their levels of *benessere* (wellbeing in general, not only with regard to wealth). The top five were Trieste (which ironically also had the highest suicide rate), Bologna, Ravenna, Florence and Reggio Emilia. Milan was in 18th place, Rome 35th, Venice 41st, Palermo 80th and Naples 81st.

Official statistics published in late 1988 revealed that, of the average Italian family's expenditure, 23% went on food, drink and tobacco, 15% on housing, gas and electricity, 13% on transport and telephone, 9.5% on clothing, 8% on recreation and 6% on health care.

Good food is of the greatest importance to Italians. They will never skimp when it comes to spending on meals, whether in restaurants or at home. They are conservative in their tastes, suspicious of foreign cuisines, and devoted to the dishes and wines of their own region, or even town.

Eating out in restaurants is often a family affair, particularly on Sundays, when even the youngest children are included in the party. Young people, couples or groups of friends, now eat out regularly, although this was uncommon a generation ago.

Wine Italy is the world's leading producer of wine and Italian males over 50 consume an average of half a litre a day. Younger Italians drink much less wine, and a few have taken to beer and even carbonated beverages with their meals. Wine is considered always as part of a meal. It is very rare to encounter street drunkards (other than the tourist variety). Smart families have private supplies of wine, often brought in demijohns from their home towns.

Too many cars The proudest possession an Italian family could have coveted 40 years ago was a small car. Since then increasingly widespread car ownership (Rome has one car for every 2.3 inhabitants) has created traffic chaos and contributed to the destruction of ancient monuments in historic centres. Once this was taken as the price of progress, but there is now a strong anti-car lobby.

Health

The national health service was introduced in the late 1970s, replacing a system under which patients were partially reimbursed with the cost of health care and medicines through a state insurance scheme. Visits to the family doctor are now free but patients, with the exception of those on low incomes and retired people, pay a proportion of the cost of treatment such as X-rays or blood tests, and of prescribed medicaments, plus a fixed fee on each prescription. Hospital care is free and there are long waiting lists for admission; better-off people sometimes opt for a private hospital. A common ploy is to pay to see the hospital consultant (*primario*) privately, who might then arrange for the patient to go to the top of the waiting list.

Each Italian pharmacy is said to stock between 2,200 and 3,000 pharmaceutical products, many of them duplicates under different brand names, and most are available without prescription.

Leisure and entertainment

More money is spent on soccer tickets than on any other spectacle. Basketball is the second most popular sport. The main participation sports are swimming, skiing and tennis. Outside the large cities, public sports facilities are meagre.

Before the advent of TV, many Italians went to the cinema at least twice a week but now they prefer to watch videos at home. Theatre and opera are attracting bigger audiences than ever before. Good concerts (with works of major, but not modern, composers) are sold out. In spite of Italy's contribution to music over the centuries, amateur music-making was almost unheard of until very recently, but now there is something of a boom in music – amateur as well as professional. After the Spanish, the Italians buy fewer books and newspapers than any other Western Europeans, but every family reads one or two of the innumerable illustrated magazines, several of which sell one or two million copies a week. Adults buy and read in public copies of Peanuts and Donald Duck comics.

Holidays and weekends

Like the French, the Italians have adopted the English word "weekend." The family climbs into the car and sets off for the second (sometimes larger) home. The *seconda casa* might be the old family farm; in most cases, however, it is an apartment in a modern condominium, either in the mountains or at the seaside. The weekend is relatively new: most Italians worked on Saturdays until the late 1960s, when the trade unions won for them *il sabato inglese*.

For the annual vacation, about half the people go to the seaside and the other half to the mountains. Safaris in Kenya and *lo shopping* in New York are popular options for the better-off.

Education

Italy's education system was dominated by the Roman Catholic church until the last decades of the 19th century. Today, education is compulsory between the ages of six and 14 and the great majority of children attend state-run schools. The system is highly centralized and school curricula and examinations are set by the Ministry of Education. Children who fail an end-of-year examination normally have to repeat that year.

Schools

Pre-school Children between the ages of three and six may go to a *scuola materna*, most of which are run by local authorities. Although the concept is relatively new in Italy, the number of available places is high.

Elementary All children attend *scuola elementare* for five years from the age of six. Pupils are required to wear smocks with starched white collars (over their blue jeans). About 4% of elementary-age children go to private schools, most of them run by religious orders; on the whole their academic standards are not higher than those of state schools, but their discipline is reputedly more firm.

Middle school Until 1963 obligatory schooling ended after the elementary level. Children now spend three years in a *scuola media unificata*. Of the 6.5m children in compulsory schooling, 53% leave at the age of 14.

High school An examination at the end of the *scuola media unificata* leads to various types of higher secondary education (*scuola secondaria superiore*). The choice is between a classical, artistic, scientific or linguistic *liceo* (lycée), an elementary teacher training institute, or one of the technical or vocational institutes. After five years at a *liceo*, the student sits an examination for the *maturità*, the higher school certificate which allows automatic entry into any university faculty. Students rarely pass all the exams in all subjects at first try. Final exams for *maturità* are both written and oral. Students at the various technical and commercial institutes take qualifying examinations but in some cases can also proceed to specialized university faculties, such as the *magistero* (faculty of education).

School life

A falling birthrate has meant that schools with younger children are now sometimes over-staffed, while the reverse is true of some of those with the older age-groups. Many schools operate a shift system and Saturday morning attendance is still the norm.

Religion Although Roman Catholicism is no longer the official state religion, instruction in religion was admitted in 1986 as an optional two-hours-a-week course, under the new concordat signed with the Vatican in 1984. State schools do not have prayers at morning assembly, but every classroom must have a crucifix.

Foreign languages are, in general, badly taught, by ill-prepared teachers. French once occupied first place but now the majority of pupils (and their parents) opt for English. However, the system has not adapted and there is a severe and much criticized shortage of competent English teachers. In the meantime, Italian youngsters learn English, or so they think, from listening to rock music.

Facilities Many long-established schools occcupy magnificent Renaissance palaces with frescoed ceilings, but with none of the facilities usually found in Italy's modern surburban schools, such as assembly halls, modern kitchens and playgrounds.

There is no sports instruction in the curriculum and the parish church is more likely than the local school to have a soccer pitch. There is no musical education until the *scuola media* and, even then, it is at a very basic level. In general, schools are poorly provided with scientific equipment and computers.

Universities

There are 55 officially recognized universities, of which 43 are state run. Since the state universities have no system of selective admission (except, since the late 1980s, for medicine) and impose no time limits on students' period of study, they suffer from chronic overcrowding. About 24% of girls and 28% of boys leaving school go on to university. Italy has nearly 750,000 full-time and 350,000 part-time university students.

Teaching through tutorials does not exist, and attendance at lectures is not compulsory. Exams can be passed by reading the professor's books or bound copies of his or her lectures. Obtaining a *laurea* (university degree) usually takes five years, but by postponing (or failing) the final exam in a required subject it can take several more years. The *laurea* (referring to the crown of laurel leaves) entitles one to be called *dottore* or *dottoressa*. It is obtained through oral examinations and a written thesis.

Some scholarships (*borse di studio*) are available but most parents have to bear the bulk of the cost of their children's university education.
Private Of the privately endowed universities, three stand out for their high reputation: Luigi Bocconi and Università Cattolica in Milan, and the Scuola Normale in Pisa.

Bocconi is unique in Italy in that it has a business school, offering courses in business management (*direzione aziendale*). The school has become the training ground for a large proportion of Italy's top managers. In 1988, 12% of the school's students were from overseas, including the USA and Japan. The plan is to increase this to 50%, and English will become the main language of instruction. Bocconi has also started an exchange of teachers and students with the USSR.

Pisa's Scuola Normale was founded by Napoleon in 1810, on the lines of the Ecole Normale just established in France. Courses are run partly at Pisa University and partly through the Normale's own seminars. Competition for places is tough: in 1988, only 26 students were accepted for science courses out of 380 candidates, and only 15 out of 150 for courses in the humanities. Total enrolment is only 220. All students are given free board and lodging and a modest living allowance. One of the Normale's most illustrious graduates was the atomic scientist Enrico Fermi.
Top universities For engineering, Milan, Turin and Pisa universities are generally rated the best; for economics, Bocconi, Rome and Bologna; for political science, Bologna, Milan and Florence; and for law, Rome, Milan and Florence. The universities of the centre and North have large numbers of bright students from the South who have won scholarships in order to get a better education than their local universities can offer.
Degrees In 1987, Italian universities gave 15,800 degrees in the humanities (*lettere*), 12,600 in medicine, 10,400 in sciences, 9,800 in engineering and 10,000 in law.
Future plans A government bill proposes far-reaching reforms which would give each university the freedom to set its own curricula and appoint its staff, and would encourage the growth of postgraduate research.
Research at university level was sorely lacking until 1983 when some universities were authorized to offer *post-laurea* degrees in research. However, most research is still carried out by the national research council *Consiglio Nazionale delle Ricerche*, or by private companies. Many university graduates have to go abroad to continue their research work. All Italian Nobel prize winners have carried out their research in other countries.
Academies Italy also has state-run academies of music, drama, design – industrial and fashion, art – painting and sculpture, art restoration and film-making.

City by City

The city guides' section is organized by region, though in some instances combines several of the country's regions under a single heading. The map at the bottom of the facing page highlights the cities featured in detail. Each of these follows a standard format: an introduction, information on arriving, getting around, city areas, hotels, restaurants, bars, entertainment, shopping, sightseeing, sports and fitness, and a directory of local business and other facilities such as secretarial agencies, couriers, hospitals, convention and exhibition centres and florists. There is also a map locating recommended hotels and restaurants, and important buildings and sights. Other cities in each region are covered in less detail, concentrating on the main commercial and industrial activities, hotels, restaurants, opportunities for relaxation and the most useful information sources.

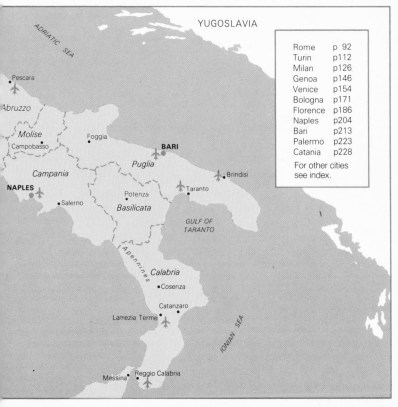

YUGOSLAVIA

ADRIATIC SEA

Pescara

Abruzzo

Molise

Campobasso

Foggia

BARI

Puglia

Brindisi

Campania

Taranto

NAPLES

Potenza

Salerno

Basilicata

GULF OF TARANTO

Apennines

Calabria

Cosenza

Catanzaro

Lamezia Terme

IONIAN SEA

Messina

Reggio Calabria

ROME (Roma)   *City codes* zip 00100 ☏ 06

Rome was a provincial town of some 200,000 inhabitants before becoming the capital of Italy just over a century ago. Today it covers more than 1,500 sq km/580 sq miles and is the largest Italian city in population (3m, plus some 1.3m visitors a year) and in area. Rome struggles to preserve the mystique (and fabric) of the ancient centre of civilization and of the Eternal City, focal point of the Roman Catholic faith, alongside its role of modern European capital.

Although the main international financial market is in Milan and industry is concentrated in the North, Rome remains the decision-making base. It is the seat of government, the embassies, the Banca d'Italia, the state-controlled holding companies, ENI (hydrocarbons), EFIM and IRI (Institute for the Reconstruction of Industry), with the head offices of its subsidiaries Alitalia, RAI (television and radio) and Finsider (steel). National corporations have administrative headquarters here and most Northern companies have an agent or office in Rome. Many international companies are based at Mussolini's planned suburb, EUR (Esposizione Universale di Roma), or at nearby Castello della Magliana: these include Colgate, Digital, Esso, General Motors, Hewlett Packard, Mobil, Procter & Gamble and Squibb.

Rome is Italy's third largest industrial conurbation in terms of employees in industry. Pomezia, about 40 minutes' drive to the south, is the main industrial complex; factories, notably pharmaceutical (Johnson & Johnson) and electronic, were set up here with aid from the Cassa per Il Mezzogiorno. High technology is concentrated along the Via Tiburtina, towards Tivoli, and includes the state-owned Selenia and Contraves, a subsidiary of Oerlikon.

Roman laziness and lethargy are legendary. But while it is true that the average Roman has something of a Southern mentality – liking siestas, street life and feast days – there is more of a get-up-and-go spirit in the city today. Public Rome and private business are sharply divided. While bureaucracy remains slow moving and corrupt, lots of thriving small businesses have sprung up since the early 1980s. These new Romans work normal business hours, and like everyone else, civil servants included, criticize state inertia and inefficiency.

In business, string-pulling is necessary, and personal clout counts for everything: foreigners usually need to operate through agents, especially as English is less widely spoken than in Milan. Romans are more easy-going (and less punctual) than the Milanese, but getting things done can be stressful. Meetings with bureaucrats and politicians (only available midweek) should be before lunch.

The 1970s and early 1980s were depressing. Terrorism was rife, governments came and went more frequently than ever, and the famous film industry based at Cinecittà declined. Now the Brigate Rosse ringleaders are behind bars, Cinecittà is back in business (just), monuments are being restored (slowly) and problems are being recognized if not resolved. The Rome capital project includes the transfer of all government ministries to Centocelle, due east of the centre, and the development of the Tiber into a navigable waterway. Funds are awaited. Vast improvements to the airports are planned for the early 1990s but it has been estimated that by the year 2005 air traffic will have doubled.

Arriving

The main airport, Leonardo da Vinci airport at Fiumicino, is often strikebound. Ciampino, which handles domestic and international charter flights, is closer to the centre but has poor transport links. Rome is connected to the North (via Florence and Milan), to the South and east of Italy by autostrada but the national rail network provides faster and more convenient access to other centres (4hrs from Milan).

Leonardo da Vinci airport (Fiumicino)

Europe's fourth busiest airport handles up to 50,000 passengers a day, nearly half on domestic flights. It is being greatly enlarged and a rail link with central Rome is under construction.

Facilities at the international terminal are not very convenient for arriving passengers. Airside, near passport control, are a bank (very high commission charges, open 7.30–11pm) and tourist information and hotel desks (not always staffed); baggage collection is near the exit. In the main arrivals hall facilities are basic: one bar, telephones, a bureau de change (24hr; more convenient than the bank). The bus ticket counter is beyond the exit (there is an automatic machine near baggage reclaim, sometimes out of order). The departures hall has a pharmacy, post office and telephone room. The departures lounge has two new duty-free shopping centres (one for designer fashion), the only airport restaurant (closes 10.30pm), a 24hr bar, a telex and telegram service (8–noon) and a VIP lounge.

Flight information inquiries ☎ 60123640; passenger information and airline offices ☎ 6010; Alitalia international flights ☎ 60103358,

national flights ☎ 60103204; recorded information on Alitalia flights 5456; baggage information 60124252. All numbers are often busy.

Nearby hotels *Satellite Palace*, Vle delle Antille 49, 00121, Roma Lido ☎ 5693941 ⊠ 611469 • Fezia Hotels • *AE DC MC V*. Large modern hotel with pool, convention facilities and airport shuttle (takes 20mins). *Sheraton* (see *Hotels*).

City link Fiumicino is 36km/22 miles southwest of Rome. Until the railway is completed, a taxi is the best way to get into the city, but beware the "pirate" versions.

Taxi The ride into central Rome takes about 45mins and costs around L65,000. Official ranks are outside the terminals. Reservations from the airport ☎ 60124310.

Limousine There is a limousine desk in the arrivals hall.

Car rental Not recommended for central Rome, but convenient for business at EUR or at Pomezia (30km/18 miles south). Major companies have offices in the arrivals hall.

Bus The ACOTRAL airport bus runs every 10mins 7–12.45, then on the hour; tickets (L5,000) from counters in both arrivals halls (or from automatic machines in the international arrivals hall). Allow 1hr for the journey. The terminal is in Via Giolitti, beside the main Stazione Termini.

Ciampino airport

Ciampino handles international charters and some domestic and private flights. Strikes here are very uncommon. Passenger inquiries ☎ 724241.

City link Ciampino is 16km/10 miles southeast of Rome. It is simplest to take a taxi to the centre as there are no airport shuttle buses and public transport is slow and inconvenient.

However, you may have to wait for a cab.

Taxi The journey to the city centre takes about 40mins and costs L25-30,000.

Car rental Avis, Budget, Hertz and Maggiore have desks.

Bus and train The ride by ACOTRAL bus to Anagnina takes 20mins; from there take the subway to the centre.

Urbe airport
Small airport for private and military planes, north of the city. It is 30mins by taxi from the centre ☎ 8120524 or 8120571.

Railway stations
Stazione Termini A huge monument of 20thC architecture, and the hub of the country's rail network. There are good, fast trains from Milan every hour during the day taking 5hrs 10 mins, and the Pendolino leaves at 7am and 7pm and takes 4hrs. Reserve sleepers on services to major cities through travel agents. The tourist information office is accessible only from the platforms and facilities are poorly indicated. There is access to both subway lines and outside in the Piazza dei Cinquecento is a bus terminal for city and suburban services. Buses from both airports arrive alongside the station in Via Giolitti. This is a seedy area; beware pickpockets and pirate cabs. There are often long lines waiting for taxis.

Inquiries ☎ 4775 but usually busy; reservations ☎ 110 but it is more reliable to use a travel agent; sleeper information ☎ 4741750.

Getting around
Rome's traffic is notoriously noisy and congested; it is a relief to walk in the traffic-restricted parts of the historic centre. Taxis are most useful for business appointments since the subway system is too limited and, at rush hours, buses are too crowded.

Taxis Taxis usually wait at ranks on main piazzas but they can be hard to find when shifts change (1–3.30pm and 8.30–9pm). A small tip (10%) is

normal practice. To order in advance consult the Yellow Pages for the local rank or call *Radio Taxi* ☎ 3570, *Radio Taxi Roma* ☎ 3875, *Radio Taxi La Capitale* ☎ 4994 or *Radio Taxi Cosmos* ☎ 8433.

Limousines Sapres ☎ 4745389, *Avis* ☎ 31512143 or 6441969, *Bevilacqua* ☎ 462896.

Driving Traffic jams are endemic and the centre is closed to nonresidents. There is 24hr parking at Villa Borghese and Piazza San Bernardo (others are open 7–9) costing about L2,000 per hour, L10,000 per day.

Walking is the best (often the only) way to get around the fairly compact but confusing historic centre; elsewhere the noise, the hills and, in summer, the heat can be wearing. It is usually safe to walk in the centre at night but it is sensible to avoid ill-lit or empty streets. The station area and backstreets of Trastevere can be sinister: dropouts and *drogati* congregate here. Bag-snatching is now less prevalent (the current sport is to snatch casually-flung fur coats) but shoulder bags are at risk, even in daylight. Avoid wearing valuable jewellery.

Bus The bus system is useful for the longer-term visitor and those who know the city well. Tickets are bought from main bus terminals, tobacconists, newsstands and bars and half-day tickets are available. Most buses run till midnight.

Subway There are two lines: A is useful for short hops from the Prati area or Piazza di Spagna to the business area (Barberini, Repubblica, Termini), B for EUR. Tickets are available from machines at some stations or the usual outlets like bars. Services stop before midnight.

Area by area
Ancient Rome was defined by the river Tiber (Tevere) and the city walls, of which there are extensive remains. The focus of life has shifted gradually north from the medieval, Renaissance and baroque heart of the city towards the northeast,

redeveloped in the 19th century.

Much of business, commercial and diplomatic Rome lies north of the walls, where smart residential areas extend beyond the Tiber. Planned suburbs and industrial areas have been developed to the south and southwest, notably at EUR, with several state companies and ministeries. The city (including EUR) is enclosed by the Grande Raccordo Anulare (GRA), or ring road.

Ludovisi, Borghese and the station
The curving, café-lined Via Veneto, scene of the *dolce vita* of the 1960s, is no longer very glamorous. But the *Ludovisi quarter* (either side of the Via Veneto) has the largest number of traditional hotels in Rome. Most major international airlines are in Via Bissolati, Via Barberini or Via Veneto and the Ministero dell'Industria and IRI are on Via Veneto.

The Ludovisi quarter extends to Via XX Settembre, site of important government ministries (notably Agriculture, Defence and the Treasury), and Via del Quirinale, with the presidential palace. Beyond is a busy commercial district around the Via Nazionale, with the Banca d'Italia, Via Cavour and the run-down area around the station. To the east, Via Tiburtina leads towards the Tiburtina Valley and Rome's burgeoning high-tech industry.

North of the ancient walls and the main traffic artery, Corso d'Italia, is a lively commercial district around Via Po (banks and trades union offices) and Via Salaria. East is *Nomentana*, mainly residential but with hospitals and the university nearby.

North of the large heart-shaped park of Villa Borghese (which has several museums) is *Parioli*, long the smartest address in Rome. In this area, which is becoming popular for offices, many of the detached villas are embassies. Farther north is the Olympic village, where some 8,000 government employees are now housed.

The historic centre The Corso, which the ancient Romans used for

horseracing, is still the capital's main high street, lined with shops, bars, the head offices of banks and the scene of the evening *passeggiata*. It runs from Piazza del Popolo (designed as a triumphal entrance to the city) to Piazza Venezia (with the hideously prominent monument to Victor Emanuel II known as the "Typewriter"). Half is closed to traffic; most of the streets off it are also traffic-restricted. On the Corso, Piazza Colonna and the adjacent Piazza Montecitorio are the centre of political life: Palazzo Chigi is the prime minister's headquarters and Palazzo Montecitorio houses the Chamber of Deputies. A few minutes' walk away, in Palazzo Madama, is the Senate.

West of the Corso, Renaissance and baroque Rome nestle in a kink of the Tiber. Here are narrow lanes full of artisans' workshops, piazzas, stately palaces (notably Palazzo Farnese, now the French Embassy) and famous churches. Café tables overlook the lively baroque Piazza Navona and the ancient Pantheon. The Borsa is incorporated in the ruins of an ancient temple behind the Piazza del Parlamento. The remains of the so-called Jewish ghetto are also in this corner of old Rome. The area west of the Corso is a popular place to live, especially among well-to-do single people and expatriates.

East of the Corso life revolves around the colourful Spanish Steps and the fashionable shopping streets around Via Condotti and Via Frattina. Newspaper offices are by Piazza San Silvestro and the Corso.

Most of the remains of ancient Rome, including the Colosseum and the Forum (but not the Pantheon), lie to the south around the Aventine, Palatine and Esquiline hills. *Aventino* is a peaceful residential district.

Trastevere and Prati *Trastevere* has a bohemian reputation but is now fashionable. Although artists and intellectuals live here, the Trasteverini, who claim to be the original Romans, are largely a

CITY BY CITY

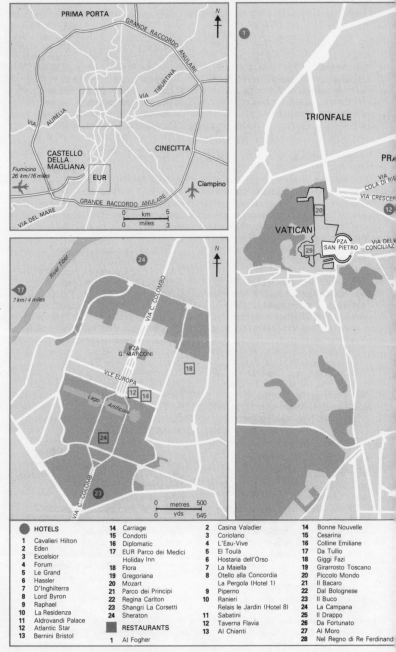

HOTELS

1 Cavalieri Hilton
2 Eden
3 Excelsior
4 Forum
5 Le Grand
6 Hassler
7 D'Inghilterra
8 Lord Byron
9 Raphael
10 La Residenza
11 Aldrovandi Palace
12 Atlantic Star
13 Bernini Bristol
14 Carriage
15 Condotti
16 Diplomatic
17 EUR Parco dei Medici
   Holiday Inn
18 Flora
19 Gregoriana
20 Mozart
21 Parco dei Principi
22 Regina Carlton
23 Shangri La Corsetti
24 Sheraton

RESTAURANTS

1 Al Fogher
2 Casina Valadier
3 Coriolano
4 L'Eau-Vive
5 El Toulà
6 Hostaria dell'Orso
7 La Maiella
8 Otello alla Concordia
  La Pergola (Hotel 1)
9 Piperno
10 Ranieri
   Relais le Jardin (Hotel 8)
11 Sabatini
12 Taverna Flavia
13 Al Chianti
14 Bonne Nouvelle
15 Cesarina
16 Colline Emiliane
17 Da Tullio
18 Giggi Fazi
19 Girarrosto Toscano
20 Piccolo Mondo
21 Il Bacaro
22 Dal Bolognese
23 Il Buco
24 La Campana
25 Il Drappo
26 Da Fortunato
27 Al Moro
28 Nel Regno di Re Ferdinand

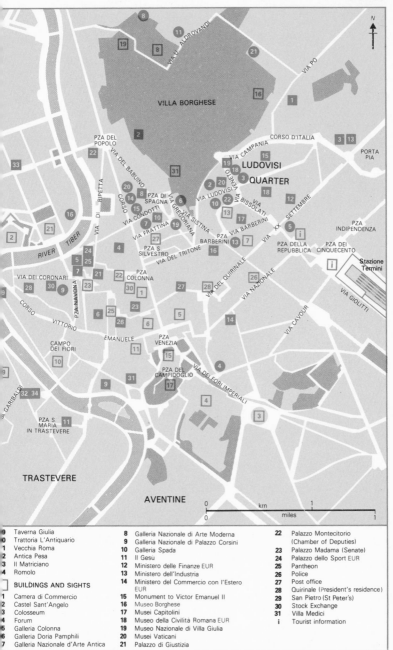

N

VILLA BORGHESE

CORSO D'ITALIA

LUDOVISI
QUARTER

PORTA
PIA

PZA DEL
POPOLO

VIA CAMPANIA

PZA
INDIPENDENZA

PZA DELLA
REPUBBLICA

PZA DEI
CINQUECENTO

Stazione
Termini

PZA DI
SPAGNA

VIA DEL BABUINO

VIA DI RIPETTA

CORSO

VIA CONDOTTI

VIA FRATTINA

PZA S
SILVESTRO

VIA DEL TRITONE

PZA VIA BARBERINI
BARBERINI

VIA DEL QUIRINALE

VIA NAZIONALE

VIA CAVOUR

VIA GIOLITTI

VIA XX SETTEMBRE

VIA BISSOLATI

VIA LUDOVISI

VIA VENETO

PZA
COLONNA

VIA DEI CORONARI

PZA NAVONA

CORSO
VITTORIO

EMANUELE

CAMPO
DEI FIORI

RIVER TIBER

PZA
VENEZIA

PZA DEL
CAMPIDOGLIO

VIA DEI FORI IMPERIALI

VIA GARIBALDI

PZA S.
MARIA
IN TRASTEVERE

TRASTEVERE

AVENTINE

0   km   1
0   miles   1

9   Taverna Giulia
10 Trattoria L'Antiquario
1   Vecchia Roma
2   Antica Pesa
3   Il Matriciano
4   Romolo

    BUILDINGS AND SIGHTS

1   Camera di Commercio
2   Castel Sant'Angelo
3   Colosseum
4   Forum
5   Galleria Colonna
6   Galleria Doria Pamphili
7   Galleria Nazionale d'Arte Antica

8   Galleria Nazionale di Arte Moderna
9   Galleria Nazionale di Palazzo Corsini
10 Galleria Spada
11 Il Gesu
12 Ministero delle Finanze EUR
13 Ministero dell'Industria
14 Ministero del Commercio con l'Estero
    EUR
15 Monument to Victor Emanuel II
16 Museo Borghese
17 Musei Capitolini
18 Museo della Civiltà Romana EUR
19 Museo Nazionale di Villa Giulia
20 Musei Vaticani
21 Palazzo di Giustizia

22 Palazzo Montecitorio
    (Chamber of Deputies)
23 Palazzo Madama (Senate)
24 Palazzo dello Sport EUR
25 Pantheon
26 Police
27 Post office
28 Quirinale (President's residence)
29 San Pietro (St Peter's)
30 Stock Exchange
31 Villa Medici
i   Tourist information

working-class community. North of the Vatican is *Prati*, a professional residential area, with apartments and rather dilapidated 19thC villas, and a popular shopping street, Via Cola di Rienzo. There is a subway connection to the centre.

Many lawyers are based here, close to the grandiose Palazzo di Giustizia (Italy's supreme court) and to the Tribunale and Prefettura (lower courts). The head office of RAI 2 (television) is in Via Mazzini. Farther north are the residential areas of *Trionfale* and airy *Monte Mario*, with apartment blocks overlooking the city. **The Vatican** On the west side of the Tiber, the Vatican covers about 44ha/100 acres, most of it inaccessible to the public. A ceremonial approach, the Via della Conciliazione, was cut through the original medieval quarter in 1929 to commemorate the establishment of a separate city state. This leads to the magnificent Piazza San Pietro, designed by Bernini.

The suburbs

To the north are the smart residential districts of *Fleming* and *Vigna Clara* around the Via Cassia and Via della Camilluccia. Here detached villas with gardens and condominiums with pools are popular with foreign residents. The Ministry of Foreign Affairs is nearby. *Olgiata* is a security-guarded suburb with villas and a famous golf club.

To the south, EUR, planned by Mussolini as a modern civic showcase for Fascism, was completed in the 1950s. This is an orderly, spacious but soulless business and residential district with ministries (notably Finance, Foreign Trade, and Post and Telecommunications) and headquarters of major companies. It is about 20mins by subway from the city centre and about 20mins drive from Fiumicino airport.

Castello della Magliana, with other company headquarters and hotels, is some 6km/4miles to the west of EUR.

Hotels

Rome's proudest old hotels are in or around the Via Veneto and the wide 19thC thoroughfares of the business district, especially Via Cavour. Many are relics of a grander age; period interiors have become shabby and double-glazing fails to keep out the noise of traffic. Still in the top league however are the Grand, Excelsior, Eden and, nearby, the Hassler. For more modern luxury, and quiet bedrooms, the two best hotels are a short taxi ride from the centre: the small, elegant Lord Byron, or the vast, airy Hilton. Hotels in the Borghese and Nomentana areas are not as grand as some of their names suggest (like Aldrovandi Palace and Parco dei Principi). A new Holiday Inn, in the shell of an old hotel on Piazza Minerva, is due to open by early 1990.

Around the traffic-restricted Piazza di Spagna there are several attractive places to stay. Rooms in these smaller hotels should be reserved well ahead in the peak tourist season (Easter to September). At EUR and Castello della Magliana most needs are catered for by a Holiday Inn and Sheraton and several smaller hotels.

Luxury and most other better hotels are air-conditioned and offer 24hr room service, concierge, currency exchange and a daily laundry service. Parking is usually with a local garage. Standard features in bedrooms are IDD telephones, radio and TV (often with foreign news channels and/or video) and minibars. Major hotels will do photocopying and send telexes and fax messages for clients, but, except for the Hilton and the Sheraton which have convention centres, will use agencies for full secretarial services. Most luxury hotels charge 19% IVA (VAT) and a small city tax on top of rates, and breakfast is usually extra.

Cavalieri Hilton [L]/////
Via Cadlolo 101, 00136 ☎ 31511
⊠ *625337 fax 3151 • AE DC MC V •*
355 rooms, 19 suites, 2 restaurants,
2 bars
The Hilton scores high among business people for its facilities and efficient service. It is in Monte Mario but there is a frequent air-conditioned shuttle bus service to the centre (15mins), and regular visitors appreciate the space and the quiet, especially in summer when there is often a cool *ponentino* (westerly) breeze. The beautifully landscaped pool, surrounded by palm trees, attracts incentive tours, and convention delegates can get their hair cut or buy newspapers and presents without having to go into the centre at all. Recent renovations to the decor have cost US$12m. Old Masters and antiques add class to the huge lobby, and bedrooms have been stylishly updated. They are spacious and restful, well-equipped without being too functional. The La Pergola restaurant has superb views (see *Restaurants*). Hairdresser, newsstand, travel agent, car rental offices, boutiques, shuttle bus to centre and airport • pool, sauna, tennis, jogging track, massage, Turkish bath • convention centre with secretarial and translation services, 5 meeting rooms (capacity up to 350, 2,000 in convention centre).

Eden [L]////
Via Ludovisi 49, 00187 ☎ 4743551
⊠ *610567 fax 4742401 • THF • AE DC MC V • 93 rooms, 17 suites,*
2 restaurants, 2 bars
The Eden (pronounced "Edden"), near the Villa Borghese and now run by Britain's Trusthouse Forte group, has been one of Rome's top hotels for a century, attracting diplomats and top business people. Ministers, and even the president, often lunch in the delightful roof terrace restaurant.

Public rooms and the majority of bedrooms are large and old-fashioned with some "modern" additions already showing their age; newer bedrooms (about 40%) are more sophisticated (marble bathrooms, push-button telephones). The suites are the height of luxury; some have enormous baths with hydro-massage. Hairdresser • 3 meeting rooms (capacity up to 120).

Excelsior [L]////
Via Veneto 125, 00187 ☎ 4708
⊠ *610232 fax 4756205 • CIGA •*
AE DC MC V • 325 rooms, 45 suites,
1 restaurant, 1 bar
Opened with ceremony in 1906, the Excelsior is the most famous hotel on the Via Veneto. It featured in Fellini's *La Dolce Vita*, and was long the haunt of film stars and exiled heads of state. Now it is an efficient hotel with more *movimento* (action) than the even grander Grand. Public rooms retain the original opulent neo-classical decoration; the balcony of the small Sala d'Oro dining room offers some privacy for business lunches and the winter garden is used for fashion shows. The best bedrooms have been refurbished in the standard CIGA Empire style; rooms overlooking the US Embassy and Via Boncompagni are the quietest; singles tend to be small. Most bedrooms are classified de luxe or super de luxe; opt for standard and you will be upgraded subject to availability. The Caffè Doney outside on Via Veneto is now owned by CIGA. Hairdresser • sauna, Turkish bath • 11 meeting rooms (capacity up to 1,500).

Forum [L]////
Via Tor de' Conti 25, 00184 ☎ 6792446
⊠ *622549 fax 6799337 • AE DC MC V*
• 74 rooms, 6 suites, 1 restaurant, 1 bar
A converted villa incorporating an old church tower, the Forum is one of Rome's most unusual hotels, with good views of the main trading place

of the ancient Romans. Its mainly business clientele includes employees of Fiat, General Motors, IBM and the World Bank; corporate rates are offered and the location is relatively convenient for EUR. Politicians and other VIPs appreciate the security here (police are in evidence outside) and the service is deferential and personal. Bedrooms are comfortable and elegant with antique desks and Murano chandeliers. The roof restaurant (genuine local cooking) is chic, with parquet floors, cane-backed chairs and cool dove-grey tones; there is a separate room (no view) for private meals. Shuttle bus to airport • 3 meeting rooms (capacity up to 100).

Le Grand   L|||||
Via V.E. Orlando 3, 00185 ☎ *4709* ☒ *610210 fax 4747307 • CIGA •* *AE DC MC V • 133 rooms, 35 suites, 2 restaurants, 1 bar*
Still the most prestigious hotel in Rome, the Grand is in a narrow, noisy street off Via XX Settembre. It is not a chic area at night but the sort of people who stay here – royalty and heads of state, politicians, diplomats and top-ranking business people – are usually cocooned in limousines as soon as they step outside. Inside, all is reassuringly civilized from the vast, formal salon (rather dowdy for some tastes) to the intimate panelled restaurant and the more informal, summery Pavillion, where buffet lunches are served. Bedrooms are mostly old-fashioned, dark and rather noisy, bathrooms are big but not luxurious. Unless you can afford a suite, you stay here for the service (impeccable) and the status, not the standard or style of the bedrooms. Hairdresser • sauna, massage • 13 meeting rooms (capacity up to 650).

Hassler   L|||||
Pza Trinità dei Monti 6, 00187 ☎ *6782651* ☒ *610208 fax 6799278 •* *AE • 87 rooms, 12 suites, 4 restaurants, 1 bar*
The legendary Hassler occupies a prime site at the top of the Spanish

Steps, a peaceful refuge from the city. The faithful customers (45% from the USA) know that little changes at this comforting hotel where the staff take a pride in personal service. Furnishings may be unfashionable and worn, the food may be notoriously dull and expensive, but the place has character and the views from the rooftop restaurant and suites are beyond price. Romans will be impressed if you stay here. Favourite rooms are often reserved several months in advance (singles are all on the back; request single occupancy in a double on the front for a better room). Only the suites are luxurious and some are very pretty with sparkling bathrooms; the presidential suite and roof terrace can be rented for meetings. Room service, 7–11, hairdresser • 3 meeting rooms (capacity up to 50).

D'Inghilterra   L|||||
Via Bocca di Leone 14, 00187 ☎ *672161,* ☒ *614552 fax 672161 •* *AE DC MC V • 95 rooms, 8 suites, 1 restaurant, 1 bar*
This exclusive, rather aristocratic hotel does not encourage an ordinary expense-account clientele. It has a long tradition of hospitality to intellectuals, artists, politicians and men of letters, as well as royalty and popes. But for those who appreciate the atmosphere of a country residence, full of antiques, paintings and fresh flowers, with courteous service, this is a most civilized base in a convenient and smart district. The tiny, club-like Morland bar and the small, enchanting Roman Garden restaurant, with separate meeting room, are suitable for business encounters. Limited parking facilities. 2 meeting rooms (capacity up to 20).

Lord Byron   L|||||
Via G. de Notaris 5, 00197 ☎ *3609541* ☒ *611217 fax 3609541 • Ottaviani •* *AE DC MC V • 44 rooms, 6 suites, 1 restaurant, 1 bar*
For luxury in a friendly atmosphere, the Lord Byron has no equal in Rome. A rather ordinary villa in quiet

Parioli has been converted into an immaculate little hotel without losing the charm of a private residence. There are gracious flower-filled public rooms (a delicious buffet breakfast is served in the bar) and spacious, fresh-looking bedrooms with splendid marble bathrooms. Service is superlative. The elegant Relais le Jardin restaurant (see *Restaurants*) is the best place to take important Roman clients. 1 meeting room (capacity up to 40).

Raphael 💷///
Largo Febo 2, 00180 ☎ *650881* ⊤ₓ *622396 fax 6878993 • AE DC MC V • 85 rooms, 1 restaurant, 1 bar*
A good mid-price choice, the Raphael is the best hotel in the Piazza Navona area. Regular guests include lawyers, senators, people in media and entertainment and foreign business guests as well as tourists. Ex-Prime Minister Bettino Craxi lives in the penthouse apartment, so the entrance is guarded by armed police. Restructuring will be complete by the end of 1990. Public rooms are individual, with a cluttered assortment of antiques and oil paintings.

La Residenza 💷/
Via Emilia 22-24, 00187 ☎ *460789* ⊤ₓ *410423 fax 972565 • no credit cards • 21 rooms, 6 suites, 1 bar*
A small hotel close to the US Embassy patronized by a cosmopolitan clientele. The decor combines casual modern with antique. The atmosphere is that of an elegant but unstuffy private house; hence the name. Bedrooms are well-equipped and some have small balconies. Splendid buffet breakfasts make a good start to the working day.

OTHER HOTELS
Aldrovandi Palace 💷//// *Via Ulisse Aldrovandi 15, 00197* ☎ *8841091* ⊤ₓ *616141 fax 879435 • AE DC MC V*. Old-fashioned, rather drab Parioli hotel with new convention centre, used mainly by

Italian companies. The pool and Relais Piscine restaurant attract outsiders.
Atlante Star 💷/// *Via Vitelleschi 34, 00193* ☎ *6564196* ⊤ₓ *622355 • AE DC*. Smart, well-equipped hotel near the Vatican, with roof-garden restaurant, conference and business facilities.
Bernini Bristol 💷/// *Pza Barberini 23, 00187* ☎ *463051* ⊤ₓ *610554 fax 4750266 • AE DC MC V*. Sound business-oriented hotel in a noisy location. Standard bedrooms, quite elegant public rooms and well-equipped meeting rooms; used by major Italian companies.
Carriage 💷/// *Via delle Carrozze 36, 00187* ☎ *6794106* ⊤ₓ *626246 fax 6799106 • AE DC MC V*. Appealing small hotel with smartly refurbished rooms in fashionable area near the busy Spanish Steps; comfortable and quiet.
Condotti 💷/ *Via Mario de' Fiori 37, 00187* ☎ *6794661* ⊤ₓ *611217 • Ottaviani • AE DC MC V*. Simple but personal, welcoming and quiet, with an elegant entrance hall.
Diplomatic 💷// *Via Vittorio Colonna 28, 00193* ☎ *6542084* ⊤ₓ *6561734 • AE DC MC V*. Well-run small hotel near the Vatican.
EUR Parco dei Medici Holiday Inn 💷/// *Via Castello della Magliana 65, 00148* ☎ *5475* ⊤ₓ *613302 • AE DC MC V*. Well-equipped modern block close to Esso at Castello della Magliana.
Flora 💷//// *Via Veneto 191, 00187* ☎ *497821* ⊤ₓ *622256 • AE DC V*. A traditional hotel with a good reputation.
Gregoriana 💷/ *Via Gregoriana 18, 00187* ☎ *6794269 • no credit cards*. Sophisticated small hotel in high-fashion street with spacious bedrooms. No restaurant.
Mozart 💷/ *Via dei Greci 23b, 00182* ☎ *6787422 • no credit cards*. Elegant and popular small hotel; rooms on the Corso can be noisy.
Parco dei Principi 💷/// *Via Mercadente 15, 00198* ☎ *8841071 • AE DC V*. Dated 1960s block near the

Villa Borghese, with pool.

Regina Carlton ☐||| *Via V.
Veneto 72, 00187* ☎ *476851*
☒ *610517 fax 8445104* • *AE DC MC V.*
A comfortable, classic Via Veneto
hotel.

Shangri La Corsetti ☐|| *Vle
Algeria 141, 00144* ☎ *5916441*
☒ *614664* • *AE DC MC V.* At EUR and
well-positioned for Squibb, Procter &
Gamble and Colgate. Pool.

Sheraton ☐|||| *Vle del Pattinaggio,
00144* ☎ *5453* ☒ *626073* • *AE DC MC
V.* Ugly situation off the main road to
Fiumicino airport, but convenient for
Castello della Magliana and EUR. Pool.
Alitalia check-in. Conference halls.

Clubs

The most aristocratic and exclusive
men's clubs in Rome are the *Circolo
della Caccia* and the *Circolo degli
Scacchi* but nonmembers enter by
invitation only. It is smart to belong
to a rowing or golf club, and business
discussions are often held over a
round of golf. Those who want their
own working base in Rome should
consider membership of the American
Express *Consul Club*, Pza di Spagna 35
tel 6786795, with business services,
formal and informal meeting rooms and
a small roof terrace.

Restaurants

Rome does not offer as great a range of restaurants in type and cuisine as
some other European capitals or even Milan. The roof-top restaurants of
the major hotels – the Eden, Forum, Hassler and Hilton – are prestigious
places for business entertaining. The garden theme restaurants at the
D'Inghilterra and Lord Byron hotels are also pleasant.

It is acceptable to take local business guests to good trattorias for less
expensive meals, and for appealing surroundings the best restaurants are
behind the Pantheon and Piazza Navona. In summer many restaurants
offer al fresco dining; but the outside tables attract tourists. Similarly,
some widely advertised trattorias in Trastevere are to be avoided. Many
restaurants are closed on Sundays. For a quick business lunch in the Via
Veneto try the Café de Paris or Harry's Bar. At EUR most people go to the
Shangri La or Sheraton.

Roman cooking is robust rather than refined. Typical dishes include
pasta with bacon (*spaghetti alla carbonara* or *all'amatriciana*), oxtail (*coda
alla vaccinara*) and *saltimbocca alla romana*. Deep fried artichokes (*carciofi
alla giudea*) are often served as a first course. A popular new summer
starter is cold pasta with tomato and basil. Some of the best restaurants
specialize in regional cuisines, from Abruzzo to the Veneto. For fish, and
especially shellfish, stick to restaurants with a good reputation.

Lunch (around 1.30pm) is the main business meal, dinner (8.30 or
9pm, often later in summer) being mainly for friends and family. Same
day reservations will often suffice, but for a choice of table reserve further
ahead.

Al Fogher ☐|
Via Tevere 13b ☎ *857032* • *closed Sun*
• *AE DC* • *jacket and tie* • *reservations
essential*
In the business district, convenient for

the major hotels, the small (but not
cramped) Al Fogher has a pleasantly
countrified atmosphere: antique
furniture and cooking from the
Veneto region, with Friulian wines.

Signora Gaspardis d'Eva, the extrovert, blonde proprietress, welcomes her business custom mainly at lunch time and will organize fixed menus for groups.

Casina Valadier   *[L]////*
Al Pincio, Villa Borghese ☎ *6792083 •* *closed L, Mon, Aug • AE DC MC V •* *jacket (and tie preferred) for D*
High prices and indifferent food do not deter smart Romans from this delightful restaurant in a Napoleonic villa on the airy Pincian hill. Those staying in the best hotels eat here in the company of ministers and Banca d'Italia chiefs; and the chic lunch-time crowd on the terrace is likely to include artists, journalists, politicians and aristocrats. Favoured customers get the inner tables which have the most shade; in cold weather, or for greater privacy, they can retreat to the elegant Empire-style *sala romana*. The evening ambience is serious and formal; romantic on the candlelit upper terrace, or cloistered in the private salons.

Coriolano   *[L]////*
Via Ancona 14 ☎ *8449501 • closed* *Sun, Aug • AE DC MC • reservations* *essential*
Convenient for the Via Po and for Via XX Settembre, this civilized small restaurant, seating just 40, is appreciated by bankers, industrialists and politicians for its calm atmosphere and good food. Produce fresh from the market includes *funghi porcini* (from October to January) and fish; pasta is home-made. Gleaming silver plates, large sparkling glasses and fresh flowers indicate attention to detail.

L'Eau-Vive   *[L]/*
Via Monterone 85a ☎ *6541095 • closed* *Sun, Aug • AE MC V • jacket and tie* *preferred • no smoking*
In an old *palazzo* close to the Pantheon, this is a French restaurant run by missionaries, popular for business lunches; converts include local politicians. Dishes number many

French classics – try the *tournedos* with champagne and mushrooms or the *crêpes Grand Marnier* – accompanied by specially imported wines including exclusive *grands crus classés*. Waitresses are multilingual (Spanish-speaking from South America, French-speaking from Africa, English-speaking from the Philippines), and an Ave Maria is sung at about 10.30pm. Despite the original decorated ceilings, the atmosphere upstairs is canteen-like; opt instead for a ground-floor table or reserve in advance the small private room (up to 8 people). Classical music.

El Toulà   *[L]////*
Via della Lupa 29b ☎ *6873498 •* *closed Sun, Aug • AE DC MC V • jacket* *and tie*
A classic business venue offering international and Venetian cuisine and an impressive wine list. The surroundings are luxurious, the service faultless.

Hostaria dell'Orso   *[L]////*
Via dei Soldati 25 ☎ *6864250 • closed* *L, Sun, mid Jul–end Aug • AE DC V •* *reservations essential*
An opulent establishment guaranteed to impress – unless your guest is a gourmet. In this 15thC *palazzo*, a one-time simple tavern now offers palatial decor, a piano bar and nightclub (upstairs). Popular with tycoons and trendies, stargazers and American tourists, but open only in the evenings.

La Maiella   *[L]/*
Pza Sant'Apollinare 45 ☎ *6864174 •* *closed Sun, 2 weeks Aug • AE DC V •* *reservations essential*
A well-known and respected restaurant near Piazza Navona, with tables outside in fine weather. Politicians and other public figures are often seen here on weekdays and the place is usually packed in the evenings as well as at lunch time. Cooking is from Abruzzo, with truffles and seafood in season.

Otello alla Concordia *[L]|*
Via della Croce 81 ☎ *6791178 • closed Sun • DC*
This well-known Roman trattoria does a brisk trade; arrive early to sit in the pleasant covered courtyard (for which reservations are not taken). Journalists, artists, tourists and people from the nearby centres of the fashion and the antiques trades find Otello convenient for a quick, cheap lunch; sit inside (in the older, more characteristic part) if you prefer not to feel hurried or overheard. Food is usually quite good, seldom outstanding; wines are simple -- from Tuscany or the Castelli Romani.

La Pergola *[L]||||*
Cavalieri Hilton ☎ *31511 • closed Sun • AE DC MC V • reservations essential*
Although the Hilton's roof terrace restaurant has been closed for security reasons, La Pergola still offers splendid penthouse views over Rome. The reputation for superb cooking and fine wines attracts Roman diners as well as hotel guests. Piano bar.

Piperno *[L]||*
Monte Cenci 9 ☎ *6540629 • closed Sun D, Mon, Aug • AE DC • D reservations essential*
The best of the restaurants in the so-called Jewish ghetto area. Both food and service here are reliable and there is plenty of space, with tables outside on the tiny piazza in summer. Popular with locals as well as tourists.

Ranieri *[L]||*
Via Mario de' Fiori 26 ☎ *6791592 • closed Sun • AE DC MC V • jacket and tie*
This conservative establishment is named after Queen Victoria's cook (who started it in 1843). The interior is little changed: several small rooms with brocaded silk walls, gilded mirrors and crystal chandeliers. Cooking has recently been rejuvenated by the arrival of a new chef. Regulars include politicians, financiers and diplomats, elderly aristocrats and tourists. Private rooms are available.

Relais le Jardin *[L]||||*
Lord Byron Hotel ☎ *3609541 • closed Sun • AE DC MC V • ties preferred • reservations essential*
Considered by some the best restaurant in Rome, Le Jardin attracts a clientele which includes the president, ministers and top business people. Its airily elegant atmosphere is just right for lingering business lunches or romantic dinners, and the adjacent bar is a delightful place for an *aperitivo* or coffee. Expect imaginative, Italianized *nouvelle cuisine* and outstanding service.

Sabatini *[L]||||*
Pza Santa Maria in Trastevere 18 ☎ *5818307 • closed Tue • AE DC MC V • D reservations essential*
The best restaurant in Trastevere, a good choice for business entertaining, but also touristy. Roman cooking.

Taverna Flavia *[L]||*
Via Flavia 9 ☎ *4745214 • closed Sun • AE DC V • reservations essential*
A favourite with IRI bosses, politicians from the nearby ministries, journalists and guests of the Grand Hotel, this simple but expensive taverna has stayed fashionable since the 1950s when it was patronized by the film stars whose signed photographs still hang on the walls. *Insalata Veruschka*, a salad with truffles, is the pride of this high-class establishment, and the wine list is outstanding.

OTHER RESTAURANTS
The following restaurants, listed by area, all offer reliable cooking.

Ludovisi/Borghese
Al Chianti, Via Ancona 17 ☎ 861083. Tuscan cooking in Porta Pia district.
Bonne Nouvelle, Via del Boschetto 73-74 ☎ 486781. Fish restaurant behind the Banca d'Italia.
Cesarina, Via Piemonte 109 ☎ 460073. Bolognese cooking.
Colline Emiliane, Via degli Avignonesi 22 ☎ 4817538. Quiet trattoria off noisy Via del Tritone; cooking from Emilia-Romagna.

Da Tullio, Via S. Nicola da Tolentino 26 ☎ 4745560. Tuscan cooking, near Piazza Barberini.

Giggi Fazi, Via Lucullo 22 ☎ 464045. Near the US Embassy, Roman food.

Girarrosto Toscano, Via Campania 29 ☎ 493759. Touristy, Tuscan restaurant convenient for the Ludovisi quarter.

Piccolo Mondo, Via Aurora 39d ☎ 485680. Well-known Ludovisi quarter restaurant; hotly-contested outside tables, elegant interior, Roman cooking.

Central Rome

Il Bacaro, Via degli Spagnoli 27 ☎ 6864110. Fine wines and good food; popular with journalists; evenings only except Sun.

Dal Bolognese, Pza del Popolo 1 ☎ 3611426. Bolognese cooking; convenient for RAI, the art galleries of Via del Babuino and the cocktail set from Rosati's (see *Bars and cafés*).

Il Buco, Via Sant'Ignazio 7–8 ☎ 6793298. Excellent Tuscan trattoria near the Borsa, with outside tables.

La Campana, Vicolo della Campana 18 ☎ 6867820. Sound, old, no-frills Roman trattoria between the Tiber and the Parliament.

Il Drappo, Vicolo del Malpasso 9 ☎ 6877365. The best Sardinian restaurant in Rome.

Da Fortunato, Via del Pantheon 55 ☎ 6792788. Classic Roman trattoria frequented by politicians and business people.

Al Moro, Vicolo delle Bollette 13 ☎ 6783495. Crowded restaurant near Trevi fountain; sound Italian cooking.

Nel Regno di Re Ferdinando, Via dei Banchi Nuovi ☎ 6541167. A rustic but sophisticated Neapolitan taverna; evenings only.

Taverna Giulia, Vicolo dell'Oro 23 ☎ 6869768. Elegant, good service and Genoese food; till 2am.

Trattoria dell'Antiquario, Pza San Simeone 27 ☎ 6879694. Good service and quite good traditional food; pleasant tables outside on the Via dei Coronari; evenings only.

Vecchia Roma, Pza Campitelli 18 ☎ 6864604. Pretty restaurant in an airy Renaissance palace, with al fresco dining on a lovely square near the Jewish ghetto area; closed Wed.

Across the Tiber

Antica Pesa, Via Garibaldi 18 ☎ 5809236. Trastevere trattoria, typical Roman dishes.

Il Matriciano, Via dei Gracchi 55 ☎ 317810. Very Roman atmosphere; popular with lawyers and film industry people. Near the Vatican.

Romolo, Via di Porta Settimiana 8 ☎ 5818284. Trastevere restaurant with delightful interior garden bounded by the Aurelian wall.

Out of town

There are good seafood restaurants at Fiumicino (30km/18 miles), near the airport. Romans flock here at weekends. *Bastianelli al Molo* ☎ 6440118, in Via di Torre Clementina, is generally considered the best. Restaurants at Frascati (22km/13.5 miles) are also popular for an excursion.

Bars and cafés

Most Roman bars cater for a quick drink standing at the counter; for a business discussion it is better to meet at a hotel, preferably the *Grand*. Alternatively, sample the garden bar of the *Eden* or the drawing-room atmosphere of the *Lord Byron* or the *D'Inghilterra*. *Casina Valadier* (see *Restaurants*) is a smart place to be seen. Romans prefer *spumantino* or white wine to spirits before dinner.

There are some café-bars suitable for a business encounter. The old-fashioned *Rosati* on Piazza del Popolo is a classy rendezvous. *Antico Caffè Greco*, Via Condotti 86, a famous haunt of 19thC *literati*, and the quaint *Babington's Tea Rooms*, at the foot of the Spanish Steps, close before dinner but are fine for an afternoon chat or an early aperitif. On the Via Veneto *Harry's Bar*, the *Café de Paris* or *Doney's* are good places for a drink or light meal.

In your leisure time you might try a chocolate *tartufo* at *Tre Scalini* on Piazza Navona or visit one of the ice-cream shops near the Pantheon.

Entertainment

The monthly newsletter and events list *Carnet* is distributed free by the tourist office. *A Guest in Rome* is also available free in hotels.

Ticket agencies Orbis, Pza del Esquilino ☎ 4744776 or 4751403.

Opera The season lasts from November to May at the *Teatro dell'Opera di Roma*, Pza Beniamino Gigli 8 ☎ 463641 (but standards are variable). In July and August there is an open-air season in the ruins of the Baths (*Terme*) of Caracalla; for good seats reserve ahead through Teatro dell'Opera or Carriani Tours ☎ 460510 or 4742501.

Theatre The season runs from October to May but in summer there are some outdoor performances. Italian classics (Pirandello and Goldoni) are regularly featured as well as Shakespeare in translation.

Music The Accademia Nazionale di Santa Cecilia plays at *Auditorio Pio*, Via della Conciliazione 4 ☎ 6541044, box office open Thu, 5–8, Fri, 9–1. In June, evening concerts are held in the beautiful setting of the Campidoglio, although the acoustics are poor. Advance tickets from Via della Conciliazione 4, Mon–Fri, 9–2.

The RAI orchestra performs from October to June at *Auditorio del Foro Italico*, Pza Lauro de Bosis 1 ☎ 6541044. The *Teatro Ghione*, Via delle Fornaci ☎ 6372294, is a venue for concerts and operettas.

Concerts are often held in the city's countless churches and at the Villa Medici (French Academy), Vle Trinità dei Monti 1 ☎ 67611; these are usually advertised on posters.

Pop and rock concerts are held in EUR at the *Pala EUR* or at the *Palaein*, Pzle dello Sport ☎ 5925205.

Cinema Pasquino, Vicolo del Piede 19 ☎ 5803662, shows frequently changing programmes of English-language films.

Nightclubs There are several stylish nightclubs and discotheques in Parioli and around Via Veneto. Most nightspots are closed in July and August.

Smart discotheques with dining include classic, touristy *Jackie' O*, Via Boncampagni 11 ☎ 461401, and *Open Gate*, Via San Nicola da Tolentino ☎ 4750464, frequented by politicians and grand Romans. *Gilda*, Via Mario de' Fiori 97 ☎ 6784838, and *Histeria*, Via R. Giovanelli ☎ 864587, are also recommended for dancing.

At *Arciliuto*, Pza Montevecchio 5 ☎ 6879419, the owner/entertainer sings poems to music, slipping from Neapolitan to English and appealing to a cosmopolitan clientele. Also in the Piazza Navona area is *Hemingway*, Pza delle Coppelle 10 ☎ 6544135, a bar popular with young Romans, actors and famous faces.

At Fregene (38km/23.5 miles) *Il Miraggio* ☎ 6462655 is a fashionable disco/nightclub, open in summer only.

Shopping

Milan may be Italy's capital of fashion but Rome still leads for *alta moda* (*haute couture*); among designers based here are Renato Balestra, Roberto Capucci, Rocco Barocco, Gianfranco Ferrè and Lancetti. The best shopping areas are compact and traffic-free. Near the Spanish Steps, and around Via Condotti, Via Borgognona and Via Frattina are the most exclusive fashion boutiques (including those selling jewellery, shoes and other accessories). *Alta moda* workshops are concentrated in nearby Via Gregoriana and Via Sistina. Via del Babuino is the best address in the city for art dealers and for Persian carpets, and parallel Via Margutta has several artists' studios and galleries. Antiques can also be found in Via Giulia and Via dei Coronari (west of the Corso there are many craftsmen making picture frames and restoring furniture).

Linens and lingerie, leather gloves and shoes are worth looking out for, as are prints and picture frames. Classic made-to-measure shirts are also good quality.

Customers from outside the EC can reclaim IVA on objects costing over L525,000 at shops displaying the "Tax Free System" sign. Take the invoice to the customs office at Fiumicino airport and obtain a cash refund at the Santo Spirito bank there (or apply by post).

Books *Lion Bookshop*, Via del Babuino 181 ☏ 3605837. *Feltrinelli*, Via Vittorio Emanuele Orlando 84–86 ☏ 484430, opposite the Grand Hotel, has an excellent English selection.

Fashion *Laura Biagiotti*, *Fendi*, *Ferrè*, *Pancaldi* and *Versace* (for men) are in Via Borgognona; *Battistoni* (made-to-measure), *Beltrami* (shoes and leathergoods), *Cucci* and *Gucci* in Via Condotti. The Milanese designer *Giorgio Armani* has shops in Via del Babuino, and top Parisian names like *Balenciaga*, *Courrèges* and *Yves St Laurent* are in Via Bocca di Leone. The most famous Roman designer is *Valentino*; his atelier is on Via Gregoriana 24 (women's boutique, Via Bocca di Leone 15; men's, Via Condotti at the corner of Via Mario de' Fiori).

Gloves *Merola*, Via del Corso 143.

Jewellery *Buccellati* and *Bulgari* are the best-known Italian jewellers in Via Condotti; also there are *Cartier*, *Capuano*, *Carlo Eleuteri* and *Massoni*. *Furst* is in Via Veneto, *Petochi* on Piazza di Spagna.

Lingerie and linens *Emilia Bellini*, Pza di Spagna 77, *Cesari*, Via Barberini 3, for the former; and *Brighenti*, Via Frattina 3, for the latter.

Street markets Lively street markets include the Sunday flea market at Porta Portese and the food market on Campo de' Fiori, daily except Sundays. On Piazza Fontanella Borghese there are stalls selling old prints and books (daily except Sun).

Sightseeing

Rome's history provides an exhausting sightseeing challenge. There are extensive remains and monuments. There are early Christian catacombs and churches (some of the most ancient being *fuori le mura*, outside the walls), and scores of important High Renaissance and baroque churches by architects such as Bramante, Bernini and Borromini. There are numerous palaces, some with extensive art collections, and the many lovely piazzas and exuberant fountains are particularly characteristic of the city. St Peter's and the Vatican are rich in art treasures and there are many museums and galleries. If you have only a limited amount of time for sightseeing you will want to take in St Peter's and the Sistine Chapel, and then perhaps some of the other sights, according to your choice.

Castel Sant' Angelo Built as a mausoleum for the Emperor Hadrian (135–39), later a medieval fortress and now an art and military museum. *Lungotevere Castello. Open Tue–Sat, 9–2; Sun, 9–1.*

Colosseum Built 72–96 by the Flavian emperors, this is the most important monument and symbol of ancient Rome, originally used for gladiatorial combats and "circuses." Nearby is the *Arch of Constantine*, built in 315 to celebrate his victory over Maxentius at Ponte Milvio. *Open daily, 9–3.30; summer 9–7.*

Forum The Roman Forum, focus of public life in the ancient capital, comprises the remains of temples, triumphal arches, public buildings and private villas overlooked by the Palatine hill. *Via dei Fori Imperiali. Open Tue–Sat, 9–3; summer, 9–6; Sun, 9–1.*

Galleria Colonna Rich Renaissance art collection of the Colonna princes. *Via della Pilotta 17. Open daily, 9–1; closed Aug.*

Galleria Doria Pamphili Superb private collection of 15th–17thC Italian and other European works of art. *Pza del Collegio Romano 1a. Open Tue, Fri–Sun, 10–1.*

Galleria Nazionale d'Arte Antica The National Gallery, housed in Palazzo Barberini. Mainly 13th–16th centuries. *Via IV Fontane 13. Open Tue–Sat, 9–2; Sun, 9–1.*

Galleria Nazionale d'Arte Moderna
19th and 20thC Italian art, beside the Villa Borghese gardens. *Vle delle Belle Arti 131. Open Tue–Sat, 9–2; Wed, Fri, 3–6; Sun, 9–1.*

Roman churches
Among the many churches worth visiting, the following is a selection of the most outstanding.
Early Christian and Byzantine
Santa Maria in Trastevere, Santa Prassede and *San Clemente* for Byzantine-influenced mosaics; the best are at *Santa Costanza,* Via Nomentana, about 2.5km/1.5 miles from the centre. *Santa Maria Maggiore* has early Christian mosaics.
Renaissance Bramante's *tempietto* at San Pietro in Montorio; a perfect Renaissance building.
High Renaissance/baroque *Il Gesù,* the main Jesuit church in Rome, and a prototype of the baroque style, famous for its façade and exuberant ceiling painting; exquisite *Santa Maria della Pace;* the façade by Carlo Maderno of *Santa Susanna;* Borromini's *Sant'Ivo alla Sapienza* and *San Carlo alle Quattro Fontane,* both masterpieces of virtuoso design; *Sant'Andrea al Quirinale* by Bernini; *Sant'Andrea della Valle* and *Sant'Ignazio,* both with unbelievably opulent ceilings.
    Among those with great works of art are *Santa Maria sopra Minerva* (Michelangelo's *Redeemer;* frescoes by Filippino Lippi); *San Pietro in Vincoli* for Michelangelo's *Moses; San Luigi dei Francesi* (famous early works of Caravaggio); *Santa Maria del Popolo* (frescoes by Pinturicchio, masterpieces of Caravaggio); *Santa Maria della Vittoria* (Bernini's *Ecstasy of Saint Teresa*); and the 16thC ceilings in *San Giovanni in Laterano.*

Galleria Nazionale di Palazzo Corsini Corsini collection of 16th and 17thC art now belonging to the state, but displayed in the family *palazzo. Via della Lungara 10. Open Tue–Sat, 9–7; Mon, 9–2; Sun 9–1.*

Galleria Spada A small but fine collection of baroque paintings in the same *palazzo* as the Council of State. *Pza Capo di Ferro 3. Open Tue–Sat, 9–2; Sun, 9–1.*

Museo Borghese In the palace of the Villa Borghese gardens. Only the sculpture rooms are open. *Pza Scipione Borghese 5. Open Tue–Sat, 9–7; Sun–Mon, 9–1.30.*

Musei Capitolini Large collection of antique sculpture in Palazzo Nuovo; more sculpture and paintings in the *Museo del Palazzo dei Conservatori* opposite. *Pza del Campidoglio 1. Open Tue–Fri, 9–2; Sat, Sun, 9–1; Tue, Thu, 5–8; Sat, 8.30pm–11pm.*

Museo della Civiltà Romana The history of Rome and its influence; worth seeing if you are at EUR. *Pza G. Agnelli 10. Open Tue, Wed, Fri, Sat, 9–1; Thu, 9–1.30, 4–7; Sun, 9–1.*

Museo Nazionale di Villa Giulia Important pre-Roman, notably Etruscan, remains in a 16thC papal villa. *Pzle di Villa Giulia 9. Open Mon–Sat, 9–2; Sun, 9–1.*

Musei Vaticani Extensive papal collections, many museums, and Michelangelo's ceiling in the Sistine Chapel, recently and controversially cleaned. Raphael's *Stanze* and the Borgia apartments can be visited on the way. Treasures of the picture gallery (*Pinacoteca*) include works by Giotto, Florentine masters, Raphael (*Transfiguration*) and Caravaggio. The *Pio-Clementino museum* contains important classical sculpture including the *Apollo Belvedere,* the *Belvedere Torso* and the *Laocoon.* Other museums show ancient art (*Museum of Ancient Egypt, Etruscan Museum*) and religious subjects. *Vle Vaticano. Open Mon–Sat, 8.45–1; last Sun in month 9–1; Easter, summer, Mon–Fri, 8.45–4.*

Pantheon Marvellously preserved 2ndC BC temple, consecrated as a Christian church in 606 and

containing the tomb of Raphael. The dome, whose diameter is equal to its height, is an extraordinary engineering feat. *Pza della Rotonda. Open Mon–Sat, 9–1, 2–5; Sun, 9–1.*
San Pietro (St Peter's) This magnificent focus of the Catholic faith, built over the tomb of St Peter, is the largest church in the world, with a dome by Michelangelo and colonnades by Bernini. Inside see Michelangelo's *Pietà* and Bernini's ornate *baldacchino*. Fine views from the roof. *Open daily, 7–6.*

Guided tours
American Express, Pza di Spagna 38 ☎ 67641; *Carrani Tours*, Via V.E. Orlando 95 ☎ 460510; *CIT*, Pza della Repubblica 68 ☎ 47941; *Pioneer Line*, Via Filippo Turati 43 ☎ 734234. Half- and full-day coach tours include entry to selected sights. For a surface-scratching view of the city ATAC operates an unguided 2hr tour on bus route 110 from Piazza dei Cinquecento ☎ 46954444.

For authorized guides contact the tourist office or *Sindicato Nazionale CISL Guide Turistiche*, Rampa Mignanelli 12 ☎ 6789842. For incentive tours contact *Eurotravel* ☎ 5926025 (EUR office) or ☎ 858592 (Parioli office).

Out of town
Typical tours include Tivoli (Roman Villa Adriana, gardens of the Villa d'Este), and the Castelli Romani (towns of the Alban Hills, known for their wines). There are also day trips by coach to Assisi, Florence and Naples.

Spectator sports
Major sporting events are held at several grounds equipped for indoor and outdoor sports from swimming to athletics and skating to soccer: the *Foro Italico*, at the foot of Monte Mario, the *Palazzetto dello Sport* and stadium at Flaminio and the *Palazzo dello Sport* and *Tre Fontane* at EUR.

Soccer Local teams are Roma and Lazio. They play at *Stadio Olimpico* ☎ 36851 or 3966733 or at Flaminio. Tickets available at the stadium.
Racing *Ippodromo delle Cappanelle*, Via Appia Nuova 1255 ☎ 7993143 or 794359; *Ippodromo di Tor di Valle*, Via del Mare ☎ 5924205 (trotting); some evening races.

Keeping fit
The sporting facilities at Foro Italico, at EUR and at Acqua Acetosa, Via dei Campi Sportivi 48 ☎ 36851, are open to all. There are several exclusive golf, rowing and tennis clubs where visitors might be invited: the snobbiest is the *Circolo Aniene*, which does not allow women.
Fitness centres *American Workout Studio*, Via Massimo d'Azeglio 3 ☎ 6799751. *American Health Club*, Largo Somalia 60 ☎ 8394488, has reciprocal membership arrangements and is associated with *Roman Sport Center*, Via del Galoppatoio 33 ☎ 3601667. *Navona Health Center*, Via dei Banchi Nuovi 39 ☎ 6530104.
Golf To play at *Circolo del Golf di Roma*, Via Appia Nuova 716a (Acquasanta) ☎ 783407, *Country Club Castelgandolfo*, Via Santo Spirito 13 ☎ 93112301 or *Golf Club Olgiata*, Largo dell'Olgiata 15 ☎ 3789141, you need membership of any other golf club in the world.
Riding *Villa Borghese*, Via del Galoppatoio 25 ☎ 360679, requires membership.
Swimming The pools at the Cavalieri Hilton and Aldrovandi Palace (see *Hotels*) can be used by visitors. There is an outdoor pool at EUR, *Piscina delle Rose*, Vle America ☎ 5926717. The best beaches are at Circeo, a 2hr drive south of Rome, and 2hrs north at Ansedonia.
Tennis *Tennis Club Parioli*, Largo de Morpurgo Umberto 2 ☎ 836408, is the most exclusive tennis club (also with pool and gym; by invitation only). *Circolo Canotieri e Tennis Lazio*, Lungotevere Flaminio 25 ☎ 3606853, offers 15-day season tickets, at the invitation of a member. *Società*

Ginnastico di Roma, Via Muro Torto 5 ☎ 465566, was opened in 1890 and is used by MPs, US diplomats, actors and journalists. *Circolo della Stampa*, Via Brunelleschi 13 ☎ 3960790, owned by a team of journalists, requires only a fee of L12,000. Anyone with government contacts might be invited to play at the *Circolo di Montecitorio* or the Foreign Ministry's sports centre at Acqua Acetosa. *Circolo Tennis EUR*, Vle dell'Artigianato 35 ☎ 5924693, is a prestigious club (members and guests only).

Local resources

Business services

Consul Club, Pza di Spagna 35 ☎ 6786795; *Executive Service*, Via Savoia 78 ☎ 853241, rents offices, equipment and staff; *Pinciana Office*, Via di Porta Pinciana 4 ☎ 4814143 ⬛ 621489 (instant offices).
Photocopying Photocopying is available at hotels; otherwise use office suppliers or business services.
Secretarial *Rome at your service*, Via Orlando 75 ☎ 484583.
Translation *World Translation Centre*, Via XX Settembre 1 ☎ 4812723; *EGA Congressi*, Vle Tiziano 19 ☎ 3960341; *Centro Pilota*, Via Palestro 68 ☎ 4453317; *Congressi* (*STOC*), Via Laurentina 203 ☎ 5401758.

Communications

Local delivery *Pony Express* ☎ 3309; *Roman Express* ☎ 3398048. *Piana* ☎ 7316451 delivers nationally.
Long-distance delivery *DHL* ☎ 72421; *Emery International Cargo System* ☎ 6454247; *Domenichelli* ☎ 43671 to Milan; *TNT Traco* ☎ 6888980.
Post offices Central office: Pza San Silvestro (24hr telex and telegram service ☎ 6795530), open Mon–Fri, 8.30–9; Sat, 8.30–noon, with facilities for international telephone calls. Area post offices open Mon–Fri, 8.15–2 (Sat to noon); principal sub post offices (including that at Fiumicino airport) open till 6pm for parcels and 8pm for telegrams and registered

letters. The Vatican post office is sometimes better for outgoing mail.
Telex and fax The telex office in the international departures lounge at Fiumicino is open daily, 8.25–1.50, 2–5 ☎ 601623 or 601631. Fax at the central post office.

Conference/exhibition centres

Rome offers a wide range of venues from convention hotels and specially built convention centres to historic buildings. The *Grand* provides splendid rooms with efficient organization. The *Sheraton Roma*, Vle del Pattinaggio, 00144 ☎ 5453 ⬛ 614223, hosts international conferences throughout the year. *International Congress Office*, Via Rubicone 27, 00198 ☎ 8441185 ⬛ 812277, organizes exhibitions.

In the centre is the *Congressi Residenza di Ripetta*, Via di Ripetta 231 ☎ 672141 (capacity up to 300); *Castel Sant'Angelo* and *Palazzo Barberini* (capacity up to 200); *Palazzo Brancaccio* can take conferences of at least 120 participants; and *Villa Miani* at Monte Mario is popular for gala dinners and receptions.

At EUR, the *Auditorium della Tecnica* (capcity up to 1,000), the *Fiera di Roma*, *Pala EUR* (capacity up to 14,000) and the *Palazzo dei Congressi* (capacity up to 1,500) cater for enormous international conferences.

Emergencies

Bureaus de change Open outside normal office hours and Sat: *Banca Nazionale del Lavoro*, Pza Venezia 6 (also open Sun), *Credito Italiano*, Pza di Spagna 19. Bureaus de change at Termini station and *American Express*, Pza di Spagna 38, are open all day weekdays and Sat am and 24hrs at Fiumicino airport.
Hospitals Ambulance (Red Cross) ☎ 5100. 24hr medical service ☎ 4756741. For private medical treatment *Salvator Mundi International Hospital*, Vle delle Mure Gianicolensi 67 ☎ 586041 (telephone in advance). *Policlinico Umberto I*, Vle del

Policlinico 155 ☏ 49971, *San Camillo*, Circonv. Gianicolense 87 ☏ 58701, *San Giovanni*, Via Amba Aradam 9 ☏ 7705, and *Sant'Eugenio*, Pzle dell'Umanesimo (EUR) ☏ 5904, have emergency facilities.

Pharmacies For details of pharmacies open see daily newspapers or ☏ 1921. *Internazionale*, Pza Barberini 49 ☏ 462996, *Imbesi*, Vle Europa 76 ☏ 5925509 (EUR), are open all night. For English or American pharmaceutical products try *Evans*, 63 Pza di Spagna ☏ 6790626, or the pharmacy at the Vatican.

Police *Questura*: Via San Vitale 15 ☏ 4686.

Government offices

Ministero degli Affari Esteri, Pzle della Farnesina 1 ☏ 36911 (Foreign Affairs); *Ministero delle Finanze*, Vle America (EUR) ☏ 5997 (Finance); *Ministero dell'Industria, del Commercio e dell'Artigianato*, Via Vittorio Veneto 33, 00100 ☏ 4705 (Industry, Commerce and Crafts); *Ministero del Commercio con l'Estero*, Vle America (EUR), 00144 ☏ 5993 (Foreign Trade); *Ministero del Tesoro*, Via XX Settembre 97 ☏ 47611 (Treasury).

Information sources

Business information *Camera di Commercio*, Via de'Burrò 147, 00186 ☏ 6783280; *Camera di Commercio Internazionale*, Via XX Settembre 5 ☏ 462575; CED (*Centro Elettronico de Documentazione*), Via D. Chiesa ☏ 3308 (legal data bank); *Confindustria*, Vle dell'Astronomia 30, 00144 ☏ 59031 (General Confederation of Italian Industry which helps members through representation to government and other groups); *Consiglio Nazionale delle Ricerche* (National Research Council), Pzle Aldo Moro 7, 00185 ☏ 49931; *European Communities Information Office*, Via Poli 29, 00187 ☏ 6789722; *Istituto Nazionale per il Commercio Estero*, Via Liszt 21, 00144 ☏ 59921 (promotes export of Italian goods); *Istituto per la Cooperazione Economica Internazionale e i Problemi*

dello Sviluppo, Via Cola di Rienzo 11 ☏ 383169 (promotes international economic cooperation and development). The Rome Yellow Pages (*Pagine Gialle*), in English, can be bought from international bookshops.

Local media *Il Messaggero* and *Il Tempo* are the main Italian dailies published in Rome; *L'Espresso* is the main news weekly magazine. *La Repubblica* has Rome and Milan editions. Other national and international newspapers are widely available, the latter by 2pm on the day of publication.

Tele MonteCarlo broadcasts CBS evening news the next morning (7.15 and 7.45) and 24hr Cable Network News is available at major hotels. On radio the Voice of America, the BBC and Vatican News are in English.

Tourist information Via Parigi 11 ☏ 461851, and branches at Termini station, in the baggage claim area at Fiumicino airport and at autostrada exits. *Vatican City information office*, Pza San Pietro ☏ 6984866.

Public transport information, bus maps, passes from ATAC, Pza dei Cinquecento ☏ 4695.

Thank-yous

Books *Rizzoli*, Largo Chigi 15 ☏ 6796641; *Mondadori*, Via Veneto 140 ☏ 462631.

Confectionery *Moriondo & Gariglio*, Via della Pilotta 2 ☏ 6786662.

Florists *Valle Fiori*, Via V.E. Orlando 90a ☏ 460209; *Teleflor International*, Via Scirè 14 ☏ 8313447.

PIEDMONT (Piemonte)

Piedmont is the largest region of mainland Italy, bordered to the north and west by its Alpine frontiers. Commerce with the rest of Europe has fostered its steady economic development. Cars (Fiat, in Turin), office equipment (Olivetti) and wine are its most important exports. Olivetti leads the field in information technology in Europe and continues to expand, employing over 59,000 people in research and development. Piedmont has some 74,925ha/185,000 acres of vineyards and produces DOC (quality controlled) wines exported all over the world, including the famous Barolo. The vermouths of Carpano, Cinzano, Martini & Rossi and Riccadonna are also produced here.

Bisecting the region is the plain of the river Po, where wheatfields and grassland alternate with rice crops especially in the provinces of Vercelli and Novara (over half the national production). To the south the vines of the Asti area produce the famous *spumante*. Gorgonzola cheese comes from the Monferrato hills, and red wines and much-prized mushrooms and truffles from the Langhe hills around Alba. To the north of the region Lake Maggiore is a focus of the tourist industry which provides good hotel accommodation and conference facilities.

The plain is the area of densest population and greatest industrial activity, with its centre at Turin. Hydroelectric power stations constructed at the turn of the century supplied the electricity needed for industrial development, notably in heavy engineering. In addition to the car industry (and related products) concentrated around Turin and Chivasso, the region is important for textiles (wool and cotton, particularly in Biella), chemicals, electronics, metallurgy and timber (furniture, paper and printing).

TURIN (Torino)   *City codes* zip 10100 ☎ 011

Turin is Fiat. Not only is Fiat the biggest vehicle manufacturer in Europe, but Gianni Agnelli's empire is now diversified into sectors such as banking, steel mills, newspapers and leisure and employs directly or indirectly nearly half of Turin's work force. Fiat makes 80% of Italian cars (including Alfa Romeo, Lancia and Ferrari) and accounts for much of the production of commercial, agricultural and earth-moving vehicles, employing some 300,000 people overall. Also in Turin are manufacturers of car parts (ATI, MEC, Siette) and car designers (Bertone, Giugiaro, Pininfarina). The international motor show takes place in even years, drawing over 500,000 visitors.

With its population of just over 1m, Turin has overtaken Milan as the main centre of Italian industry, and not just of cars and engineering. There are many clothing and textile companies here too. Gruppo Finanziario Tessile (GFT), with Marco Rivetti at the helm, has 14 factories employing some 7,500 workers and makes garments for designers like Armani, Ungaro and Valentino. Confectionery (notably Ferrero), coffee (Lavazza) and printing and publishing are also major employers, and the famous vermouth firms, Martini, Carpano and Cinzano, have their main offices in central Turin. Insurance is another important sector (SAI, Toro and Reale Mutua among others).

Companies based in Turin have taken to sponsoring exhibitions and have poured much-publicized funds into local restoration projects, thus drawing international attention to the city and proclaiming their faith in its future. Recent projects have included the reorganization of the Egyptian Museum (Istituto Bancario San Paolo), and the restoration of Juvarra's baroque, palatial hunting lodge, Stupinigi (Fiat and the Cassa di Risparmio) and of the Accademia delle Scienze (Italgas).

The old Fiat factory at Lingotto is being transformed into a high-tech exhibition, conference and research centre with heliport and restaurant. The whole project is expected to be completed around 1994, jointly financed by public and private money with Fiat providing half the funds, estimated at L400bn. Other major projects include the new stadium for the World Cup in 1990.

But, compared with Milan, Turin is still a provincial town, with a provincial mentality. The influx of some 50,000 workers from the South in the 1960s profoundly affected its social fabric. The dwindling aristocracy retreated behind the shutters of gloomy *palazzi*, the rich industrialists barricaded themselves in their villas in the hills, with guard dogs and closed-circuit television. Still only 100,000 people live in the noble but rather run-down centre of Turin, one-time capital of the princes of Savoy and of a united Italy.

Arriving

There is direct road access to Turin from the north (St Bernard Pass, Mont Blanc tunnel) but there is still no autostrada from the French border. The city is bounded to the north, west and south by the *tangenziale* ring road and forms the westernmost apex of the triangle of autostrada routes linking the main cities of Northern Italy. Rail connections are also good. There are flights from some European cities but many business visitors fly to Milan.

Caselle airport

Scheduled direct flights link Turin daily with Frankfurt, London and Paris, several times a week with Munich, Düsseldorf, Stuttgart and Zurich and with Rome, Naples, Palermo and Pisa. Facilities are fairly basic but a staffed business centre, the first of its kind in the country, is planned and general improvements are under way to cope with the growing traffic. The bank on the main

concourse is open Mon–Fri, 6.25–4.50, 5.25–11.15. Inquiries ☎ 5778431, recorded flight information ☎ 577831/2/3/4 and ☎ 57781 (12–6am). Reservations ☎ 5778372.

Nearby hotels Atlantic, Via Lanzo 163, Borgaro Torinese 10071 ☎ 4701947 ☒ 22140 fax 4701783 ● AE DC MC V. Modern hotel on the main road to Turin with SADEM bus stop nearby; restaurant, meeting rooms, pool, sauna and gym. *Jet Hotel*, Via della Zecca 9, Caselle Torinese 10072 ☎ 9963733 ☒ 215896 fax 9961544 ● AE DC MC V. Popular hotel with meeting rooms, garden and good restaurant, the Antica Zecca (see *Restaurants*).

City link The airport is 16km/10 miles northwest of Turin. It's best to take a taxi into the centre. Buses operate directly between the Alitalia terminal at Via Lagrange 35 ☎ 55911 and Milan's Malpensa airport to connect with Alitalia flights (journey time 2hrs, cost L10,000).

Taxi There are usually plenty of cabs on the rank in front of the airport; allow 25–35mins for the journey and about L30,000.

Car rental The major car rental firms have desks at the airport, but a car is a drawback in the city.

Bus SADEM runs a regular service (every 20–30mins) of air-conditioned buses to the terminal (outside the centre) in Corso Inghilterra, also stopping on request outside Porta Susa station; journey time 30–45mins.

Helicopter Interavia ☎ 4703938 or 578630 is based at Caselle; 2-seaters cost from L600,000 an hour.

Railway station

Stazione Porta Nuova is very central, opposite the end of Via Roma, and serves national and continental destinations. In the reservations hall there are separate windows for sleepers, for international services and for credit card payment (AE V). The best facilities are on the modern main concourse. The taxi rank on the left of the exit is a better bet than the one on the other side. Hotel reservations can be made at the information desk (open 9–3) ☎ 531327. Rail inquiries ☎ 517551.

Getting around

Visitors staying for only a day or two will find walking (in the centre) and taxis (for farther afield) the easiest answer. For longer visits it is worth mastering the bus and train systems.

Taxis wait at ranks (in main squares and streets, marked with blue-and-white signs) and can be ordered by telephone: *Central Taxi* ☎ 5744 (AE, free wake-up call), *Radio Taxi* ☎ 5730, *Pronto Taxi* ☎ 5737. For advance reservations, *Radio Taxi Avvenire* ☎ 5748. Surcharges are levied for baggage and at weekends, and journeys to the hills round Turin are double rate for single trips.

Limousines *Autoservizi Mentana* ☎ 446027 or 6691229.

Driving Not recommended; parking is difficult and buses and taxis have priority lanes.

Walking is convenient (and the many arcades offer shelter from sun and rain) but the main through streets are extremely noisy and you can encounter drunks, tramps and hawkers in some areas.

Bus and tram Routes are constantly changed in an effort to improve the system so get an up-to-date map from the tourist office or the ATM headquarters at Corso Turati 19b ☎ 500900. Tickets are sold by tobacconists displaying the blue-and-white ATM sign and at the kiosk in the underground passage in front of Porta Nuova station.

Sleek modern trams (*metropolitana leggera*) are replacing the old-fashioned ones now that plans for a subway have been shelved.

There are bus services to the main provincial towns, mostly from the terminals in Corso Inghilterra and Corso Marconi.

Area by area

The centre of Turin, laid out in a grid, lies west of the river Po and south of the river Dora Riparia, its main axis being the Via Roma, leading from the station to the Piazza Castello. The banking and business area is to the west of the Via Roma, around Piazza Solferino. West of the station is Crocetta, the most prestigious residential area in the centre, where rich Torinese live in detached villas with gardens.

The outskirts of Turin have distinct characteristics. North of the Corso Regina Margherita is the Barriera di Milano, home to immigrants from the South of Italy, as is Le Vallette, to the northwest, site of the World Cup soccer stadium. To the south are densely-populated areas close to the Fiat factory at Mirafiori, and the former Fiat factory at Lingotto, now an exhibition centre, used for the international motor show. Further development will include a research centre for industry, incorporating the scientific departments of Turin university, a conference centre, apartments and shops.

A contrast to the dreary suburbs is the area east of the Po where the remains of Turin's aristocracy and the newer rich have their villas. The Pre Colline, immediately east of the centre, is a residential extension of it, a district of restored old buildings inhabited by artists and successful single people.

The suburbs

The conurbations of Beinasco (metallurgy), Collegno and Grugliasco to the west; Moncalieri and Nichelino to the south; Settimo Torinese (with GFT's largest single ready-made clothing factory in Europe) and Venaria to the north are all now incorporated in Turin. They are close to the ring road, and have a population of around 300,000. The aeronautics (Alitalia) zone is around Corso Francia, towards Collegno to the west.

Hotels

There is a wide gap between Turin's best hotels – the Turin Palace and the Principi di Piemonte in the centre vie for top spot – and the rest. In general, officially classified 4-star hotels are fairly well equipped for the business traveller, with modernized bedrooms and several meeting rooms, but 3-star hotels are of a poor standard.

All the hotels listed have IDD telephones, a concierge, but rarely 24hr room service, and at least one meeting room. Those with a full entry also have air conditioning, several conference rooms and parking facilities. None have shops, sports or keep-fit equipment or on-site business facilities – and changing money may not be easy.

It is not difficult to find a room except during major fairs, but it is essential to reserve accommodation well in advance for the bi-annual international car show.

Concord ⃞///
Via Lagrange 47, 10123 ☎ *5576756*
⃞ *221323 fax 5576305 • Atahotels •*
AE DC MC V • 140 rooms, 4 suites,
1 restaurant, 1 bar
A rather impersonal but quite comfortable and central hotel used by business travellers which prides itself on its well-equipped convention centre. Bedrooms, of which about half are singles, are spacious with high ceilings and modern comforts. All are sound-proofed but it is still advisable to request one on the courtyard. The lobby (writing desk, newspapers) is a good meeting place and the Lagrange restaurant, although rather claustrophobic, is suitable for business lunches. Popular with visiting soccer teams. 6 meeting rooms (capacity up to 230).

Grand Sitea ⃞///
Via Carlo Alberto 35, 10123
☎ *5570171* ⃞ *220229 fax 548090 •*
AE DC MC V • 117 rooms, 3 suites,
1 restaurant, 1 bar
A well-established hotel in the grand style, in a rather dour 19thC building. It has been modernized but retains some period features and a sedate atmosphere. Recent renovation has included the restaurant, in imperial style. The Sitea is close to the Teatro Regio and attracts visiting actors and musicians. Courtyard garden. 5 meeting rooms (capacity up to 100).

Jolly Principi di Piemonte ⃞////
Via P. Gobetti 15, 10123 ☎ *532153*
⃞ *221120 • AE DC MC V • 99 rooms,*
8 suites, 1 restaurant, 1 bar
A marble-faced detached block set back from the central Via Roma, this is the flagship of the Jolly chain. Although it does not enjoy official luxury status, like the Palace, its public rooms and meeting rooms have

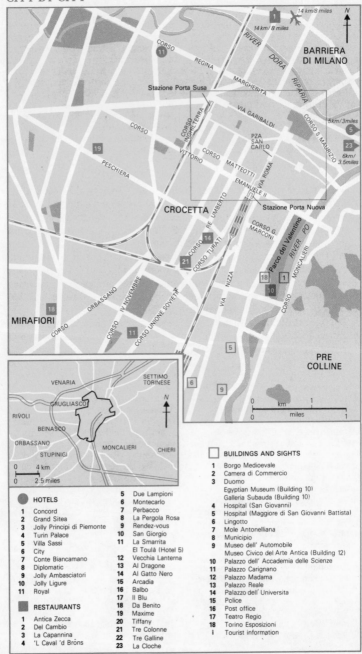

BUILDINGS AND SIGHTS

1 Borgo Medioevale
2 Camera di Commercio
3 Duomo
  Egyptian Museum (Building 10)
  Galleria Subauda (Building 10)
4 Hospital (San Giovanni)
5 Hospital (Maggiore di San Giovanni Battista)
6 Lingotto
7 Mole Antonelliana
8 Municipio
9 Museo dell' Automobile
  Museo Civico del Arte Antica (Building 12)
10 Palazzo dell' Accademia delle Scienze
11 Palazzo Carignano
12 Palazzo Madama
13 Palazzo Reale
14 Palazzo dell' Universita
15 Police
16 Post office
17 Teatro Regio
18 Torino Esposizioni
i Tourist information

HOTELS

1 Concord
2 Grand Sitea
3 Jolly Principi di Piemonte
4 Turin Palace
5 Villa Sassi
6 City
7 Conte Biancamano
8 Diplomatic
9 Jolly Ambasciatori
10 Jolly Ligure
11 Royal

RESTAURANTS

1 Antica Zecca
2 Del Cambio
3 La Capannina
4 'L Caval 'd Bröns
5 Due Lampioni
6 Montecarlo
7 Perbacco
8 La Pergola Rosa
9 Rendez-vous
10 San Giorgio
11 La Smarrita
  El Toulà (Hotel 5)
12 Vecchia Lanterna
13 Al Dragone
14 Al Gatto Nero
15 Arcadia
16 Balbo
17 Il Blu
18 Da Benito
19 Maxime
20 Tiffany
21 Tre Colonne
22 Tre Galline
23 La Cloche

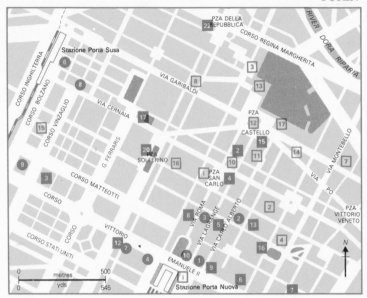

more old-fashioned elegance and charm. The recently refurbished bedrooms are very comfortable and well-equipped with desks and hairdryers and telephones in the bathrooms. The few single rooms, although spacious, have small bathtubs. Suites include marble bathrooms and small sitting-rooms. There are panoramic views from the upper floors; ask for a north or east facing room. 4 meeting rooms (capacity up to 250).

Turin Palace □////
Via Sacchi 8, 10128 ☎ *515511*
TX *221411 fax 5612187 • Italhotels •*
AE DC MC V • 121 rooms, 2 suites,
1 restaurant, 1 bar
Turin's only 5-star hotel is, although opposite the station, considered the smartest place to stay. The guestbook lists VIPs from rock stars to royalty. The lacquered, oriental-style bar is a calm venue for business meetings. The restaurant, serving regional and international cuisines, has a separate banqueting room and offers a sensibly priced set meal and *à la carte.* • 5 meeting rooms (capacity up to 200).

Villa Sassi □////
Strada Traforo del Pino 47, 10132
☎ *890556* TX *225437 fax 890095 •*
Relais et Châteaux • AE DC MC V •
16 rooms, 1 suite, 1 restaurant, 1 bar
Only a short taxi ride from the centre, Villa Sassi is a noble 18thC villa, secluded in its own tranquil parkland. It retains the atmosphere of a country house, with antique furniture and Old Master paintings. A comfortable place to stay, and a prestigious venue for dining, club reunions, and fashion shows or conferences. 4 meeting rooms (capacity up to 500).

OTHER HOTELS
City □/// *Via Filippo Juvarra 25,*
10122 ☎ *216228* TX *216228 • AE DC*
MC V. Small, neat, modern hotel near Porta Susa station.
Conte Biancamano □/// *Corso*
Vittorio Emanuele 73, 10128 ☎ *513281*
fax 513281 • AE DC MC V. Appealing little family-run hotel with elegant sitting-room and bar and modern bedrooms (ask for one at the back). No restaurant.
Diplomatic □/// *Via Cernaia 42,*
10122 ☎ *5612444* TX *225445 fax*

117

540472 • *AE DC MC V*. A new hotel near the business area and main bus terminal, with comfortable well-decorated and equipped bedrooms (mostly singles, with shower only) and 4 meeting rooms. No restaurant.

Jolly Ambasciatori *[L]||* *Corso Vittorio Emanuele 104, 10121* ☎ *5752* ⊠ *221296 fax 544978* • *AE DC MC V*. Near the bus terminal.

Jolly Ligure *[L]|||* *Piazza Carlo Felice 85, 10123* ☎ *55641* ⊠ *220617*

fax 535438 • *AE DC MC V*. Second choice in the Jolly trinity. Central, comfortable and functional, with a spacious lobby lounge and 2 meeting rooms.

Royal *[L]|* *Corso Regina Margherita 249, 10144* ☎ *748444* ⊠ *220259 fax 748393* • *AE DC MC V*. Well-equipped but charmless hotel on the way out to the western *tangenziale* and the aeronautics area. Conference room for up to 600.

Restaurants

Turin executives avoid long business lunches and most restaurants are closed by 3pm. Favoured places are brisk Tuscan trattorias, but there are many more formal places suitable for confidential discussions or for evening entertaining. Restaurants and old Torinese trattorias are concentrated near the markets, east of Via Roma and around Porta Palazzo. It is advisable to make reservations in advance for dinner and the same day for lunch.

Summer dining in the hills east of the Po is popular, and there are some excellent restaurants around Alba, 59km/36.5 miles south of Turin; Italian guests will appreciate a gastronomic excursion there during the autumn truffle season.

Piedmontese cooking is regaining favour but now chefs try for quality rather than quantity. Traditional dishes tend to be rich, and include *agnolotti* (ravioli filled with truffles) and *brasato al Barolo* (beef braised in Barolo wine).

Antica Zecca *[L]||*
Via della Zecca 9, Caselle Torinese
☎ *9961403* • *closed Mon, Aug* • *AE DC MC V*
Near the airport at Caselle, this is a sophisticated restaurant, in a converted old mint, often crowded with business people, especially at lunch. Cooking, which is superb, features unusual Piedmontese dishes and excellent local wines.

Del Cambio *[L]|||*
Pza Carignano 2 ☎ *546690* • *closed Sun, Aug* • *AE DC V* • *jacket and tie*
A famous restaurant with original late 18thC mirror and gilt interior. Under the present ownership, Del Cambio's flagging gastronomic reputation has been revived: dishes (like *brasato al Barolo*) are traditional but interpreted

with flair, and the wine list has been improved. Service is formal without being starchy. Foreign visitors come here out of curiosity, especially in the evenings.

La Capannina *[L]||*
Via Donati 1 ☎ *545405* • *closed Sun, Aug* • *no credit cards*
The Gallina brothers run a rustic-style trattoria famous for its Piedmontese food from the Langhe region, south of Alba (where there is another branch). A good place for an informal evening.

'L Caval 'd Brôns *[L]|||||*
Pza S. Carlo 157 ☎ *553491* • *closed Sun, Aug* • *AE V* • *jacket and tie* • *reservations essential*
Turin's most exclusive restaurant, on the *piano nobile* above the café of the

same name, was restored in 1988 after ten years of neglect. The atmosphere is discreet and club-like; there is no name or menu outside, just a doorbell. Bankers from the Banca San Paolo opposite snap up the tables (there are only 8) at lunch time.

Due Lampioni   *L*||
Via Carlo Alberto 45 ☎ *546721 • closed Sun, Aug • V • jacket and tie • reservations essential*
Carlo Bagatin's long-established restaurant has well-spaced tables, is ideal for groups of four people, and serves regional and international cooking in comfortable though not grand surroundings.

Montecarlo   *L*||
Via San Francesco da Paola 37 ☎ *830815 • closed Sat L, Sun, Aug • AE DC MC V • reservations essential*
A vaulted restaurant with a serious atmosphere and modern cooking, much frequented for mid-price business lunches and dinners. Good wine list.

Perbacco   *L*|
Via Mazzini 31 ☎ *882110 • closed Mon L, Sun, Aug • AE DC V*
An attractive and fashionable new restaurant in an old mansion, but with a no-frills interior and fairly cramped tables. The menu is inventive, with surprising culinary combinations. Popular with journalists.

La Pergola Rosa   *L*|
Via XX Settembre 18 ☎ *546534 • closed Sun, Aug • V*
A simple Tuscan trattoria with 1940s decor and snob appeal. Fiat directors lunch here.

Rendez-vous   *L*||
Corso Vittorio Emanuele 38 ☎ *8396961 • closed Sat L, Sun, Aug • AE DC MC V • jacket and tie • reservations essential*
This is a large restaurant, frequented by business people and ladies out for lunch. Tables are well spaced, but it can be noisy; there is a separate private room (10–14 people).

San Giorgio   *L*|||
Borgo Medioevale al Valentino ☎ *6692131 • closed Wed L, Tue, Aug • AE MC V*
An elegant restaurant in the mock medieval castle on the Po. Candlelit dining (till 2am), with an orchestra and formal service, attracts the tourists. There are special salons for banquets and receptions.

La Smarrita   *L*|||
Corso Unione Sovietica 244 ☎ *328488 • closed Mon • AE DC MC V • reservations essential*
Close to Fiat and sometimes used by Gianni Agnelli, La Smarrita is a small, smart place for *nouvelle* Tuscan food. The waiters are dressed like monks. Good wines.

El Toulà   *L*||||
Villa Sassi Hotel ☎ *890556 • closed Sun, Aug • AE DC MC V*
A calm, countrified setting close to the centre for formal business gatherings or a romantic summer evening. Reserve well in advance for a table on the terrace.

Vecchia Lanterna   *L*|||
Corso Re Umberto 21 ☎ *537047 • closed Sat L, Sun, 10–20 Aug • AE DC MC V • jacket required • D reservations essential*
Armando Zanetti is one of Italy's best-known chefs and attracts those with a palate for the 7-course *menu degustazione* (changed every 15 days). Senior business executives and ministers lunch here (the round tables are good for small groups), and in the evening the clientele is often younger. Brocaded walls and Venetian lace tablecloths create a traditional atmosphere but the cooking is modern and seasonal. Downstairs, opposite the kitchens, is the Sala Inglese, used for private banquets.

OTHER RESTAURANTS
Al Dragone, Via Pomba 14 ☎ 547019, is a brick-vaulted, taverna-type trattoria. *Al Gatto Nero*, Corso Turati 14 ☎ 590414, is a well-known seafood

restaurant with a Tuscan chef. The
Arcadia, Galleria Subalpina 16
☎ 532029, is pretty and smart and
full of executives at lunch time.
Balbo, Via Andrea Doria 11
☎ 511743, serves international and
local cuisine. *Il Blu*, Corso Siccardi 15b
☎ 545550, specializes in salads, and is
chic and speedy. For the best fish try
the informal *Da Benito*, Corso
Siracusa 142 ☎ 3090353, close to the
Fiat factory, and *Maxime*, Via
Verzuolo 40 ☎ 4475677, whose
Egyptian owner adds exotic spices. The
elegant *Tiffany*, Pza Solferino 16
☎ 540538, is near the business and
banking area; *Tre Colonne*, Corso
Rosselli 1 ☎ 587029, with summer
service in the garden, is another safe
choice. *Tre Galline*, Via Bellezia 37
☎ 546833, is a typical old Torinese
trattoria. *La Cloche*, Strada al Traforo
del Pino 106 ☎ 894213, serves good
Piedmontese cooking on a rustic
covered verandah.

Bastian Contrario, Strada Moncalvo
102, Moncalvieri ☎ 6968388,
panoramic views, vast array of
antipasti. *Il Ciacolon*, Vle XXV Aprile
11 ☎ 6610911, Venetian cooking and
antipasti, good fixed-price menus.
Pigna d'Oro, Via Roma 130, Pino
Torinese ☎ 841019, lovely terrace,
exclusive atmosphere, average food.
Tromlin, Via alla Parrocchia 7,
Cavoretto ☎ 697804, intimate, family-
run, with typical Piedmontese food;
open weekends and evenings. *Villa
Montforts*, Strada de' Luogo 29,
Castiglione Torinese ☎ 9606214,
18thC villa with classic cooking and
fine French wines (about 15km/9
miles from Turin).

Bars and cafés
Turin's delightful 19thC coffee houses
are civilized places for semi-formal
business discussions where you can
drink the vermouth, take a light lunch
or snack and try the local confections.
San Carlo and *Caffè Torino* in Piazza
San Carlo and *Baratti* and *Mulassano*
in Piazza Castello have splendid

original interiors, with chandeliers,
mirrored or wood-panelled walls, and
a profusion of gilt, velvet and stucco.
The brasserie in *Caffè Platti*, Corso
Vittorio Emanuele 72, has just the
right atmosphere for longer lunch-
time meetings.

Entertainment
Turin is rather quiet at night; the
Torinese like to meet in cafés and
piano bars.
  In July and August there are open-
air performances (*punti verdi*) in the
parks and there is a music festival in
September.
Theatre, opera, dance Teatro Regio,
Pza Castello 215 ☎ 548000, puts on
opera, concerts, ballets and plays
Nov–mid Jun.
  The other main theatres are the
Teatro Alfieri, Pza Solferino 4
☎ 535440, and the *Teatro Carignano*,
Pza Carignano 6, which stages plays
that require a good knowledge of
Italian (tickets ☎ 544562).
Music Concerts are given at the
recently facelifted *Conservatorio
Giuseppe Verdi*, Via Mazzini 11
☎ 878458, and in the *RAI* auditorium,
Via Rossini 15 ☎ 8800.
Discotheques Bogart, Via Sacchi 34
☎ 547530, with a piano bar, is one of
the more reliable discotheques.

Shopping
Arcaded Via Roma and the traffic-free
Via Garibaldi are the smart shopping
streets, exhibiting the designs of the
famous names in Italian fashion.
Parallel to Via Roma is Via Lagrange,
with mouth-watering food shops
including *Defilippis* (for pasta), *Baita
del Formagg* (for cheese) and *Castagno*,
a superb delicatessen. At *Casa del
Barolo*, Via Andrea Doria 7
☎ 532038, you can taste and buy a
large range of Italian wines. All over
Turin are *pasticcerie*, displaying the
confectionery, especially *gianduie*
(chocolates), for which the city is
famous. *Peyrano*, Corso Vittorio
Emanuele II 76 ☎ 538765, sells
probably the best chocolates in Turin;
just up the road is *Platti*, a close rival.

Street markets *Porta Palazzo* is a
general market, the *Fiera del Gran
Balon* an antique market held the
second Sunday in the month. Both are
not too far from the Piazza della
Repubblica.

Sightseeing

Turin is a city of museums,
monuments, churches and palaces.
Duomo The *Cappella della Santa
Sindone*, containing the rarely
displayed Holy Shroud, dated in 1988
to medieval times, is inside the
cathedral. *Pza San Giovanni. Chapel
open Tue–Fri, 8.30–12, 3–7; Sat–Sun,
9.45–10.30, 11.30–12.*
Mole Antonelliana Turin's odd
pagoda (city emblem) affords fine
views of the Alps on a clear day. *Via
Montebello 20. Elevator Tue–Sun, 9–7.*
Museo dell'Automobile A fine
collection of historic cars. *Corso Unità
d'Italia 40. Open Tue–Sun,
9.30–12.30, 3–7.*
Palazzo dell'Accademia delle Scienze
Palace by Guarini containing, in the
Galleria Sabauda, an important
picture collection with Italian and
Flemish masterpieces, and the
outstanding *Egyptian Museum. Via
Accademia delle Scienze 6. Open
Tue–Sat, 9–2, 3–7; Sun, 9–2.*
Palazzo Carignano Also by Guarini,
the birthplace of Victor Emanuel II
and seat of the first parliament of a
united Italy. *Pza Carignano. Open
Mon–Sat, 9–7; Sun, 9–1.*
Palazzo Madama Juvarra's majestic
baroque façade hides a fortified
medieval palace containing the Gothic
and Renaissance collection of the
*Museo Civica d'Arte Antica. Pza
Castello. Open Tue–Sat, 9–7; Sun,
10–1, 2–7.*
Palazzo Reale Royal palace of the
princes of Savoy, with opulent
decoration and furniture. *Pza
Castello. Open Tue–Sun, 9–2.*
Parco Valentino Broad park on the
banks of the Po with a French-style
château and the *Borgo Medioevale*, a
19thC reconstruction of a feudal
village and castle. *Open Tue–Sat, 9–4;
Sun, 10–4.*

Guided tours
Tours, some including lunch and a
boat trip on the Po, leave in summer
and during exhibitions from the
station and some major hotels. Details
at the tourist office and travel agents.
    A private half-day tour of the
robotic-assembly Fiat factory at
Mirafiori can be made Mon–Sat.
Chambers of commerce will organize
group visits ☎ 33331.

Out of town
Basilica di Superga Juvarra's
imposing basilica contains the tombs
of the Savoy dynasty and the kings of
Sardinia; 10km/6 miles to the east.
Open Sat–Thu, 10–12.30, 3–5
☎ 890083.
Castello di Rivoli Museum of
contemporary art in handsome
baroque interiors; 14km/8.5 miles
west. *Open Tue–Sun, 10–7*
☎ 9581547.
Sagra di San Michele Impressive
fortified monastery at the entrance to
the Susa valley, 25km/15.5 miles to
the east.
Stupinigi Hunting lodge conceived on
a grand scale by Juvarra, also known
as a *palazzo*, now gloriously restored,
9km/5.5 miles southwest of Turin
☎ 3581220.

Spectator sports

Soccer Juventus, Turin's most
successful team, is sponsored by
Agnelli and supported by most middle
management. Torino is the people's
team. Matches are played at the
Studio Comunale ☎ 352600.
Basketball, played at the Palazzo dello
Sport ☎ 337416, and rowing (on the
Po) are also popular spectator sports.
Horseracing and polo take place at
the *Ippodromo*, Vinovo, near
Stupinigi, mostly at weekends
☎ 9651356.

Keeping fit

Fitness centres *The Gym and Squash
Club*, Corso Trapani 57 ☎ 380835,
and *Sport City*, Corso Dante 17a
☎ 3190884. *The American Club*, with
4 branches (including Corso Trapani

46 ☎ 337109), offers monthly
membership and pools and tennis
courts.

Golf Visitors who are members of
other clubs may play at *I Roveri*, La
Mandria ☎ 9235667, 18km/11 miles
to the north. There are other courses
at Stupinigi and Vinovo.

Skiing Sestrière and Sauze d'Oulx are
within a 2hr drive of Turin.

Local resources

Business services

Multilingual secretaries, telex and fax,
word processing and other office
facilities are offered by *AV*, Corso
Siccardi 15 ☎ 533740 ⊤⊠ 225557
fax 515563, and *Executive Service*, Via
Magenta 44a ☎ 531740, both with
branches in other major cities. A local
set-up is *CFT*, Via Ceva 47
☎ 4731113. *International Office
Service*, Via Egeo 18 ☎ 55811, is
equipped for meetings and
conferences.

Photocopying and printing Most
hotels will photocopy for guests and
there are numerous copy shops near
the university and in business areas.
Elektra, Pza Solferino 3 ☎ 531961, is
central and open Mon–Fri, 8.30–7,
Sat, 8.30–12.30. *TarServi* is near the
aeronautics zone, Corso Marche 12
☎ 715346.

Secretarial *Copisteria Agostino*, Via S.
Agostino 4 ☎ 535657, offers word
processing, translating (and offset
printing) and will collect and deliver.

Translation *ATID*, Via Vittorio
Amedeo II ☎ 519571, for notarized
translations. *Inlingua*, Corso Vittorio 68
☎ 532912 ⊤⊠ 225272 fax 5576297.

Communications

Local delivery *Defendini*, Via San
Francesco d'Assisi 23d ☎ 55401;
Pony Express, Via San Francesco di
Paola 15-17 ☎ 8123618.

Long-distance delivery There are
firms specializing in transporting
anything from cars to computers to
pianos; see the Yellow Pages. *DHL*,
Via Saluzzo 42 ☎ 6502275, for letters
and packets.

Post office Main office: Via Alfieri 10

and Via Arsenale 13, open Mon–Sat,
8–8 ☎ 547097.

Telex and fax At the main post
office.

Conference/exhibition centres

The main exhibition hall, *Torino
Esposizioni*, Corso Massimo d'Azeglio
15, 10126 ☎ 6569 (during exhibitions
6504970) ⊤⊠ 221492 fax 6509801, has
9 meeting rooms and conference
facilities for up to 3,000. Among the
most important international shows
held here are those on new
technology, leisure and sport and food
equipment. Other central conference
venues include the *Centro Incontri
della Cassa di Risparmio di Torino*,
Corso Stati Uniti 23 ☎ 57661, with a
capacity of up to 300; the *Centro
Congressi SEAT*, Via Bertola 34
☎ 541096, which has 4 meeting
rooms with a capacity of up to 300;
and the *Sala Congressi dell'Istituto
Bancario di San Paolo*, Via Santa
Teresa ☎ 5551, with a meeting room
accommodating up to 290 people;
they have more conference facilities
(capacity up to 200) at Via Lugaro 15
☎ 5551. The *Museo dell'Automobile*,
Corso Unità d'Italia 40 ☎ 677666, has
2 rooms (capacity up to 340). The
international motor show is held every
two years at *Centro Espositivo Lingotto*,
Corso G. Ferraris 61, 10128 ☎ 5761.

Outside the centre there are
attractive convention facilities at *Villa
Gualino*, Vle Settimio Severo 65
☎ 6502565, with panoramic views,
and a meeting room for 80 people at
Castello di Rivoli, Pzle Castello
☎ 9587256 (see *Sightseeing*), and at
Villa Sassi (see *Hotels*). Receptions can
be held at *Stupinigi* (see *Sightseeing*).

The *Centro Congressi Internazionale*,
Corso Tassoni 32 ☎ 761870, will
organize conferences.

Emergencies

Bureaus de change Porta Nuova
station information office, open 7–9,
12–2 and 3–9.30.

Hospitals Ospedale San Giovanni, Via
Cavour 31 ☎ 57541; *Ospedale
Maggiore di S. Giovanni Battista*,

Corso Bramante 88–90 ☎ 6566, is the main university hospital; in emergency ☎ 5747, emergency surgery ☎ 633722.
Pharmacies Open at night and on holidays: *Boniscontro*, Corso Vittorio Emanuele 66 ☎ 541271, *Maffei*, Pza Massaua 1 ☎ 793308, and *Pescarmona*, Via Nizza 65 ☎ 6699259. Some others stay open until 10.30.
Police *Questura*: Corso Vinzaglio 10 ☎ 55881.

Business information *Camera di Commercio*, Via San Francesco di Paola 24 ☎ 57161. *Centro Estero Camere Commercio Piemontesi*, Via Ventimiglia 165 ☎ 6960096 ☒ 214159 fax 6965456 (chamber of commerce for Piedmont region). *Centro Internazionale di Perfezionamento Professionale e Tecnico*, Corso Unità d' Italia 125 ☎ 633863. *Federazione delle Associazioni Industriali del Piemonte*,

Corso Stati Uniti 38 ☎ 549246 (federation of industrial associations of Piedmont). *Biblioteche Civiche e Raccolte Storiche*, Via della Cittadella 5 ☎ 7653900 (public library).
Local media The influential Turin-based *La Stampa* is read all over Italy. The supplement *Torino Sette* details the week's cultural events. *RAI* television headquarters are also in Turin.
Tourist information Tourist offices are at at Via Roma 226 ☎ 535181 and Porta Nuova station ☎ 517551 or 531327. *A Guest in Torino* is distributed free in hotels and has information and advertising.

Confectionery *Peyrano* (see *Shopping*).
Florists *T. Cichetti*, Via Cernaia 34–36 ☎ 540054, *Fiorir di Fiori*, Corso Vittorio Emanuele 78 ☎ 544775; *Gabri*, Corso Palermo 25 ☎ 237993 or 284544.

OTHER CITIES

ALESSANDRIA
codes zip 15100 ☎ 0131
An important agricultural market with a population of over 96,000, Alessandria is known for its hat factory, Borsalino. There are also chemical, engineering, footwear and wood industries. Guala is a leader in the production of plastics, including patent bottle-stoppers, and Graziano makes precision machine tools.

In the province, the town of Valenza Po is known for its goldsmiths, of which there are over 1,000. In Quattordio are Alfacavi (cables), Ivi (paint dyes) and Invex (wires). At Cassine, Tacchella produces machine tools.

Alli Due Buoi Rossi, Via Cavour 32 ☎ 445252, is the best hotel, with a well-known restaurant and a meeting room for up to 130 people. *Lux*, Via Piacenza 72 ☎ 51661, is an

alternative, and *Il Grappolo*, Via Casale 28 ☎ 53217, an appealing restaurant in a 17thC palace.

Sightseeing includes the 18thC *fortress*, several churches and the neo-classical *Duomo* as well as the *Museo Civico* and *Pinacoteca*. There is also a *Museo del Cappello* (hat museum). A gastronomic festival is held in the autumn. Visit the wine-growing Monferrato hills, where Montcalvo has wine and truffle festivals.

Conferences can be held at the *Sale Convegni dell'Azienda Teatrale Alessandrina*, Via Savona ☎ 441872 (capacity up to 170). *Camera di Commercio*, Via S. Lorenzo 21 ☎ 54001.
Tourist information, Via Savona 26 ☎ 51021, open Mon–Fri, 8–12, 3–5.30; Sat, 8–12.

ASTI *codes* zip 14100 ☎ 0141
Known principally for wine and
spirits, Asti is also an agricultural and
industrial centre. The famous Asti
Spumante is actually produced at
Canelli by the family firm of
Riccadonna (also vermouths), Gancia
and others. Population 75,000.

Hotels and restaurants
The best hotels are the *Hasta*,
Località Valle Benedetta 25
☎ 213312, and the *Salera*, Via Mons.
Marello 19 ☎ 211815. The most
popular restaurant is *Gener Neuv*,
Lungo Tanaro 4 ☎ 57270. At Canelli,
the best hotel is *Al Grappolo d'Oro*
☎ 833812.

Relaxation
There are two major events in
September: the Douja d'or wine
festival and the Palio (medieval horse
race). The main sights (churches and
palaces) are in the old centre (*recinto
dei nobili*).

Information sources
Camera di Commercio, Pza Medici 8
☎ 53011 (with conference facilities
for up to 130). A prestigious venue for
conferences (capacity up to 100) is the
Palazzo Ottolenghi, Corso Alfieri 350
☎ 3991.
Tourist information, Pza Alfieri 34
☎ 50357, open Mon–Fri, 9–12.30,
2.30–5.30.

BIELLA *codes* zip 13051 ☎ 015
A very important centre for the textile
and garment industry, notably fine
wool fabrics; famous names include
Cerruti, Loropiana and Zegna.
Aiazzone is a well-known producer of
cheap furniture. The population is
nearly 52,000.

Hotels and restaurants
Biella has comfortable hotels: *Astoria*,
Vle Roma 9 ☎ 20545, is elegantly
decorated; *Augustus*, Via Orfantrofio
☎ 27554, comes a close second. *Prinz
Grill*, Via Torino 14 ☎ 30302, is the
best restaurant for business
entertaining.

Relaxation
An interesting town to explore, with
the main monuments around the
Gothic *cathedral* of Biella Piano, the
lower town. In Biella Piazza, the
upper town, there are villas built by
textile merchants in the Renaissance,
a 19thC cotton mill and the
*International Museum of Alpine
Photography*.

Information sources
Unione Industriale Biellese, Via Torino
56 ☎ 35021. *Camera di Commercio*,
Via N. Sanzoi ☎ 21600.
Tourist information, Via Quintino Sella
12 ☎ 8491577, open Mon–Thu,
8–12.30, 2–5.30; Fri, 8–12.

IVREA *codes* zip 10015 ☎ 0125
Ivrea (population 26,600) is known
principally for the Olivetti factory
(just south of the river), run by the
Milan-based entrepreneur Carlo De
Benedetti.

Hotels and restaurants
The functional *La Serra*, Corso Carlo
Botta 30 ☎ 44341, has convention
facilities, restaurant, pool, sauna and
gym. *L'Aranciere*, Pza Ottinetti
☎ 422443, which serves Piedmont
food, is the most convenient
restaurant for business entertaining.

Relaxation
The pleasant old town, with its
medieval *cathedral* and *castle* is worth
exploring. See also the church and
monastery of *San Bernardino*, at the
heart of the Olivetti factory complex,
and now a cultural centre for concerts,
exhibitions and other events.

Information sources
Camera di Commercio, Via Jervis
☎ 423201 or 49013.
Tourist information, Corso Vercelli 1
☎ 424005.

NOVARA *codes* zip 28100 ☎ 0321
Novara, situated between Turin and
Milan, has thriving industrial and
service sectors. The province is
important for rice, for food (Alivar

Pavesi factory) and for the industry and tourism centred on the Lakes, where Arona is the most important centre. The Istituto Geografico De Agostini, mapmakers and publishers, is based here.

Hotels and restaurants

Italia, Via Solaroli 10 ☎ 399316, is the grandest hotel in Novara, with an elegant and popular restaurant, La Famiglia. Also convenient are the modern *Maya*, Via Boggiani 54 ☎ 450810, and *La Rotonda*, Baluardo Massimo d'Azeglio ☎ 23691. All have conference facilities. A simple family-run restaurant serving local dishes is *Trattoria dell'Amicizia*, Via Sottile 23 ☎ 23247.

Out of town There are several resorts on Lake Maggiore. At Arona (40km/ 25 miles) the *Atlantic*, Corso Repubblica 124 ☎ (0322) 46521, is the best hotel. Stresa (56km/35 miles), has many hotels: *Des Iles Borromées*, Lungolago Umberto I 67 ☎ (0323) 30431, is the most luxurious and expensive and provides conference facilities. Also on Lungolago Umberto I are the *Astoria* ☎ (0323) 32566, the *Bristol* ☎ (0323) 32601, *La Palma* ☎ (0323) 32401 and *Regina Palace* ☎ (0323) 30171, all with pools and conference facilities, but closed during the winter.

Relaxation

Novara has some interesting churches – you can't miss the soaring spire of *San Gaudenzio* – and a few medieval civic buildings. But those with more than an hour or two to spare should head for *Lake Maggiore* or the quieter *Lake Orta*.

Information sources

Camera di Commercio, Via degli Avogadro 4 ☎ 20671.
Tourist information, Corso Cavour 2 ☎ 23398, open daily, 8.30–12.15, 1.15–4.30.

VERCELLI *codes* zip 13100 ☎ 0161
Vercelli is dependent largely on rice and agriculture. It also has engineering (Claas Italia), textile (ITV), chemical and timber industries. The population is about 51,000.

Hotels and restaurants

Accommodation is basic (*Modo*, Piazza Medaglio d'Oro 21 ☎ 57481, is near the *strade statale*); it is better to stay at Biella or Novara. *Il Paiolo*, Via Garibaldi 72 ☎ 53577, serves a respectable risotto.

Relaxation

The basilica of *Sant'Andrea*, the *cathedral* and *Santa Chiara* are worth visiting and there are several Renaissance buildings in the centre. You can visit the *Borsa Risi* (rice exchange) by arrangement ☎ 5981.

Information sources

Camera di Commercio, Pza Risorgimento 12 ☎ 5981 (with conference centre for up to 250).
Tourist information, Via Garibaldi 90 ☎ 64631, open Mon–Fri, 8.30–12.30, 2.30–5.30.

LOMBARDY (Lombardia)

Extending from the central Po valley to the Alps, Lombardy's position has always favoured trade between Europe and the Mediterranean. It is now Italy's most densely populated region (total population near 9m), responsible for one third of the country's total GDP of $580bn and more than 30% of the country's exports.

The area between Milan, Como and Varese is now almost completely built up, and the Milanese urban sprawl engulfs nearby towns, including, in the province, Vimercate (IBM), Cinisello Balsamo (Toshiba), Legnago (Montedison chemicals, Eliolona textiles), Arese (Alfa-Romeo) and Monza, an important centre in its own right with SGS, Singer, Candy (washing machines) and Star (food processing). The province of Milan has a population density of 1,442 inhabitants per sq km. In the Brianza district rows of mulberry trees testify to the importance of silk production based at Como, and Brianza itself is known for furniture manufacture. To the north the mountainous, underpopulated Sondrio and parts of the areas around the Lakes have retained some rural beauty.

Fertile Lombardy, watered by the lakes and tributaries of the Po, has always been systematically cultivated. Here farming has become an industry in itself, with the southwest part of the region, around Mantua and Cremona, still dedicated mainly to agriculture. Artificial pastures have created a modern dairy products industry and the Lomellina area west of Pavia is given over to rice fields. Sugar beet, cereals and vegetables are cultivated extensively, and Lombardy has more cattle and more pigs (especially round Mantua) than any other region of Italy. However, rural Lombardy is suffering gradual depopulation in favour of the industrial zones and expanding service sectors of the cities.

Elsewhere on the Lombard plain, around the provincial capitals of Bergamo, Brescia and Pavia, engineering and other industries flourish, to the detriment of the environment. The famous Lombardy fogs are as much due to atmospheric pollution as to the climate.

Although the cities have a rich heritage of art and architecture, it is the Lakes which continue to attract most of the foreign tourists.

MILAN (Milano)   *City codes* zip 20100 ☎ 02

Milan is essentially a central European city, just 48km/30 miles south of the Alps and a strategic trading post for centuries. Successive domination by the Spanish, Austrians and French has helped to shape a cosmopolitan city which commercially and financially is the capital of Italy. With a population of 1.7m (3.1m including suburbs), Milan is second to Rome in size but accounts for much more of Italy's national income; the average Milanese is over twice as rich as the average Southerner.

Milan's economy is now based on the service sector which employs more than half the work force. It is the centre of banking and the Milan Borsa is the main stock market in Italy. The Americans, British and Swiss (and increasingly the Japanese) are the chief foreign investors.

Tertiary industries like advertising, marketing, PR and broadcasting, particularly private television companies, flourish. Silvio Berlusconi, the media magnate, is one of several dynamic business figures. Carlo De Benedetti, of Olivetti fame, directs his wide-ranging business empire from here and Raul Gardini heads several of the heavier industries. There are five universities, three of which are private, including Luigi Bocconi, a business and economics university.

Local industries include machine tools, car components, furniture and paper, textiles and garments, gold and silver jewellery, leather goods and foodstuffs. Firms employing under 100 people are still the backbone of Milan's commercial success. The annual April Fiera is the largest general trade fair in Europe with well over 1m visitors. Specialist trade fairs, especially fashion, are of increasing importance.

Among the major industries are chemicals and petrochemicals (Montedison, now controlled by Gardini), bio-engineering and textiles (SNIA), electro-engineering (Magneti Marelli at Sesto San Giovanni, employing over 8,000 people), steel (Falck, employing 10,000), rubber and cables (Pirelli, Italy's fourth largest private-sector company, employing over 30,000 here, with a tyre factory at Bollate) and agro-industrial products (notably Ferruzzi, also run by Gardini). Pharmaceuticals include Carlo Erba at Limito, Enichem at San Donato Milanese and Formenti at Vimodrone plus Beecham, Glaxo and ICI. IBM employs over 12,000.

For ready-to-wear (*pronta moda*) fashion, many cognoscenti say that Milan has overtaken Paris; the biggest name is Giorgio Armani. Milan leads Europe in furniture design (Artemide's research headquarters are at Pregnara) and manufacture with factories in the Brianza area. Publishing is important (Fabbri, Feltrinelli, Garzanti, Mondadori – at Segrate – Olympia Press, Rizzoli, Rusconi, *La Repubblica*, Sperling & Kupfer and others), and the Italian art market is also based here.

A relatively small proportion of inhabitants are true *milanesi* (the descendants of at least three generations). After the war there was a concerted emigration from the poor Mezzogiorno and Southerners still comprise much of the work force (and many of those out of work) at the bottom of the social pile. Next come the industrious *piccoli borghesi*, then the English-speaking, Burberry-wearing, go-getting workaholics and yuppies (*rampanti*). Old aristocrats, entrepreneurial industrialists and *nuovi ricchi* head the hierarchy.

The Milanese work feverishly hard, enjoy making deals, pride themselves on their efficiency and are frustrated that the lazier Romans make the decisions. They joke that the Mediterranean, if not Africa, begins at Rome and complain that they are the Romans' new slaves. It is important, at all costs, to cut a *bella figura*: fur coats are more than a protection against the cold winters; high-profile security is a status symbol. Smart *milanesi* have villas on the Lakes and yachts at Portofino, and, when the city closes down in August, are seen at St Tropez or on the Costa Smeralda.

Research and technology are to be boosted with the creation of

Monte-city (for Montedison's chemical works) and Centro-direzionale. Pirelli's old plant at Bicocca will become Tecno-city, Europe's largest science park for high-tech firms, by the early 1990s. And by 2000 airport facilities will be improved and Malpensa connected to Milan by train.

Arriving

Milan has two international airports, neither very large nor well-equipped for the volume of business-oriented traffic which comprises nearly 90%, some 10m passengers a year. Malpensa is 1hr by road from central Milan (but well-placed for Varese or Como); Linate is more convenient. There is no regular link between the two airports, although Alitalia can arrange transfers for groups if its connecting flights are involved. General flight information (both airports but the line is often busy) ☎ 74852200; recorded information on operations and check-in times ☎ 7491141.

Autostrada and rail connections with Europe and the rest of Italy are excellent; Milan is 1hr by road from the Swiss border (60km/37 miles) and 4hrs by high-speed train from Rome (570km/354 miles).

Linate airport

Linate handles European and domestic flights, plus Middle Eastern destinations, with regular flights from capitals and other major cities. Facilities are often very crowded. They include a restaurant, pharmacy, bars, limited shops (but an excellent food emporium for last-minute gifts), car rental and a tourist office. There is a Visa automatic cash dispenser in the baggage collection area; expect a wait (though not necessarily poor rates of exchange) at the banks, which are open 8–9. The Fiera welcome desk on the left of the exit provides information and advice on major trade fairs.

Linate is often plagued by strikes and understaffing may cause delays at passport control or baggage collection. Allow 1hr or more for check-in on departure as passengers are often "bumped." Those with hand baggage only may collect boarding passes in the boarding area and so avoid the check-in procedures. Inquiries ☎ 7485313 or 3129; (tickets) ☎ 74852250, (international departures) ☎ 7381312, (freight) ☎ 7384393.

City link The airport is just 10km/6 miles east of the centre; a taxi to Piazza Duomo or a bus to the Stazione Centrale take about 20mins in average traffic. Bus tickets are sold inside the airport (left of the exit).

Taxi There are usually plenty of taxis outside the terminal. The fare to central Milan is at least L20,000 and to the Fiera allow 40mins and L25,000. There is an extra charge of L15,000 to the Padiglione Sud exhibition pavilion (30km/18 miles). A "private taxi" service charges double for journeys into central Milan.

Car rental A car is no use in central Milan but Hertz (open 7.30–11.30 ☎ 868001) and other car rental firms are represented here.

Bus The blue SEAV bus service to the central station (and Porta Garibaldi) runs every 15–20mins and costs L2,000. The orange ATM (public transport) bus No. 73 goes to the central Piazza San Babila. There is a free bus service to Padiglione Sud during major fairs.

Helicopter ATA ☎ 7381051.

Malpensa airport

Flights from major US cities, notably New York (several daily), some other international and long-haul destinations and charter flights from Europe arrive here. Facilities include a post office, restaurant, bar, car rental desks and bureau de change. Inquiries ☎ 868028, (air freight) ☎ 868096, (passengers) ☎ 748 52200.

Nearby hotels Jet Hotel, Via Tiro a Segno 22, Gallarate 21013 Varese ☎ (0331) 785534 (with pool), takes major credit cards. *Astoria*, Vle Duca d'Aosta 14, Busto Arsizio, 21052 Varese ☎ (0331) 636422, has a restaurant and meeting room (AE only).

City link The airport is 46km/29 miles northwest of Milan, so a taxi is expensive; the bus service, which connects with flights, is much cheaper and scarcely less convenient.

Taxi Allow 1hr for the journey to central Milan, and at least L80,000.

Car rental It can be cheaper to rent a car for a day than take a taxi to central Milan if you are sure you can park and deliver it. Europcar ☎ 868017, Hertz ☎ 868001, InterRent ☎ 868124, Maggiore ☎ 868036, Tirreno ☎ 868023.

Bus The bus to Stazione Centrale (via Porta Garibaldi station) takes 45mins and costs L5,000. For outward journeys report to Stazione Centrale 2hrs 30mins before flight departure.

Helicopter or jet Executive Jet ☎ 7380951, Ciga Aviation ☎ 733316, Gitanair ☎ 717468 or 7426954.

Railway stations

Stazione Centrale Milan's grandiose main station in Piazza Duca d'Aosta provides national and international services. Despite the name it is not in the city centre, although conveniently close to some major hotels. It provides a tourist office, bars, restaurants, newsstands, photocopying facilities, multilingual information booths and information desks for different foreign languages. The shops, bank and tourist office are closed at lunch time. Travel agencies, on the concourse or just outside, will make wagon-lits and hotel reservations.

The nonstop Milan–Rome express (Il Pendolino) runs at 6.55am and 7pm and takes 4hrs. It has first-class carriages, restaurant cars and multilingual stewardesses. A faster version, the ETR 500, due for inauguration in 1990, will have telephones, telex and fax.

There are buses to both airports (tickets from Agenzia Doria, Piazza Luigi di Savoia, to the east of the building). Take a taxi to the city centre; there is usually a steady flow of cabs. Until the completion of line 3, the subway journey involves changing lines. Rail inquiries ☎ 67500.

Porta Garibaldi Some international arrivals from the north (especially motorail from, for example, Paris); also from Turin, Pavia, Rome and Florence.

Stazione Nord Commuter trains from Brianza, Como and Varese.

Getting around

In the centre of Milan restricted traffic makes walking easy but taxis are plentiful. The public transport system is comprehensive, well integrated and cheap but you need time to buy tickets and work out routes.

Despite or perhaps because of the layout of Milan, with its concentric ring roads and streets radiating from the Duomo, the city is confusing to drive in. One-way systems, tramlines and the restricted central zone (closed to nonresidents 7.30–1, 7.30–6 in summer) are additional complications. *Piste ciclabili* (cycle lanes) have been added to some roads.

Public transport runs from 6.15am to just after midnight (some buses until 1am). Day tickets for unlimited travel on both the ATM (bus and tram) and MM (subway) can be bought at the ATM offices in the subway stations at Piazza Duomo (open Mon–Sat, 8–8) and the Stazione Centrale. ATM information ☎ 89010797.

Taxis There are always plenty of taxis in the centre and at ranks in the main piazzas. They can sometimes be hailed on the street. They are metered but fares are usually rounded up, so tipping is not obligatory. Drivers rarely speak English and may look up quite straightforward destinations. Radio taxis: *Arco* ☎ 6767, *Autoradiotaxi Velasca* ☎ 8585, *Esperia* ☎ 8388.

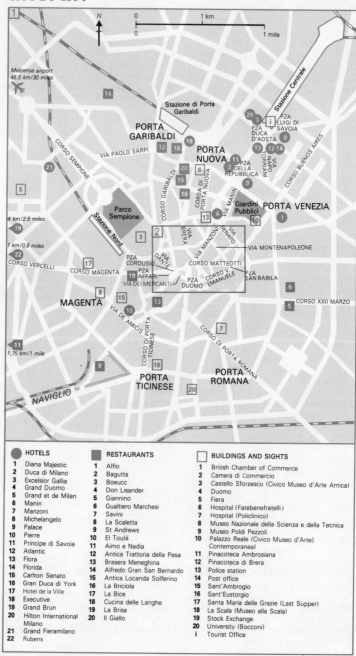

HOTELS

1 Diana Majestic
2 Duca di Milano
3 Excelsior Gallia
4 Grand Duomo
5 Grand et de Milan
6 Manin
7 Manzoni
8 Michelangelo
9 Palace
10 Pierre
11 Principe di Savoia
12 Atlantic
13 Flora
14 Florida
15 Carlton Senato
16 Gran Duca di York
17 Hotel de la Ville
18 Executive
19 Grand Brun
20 Hilton International Milano
21 Grand Fieramilano
22 Rubens

RESTAURANTS

1 Alfio
2 Bagutta
3 Boeucc
4 Don Lisander
5 Giannino
6 Gualtiero Marchesi
7 Savini
8 La Scaletta
9 St Andrews
10 El Toulà
11 Aimo e Nadia
12 Antica Trattoria della Pesa
13 Brasera Meneghina
14 Alfredo Gran San Bernardo
15 Antica Locanda Solferino
16 La Briciola
17 La Bice
18 Cucina delle Langhe
19 La Brisa
20 Il Giallo

BUILDINGS AND SIGHTS

1 British Chamber of Commerce
2 Camera di Commercio
3 Castello Sforzesco (Civico Museo d'Arte Antica)
4 Duomo
5 Fiera
6 Hospital (Fatebenefratelli)
7 Hospital (Policlinico)
8 Museo Nazionale della Scienza e della Tecnica
9 Museo Poldi Pezzoli
10 Palazzo Reale (Civico Museo d'Arte Contemporanea)
11 Pinacoteca Ambrosiana
12 Pinacoteca di Brera
13 Police station
14 Post office
15 Sant'Ambrogio
16 Sant'Eustorgio
17 Santa Maria delle Grazie (Last Supper)
18 La Scala (Museo alla Scala)
19 Stock Exchange
20 University (Bocconi)
i Tourist Office

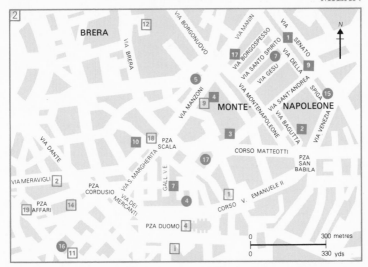

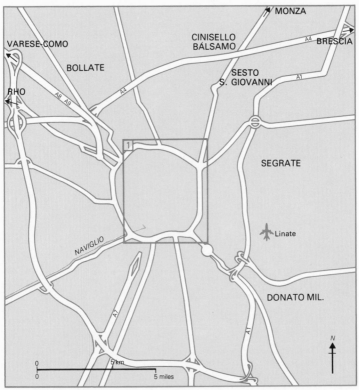

Limousines *Pacifico Deluxe cars*
☎ 864664, *Mose' Bellina* ☎ 3080180,
VIP Limousine ☎ 6592158 (including
cars with telephones).

Driving Not only is driving restricted
and complicated but break-ins are
common. Hotels should issue permits
to enter the central zone. Car rental
from *Hertz* ☎ 6598151, *Eurodrive*
☎ 6704582, *Avis* ☎ 6981. Guarded
car-parking is indicated by a white P
on blue background in the city centre,
near the station and in the Fiera
districts.

Walking Milan's streets are relatively
safe and pleasant, although you may
be bothered by hawkers, especially
near the station. Women alone at
night, especially in the Castello and
Parco Sempione areas, may be
propositioned.

Bus and tram The surface transport
system is efficient and the same stops
are used by bus and tram. Useful lines
include the *circonvallazione* tram line
(Nos 29 or 30) which runs around the
viali (until 1am). A bus tours the vast
Fiera area during exhibitions.

Tickets are bought from bars,
tobacconists or newsstands displaying
the ATM sign and from coin-operated
machines at some bus-stops. They are
valid for 75mins from the moment
they are time-stamped.

Subway The Metropolitana Milanese
(MM) system is simple to use, with
swift, frequent and clean trains. There
are two lines, 1 (red) and 2 (green),
and a third (yellow) is due to open in
the first half of 1990.

Tickets are valid for the bus and
tram. They can can be used for more
than one trip within 75mins, but only
for one metro journey, which must be
the first. They can be bought from
machines at stations and from bars.

Area by area

Milan is laid out like a target, with the
Piazza Duomo as the bull's-eye.
Within the inner circle or Cerchia dei
Navigli (following the original
medieval walls) are the banking and
business areas, the smartest shopping
streets, the main historical sights and
the most expensive residential
districts. A second *circonvallazione*,
the *viali* or *bastioni*, encloses other
fashionable residential and business
areas.

The areas between the *viali* and the
circonvallazione esterna (ring road), are
becoming more acceptable as districts
to live in. The gates of the original
walls have given their names to the
surrounding areas.

Beyond the ring road are working-
class suburbs, factories and modern
office and residential complexes such
as Milanofiori to the southwest,
Segrate, Milano San Felice and
Milano 2 to the east, near Linate
airport. These areas are now
incorporated in Greater Milan.

Piazza Duomo/the centre The
Duomo is still the heart of the city.
From it the vaulted Galleria Vittorio
Emanuele II, a popular meeting-place
with cafés and shops, leads to La
Scala. To the west is the banking and
business area around Piazza Affari
(site of the Stock Exchange), Via dei
Mercanti and Piazza Cordusio. To the
east a traffic-free shopping street,
Corso Vittorio Emanuele, leads to the
modern Piazza San Babila, with
insurance and other offices.

Brera A small area north of the
Duomo and around the Brera gallery.
Derelict and the home of penniless
artists and drug addicts in the 1970s,
it is now gentrified and trendy,
Milan's answer to Greenwich Village.
Corriere della Sera and other
newspaper offices are based here.

Montenapoleone Fashionable central
Milan around Via Montenapoleone,
with exclusive shops and aristocratic
palace façades hiding courtyards and
gardens.

Magenta Wide avenues and turn-of-
the century apartment blocks give this
area west of the Duomo a rather
Parisian feel. It has long been a
fashionable residential district,
traditionally the home of Lombard
nobility.

Porta Romana Shops, offices and
housing; a fairly well-to-do district
south of the Duomo.

Porta Garibaldi This commercial district by the station is developing fast, thanks to rocketing prices. Via Paolo Sarpi is Milan's Chinatown.

Stazione Centrale The central station area (Porta Nuova and Porta Venezia) is also commercial, and the base for the wholesale rag trade. Corso Buenos Aires is the main traffic artery and shopping street with a large population of Moroccan immigrants. The elegant Pirelli building became a symbol of modern architecture after it was completed in 1960.

Fiera A residential and business area around the Fiera exhibition halls.

Porta Ticinese Run-down until five years ago, this is the area for the unconventional, artists and even young brokers and yuppies. There are some expensive bars and nightclubs and good restaurants. Along the *Naviglio* (canal) are dilapidated shuttered *palazzi* with balconies.

The suburbs
Commuting is relatively new, although the wealthy Milanese have traditionally kept villas near the Lakes. Monza and Brianza have become virtual suburbs of Milan. Como and Varese, less than 1hr by train from Milan, are becoming dormitory towns.

Hotels

Milan has nearly 400 hotels, and most of the guests are here on business. Hotels are generally well-equipped and comfortable, with meeting rooms for conferences, and employees normally speak excellent English. In-house business services are rare but staff will arrange photocopying, telex and fax for you.

The most prestigious hotels are those in the CIGA chain (but none is really central) and some grand old hotels (the elegant Marino alla Scala is being renovated). Prices tend to be very high but there are comfortable, efficient and moderately priced hotels near the Stazione Centrale.

For major international fairs (especially the April trade fair and September furniture fair), reserve accommodation up to a year ahead; for minor fairs a month should suffice. Those who have not made reservations may have to stay outside Milan in Bergamo, Como or Varese, all within about 55km/35 miles. Rooms can be reserved at the tourist office in the Stazione Centrale, at Linate airport and through Hotel Reservation Milan ☎ 706095. As a rule, breakfast is not included in room prices. Many hotels are closed for two weeks in August.

Diana Majestic *[L]||*
Vle Piave 42, 20129 ☎ *202122*
☒ 333047 • CIGA • AE DC MC V • 94 rooms, 1 bar
A comfortable old-fashioned hotel being upgraded to CIGA standards but retaining some of its Art Deco features. For six months of the year, the hotel is used by models, designers and others in the fashion trade. 24hr room service.

Duca di Milano *[L]|||||*
Pza della Repubblica 13, 20124
☎ *6284* ☒ *325026 fax 6555966 •*
CIGA • AE DC MC V • 10 rooms, 50 suites, 1 restaurant, 1 bar
Quieter and calmer than its grander neighbour the Principe, the Duca is ideal for those needing a working base and popular with merchant bankers. Each of the comfortable suites has a separate desk and seating area suitable for small meetings; the single rooms are unusually spacious. Civilized public rooms include a dining area. Stock exchange prices are transmitted for the benefit of business guests.

Excelsior Gallia 🛏////
Pza Duca d'Aosta 9, 20124 ☎ *6277*
🖅 *311160 fax 6277* • *THF* • *AE DC MC
V* • *266 rooms, 14 suites, 1 restaurant,
1 bar*
This traditional grand old hotel,
whose heyday was in the 1930s, has
recently been taken over by Trust
House Forte. Although the grandeur
is faded in places the Excelsior is still
a prestigious business hotel, with good
facilities. It is a few minutes' walk
from the bus terminal for the airports
and from the station. Sauna, massage,
solarium • 7 meeting rooms (capacity
up to 400).

Grand Duomo 🛏///
Via San Raffaele 1, 20121 ☎ *8833*
🖅 *312086 fax 872752* • *MC V* • *160
rooms, 18 suites, 1 restaurant, 1 bar*
The central location of this well-
known hotel overlooking the Piazza
del Duomo attracts many foreign
business people and tourists, and the
spacious lobby is a good meeting
place. Rooms (with some inadequate
small exceptions) are well-equipped
for the working visitor and some have
splendid views. The split-level suites
have ideal facilities for small
meetings.

Grand et de Milan 🛏////
Via A. Manzoni 29, 20121 ☎ *801231*
🖅 *334505 fax 872526* • *AE DC MC V* •
*79 rooms, 10 suites, 1 restaurant,
1 bar*
The Grand is an aristocratic hotel;
tradition (since 1865) and old money
mingle with the new fashion brigade.
The *belle époque* interior is being
completely restructured. Verdi was
among the illustrious guests and
composed some of his masterpieces in
the ornate studio (in which he also
died): the hotel is a traditional
favourite with La Scala stars. The tiny
restaurant is primarily for the
convenience of guests. No hotel
parking.

Manin 🛏///
Via Manin 7, 20121 ☎ *6596511*
🖅 *320385 fax 655216* • *AE DC MC V* •

*105 rooms, 5 suites, 1 restaurant,
1 bar*
Well-respected as a sound family-run
hotel, giving good value and personal
service and with a pleasant location
opposite the public gardens. There is
an open bar area suitable for quiet
meetings and a formal restaurant.
Bedrooms are spacious and plain
(quietest at the back, but with terraces
on the front). A covered verandah
leads to a private garden and the
conference rooms. No hotel parking.
3 meeting rooms (capacity up to 230).

Manzoni 🛏/
Via Santo Spirito 20, 20121 ☎ *705697*
• *no credit cards* • *52 rooms,
1 bar*
A superior small hotel with a good
address. The Manzoni offers few
facilities and services but has
comfortable bedrooms at a sensible
price. Old photographs of Milan add
charm and atmosphere; there is a
garage.

Michelangelo 🛏////
Via Scarlatti 33, 20124 ☎ *6755*
🖅 *340330 fax 6694232* • *AE DC MC V*
• *250 rooms, 10 suites, 1 restaurant,
1 bar*
A tall modern hotel with its own
high-tech convention centre. In the
basement is the Ghirlandaio
restaurant, with a menu created by
Gualtiero Marchesi (see *Restaurants*).
Bedrooms (nearly half of which are
singles) are functional and well
equipped; they are being gradually
refurbished from the top floor, which
has fine views, downwards. Bus
service to both airports • 8 meeting
rooms (capacity up to 750).

Palace 🛏////
Pza della Repubblica 20, 20124
☎ *6336* 🖅 *311026 fax 654485* • *CIGA*
• *AE DC MC V* • *184 rooms, 7 suites,
1 restaurant, 1 bar*
The best-known business hotel in
Milan (many visiting stockbrokers
stay here) is a stark modern block
opposite the Principe. The public
areas are modern, but dated. By

contrast bedrooms (and the Casanova restaurant) are luxurious, in neo-classical style. The roof garden is used for receptions.

Pierre 📷|||||
Via de Amicis 32, 20123 ☎ *8056221 fax 8052157 • AE DC MC V • 47 bedrooms, 6 suites, 1 restaurant, 1 bar*
A sophisticated, chic new hotel which has yet to establish its market. The Pierre is not geared to executive-level meetings but aims to combine ultra-luxurious accommodation with friendly personal service. For those who enjoy remote-control gadgetry and monogrammed towelling robes. No hotel parking. 1 meeting room (capacity up to 30).

Principe di Savoia 📷||||||
Pza della Repubblica 17, 20124 ☎ *6230* ☒ *310052 fax 6595838 • CIGA • AE DC MC V • 269 rooms, 18 suites, 1 restaurant, 2 bars*
If the Palace is for business, then the Principe, a good 20min walk from the centre, is for VIPs. The presidential suite is just that. The 85 or so super de-luxe rooms have Empire-style furniture and pastel ragged walls and 100 modern de-luxe rooms have teak walls and fittings. The rest (merely "superior," although some are very small) are being refurbished. A very busy hotel whose services can be variable.

OTHER HOTELS
Near the station there are some efficient and pleasant small hotels with good facilities:
Atlantic 📷|| *Via Napo Torriani 24, 20124* ☎ *6691941* ☒ *321451 fax 6706533 • AE MC V.*
Flora 📷 *Via Napo Torriani 23, 20124* ☎ *650242* ☒ *312547 • AE DC V.*
Florida 📷 *Via Lepetit 33, 20124* ☎ *6705921* ☒ *314102 • Best Western • AE DC MC V.*
In the centre but reasonably priced are:
Carlton Senato 📷|| *Via Senato 5, 20121* ☎ *798583* ☒ *331306 fax*

5456043 • AE MC V. Bright and modern; quiet back bedrooms overlook Via della Spiga.
Gran Duca di York 📷| *Via Moneta 1a, 20100* ☎ *874863 • AE.* Modest, old-fashioned hotel near the Borsa.
Hotel de la Ville 📷|| *Via Hoepli* ☎ *867651* ☒ *312642 fax 866609 • AE DC MC V.* Central and convenient, if a bit dated.
Well-equipped for the business visitor, but not within walking distance of the centre are:
Executive 📷|||| *Vle Sturzo 45, 20154* ☎ *6294* ☒ *310191 fax 653240 • Interhotel • AE DC MC V.* Opposite Porta Garibaldi station. Adjacent convention centre with facilities for up to 1,200.
Grand Brun 📷|||| *Via Caldera 21, 20153* ☎ *45271* ☒ *315370 fax 4526055 • Gamma hotels • AE DC MC V.* Luxury modern hotel near San Siro and 3 km/2 miles from the western *tangenziale.*
Hilton International Milano 📷|||||
Via Galvani 12, 20124 ☎ *6983* ☒ *330433 fax 6071904 • AE DC MC V.* Standard Hilton, with plans under way for an up-to-date executive business centre.
Near the Fiera are two functional hotels:
Grand Fieramilano 📷|||| *Vle Boezio 20, 20145* ☎ *3105* ☒ *331426 fax 314119 • Interhotel • AE DC MC V.*
Rubens 📷|| *Via Rubens 21, 20148* ☎ *405051* ☒ *333503 fax 48193114 • AE DC MC V.*

Clubs

There are several exclusive men's clubs to which visitors might be invited, and which have affiliations with a few similar clubs abroad. The *Società del Giardino,* Via San Paolo 10, is the oldest with the finest decor (see the fencing room) and a garden. It has some women members. *L'Unione,* Via Borgonuovo, is the most aristocratic and old-fashioned. *Il Clubino,* Via Omonima 3, has a separate dining room where women may be entertained.

Restaurants

There are typically old-fashioned Milanese restaurants (where the reputation is more legendary than the food) and friendly trattorias serving traditional Lombard cooking, although *nouvelle cuisine* (or *la cucina nuova*) has several brilliant disciples, in particular Gualtiero Marchesi. Perhaps surprisingly, Milan has the best fish restaurants in the country (but fish is very expensive). Hotel restaurants are not generally highly regarded, and it would not be considered good form to entertain Italian guests at a foreign restaurant. Most of the best restaurants are closed in August.

Reservations are not necessary for lunch. Most Milanese now prefer a quick snack at a bar to the traditional midday meal. However, at the top business lunch venues it is sensible, and sometimes essential, to make a reservation in the morning. Friday and Saturday nights are busiest and, in the evenings, it is quite usual for businessmen to entertain without their wives. Because of the fashion clientele, suits are not usually *de rigueur* but jackets should be worn in smarter restaurants.

Traditional Milanese dishes are saffron risotto, *cotoletta alla milanese* (*Wiener Schnitzel*) and *vitello tonnato* (veal in cold tuna sauce) plus various stews (including *osso buco*, *cassoeula*). Lighter food is generally appreciated now, especially at lunch time, but it is worth remembering that some Italians remain suspicious of *nouvelle cuisine*.

Alfio [L]////
Via Senato 31 ☎ 700633 • closed Sun L, Sat • AE DC MC V
One of the top restaurants in Milan, attracting US and Japanese bankers, Italian industrialists and brokers and journalists from nearby Piazza Cavour. Alfio serves excellent pasta and the best seafood in town; choose swordfish, salmon or a *misto*. The splendid buffet and light setting are most attractive in summer.

Bagutta [L]//
Via Bagutta 14 ☎ 702767 • closed Sun, Aug, Xmas • AE DC MC V • reservations essential
A large, casual and cluttered Tuscan trattoria, with walls decorated with caricatures and a garden at the back. Literati, art collectors and dealers, media and PR people, stars from the opera and ballet, and some publishers and journalists, are attracted by the atmosphere rather than particularly special food. Ask for a table at the rear if you want to talk business in private.

Boeucc [L]//
Pza Belgioioso 2 ☎ 780224 or 782880 • closed Sun L, Sat, Aug, Xmas • AE • reservations a day in advance
Used by grand old businessmen, by politicians (Craxi, Goria), journalists, the Mayor of Milan, La Scala stars and Raul Gardini, whose office is next door. Boeucc is elegant and understated with well-spaced tables, ideal for confidential business discussions (request a quiet table). The seafood is good and the verandah and garden are a bonus. There is a private room for parties of 20–30.

Don Lisander [L]//
Via Manzoni 12a ☎ 790130 • closed Sat D, Sun • AE DC MC V • reservations essential
Known as a business restaurant, elegant remodelled Don Lisander is popular with top bankers and Fiat executives from Turin. Tables are close together but al fresco dining in a delightful garden courtyard is a major attraction in summer. Cooking is traditional but leans towards *la cucina*

nuova; fixed-price menus are suitable for a quick lunch, and a 7-course *menu degustazione* is on offer.

Giannino *L*////
Via Amatore Sciesa 8 ☎ *5452948* •
closed Sun • *AE DC MC V*
A favourite with foreign bankers, business guests and tourists rather than locals. The layout is spacious, with a winter garden and several large private rooms. Representative dishes from all the Italian regions come out of the open-plan kitchen. Suitable for an extended lunch or dinner, especially for groups of 6–10 people.

Gualtiero Marchesi *L*/////
Via Bonvesin de la Riva 9 ☎ *741246* •
closed Mon L, Sun, Aug • *AE DC MC V*
• *jacket and tie*
Ultra-expensive, ultra-serious temple of modern Italian cooking, the only restaurant in the country to boast three Michelin rosettes. From the individual modern sculptures on each table to the saffron risotto with gold leaf, everything is calculated to challenge conventional tastes. The *atto unico* is a theatrical single fixed-price dish suitable for a business lunch. Marchesi is more popular with Americans than the *milanesi*, but the ambience is suitable for business entertaining.

Savini *L*////
Galleria Vittorio Emanuele II
☎ *8058364* • *closed Sun, mid Aug, Xmas* • *AE DC MC V* • *jacket and tie* •
D reservations advisable Sep–Nov
Legendary Savini's offers bland cuisine in velvet, mirror and gilt surroundings little changed since the 19th century. This is definitely the safest place to invite local business contacts if you want to impress, but may be too stuffy and uninspiring for some tastes. The glassed-in area under the awning is more public, and slightly less formal than the exclusive interior. Upstairs there are several elegant private dining rooms. The formidable wine list includes 100 French wines.

La Scaletta *L*////
Pzle Stazione Genova 3 ☎ *8350290* •
closed Sun, Mon • *no credit cards* • *D reservations essential*
Pina Bellini's delicious, highly inventive cooking is considered by some to be the best in Milan. The elegant but informal surroundings, with just nine tables, and the off-centre location make La Scaletta more suitable for a leisurely dinner than a business lunch. For some privacy request the table by the bar. Selection of excellent, often unusual wines.

St Andrews *L*////
Via Sant'Andrea 23 ☎ *793132* • *closed Sun* • *AE DC MC V* • *jacket and tie* •
reservations essential
The sombre modern decor of this international-style restaurant makes it ideal for business lunches. Food is excellent, with the emphasis on luxuries (caviar, oysters, Scotch smoked salmon); menus come in five languages and wines vary from local to French *grands crus*. The location, on the corner of Via della Spiga, attracts the fashion fraternity as well as business people. The dark *enoteca* in the cellars is an excellent place for confidential meetings or parties of 25–30 people.

El Toulà *L*////
Pza Paolo Ferrari 6 ☎ *870302* • *closed Sun* • *AE DC MC V* • *D reservations essential.*
Second only to Savini in prestige, sophisticated El Toulà has a conventional, club-like atmosphere conducive to top-level business discussions (Agnelli and De Benedetti lunch here). Proximity to La Scala also attracts evening opera-goers for whom there is an after-theatre supplement. Inoffensive continental cuisine – the *filet mignon* could be in London or New Jersey – but a superb wine cellar.

OTHER RESTAURANTS
Superb creative cooking in elegant surroundings 15mins by taxi from the centre is provided by *Aimo e Nadia*,

Via Montecuccoli 6 ☎ 416886: an excellent place for an evening excursion when enjoyment is more important than business. *Antica Trattoria della Pesa*, Vle Pasubio 10 ☎ 6555741, is an old favourite, serving typical, rather heavy Lombard cooking. *Brasera Meneghina*, Via Circo 10 ☎ 808108, is similar, with a pleasant garden. *Alfredo Gran San Bernardo*, Via G.A. Borghese 14 ☎ 3319000, offers the best in classic Lombard cooking, a little way from the city centre. In the Brera area, *Antica Locanda Solferino*, Via Castelfidardo 2 ☎ 6599886, is a chic bistro. Nearby, *La Briciola*, Via Solferino 25 ☎ 6551012, is popular with media people.

Fashion-crowd favourites include *La Bice*, Via Borgospesso 12 ☎ 702572/795528, now with a twin in New York, and *Cucina delle Langhe*, Corso Como 6 ☎ 6595180, with conservatory dining. In the evening trendies eat late at chic but pretentious *La Brisa*, Via Brisa 15 ☎ 872001, which has a garden (popular at weekends), or at *Il Giallo*, Via Milazzo 6 ☎ 6571581, in the Brera area.

Out of town

For a gastronomic excursion make the short journey (20km/12.5 miles) southwest to *Antica Osteria del Ponte* ☎ (02) 9420034 at Cassinetta di Lugagnano, which is regarded by Italian and foreign gourmets as the best restaurant in Italy.

Bars and cafés

Hotel bars are convenient for business meetings and are generally quiet in the afternoon. The atmospheric and elegant old cafés (*Sant' Ambroeus, Cova, Del Bon, Taveggia*) are good places to meet over an *aperitivo* and there are also several cafés in the Galleria, for example *Biffi. Baretto*, Via Sant'Andrea 3, is popular with merchant bankers; in the same street the bar of *St Andrews* restaurant is a good place to meet for discussions (open outside mealtimes).

Entertainment

If you are lucky enough to get tickets for an evening of opera at *La Scala*, from personal contacts, you have a scoop. Ticket agencies do not exist.

For listings see the free fortnightly *Night and Day Milano* or the monthly *Spettacolo a Milano* or *What's On in Milan*.

Opera The season runs from 7 Dec (St Ambrose Day) to the end of May. For tickets you can try writing 60 days in advance to the box office: Botteghino, La Scala, Via dei Filodrammatici 2. If international stars have cancelled at short notice try the box office (open daily 10–12.30, 3.30–5.30, performance days 5.30–9.30 ☎ 807041) for returns.

Theatre The main theatres are *Teatro Manzoni*, Via Manzoni 42 ☎ 790543, *Teatro Nazionale*, Pza Piemonte 12 ☎ 4396700 (classic Italian drama and visiting international companies), *Piccolo Teatro*, Via Rovello 2 ☎ 8690631, under the brilliant manager/director Giorgio Strehler, and *Teatro Lirico*, Via Larga 14 ☎ 866418, the largest in Lombardy.

Music There are concerts at the *Angelicum*, Pza Sant' Angelo 2 ☎ 6592748, the *Conservatorio Giuseppe Verdi*, Via Conservatorio 12 ☎ 701755, and the *Piccolo Scala*, Via Filodrammatici. The concert season at La Scala is June and Sep–Dec. The main venue for rock concerts is the *Palatrussardi* close to the Fiera district ☎ 3340055.

Cinema Films in the original language are shown at *Angelicum*, Pza Sant' Angelo 2 ☎ 6551712 (Wed–Sun). *Cinema Anteo*, Via Milazzo 9 ☎ 6597732, is among the art cinemas (*cinema d'essai*).

Nightclubs One of the most exclusive members-only nightclubs is *Agora*, Via San Marco 33a. Discotheques include *Nepentha*, Pza Diaz 1 ☎ 804837, and *Plastic*, Vle Umbria 20, the current hits among the gilded (and sometimes tarnished) youth of Milan. Otherwise nightlife revolves mainly around the bars (open until about 2am) of the Brera and Naviglio areas. Friendly jazz bars (*locali*) and piano bars include *Biblo's*, Via Madonnina 17 ☎ 8051860 (with a basement discotheque).

Shopping

Shops in Milan are now among the finest in Europe, and are comparable with the best in New York. The most sophisticated and elitist shopping streets are the Via Montenapoleone and surrounding streets (between Via Manzoni, Corso Matteotti and Via della Spiga). Fashion boutiques predominate but there are also furriers, jewellers, shops selling fine leather goods and antique dealers.

The arcaded, traffic-free Corso Vittorio Emanuele is another major shopping street.

Shops open Mon–Sat, 9 or 9.30–12.30 or 1 and 3.30–7 or 7.30.

Antiques Antique shops are in the Montenapoleone, Brera and Naviglio areas. The Brera market is held every third Sat in the month from 10am between Via Fiori Chiari and Via Madonnina.

Art galleries Milan is the leading city in Italy for contemporary art, with hundreds of commercial galleries. *Studio Marconi*, Via Tadino 15, is well established. More avant-garde are *Studio Carlo Grossetti*, Via dei Piatti 9, *Cannaviello*, Via Cusani 10, and *Toselli*, Via del Carmine 9. *Philippe Daverio*, Via Montenapoleone, shows good Italian 20thC art.

Bookshops There are bookshops all over town, but conveniently in the Galleria Vittorio Emanuele (*Garzanti*, *Rizzoli*), Via Manzoni (*Feltrinelli*) and Corso Vittorio Emanuele (*Mondadori*). *The American Bookstore* is opposite the Castello Sforzesco and *The English Bookshop* is at Via Mascheroni 12.

Fashion Among the famous names in Italian fashion (for women) in the Via Montenapoleone area are *Giorgio Armani* (Via Sant'Andrea), *Laura Biagiotti* (Via Borgospesso), *Gianfranco Ferrè*, *Krizia* and *Gianni Versace* (Via della Spiga), *Mila Schön* and *Missoni* (Via Montenapoleone) and *Valentino* (Via Santo Spirito).

Food Gourmets will enjoy the stores in Via San Marco, Via Spadari (*Peck*, with a restaurant in Via Victor Hugo) and Via Speronari. The irresistible *Salumaio di Montenapoleone*, Via Montenapoleone 12, also has mouth-watering window displays.

Furniture The best modern furniture showrooms are between the Brera and Piazza San Babila, in Via Borgogna, Via Durini and Via Manzoni.

Jewellery The most famous names are in Via Montenapoleone: *Buccellati*, *Calderoni*, *Faraone* and others. On Via Manzoni *Gioelli di Burma* makes copies of classic jewellery.

Leather goods The big names are *Nazareno Gabrielli*, *Gucci*, *Trussardi* and *Valextra* in the Via Montenapoleone and Corso Vittorio Emanuele areas. Some of the best shoe shops (*Beltrami*, *Ferragamo*, *Fratelli Rossetti*, *Tanino Crisci*) are on the Via Montenapoleone.

Menswear Famous names in Italian menswear are *Armani*, via Sant'Andrea 9, and *Ermenegildo Zegna*, Via Verri 3. Italians buy English-style clothing from *Bardelli*, Corso Magenta 13; and *Brigatti*, with shops in Corso Venezia and Galleria Vittorio Emanuele, is famous for classic sportswear. Tailors include *Tindaro de Luca*, Via Durini 23 ☎ 794394. *Truzzi*, Corso Matteotti 1, is the smartest shirt-maker. *Cravatti Nazionali*, Via San Pietro all' Orto, has a vast range of ties and *Lorenz*, Via Napoleone 12, sells masculine accessories made from horn, leather and other natural materials.

Pasticcerie The best confectionery and pastry shops are *Galli*, Corso Porta Romana 2 (for *marrons glacés*), *Marchesi*, Via Santa Maria alla Porta 13, and *Taveggia*, Via V. di Modrone 2. *Cova*, Via Montenapoleone 8, and *Sant'Ambroeus*, Corso Matteotti 7, have prettily packaged chocolates.

Wine At the atmospheric old *Taverna Moriggi*, Via Morigi 8 ☎ 807752, you can buy and taste fine wines with salami and cheese. *N'Ombra de Vin*, Via San Marco 2 ☎ 6552746, is another good wine merchant.

Sightseeing

Although not primarily a tourist city, Milan has important museums and art collections and some fine churches. Top priority for those with little time is Leonardo da Vinci's *Last Supper*, in the refectory of the church of Santa Maria delle Grazie (about 15mins by taxi from the Piazza del Duomo).

Castello Sforzesco The castle of the Sforza dynasty houses the *Civico Museo d'Arte Antica*. Lombard painting and sculpture, furniture and tapestries, musical instruments, ivories, glass and ceramics, mainly from the Renaissance and later, and Michelangelo's last work, the Rondanini Pietà. *Pza Castello. Open Tue–Sun, 9.30–12.15, 2.30–5.30.*

Duomo Vast, ornate Gothic cathedral begun in 1386 (the façade was completed only in 1809). Splendid views from the roof (elevator). *Pza Duomo.*

Museo Poldi Pezzoli Charming city collection, with paintings (by Bellini, Botticelli, Guardi, Pollaiuolo), glass, ceramics, Persian rugs, clocks, bronzes and other treasures. *Via Manzoni 12. Open Tue–Sat, 9.30–12.30, 2.30–5.30 or 6 (Thu, 9–11pm); Sun, 9.30–12.30.*

Pinacoteca Ambrosiana Old Master collection of Cardinal Federico Borromeo, with rooms devoted to Leonardo da Vinci and his followers and to Venetian and Dutch art. Fine paintings by Titian and Caravaggio. *Pza Pio XI 2. Open Sun–Fri, 9.30–5.*

Pinacoteca di Brera One of the world's greatest art collections with many Italian masterpieces. *Via Brera 28. Open Tue–Thu, 9–5.30; Fri, Sat, 9–1.30; Sun, 9–12.30.*

Santa Maria delle Grazie Renaissance church with a dome by Bramante and the refectory where in 1495 Leonardo painted the *Last Supper. Pza Santa Maria delle Grazie. Refectory open Tue–Sat, 9–1.30, 2–6.30; Sun, 9–3.*

Other museums include the *Museo alla Scala*, Pza della Scala, with opera memorabilia, the *Museo Nazionale della Scienza e della Tecnica*, Via San

Vittore 21, with models by Leonardo, and the *Civico Museo d'Arte Contemporanea*, an expanding collection of modern art in the Palazzo Reale.

Romanesque churches include the 9thC *Sant'Ambrogio*, a superb example of the style, and *Sant'Eustorgio*, with the fine Renaissance Portinari chapel.

Guided tours

Basic guided tours of the city by bus leave from Piazza Duomo.

The Stock Exchange can be visited on weekday mornings: arrangements by the *Comitato Direttivo Agenti di Cambio di Milano*, Pza degli Affari 6 ☎ 85344632.

Out of town

A number of interesting smaller cities are within easy reach, *Bergamo* being the most appealing and nearest (see *Other Cities*). About 30km/18.5 miles to the south is the famous *Certosa di Pavia*, an ornate Renaissance monastery.

Lake Como is the nearest of the major Italian Lakes, although traffic is bad at weekends and *Lake Maggiore* (with resort accommodation at Stresa) may be more easily accessible. *Lago d'Orta* is one of the most charming lakes and less visited than its larger neighbours. Day trips to the Lombard Lakes (bus and boat) depart daily Apr–Oct from Piazza Castello or the Stazione Centrale. *Bellagio*, on a promotory between Lake Como and Lake Lecco, is a pleasant weekend resort with spectacular scenery.

Spectator sports

Soccer is the most popular spectator sport, followed by "basket," of which the Italians are European champions.

Horseracing Racing and trotting at *Ippodromo di San Siro* ☎ 4084350.

Motor racing The Grand Prix circuit at Monza is 15km/10 miles from the centre of Milan ☎ (039) 22366.

Soccer Milan and Inter play on Sundays on the western outskirts at the *Stadio San Siro*, Via Piccolomini 5 ☎ 4077279 or 4031235.

Keeping fit

The Milanese are becoming fanatical about keeping fit. The best municipal sports centre (with gyms, tennis courts, pools, skating rinks and more) is the SAINI, Via Corelli 136.

Fitness centres American Contourella at Via Montenapoleone 10 ☎ 705290 and Pza della Repubblica 1a ☎ 6552728 (aerobics, body-building, yoga, swimming). *Club Francesco Conti*, Via Cerva 4 ☎ 700141, with several branches in other districts of the city, accepts membership by the month.

Golf Country Club Barlassina, Birago di Camnago ☎ (0362) 560621, and *Golf Club Milano*, Parco di Monza ☎ (039) 303081, are the nearest full golf courses (green fees required). *Country Club Carimate* ☎ (031) 790226 (membership of another club required) is on the Como road.

Jogging The *Giardini Pubblici*, an English-style park, and the *Parco Sempione* are the most central parks.

Riding Contact *Associazione Nazionale Turismo Equestre*, Via Piranesi 44b ☎ 7384615 for information.

Squash Club Milano, Via Piranesi 9 ☎ 7382437 (entry fee required); *Giambellino Squash Club*, Via Giambellino 5 ☎ 4225979.

Local resources

Business services

Executive Service, Via Vincenzo Monti 8 ☎ 5456331, provides fully-equipped offices with multilingual secretaries, photocopiers, telex, fax and meeting rooms. *International Business Centre*, Corso Europa 12 ☎ 656093, has offices for rent.

Photocopying and printing There are copy shops all over Milan. *Secretarial* MGR, Pza S. Ambrogio 16 ☎ 809621, and CTI, Via Palestrina 31 ☎ 719244, offer typing in several languages. MGR also organizes conferences.

Translation Language Consulting, Via Lanzone 6 ☎ 8057846; *Cooperativa Traduttori Interpreti*, Via Don Gnocchi 19 ☎ 4044826; *Associazione Italiana Traduttori ed Interpreti* ☎ 48193195.

Communications

Local delivery Mototaxi ☎ 5434, *Pony Express* ☎ 5493.
Long-distance delivery Airborne Express ☎ 5064946, *DHL International* ☎ 5080, *ITK* ☎ 3072.
Post office Main office: Via Cordusio 4 ☎ 875452, open 8.15–7.40 and to midnight for some services.
Telex and fax Both are available at the 24hr telegraph office of the main post office.

Conference/exhibition centres

The vast *Centro Congressi Milanofiori*, 20090, Milanofiori ☎ 824791, has 9 meeting rooms for up to 2,500 people. The *Fiera di Milano*, Largo Domodossola 1, 20145 ☎ 49971, has meeting rooms for up to 500 people and is the venue for the April industrial and consumer goods fair, and for specialized international exhibitions including several for fashion.

Camera di Commercio, Industria, Artigianato e Agricoltura di Milano, Via Meravigli 9b ☎ 85151, and the *Centro Meravigli*, Via G. Negri 8 ☎ 8693520 (capacity up to 200 people), are central. The central *Palazzo Acerbi*, Corso Porto Romana 3, and *Palazzo delle Stelline*, Corso Magenta 61 ☎ 4818503, provide historic venues (capacity up to 120 and 250 respectively). *Castello di Macconago*, on the outskirts of the city at Via Macconago 38 ☎ 5694819, can accommodate up to 80 participants and is also available for receptions.

Emergencies

Bureaus de change At Linate and Malpensa airports and major stations. Open normal office hours are *Cambio Milano*, Pza Affari ☎ 8053927, *Cambival*, Via Cantù 3 ☎ 864101, *Urgnani*, Via Cordusio 2 ☎ 807490.
Hospitals Ambulance ☎ 7733, Red Cross ☎ 3883, dental assistance (9am–noon) *Odontomil*, Pza Loreto ☎ 2829808. *Fatebenefratelli*, Corsa Porta Nuova 23 ☎ 63631, has a 24hr first aid service. *Policlinico*, Via Francesco Sforza 35 ☎ 5511655.

Pharmacies *Ambreck*, Via Stradivari 1
☎ 209401, *Bracco*, Via Boccaccio 26
☎ 4695281,*Ferrarini*,Pza V. Giornate 6
☎ 5451471, and *Formaggia*, Corso
Buenos Aires 4 ☎ 203320, are open
24hrs. The *Italo-English Chemist's
Shop*, Corso Europa 18 ☎ 701828, is
open during shop hours. The
pharmacy in the departures hall at the
Stazione Centrale is open 8.30–12.30,
3.30–7.30 with an emergency night
service bell.
Police *Questura*: Via Fatebenefratelli
11 ☎ 62261; city police emergencies
77271 (*Vigili urbani*).

Information sources
Business information *Camera di
Commercio*, Via Meravigli 9b, 20123
☎ 875109; *Assistenza e documentazione
operatori esteri*, Via Ansperto 5
☎ 85155248 or 85155212 (help and
information for foreign
entrepreneurs). The *British Chamber
of Commerce for Italy*, Via Agnello 8,
20121 ☎ 877798, offers research and
business facilities to members, who
are not necessarily British.
Local media Milan publishes the

Corriere della Sera (Via Solferino), a
national heavyweight (see *The business
media*) and *La Repubblica* has editorial
offices in Milan. *Il Sole-24 Ore* is a
prestigious business daily read by
entrepreneurs and professionals,
Milano Finanza a weekly international
digest of finance, economy and
politics. *Panorama*, published by
Mondadori, is a Milanese *Time* or
Newsweek. The major publishing
group Rusconi publishes a magazine
called *GenteMoney*. There are three
major private TV networks; Canale 5,
Italia 1 and Retequattro. On *Tele
Montecarlo* the previous night's CBS
news is broadcast at 7.30 and 8am.
Tourist information The main office
is at Via Marconi 1 ☎ 809662 (open
9.45–12.30, 1.30–6), with branches in
the Stazione Centrale and at Linate
airport.

Thank-yous
Confectionery *Cova*, Via
Montenapoleone 8.
Florist *Radaelli*, Via Manzoni 16
☎ 702876.
Gifts see *Shopping*.

OTHER CITIES

BERGAMO *codes* zip 24100 ☎ 035
In this city of some 120,000
inhabitants the busy Città Bassa
(lower town) is a lively commercial
and industrial centre while the Città
Alta (upper town) is the unspoilt old
city. The building trade accounts for
the largest portion of Bergamo's
economy, followed by engineering –
including ironworks, textile
machinery and electrical equipment –
and the textile industry. Names
familiar to the trade and to many
consumers are Dalmine (steel piping),
Legler (one of the major European
producers of denim and velvet),
Radici (drapery and upholstery) and
Italcementi (cement). At Sarnico on
the shores of Lake Iseo are the
boatyards of Riva, manufacturers of
motorboats. The province of Bergamo
boasts several well-known mineral

springs where bottling plants have
been set up; the most important, San
Pellegrino, has achieved international
fame. There are three local banks as
well as branches of leading Italian
banks. Bergamo airport has twice-
daily flights to Rome. It also handles
some holiday charter traffic.

Hotels and restaurants
Excelsior San Marco, Pza della
Repubblica 6 ☎ 232132, is the most
comfortable central hotel; runners-up
are the *Arli*, Largo Porta Nuova 12
☎ 222014, and *Cappello d'Oro*, Vle
P.Giovanni XXIII 12 ☎ 242606. The
newish *Città dei Mille*, Via Autostrada
3c ☎ 221010, is handy for an
overnight stop and the *Cristallo
Palace*, Via Betti Ambiveri 35
☎ 311211, on the ring road, is
comfortable, if not very convenient.

Excelsior San Marco's restaurant is run by Tino Fontana (of Tino Fontana, New York), but competition is stiff and the Città Alta is the favourite venue for business meals. *Il Pianone*, Via per Castagneta ☏ 216016, up on the hills, has a panoramic view over the valley. *Gourmet*, Via San Vigilio 1 ☏ 256110 (a halfway house on the way up to San Vigilio), and the *Agnello d'Oro*, Via Gombito 22 ☏ 249883 (in the heart of the old town), both offer good cooking, and also have simple accommodation. *La Fontana* ☏ 220648, right in Piazza Vecchia in the heart of the old town, affords the perfect setting for a special treat after hours. In one of the older streets of the lower town, award-winning *Dell'Angelo*, Borgo Santa Caterina 55 ☏ 237103, is worth a visit.

Relaxation
The lovely walled upper town is reached by funicular or a scenic route. Behind the *Piazza Vecchia* are the *cathedral*, the ornate *Colleoni chapel* (frescoes by Tiepolo) and the church of *Santa Maria Maggiore*. In the lower town the *Accademia Carrara* has an important collection of 15th-18thC Lombard and Venetian painting and sculptures by Manzù.

Information sources
Camera di Commercio, Largo Belotti 16 ☏ 383111; *Unione degli Industriali*, Via Camozzi 70 ☏ 236046; *Consorzio Bergamo Export*, Via Zilioli 2 ☏ 216194 or 237818.
Tourist information, Vicolo Aquila Nera ☏ 232730 (open daily, 9–1, 3–6) and Vle Vittorio Emanuele 20 ☏ 210204 (open daily, 9–1, 3–6).

BRESCIA *codes* zip 25100 ☏ 030
Brescia has a spacious centre where the old Venetian-style Piazza Loggia exists alongside the modern Piazza Vittoria. But it is the sprawling development beyond the old city walls that makes this the second largest town in Lombardy with a population of nearly 200,000. It has a pugnacious

tradition and has earned for itself the nickname *leonessa d'Italia*.

During the Renaissance Brescia was renowned for fine armour, and firearms are still produced at Gardone Val Trompia (the famous Beretta pistols are now supplied to the US army and FBI). The steel industry is based in Brescia itself (Lucchini) and at Odolo and Vobarno. Light alloys are manufactured at Chiari, Rovato and at Lumezzane (where firms specializing in bathroom fittings include Bonomi, Gnutti and Teorama). At Verolanuova, Ocean makes refrigeration machinery. Footwear and knitwear is made at Manerbio and Montechiari. Chemicals, foodstuffs and textiles are also manufactured and there is marble quarrying at Botticino.

Hotels and restaurants
The *Vittoria*, Via delle X Giornate 20 ☏ 280061, is the only central and luxurious hotel. The best restaurant is *La Sosta*, Via San Martino della Battaglia 20 ☏ 295603; just outside the town, and with superb views from its park, is *Castello Malvezzi*, Via Colle Giuseppe 1 ☏ 2004224.
Out of town There are comfortable hotels with lake views and pools at Sirmione, 40km/25 miles east: *Grand Hotel Terme*, Vle Marconi 1 ☏ 916261 (closed in winter), and *Villa Cortine*, Via Grotte 12 ☏ 916021 (used for business entertaining).

Relaxation
The *Piazza della Loggia* and the *Piazza Duomo* are lovely old squares at the heart of the town. The *Pinacoteca* and many of the churches contain paintings of the Brescian School and the *Roman museum* and *Museum of Christian art* are worth visiting. *Lake Garda* and *Lake Iseo* merit an excursion; and see the villa of the poet Catullus at *Sirmione*.

Information sources
Camera di Commercio, Via Einaudi 23 ☏ 45061; *Brixia Industries Consortium*, Via V. Emanuele II 60 ☏ 294054.

Tourist information, Corso Zanardelli 34
☎ 43418 and 45052, open Mon–Fri,
9–12, 3–6.30; Sat, 9–12.

COMO *codes* zip 22100 ☎ 031
A major centre of silk production
since the 12th century, Como
produces 80% of Italy's silk fabrics
and exports more finished silk than
any other centre in the world. There
are over 400 factories in and around
the town: the giants are Canepa, Etro,
Ratti, Mantera and Stucchi. The
engineering, textile (Meccanotessile)
and service sectors are also developed.
   In the province, Erba and Lecco are
known for scissor and knife
manufacture, and 30,000 Guzzi
motorcycles a year are made at
Mandello del Lario. Cantù, towards
Milan, is known for furniture
manufacture. Hams and sausages are
processed by Vismara at Casatenovo
and by Fumagalli at Tavernerio.

Hotels and restaurants
In the centre of Como are the
Barchetta Excelsior, Pza Cavour 1
☎ 266531, and *Metropole Suisse*, Pza
Cavour 19 ☎ 269444. The best
restaurant for business entertaining is
Sant'Anna, Via Filippo Turati 3
☎ 505266; also try *Imbarcadero*, Pza
Cavour 20 ☎ 277341. At Cernobbio
(5km/3 miles north) is the *Grand Villa
d'Este* ☎ 511471, a supremely
luxurious hotel in parkland
overlooking the lake and golf course;
there are indoor and outdoor pools
and 8 tennis courts. The Ideacomo
fabric fair is held here twice a year.

Relaxation
Como has a fine late-Gothic *Duomo*.
There are frequent boat trips around
the lake, known for its natural beauty,
its villas and the resort of *Bellagio*.

Information sources
Camera di Commercio, Via Parini 16
☎ 256111; *Comoexport*, Via Volta 81
☎ 273498.
Tourist information, Pza Cavour 17
☎ 262091 and at the station
☎ 267214, open daily, 9–12.30, 2.30–6.

CREMONA *codes* zip 26100 ☎ 0372
Agriculture (cattle) and food
production are the chief occupations
here; major firms include Pietro
Negroni (hams), Auricchio (cheese)
and Sperlari (preserves including the
Mostarda di Cremona chutney). Steel
is produced by Arvedi. Birthplace of
Stradivarius, Cremona is still famous
for the manufacture of stringed
instruments. The population of the
town is about 77,000.

Hotels and restaurants
The *Continental*, Pza della Libertà 26
☎ 434141, provides adequate
accommodation. *Ceresole*, Via Ceresole 4
☎ 23322, serves splendid modern and
regional cooking in elegant
surroundings.

Relaxation
The main sight is the romanesque
Duomo, with the tallest *campanile* in
Italy, called the *Torrazzo*, and frescoes
by Pordenone. Visit the *Museo
Stradivariano* and *Palazzo Comunale*.

Information sources
Camera di Commercio, Pza Cavour 5
☎ 28301.
Tourist information, Pza del Comune 5
☎ 23233, open Mon–Sat, 9–12.30,
2.30–6.30; Sun, 9–12.

MANTUA (Mantova)
codes zip 46100 ☎ 0376
Mantua is a provincial market town,
with a population of over 56,000, now
becoming industrialized; Belleli
produces oil rigs and other large
installations, Marcegaglia steel
products and Lubiam and
Cornegliano make clothing. In the
province, the knitwear sector is
developing and Castel Goffredo is
known for hosiery manufacture.

Hotels and restaurants
San Lorenzo, Pza Concordia 14
☎ 327153, is a comfortable traditional
hotel. *Rechigi*, Via Calvi 30
☎ 320781, is more modern and also
central. For business entertaining
choose *Aquila Nigra*, Vicolo Bonacolsi 4

☎ 350651, or *Il Cigno*, Pza d'Arco 1 ☎ 327101 both in fine old buildings.

Relaxation
Allow time for the 2hr guided tour of the *Ducal Palace*, where the Gonzaga family – portrayed by Mantegna in the *Camera degli Sposi* – held one of the most brilliant Renaissance courts in Europe. The church of *Sant'Andrea* and the eccentric *Palazzo del Tè* are significant architecturally.

Information sources
Camera di Commercio, Via Pietro Fortunato Calvi 28 ☎ 322371.
Tourist information, Pza Mantegna 6 ☎ 321601 and 350681, open daily, 9–12.30, 3–6.30.

PAVIA *codes* zip 27100 ☎ 0382
This old university town has a growing service sector. Industries include mechanical engineering (Necchi), chemicals and clothing, especially furs (Annabella). It has a population of over 82,000.
   The province is known for shoemaking, notably at Vigevano (where there is also Fiscagomma, making machinery). Frugone & Preve, at Robbio, is the national market leader in rice. At Abbiategrasso is BCS.

Hotels and restaurants
The *Palace*, Via della Libertà 89 ☎ 27441, is the best hotel and has a good restaurant (La Serra). For a gastronomic treat, however, visit *Antica Osteria del Ponte* at Cassinetta di Lugagnano (35km/22 miles northeast) ☎ (02) 9420034.

Relaxation
The *Certosa di Pavia* monastery, a masterpiece of Lombard romanesque architecture, is 10km/6 miles north of Pavia. *Vigevano* has a magnificent Renaissance square, probably designed by Leonardo da Vinci.

Information sources
Camera di Commercio, Via Mentana 27 ☎ 3931.

Tourist information, Corso Garibaldi 1 ☎ 27238 and 22156, open Mon–Fri, 9–12.30, 2.30–6.

VARESE *codes* zip 21100 ☎ 0332
Varese competes with Modena as the city with the highest per capita income in Italy and is an important centre for exports. Leather goods, mechanized domestic appliances, garments and textiles are manufactured locally. Important companies include Calzurificio di Varese for shoes (factories at Tradate), IRE (formerly Philips) and Cantoni (at Castellanza) for cotton fabrics. Chemicals (Mazzuchelli) and electronics (Gemini, Delta, Orvel) are also important. Cagiva motorcycles provide strong European (and US) competition for the Japanese. Aermacchi makes military aircraft and Agusta (helicopters) is at Sammarate. The EC's atomic research centre, CERN, is at Ispra.
   Busto Arsizio and Gallarate are particularly known for cotton manufacture ("the Italian Manchester"); also here are Brancotosi (engineering), Cartiere Sottrici (paper) and Bandera (plastics machinery). At Saronno are Ilva and Lazzaroni (biscuits) and CIBA-Geigy.

Hotels and restaurants
In town, *City*, Via Medaglie d'Oro 35 ☎ 281304, is the best hotel and *Centenate*, Via Centenate 15 ☎ 310036, and *Lago Maggiore*, Via Carrobbio 19 ☎ 231183, the best restaurants. Good restaurants on Lago di Varese include *Al Passatore*, Lungolago Calcinate 30 ☎ 310318.

Relaxation
Climb the *Sacro Monte*, a pilgrimage hill, or visit *Lake Como* or *Lake Maggiore*.

Information sources
Camera di Commercio, Pza Monte Grappa 5 ☎ 284577.
Tourist information, Pza Monte Grappa 5 ☎ 283604, open Mon–Fri, 8.30–12.30, 2.30–6.30; Sat, 9–12.

LIGURIA

This small region forms a narrow arc around the Gulf of Genoa, about 250km/155 miles long and rarely over 30km/20 miles wide. It is divided into the Riviera di Ponente (from the French border to Genoa) and the Riviera di Levante, east of Genoa. The hinterland is mountainous and wooded; most of the population is crowded into the towns and resorts along the coast where employment is in industry, commerce, tourism and port-related activities such as transport and insurance.

The main industries, concentrated around the ports of Genoa, La Spezia, Imperia and Savona, are steel, engineering, metallurgy and petrochemicals, with several major oil refineries. Shipbuilding has declined in recent years, and the industry concentrates more on pleasure craft, notably yachtbuilding at Varazze (Baglietto). Slate quarrying is important locally. At Imperia, Agnesi has the most advanced pasta factory in the country and Sasso is an important olive oil producer. The mild climate of the Italian Riviera favours tourism and floriculture, which is based at San Remo.

GENOA (Genova)   *City codes* zip 16100 ☎ 010

The largest port in Italy with a population of 727,500, Genoa has a proud maritime history, although it has recently become the weak link in Italy's industrial triangle. But with the 500th anniversary of Christopher Columbus's discovery of the New World in 1492 in sight, the city is planning ambitiously for reindustrialization and urban renewal. Nearing completion are two commercial developments: the gleaming Corte Lambruschini for offices, banks, a convention centre, theatre and hotel plus shops and underground parking, and San Benigno at Sampierdarena.

Plans for 1992 include the building of an 8km/5mile subway for the Ponente (west) area and the complete restructuring of the port. There will be improved passenger terminals with airport-like facilities and a small tourist harbour with boats for recreation. The new port at Voltri will have the main container terminals for ocean-going vessels. Other projects also well under way include the rebuilding, in post-modernist style, of the historic Carlo Felice opera house; the restoration of the Ducal Palace to become a "Palace of Culture"; and the reorganization of the Palazzo Spinola as the National Gallery of Liguria.

The main companies based in Genoa are Ansaldo, Italsider (steel, with some 47,000 employees), Piaggio, Italimpianti and Elsag (electronics, radar). Marconi's Italian headquarters are here. IRI and the chief political parties are promoting a Science Park at Cornigliano; this would alleviate the unemployment caused by the threatened closure of the Italsider production centre there.

Arriving

National and international connections by road are good; the autostrada is carried over the city on stilts and exits are being improved. High-speed Eurocity trains link Genoa with the north and there are scheduled air services from some European cities.

Cristoforo Colombo airport

This small airport 7km/4 miles west of the city centre handles about 2m passengers a year. It copes with Ligurian tourist traffic in summer and flights diverted from the north because of fog in winter. London (Gatwick), Paris, Rome (several flights daily) and major Italian, German and Swiss cities are served.

Arrivals and departures share most facilities, including the bank (open Mon–Sat, 8–7.15, Sun am; 24hr automatic foreign currency changing machine), tourist office, a smart restaurant (useful for local business entertaining), a VIP lounge on the departures floor, and a superior duty-free shop. Inquiries: passengers ☎ 2690571, cargo ☎ 2690565; airport information ☎ 26901.

City link The journey into town takes 20–25mins, 35–40mins in rush hour or by bus (useful for some hotels).
Taxi There are usually plenty of cabs.
Car rental The main car rental firms have desks in the arrivals hall.
Bus The *Volabus* goes to and from Piazza della Vittoria, past Stazione Principe and Piazza De Ferrari, approximately hourly to coincide with flights. Tickets are bought on the bus.
Helicopter Aeromast ☎ 363956 and *Alitaxi* ☎ 603767 (executive jets and helicopters) have offices at the airport.

Railway stations

As the focus of the city has shifted eastwards, Stazione Brignole is now more central than the former main station, Stazione Principe. Most important services (for example the TEE) stop at both stations. The journey to Rome takes 5¼hrs by *rapido* (flight time 1hr) but the sleeper service is convenient. Facilities, inside and just outside, include car rental booths, banks, post office, restaurant. Inquiries ☎ 586350 (Brignole) ☎ 262455 (Principe).

Getting around

Central Genoa is compact and walking is often the easiest way to get around, particularly in the old part of town where streets are too narrow for vehicles. Street numbering is confusing: red numbers (indicated by an "r" in the address) are for commercial buildings and black numbers for the rest.

The linear layout of Genoa means that visits to the port, industrial and residential areas or resorts may require quite long journeys. The bus system is simple and efficient. Elevators and funiculars from Via Balbi, Largo Zecca and Piazza Portello serve the residential hill.
Taxis There are marked ranks in the main squares; for reservations ☎ 2696. A small tip is in order.
Driving Not recommended because of a confusing road system.
Walking The area around Piazza Caricamento and Via Gramsci is dangerous after dark.
Bus Boccadasse (15mins, Nos 31 or 42) and Nervi (No. 17r) are easy by bus. The main terminal is in Piazza De Ferrari.
Train There are stations at Voltri, Pra, Pegli, Sestri Ponente, Cornigliano and Sampierdarena to the west (*ponente*) and Sturla, Quarto dei Mille and Nervi to the east (*levante*). The Stazione Marittime serves the docks.

Area by area

Greater Genoa extends from Voltri to Nervi, about 35km/22 miles, but the centre is small and clearly defined. At its heart is the medieval town, a maze of steep narrow lanes or *caruggi*, bordered to the north by the palaces of Via Balbi and Via Garibaldi (many now banks and offices), to the south by the raucous, run-down docks and red-light district. To the southeast is the spacious business area; its main axis, the arcaded Via XX Settembre, runs from stately Piazza De Ferrari to downtown Piazza della Vittoria, with triumphal arch, grandiose station arcades and the Corte Lambruschini. Boulevards lined with car showrooms lead to the Fiera site, scene of the world's biggest annual boat show in late October.

The smartest, most conservative residential areas are Castelletto and Righi in the hills, where the Genoese aristocracy have some grand old villas. Albaro to the east, reaching to the unspoilt fishing village of Boccadasse, is also favoured. Poor areas are Marassi and Staglieno.

To the west the sprawling docks extend to Sampierdarena, Cornigliano and Sestri Ponente. Beyond are industrial Pegli and Voltri.

East of Boccadasse are Sturla (also a fishing village) and the poorer seaside towns of Quarto dei Mille and Quinto. Nervi, both residential and a resort, is about 20mins drive away.

The suburbs
The harbour towns to the east are places to dine or stay in or escape to. Hotels cater for international conventions as well as tourism. On the Portofino peninsula the charming fishing villages of Portofino and Santa Margherita have long been chic resorts; Camogli is a more genuine fishing port, Rapallo a sedate resort.

Hotels
The business visitor can stay in the centre or commute from the seaside resorts of Nervi or Santa Margherita, 30mins by car from the centre; but the Portofino peninsula resorts should be avoided during the holiday season. For major fairs it is essential to make reservations months ahead. The convenient and pleasant Albaro/Boccadasse area is an alternative, but accommodation here is not of a high standard.

All central hotels listed offer currency exchange, TVs and IDD telephones in the bedrooms and room service, but not always 24hr.

Bristol *[L]//*
Via XX Settembre 35, 16121
☎ *592541* ⊠ *286550 fax 592541 • AE DC MC V • 130 rooms, 5 suites, 1 bar*
A grand old central hotel, with a constant flow of business visitors, many attending conferences or sales promotions. Bedrooms are mostly very large and high-ceilinged, with antique or old furniture; about 50 have been tastefully modernized with gleaming bathrooms.

Colombia *[L]////*
Via Balbi 40, 16126 ☎ *261841* ⊠ *270423 fax 252410 • CIGA • AE DC MC V • 162 rooms, 10 suites, 1 restaurant, 1 bar*
The best hotel in Genoa is not in the best location but you can be assured of VIP treatment and the most prestigious venue for conferences. Bedrooms are spacious and traditional; those on the back are quietest. The restaurant is a safe haven for a business meal. Garage service, hairdresser • 4 meeting rooms (capacity up to 770).

Metropoli *[L]*
Pza Fontane Marose, 16123 ☎ *203524 fax 281816 • AE DC MC V • 48 rooms, 1 bar*
A simple but pleasant hotel offering good value in a central position; guests include bankers, sales reps, lawyers and consular staff. There are two comfortable lounges near the bar. Bedrooms are more basic (some with shower only); ask for a room on the interior courtyard.

OTHER HOTELS
Britannia *[L]/ Via Balbi 38, 16126* ☎ *26991* ⊠ *275069 fax 262942 • AE MC DC V.* Modernized small hotel with quiet apartments and meeting rooms.
La Capannina *[L] Via Tito Speri 7, 16145* ☎ *363205 • AE MC V.* A down-at-heel, spartan but curiously charming little hotel at Boccadasse, with a basement restaurant.
City *[L]/ Via San Sebastiano 6, 16123* ☎ *592595* ⊠ *271686 fax 586301 • AE DC MC V.* Quiet, central hotel with adequate rooms and pleasant lobby.

Savoia Majestic _⌑/||_ _Via Arsenale di Terra 5, 16126_ ☎ _261641_ _TX_ _270426 fax 261883_ • _AE DC MC V._ Traditional hotel opposite the Colombia, but without the CIGA style, used for conferences and by Italsider visitors.

Out of town

All the following have parks, pools and conference facilities: _Cenobio dei Dogi_ ☎ (0185) 770041 at Camogli (26km/16.5 miles); and the _Grand Miramare_ ☎ (0185) 287013 and _Imperial Palace_ ☎ (0185) 288991 at Santa Margherita (31km/19 miles). At Portofino (36km/22.5 miles) are the popular luxury _Splendido_ ☎ (0185) 269551 in a fine location; and the very expensive _Vetta_ ☎ (0185) 772281, often used for conferences. At Nervi (10km/6 miles east) is the _Astor_ ☎ 328325 which has a convention centre.

Restaurants

Several smart central restaurants are suitable for business entertaining. But it is more fun to eat seafood at Boccadasse. As well as fish, vegetables feature widely in Genoese cooking: in pies (_torta pasqualina_), fried in batter and combined with fish. Pasta dishes include _pansoti alla salsa di noci_ (with herbs, ricotta and walnut stuffing) and _trenette al pesto_ (with pinenuts, garlic and basil).

Aladino _⌑/||_
Via E. Vernazza 8 ☎ _566788_ • _closed Sun_ • _AE MC DC V_ • _reservations essential_
At the heart of the business area, a classic, comfortable establishment with a top-flight clientele of aristocrats and bankers. Favoured dishes include _cappon magro_ (fish and vegetable salad). Private rooms available.

Da Giacomo _⌑/|||_
Corso Italia 1 ☎ _369647_ • _closed Sun_ • _AE DC MC V_
Only the three crossed Michelin knives and forks on the awning give any exterior indication of its quality. But inside it is airy and sophisticated with food and service to match. Diners include big company bosses, insurance brokers and visitors to the nearby Fiera, particularly the boat show. Reserve a table outside for more informal meals or in the separate dining room for privacy.

Gran Gotto _⌑/||_
Via Fiume 11r ☎ _564344_ • _closed Sat L, Sun, 3 weeks Aug_ • _AE MC V_ • _formal dress_
A stylish modern restaurant (once a humble _osteria_) run by the two Bertola brothers. While Riccardo interprets and refines regional cuisine with flair, Sergio has a professional eye for the best wines. Those who choose _Stoccafisso alla Genovese_ from the fish on the menu are given a hand-painted ceramic plate.

Il Primopiano _⌑/||_
Via XX Settembre 36 ☎ _540284_ • _closed Sun_ • _AE DC MC V_
This formal but modern and welcoming upstairs restaurant has a reputation for business entertaining and is frequented by visiting politicians and senior professionals. Classic Genoese cooking plus fillet steak cooked seven different ways, and well-chosen wines.

Santachiara _⌑/||_
Via al Capo di Santa Chiara 69 ☎ _3770081_ • _closed Sun_ • _AE_
Overlooking the harbour at Boccadasse, this unpretentious-looking restaurant has a clientele of Genoese who appreciate fresh, simply cooked ingredients, mostly straight from the sea. Popular with people visiting Ansaldo or Piaggio and English working for Marconi. Inside the decor is chic and light.

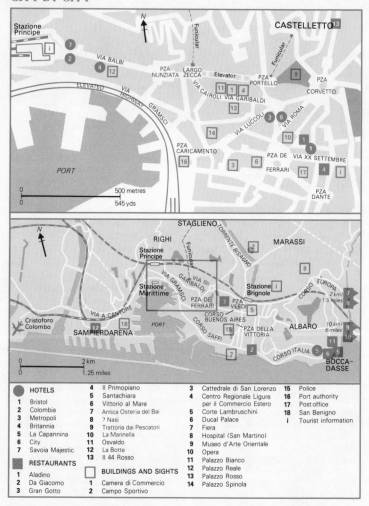

Map legend:

HOTELS

1 Bristol
2 Colombia
3 Metropoli
4 Britannia
5 La Capannina
6 City
7 Savoia Majestic

RESTAURANTS

1 Aladino
2 Da Giacomo
3 Gran Gotto
4 Il Primopiano
5 Santachiara
6 Vittorio al Mare
7 Antica Osteria del Bai
8 7 Nasi
9 Trattoria dai Pescatori
10 La Marinella
11 Osvaldo
12 La Botte
13 Il 44 Rosso

BUILDINGS AND SIGHTS

1 Camera di Commercio
2 Campo Sportivo
3 Cattedrale di San Lorenzo
4 Centro Regionale Ligure per il Commercio Estero
5 Corte Lambruschini
6 Ducal Palace
7 Fiera
8 Hospital (San Martino)
9 Museo d'Arte Orientale
10 Opera
11 Palazzo Bianco
12 Palazzo Reale
13 Palazzo Rosso
14 Palazzo Spinola
15 Police
16 Port authority
17 Post office
18 San Benigno
i Tourist information

Vittorio al Mare [L]////
Belvedere Firpo 1 ☎ *312872* • *closed Mon* • *AE DC MC V*
With its formal service and separate bar, Vittorio is appropriate for a serious business lunch. The cooking is classic local and international, with the emphasis on fish. Panoramic sea views.

OTHER RESTAURANTS

At Quarto dei Mille try *Antica Osteria del Bai*, Via Quarto 12 ☎ 387478, a famous *locale* in part of an old fort, or *7 Nasi*, Via Quarto 16 ☎ 337357, which has a good reputation locally. At Nervi (10km/6 miles to the east), *Trattoria dai Pescatori*, Via Aldo Casotti 6r ☎ 326168, is typical and reliable, *La Marinella*, Passeggiata Anita Garibaldi 18 ☎ 321429, more refined. *Osvaldo*, Via Della Casa 2r ☎ 310004, at the heart of Boccadasse, is an elegant small trattoria with delicious food. *La Botte*, Pza Gustavo Modena 6r ☎ 413017, in Sampierdarena, serves good food in a rustic marine setting.

In the centre *Il 44 Rosso*, Via Palestro 44r ☎ 885647, a favourite with actors and opera singers, is open till 2am.

Out of town
Manuelina ☎ (0185) 74128 at Recco, 23km/14 miles to the east, is a superb seafood restaurant, popular for family Sunday lunches.

Bars and cafés
The Genoese like to meet in one of their nice old cafés. These include *Ballila* (famous for ice creams), Via Cesarea 111–121r, and *Caffè Mangini*, at the top of Via Roma. *Klainguti*, Pza Soziglia 98r, and *Romanengo*, Via Soziglia 74r, also serve aperitifs and snacks.

Entertainment
Genoa has quite a lively cultural scene. *Vivi Centro Storico Colombo '92* lists city events.
Opera, theatre, music During rebuilding (due to be completed in 1990) the Teatro Comunale Dell'Opera is at the *Teatro Margherita*, Via XX Settembre 33 ☎ 589329 ⓉⓍ 286354, which is also the main venue for classical concerts. Rock concerts are held at the *Palazzo dello Sport* ☎ 53911 or the *Fiera del Mare*.
Dance The July international ballet festival takes place in the park at Nervi; tickets from the Teatro Comunale Dell'Opera from late June, or on the day from *Teatro ai Parchi* after 8pm ☎ 323233.
Cinema For information ☎ 198.
Nightclubs The smartest nightspot is the *Carillon* ☎ (0185) 286721 at Paraggi near Santa Margherita.

Shopping
The chic boutiques are in Via Roma and Via XX Settembre. Behind the latter is the covered food market. Traffic-free Via Luccoli is lined with

little shops selling local crafts; just off it is the flea market at Piazza Lavagna. Antiques are in Via Garibaldi and Via Cairoli.

Local confectionery (candied fruits and marzipan) can be found at *Canepa*, Via della Maddalena 98–100r, and *Klainguti*, Pza Soziglia 98r. For smart yachting kit try *Lucarda*, Via Sottoripa 61.

Sightseeing
Cattedrale di San Lorenzo Gothic cathedral with black-and-white striped façade and treasury. *Pza San Lorenzo. Open Tue–Sat, 9.30–11.50, 2–5.*
Museo d'Arte Orientale Edoardo Chiossone Important collection of oriental (especially Japanese) art. *Villeta Dinegro, Via Martin Piaggio. Open Tue–Sat, 9–1.15, 3–6; Sun, 9.15–12.45.*
Palazzo Bianco Flemish art and the 17thC Genoese School which it influenced. *Via Garibaldi 11. Open Tue–Sat, 9–1, 3–6; Sun, 9.15–12.45.*
Palazzo Reale Decaying palace of the house of Savoy, rulers of Piedmont, with grand rooms and baroque paintings. *Via Balbi 10. Open daily, 9–1.30.*
Palazzo Rosso Beautifully displayed North Italian and Genoese paintings and portraits by Van Dyck. *Via Garibaldi 18. Open Tue–Sat, 9–1, 3–6; Sun, 9.15–12.45.*
Palazzo Spinola Fine frescoes, furniture and some outstanding paintings (Joos van Cleve, *Adoration of the Magi*). *Via di Pelliceria 1. Open Tue–Sat, 9–5; Sun, Mon 9–1.*

Spectator sports
The rival city soccer teams are Genoa and Sampdoria ("Samp"), who play at the *Campo Sportivo L. Ferraris*, Via de Pra ☎ 873059. Genoa hosts a regatta in the first week of June, even years.

Keeping fit
Nuovo Lido, Corso Italia 1 ☎ 303726, is a vast sports complex, with pools and 9 tennis courts.
Fitness centres Sun & Gym, ☎ 312230 (at the Nuovo Lido), for

gym, aerobics, sauna and massage.
Golf At Rapallo (28km/17 miles east)
☎ 50210 (also tennis) and at
Arenzano (9 holes; 28km/17 miles
west) ☎ 9111817.
Sailing The most famous of many
clubs is at Quarto dei Mille.
Swimming *Stadio del Nuoto*, Via De
Gasperi 39 ☎ 368409.
Tennis In Albaro at Via Campanella 4
☎ 313056, and in summer at the
tennis school at Via Ricci 3
☎ 317604; both welcome nonmembers.

Local resources

Business services
Centro Congressi Palffi, Via di Brera
2–19a ☎ 586964, organizes
conventions and provides offices and
translators. *Executive Service*, Pza
Marsala 4 ☎ 885858, provides offices
and multilingual secretarial services.
Photocopying and printing *Centro
copie*, Via Ruspoli 108g ☎ 581012.
Copycolor, Via Balbi 133 ☎ 206655.
Translation *AITI*, Pza Colombo 3
☎ 593056. *Filo d'Arianna*, Via Felice
Cavalotti 21 ☎ 3991390.

Communications
Local delivery *Mototaxi* ☎ 6003,
Rapid Service ☎ 585814. *Piana*
☎ 457370 delivers within Italy.
Long-distance delivery *DHL*
☎ 600831. *Executive Express*
☎ 885858.
Post office Via G. Boccardo 2
☎ 591762, open 8.15–8pm.
Telex and fax At the post office.

Conference/exhibition centres
The *Fiera*, Pzle J.F. Kennedy 1,
16129 ☎ 53911 TX 271424, is the
venue for international trade fairs
(including catering, advanced
manufacturing systems, electronic
equipment and food as well as the
boat show) and conferences, and has 3
pavilions and a Palazzo Congressi.
The *Corte Lambruschini* plans to instal
the most up-to-date conference
facilities by 1990 ☎ 541430. *Genova
Ricerche*, in the old monastery of
Sant'Andrea (near the airport), Via
dell'Acciaio 139 ☎ 608511, provides

meeting rooms and all services.
International conferences are held
at the Colombia Hotel (see *Hotels*) or
at the large hotels in nearby resorts,
notably Santa Margherita.

Emergencies
Bureaus de change At the Principe
and Brignole stations and 24hr
machine at the airport (and bank on
Sun am and holidays).
Hospitals Ambulance ☎ 595951.
Doctor, night and holidays ☎ 354022.
Ospedale San Martino, Vle Benedetto
XV 10 ☎ 35351.
Pharmacies *Ghersi*, Corso Buenos
Aires 74r ☎ 541661, and *Pescetto*, Via
Balbi 185r ☎ 261609, are closed
12.30–3.30 but open at night.
Police *Questura*: Via Diaz 2 ☎ 53661.

Information sources
Business information *Associazione
Industriali della Provincia di Genova*,
Via F. Romani 9 ☎ 53671 ☎ 5367574
(quantity experts). *Camera di
Commercio*, Via Garibaldi 4 ☎ 20941.
*Centro Regionale Ligure per il
Commercio Estero*, Via Garibaldi 3,
16124 ☎ 2094376. *World Trade
Center*, Via De Mezini 1, 16149
☎ 2423001. *Genova Ricerche*, Via
dell'Acciaio 139 ☎ 608511
(information on research and
development projects for the city).
*Ufficio Speciale Colombiane del
Comune di Genova*, Via Garibaldi 9,
12164 ☎ 20981 (projects for 1992).
Porto di Genova, Palazzo San Giorgio,
Via della Mercanzia, 16123 ☎ 26901
(the port authority).
Local media *Il Secolo XIX* is the
local daily newspaper and leans left of
centre.
Tourist information Via Porta degli
Archi 10/5, 16121 ☎ 541541
(entrance set back from south side of
street). Information offices at the
airport and stations are often shut.

Thank-yous
Confectionery *Pietro Romanengo fu
Stefano*, Via Soziglia 74r ☎ 297869.
Florist *Pittaluga*, Pza Portello 18
☎ 298787.

OTHER CITIES

LA SPEZIA *codes* zip 19100 ☎ 0187
A modern city (badly bombed in
World War II) with extensive naval
dockyards, a NATO base and a nuclear
energy research centre. It is rapidly
expanding as one of the biggest
European container ports, on a par
with Felixstowe or Hamburg. Major
employers are the various shipbuilders
and Oto Melara (armaments). Also
important are Sangiorgio (electrical
appliances) and Termomeccanica
(desalination machinery). Population
109,000.

Hotels and restaurants
The *Jolly*, Via XX Settembre 2
☎ 27200, is central, on the seafront.
Near the autostrada there is a good
modern business hotel, the *Residence*,
Via Tino 62 ☎ 504141. The best
restaurant for business entertaining in
town is *La Posta*, Via Don Minzoni
24 ☎ 34419.
But visitors often stay at Lerici
(10km/6 miles to the northeast), at the
Shelley ☎ 968204 or at Portovenere
(12km/7.5 miles southwest) at the
Royal Sporting ☎ 900326, open April
to October, with a park and pool. At
Portovenere *Da Iseo* ☎ 900610 is a
famous seafront trattoria, with
excellent food (closed in winter).
Conchiglia ☎ 967334 at Lerici is also
highly recommended. For an
important business lunch, or a
gastronomic treat, go to *Paracucchi*
☎ 64391 at Ameglia (16km/10miles
southeast), a favourite venue of Oto
Melara directors.

Relaxation
The *Museo Tecnico Navale* is worth a
visit. Just south of La Spezia are the
unspoilt fishing villages of the Cinque
Terre, best visited by train or on a
boat trip.

Information sources
Camera di Commercio, Via V.Veneto 28
☎ 546111.
Tourist information, Via Mazzini 47
☎ 36000, open daily, 7.30–1.30,
Sun–Tue, Thu, Fri, 5.30–6.30.

SAVONA *codes* zip 17100 ☎ 019
A port on the Riviera di Ponente,
with close links to Piedmont. In the
province the Montedison group has
several facilities. Vitrofil (St Gobain
group) at Vado Ligure, 3M Italia and
Vetrerie Italiana Vetri (the second
largest glass-maker in Italy) are
important.

Hotels and restaurants
Most visitors stay on the Riviera, at
nearby Spotorno or Finale Ligure (the
Punta Est ☎ 600612 is an attractive
converted villa) or farther afield at
Loano (*Garden Lido* ☎ 669666) or
Garlenda (where *La Meridiana* ☎
(0182) 580721 is luxurious). The
obvious town centre hotel is the
Riviera Suisse, Via Paleocapa 24
☎ 820683 (dine at *Sodano*, Pza della
Maddalena 9 ☎ 38446, in an old
palazzo, closed L). For a business
lunch take guests to *Al Cambusiere*
☎ 481663 or *Ai Pescatori de Gianni*
☎ 481200 in nearby Albissola Marina
or *Da Mosè* ☎ 991560 at Celle Ligure
(7km/4 miles).

Relaxation
The medieval part of town, around
the port, is interesting, with some fine
churches and palaces. There are
Genoese School paintings in the
Pinacoteca.

Information sources
Camera di Commercio, Via Quarda
Inferiore 16 ☎ 83141.
Tourist information, Via Paleocapa 59r
☎ 820522, open daily, 8.30–12.30.

THE VENETO AND FRIULI-VENEZIA GIULIA

A bastion of agricultural traditions and conservative, Christian Democrat values (there are several Catholic-run banks), the northeast has made striking economic progress in recent years and produces over 10% of Italian GDP. With a few significant exceptions, industry is characterized by small or medium-sized concerns producing consumer goods. Between the remote mountainous north (Belluno province) and the flood-prone south (Rovigo), the plains north of the Adige river are the richest area, with the highest population, best communications and most sites of artistic interest.

The mainland area around Venice, cultural and tourist focus of the area, is highly industrialized, notably at Mestre and Marghera. The Porto Marghera complex is one of the biggest in the country. Development will shortly engulf Treviso and Padua, creating a metropolitan area with a population of 1.5m.

Industry around Verona and Vicenza is connected with Milan (and the rest of Europe) rather than with Venice. In the valleys descending from the Pre-Alps hydroelectric power is used for textile factories and woollen mills. The Benetton casual fast-fashion chain and Stefanel are run from near Treviso. Wheat and sugar beet are produced on an industrial scale on the plains of the Po and the Adige. The Veneto also exports more wine than any other Italian region and has the highest DOC (quality controlled) production in the country.

Friuli-Venezia Giulia borders Austria and Yugoslavia and lies between the Alps and the Adriatic. The government is offering inducements to businesses setting up in the provinces of Trieste (capital of coastal Venezia Giulia) and Gorizia, and the area is becoming a focus of new technology and scientific research. Friuli, now virtually recovered from the devastation of the 1976 earthquake, is more agricultural (Ferruzzi has a vast farm at Torvicosa). Industry is concentrated around prosperous Pordenone (with Zanussi) and Udine. The area has benefited from the recent completion of the Udine-Tarvisio stretch of autostrada, connecting it to central Europe.

VENICE (Venezia)   City codes zip 30100 ☎ 041

Geographically and historically, Venice is unique. Built on an archipelago of islets and mudflats in a lagoon off the Adriatic coast, it has always owed much of its prosperity to the sea. Today it is Italy's fourth port by value of trade, and capital of the Veneto region; seven centuries ago it was the greatest maritime republic of Italy, dominating the Mediterranean and trade between Europe and the East.

In the city, the leisure industry and tourism now form the basis of the economy, employing over one half of the population of 400,000. Modern Venice also embraces industrial Mestre and Marghera on the mainland. During the 1920s and 1930s a petrochemical port and factory complex were set up at Marghera, and today its shipbuilding yards have a capacity

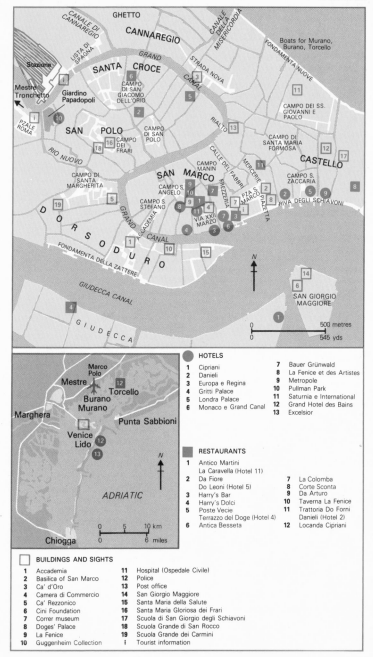

HOTELS

1 Cipriani
2 Danieli
3 Europa e Regina
4 Gritti Palace
5 Londra Palace
6 Monaco e Grand Canal
7 Bauer Grünwald
8 La Fenice et des Artistes
9 Metropole
10 Pullman Park
11 Saturnia e International
12 Grand Hotel des Bains
13 Excelsior

RESTAURANTS

1 Antico Martini
  La Caravella (Hotel 11)
2 Da Fiore
  Do Leoni (Hotel 5)
3 Harry's Bar
4 Harry's Dolci
5 Poste Vecie
  Terrazzo del Doge (Hotel 4)
6 Antica Besseta
7 La Colomba
8 Corte Sconta
9 Da Arturo
10 Taverna La Fenice
11 Trattoria Do Forni
  Danieli (Hotel 2)
12 Locanda Cipriani

BUILDINGS AND SIGHTS

1 Accademia
2 Basilica of San Marco
3 Ca' d'Oro
4 Camera di Commercio
5 Ca' Rezzonico
6 Cini Foundation
7 Correr museum
8 Doges' Palace
9 La Fenice
10 Guggenheim Collection
11 Hospital (Ospedale Civile)
12 Police
13 Post office
14 San Giorgio Maggiore
15 Santa Maria della Salute
16 Santa Maria Gloriosa dei Frari
17 Scuola di San Giorgio degli Schiavoni
18 Scuola Grande di San Rocco
19 Scuola Grande dei Carmini
i Tourist information

of 450,000 gross tonnage. Mestre and Marghera are important for metallurgy (companies such as Sava) and engineering as well as the mechanical and chemical industries.

Employment opportunities on the mainland, together with cheaper and newer housing, have prompted many native Venetians, particularly the younger generation, to leave the city, halving its population over the last 30 years. The industrial expansion has also caused serious pollution, with disastrous effects on the city's architecture; but the population decline is being halted by state subsidies for home restoration. Industrial pollution is being controlled and there are plans to develop the old docks at the Arsenale, and to build barriers against the high tides which sweep through the lagoon.

The hotel, conference and exhibition facilities of Venice provide a base from which to operate on the industrial mainland, and the city has many attractions for anyone doing business elsewhere in Italy with a day or two to spare. The city itself is not exclusively a tourist centre. Traditional Venetian handicrafts are still thriving: glass and glass-making on the island of Murano, lace-making on Burano, costume jewellery, ceramics and clothing. The Veneto teems with small and medium-sized enterprises manufacturing footwear, textile products, metals, mechanical and electrical goods, glass and glassware. Services employ significant numbers of people and large companies with their headquarters in Venice include CIGA hotels, COIN, the department store, and Supermercati, the supermarket chain.

Arriving

There are regular, though not always frequent, scheduled air services to Venice from all the major European and Italian cities. It is easily accessible by rail from Milan, Florence, Rome, Bologna and the cities of the Veneto. Through trains from Calais arrive during the summer and from Paris all year round. The A4 autostrada links Mestre (8km/5 miles northwest of the city) with Milan and with Trieste.

Marco Polo airport

For the amount of traffic it handles this mainland airport is small and ill-equipped. It is at its worst from Easter to the end of September when there is much charter traffic. Enlargement of the airport and its facilities is planned. Present facilities are concentrated in the departures hall and may be swamped with customers: currency exchange (open Mon–Sat, 10–12.30, 1.30–3.45), bank (open weekdays, 10.30–1, 2–3.30), telephone office, hotel reservation office for CIGA and AVA hotels, and one very busy snackbar. Inquiries ☎ 661111.

City link The airport is at Tessera, on the lagoon, 10km/6 miles north of Venice by boat. The most spectacular transfer to the city, and the most convenient if your hotel is in the San Marco area, is across the water. The quickest journey is by land-taxi or bus (about 12km/7.5 miles).

Watertaxi Fiendishly expensive private launches will drop you as near to your hotel as possible; journey time is about 20mins to the centre and the cost L100,000.

Water-launch A *motoscafi* service run by the Cooperativa San Marco from a landing stage near the airport terminal (tickets from the airport desk) costs about L12,000 and takes about 35mins to the Piazzetta by San Marco. You may have to take a waterbus from there to the stop nearest your hotel. Porters are expensive (there are fixed tariffs) and very rarely available, but you can make arrangements at the airport information office or call your hotel and ask for one to meet you.

Land-taxi Much cheaper than a water taxi but more expensive than the water-launch and not nearly as spectacular a ride. The drop-off point is Piazzale Roma, and the journey time about 15mins.

Car rental All the main car rental firms have desks at the airport but, since Venice has no roads, a car can only be used outside the city. There are parking facilities (at a price and sometimes full) at Piazzale Roma, opposite the station, and a short way from it in the open-air park on the island of Tronchetto, or on the mainland across the 4km/3 mile-long rail and road bridge. Waterbuses go from the mainland to Piazzale Roma (30mins) and from landing stages there to the rest of the city.

Bus All scheduled flights are met by ATVO buses but there are also public ACTV buses, which stop along the way, that run about every 30mins up to 11.30pm. Inquiries ☏ 5205530. Both services cost L4,000 and take 20–30mins to Piazzale Roma. The airport is also connected by bus to Marghera and Mestre.

Railway station
Santa Lucia station is in a modern streamlined building at the Piazzale Roma end of the Grand Canal. It is efficient and well-equipped. Apart from mainline trains from Milan (3hrs 30mins), Rome (7hrs) and Trieste there are direct services from Vienna, Munich, Belgrade and Paris. The luxury Venice-Simplon Orient-Express runs from March to October between London and Venice with stops at Paris and cities in Switzerland and Austria.

Station facilities include a bank and currency exchange (open daily, 7–10), a tourist office (with hotel reservations service), telephone office, large cafeteria and bar, and *albergo diurno*. Public waterbuses, journey time 20–40 mins to San Marco, stop outside the station. The taxi rank at Piazzale Roma is about a 3min walk. For railway information ☏ 715555.

Getting around
The city is small but it is easy to get lost in the twisting maze of corridor-like lanes (*calle*), squares (*campi*) and canals. A detailed map is essential and unless you can take short cuts by using boats you can walk a long way to reach your destination. Looking for an address is very confusing.

Buildings are sequentially numbered within each of the six *sestieri* or districts (for example San Marco 4243) and not by the streets. It is a good idea to establish the street name of the address you want or at least the nearest landmark.

Watertaxis Small launches which zip down the canals and charge outrageously. Prices are theoretically controlled but it is essential to establish the fare before boarding. "Ranks" are located at important landmarks. *Radio Taxi* ☏ 716286 and 716922.

Walking Street crime is unusual; Venice is much safer than most big Italian cities.

Waterbus The main form of transport and the most entertaining way of seeing the city, although places may be scarce 7.30–9, 4.30–8 in the rush hours. There are two main types: the *vaporetti* (slow and more comfortable) and the more crowded *motoscafi* (express). Tickets can be bought at most landing stages, any ACTV office or at authorized sellers displaying the ACTV sign, and must be stamped at the automatic machines at the entrance to the landing stage. Books of 10 or 20 are available (at no saving). Daily tourist tickets allow unlimited travel on any waterbus.

The most frequently used lines are: No. 1, the slow boat down the Grand Canal (confusingly called the *accelerato*) which provides a 24hr service; No. 2, the *diretto*, connecting both ends of the Grand Canal but taking a short cut through the Rio Nuovo; No. 4, a faster version of No.

1 (summer only); No. 5, the circle line around Venice; and No. 34, the *espresso* from Tronchetto, Piazzale Roma and the station to San Marco.
Gondola Used for pleasure rather than transport, a gondola can be picked up throughout Venice. Official prices, which are notoriously high, are published in the free tourist booklet *Un Ospite di Venezia* but many gondoliers overcharge. Check prices before you board. ☎ San Marco 5200685, Rialto 5224904.
Traghetti Gondola ferries operating in the day and into the evening take passengers across the Grand Canal.
Bus From the station at Piazzale Roma there are regular and frequent bus services to (among others) Mestre, Marghera and Padua.
Land-taxis The taxi rank is at Piazzale Roma ☎ 5237774.

Area by area

Historic Venice is built on wooden piles resting on over 100 islets and mudbanks. The modern city also comprises the whole lagoon, including ten major islands, and Mestre and Marghera on the mainland.

The Grand Canal, the principal thoroughfare of Venice, sweeps through the city following an ancient river bed. Over 100 marbled and stately *palazzi* fringe the canal, some still homes to the super-rich, others empty and sadly dilapidated. Check prices

There are six districts or *sestieri*: San Marco, Castello, Cannaregio, Santa Croce, San Polo and Dorsoduro. Most visitors rarely venture beyond the central *sestiere* of San Marco which packs in the top monuments, hotels, restaurants and shops. This is also the main area of the city for big banks, the Stock Exchange, shipping companies and other businesses.

The hub of Venetian life has always been the Piazza San Marco. Described by Napoleon as "the finest drawing room in Europe," it is dominated by the elaborate, glittering façade of the basilica and flanked by dignified arcades of shops and elegant cafés.

The Piazzetta, with the Doges' Palace, extends from San Marco to the water where there is a splendid panorama across the lagoon to the island of San Giorgio Maggiore. Some of the city's top hotels are strung along the waterfront (Riva degli Schiavoni). A jigsaw of narrow streets north of Piazza San Marco leads to the Rialto, commercial focus of both ancient and modern Venice. The bridge is a tourist magnet and lined with souvenir stalls; to the north, the colourful food and fish markets are morning haunts for the locals.

The *sestiere* of Cannaregio, forming the northern arc of Venice, is the site of the world's first Jewish ghetto, established there in the 16th century. To the east is Castello, which includes the Arsenale, once the greatest shipyard in the world, and beyond it the Giardini Pubblici, site of the Biennale. Dorsoduro, south of the east end of the Grand Canal, is a peaceful upmarket residential neighbourhood with pretty quaysides leading down to the Zattere promenade which looks across to the quiet island of Giudecca. One of the city's two main docks is at San Basilio on the Giudecca canal.

The suburbs

Industry is mainly concentrated in the dull modern town of Mestre, 8km/5 miles northwest of Venice and beside the commercial port of Marghera. Many Venetians (particularly the business community) now live in Mestre which is cheaper and more convenient than living on the island city.

The Lido, a 11.25km/7 mile-long narrow strip of land separating the lagoon from the sea, is not the chic place it was once; but it is popular for its beach, sporting facilities and comfortable hotels.

The main islands of the lagoon are glass-making Murano, Burano, a fishing village and also known for lace-making, and Torcello, famous for its 9th–11thC cathedral which contains Byzantine mosaics.

Hotels

Venice's hotel prices are notoriously high, and the Gritti Palace and the Cipriani are two of the most expensive hotels in the world. At the top end of the market you are paying for a lavishly decorated Venetian *palazzo*, washed by the waters of the lagoon or the Grand Canal. The hotels best equipped for business belong mainly to the CIGA chain (Danieli, Europa e Regina, Excelsior, Des Bains and Gritti Palace).

Reservations are essential from Easter to the end of September and during the two-week carnival before Lent in February. In an emergency, the tourist offices at the airport, railway station or Piazzale Roma (summer only) may be able to help. Failing that, Padua and Treviso are only 30mins away by train (see *Other cities*).

All the main hotels provide room service, currency exchange, IDD telephones, TV, minibars and air conditioning. The CIGA hotels have private launches to the airport and to the Lido for the use of their beach and sports facilities (see *Keeping fit*). Prices are often much higher in the summer and in February.

Cipriani   [L]|||||
Giudecca 10, 30133 ☏ *5207744*
TX *410162 fax 5203930* • *Orient-Express* • *AE DC MC V* • *closed Nov–Mar* • *73 rooms, 25 suites, 2 restaurants, 2 bars*
Commendatore Cipriani (of Harry's Bar fame) set up this luxury hotel on the island of Giudecca in the mid-1950s. A grand Venetian palace in large gardens and boasting the only private pool in Venice, it has the air of a country estate. Though mainly geared to the extremely wealthy tourist, the hotel has clear appeal for the business executive able to combine work with sport and pleasure. San Marco is only 5mins away in the hotel's launch. Bedrooms are lavish, furnished with Fortuny fabrics and equipped with sumptuous bathrooms. The main dining room overlooking the lagoon is a delight. 24hr room service, private motorboat service to San Marco • hairdresser, boutique • pool, fitness centre, tennis court, yacht harbour • 4 meeting rooms (capacity up to 170).

Danieli   [L]|||||
Riva degli Schiavoni, Castello 4196, 30122 ☏ *5226480* TX *410077 fax 5200208* • *CIGA* • *AE DC MC V* • *226 rooms, 9 suites, 1 restaurant, 1 bar*

The ancient palace of Doge Dandolo (along with its stark 1950s extension) is an unmistakable landmark on the main waterfront. Dickens, Ruskin, Balzac and foreign royalty have stayed here. Today, the setting, looking over the waters of the lagoon towards San Giorgio Maggiore, the old-fashioned splendour of the lobby and comfort of the rooms make it a firm favourite among business people and top politicians. Millions of lire have been spent since 1981 on improvements, many of them on redecorating 84 rooms in a (modernized) Venetian baroque style. For a room with a view, ask for a *de luxe superior*. The rooftop restaurant, which has one of the best views in Venice, is an attractive venue for business meetings (see *Restaurants*). 24hr room service, beauty salon, hairdresser • 1 meeting room (capacity up to 130).

Europa e Regina   [L]||||
San Marco 2159, 30124 ☏ *5200477* TX *410123* • *CIGA* • *AE DC MC V* • *200 rooms, 10 suites, 1 restaurant, 1 bar*
This large CIGA hotel on the Grand Canal may not have the cachet of the group's other hotels in the city but it is more modestly priced and scores high for space, comfort and conference facilities. The building

consists of two adjacent palaces, one with accommodation in classic Venetian style (carved furniture, mirrors and glass), the other with more modern rooms overlooking the canal. 24hr room service • 6 meeting rooms.

Gritti Palace   ⬜//////
Campo Santa Maria del Giglio, San Marco 2467, 30124 ☎ *794611* ⊠ *410125 fax 5200942* • CIGA • AE DC MC V • *88 rooms, 9 suites, 1 restaurant, 1 bar*
Once the home of a doge, the Gritti still maintains the air of a private palace. Important people have always featured on the guest list, attracted by the discreet, attentive service, classical Venetian furnishings and meticulous attention to detail. And the setting too, with bar and restaurant terrace (see *Restaurants*) perched over the Grand Canal and across the water from the Salute church, is memorable, even for Venice. This is not primarily a business hotel, but small meetings can be arranged for top-notch executives and the bar is suitable for informal discussions. Public rooms are furnished with antiques, crystal chandeliers and Persian rugs on marble floors. Bedrooms range from luxurious suites with marble bathrooms to the much smaller "courtyard" rooms, newly decorated in damask and silk. 24hr room service, beauty salon • 2 meeting rooms (capacity up to 30).

Londra Palace   ⬜///
Riva degli Schiavoni, Castello 4171, 30122 ☎ *5200533* ⊠ *431315 fax 5225032* • *Space Hotels* • AE DC MC V • *69 rooms, 1 restaurant, 1 bar*
The smallest of the luxury establishments, the Londra Palace has more the air of a club than of an international hotel. Rooms are furnished in sober good taste and the hotel boasts "100 windows overlooking the lagoon." The stylish rooftop conference room has wide views of the Grand Canal. Food at the Do Leoni Restaurant is definitely a cut above average (see *Restaurants*). 1 meeting room (capacity up to 200).

Monaco e Grand Canal   ⬜///
Calle Vallaresso, San Marco 1325, 30124 ☎ *5200211* ⊠ *410450 fax 5200501* • AE V • *75 rooms, 4 suites, 2 restaurants, 1 bar*
A charming, understated hotel at the San Marco end of the Grand Canal. This is a good choice for executives for whom individuality and a prime location come before on-the-spot business facilities. Public areas consist of small salons, a prettily furnished restaurant and waterside terraces looking across the lagoon to Giudecca. The San Marco landing stage is on the doorstep and Harry's Bar across the street. 1 meeting room (capacity up to 40).

OTHER HOTELS
Bauer Grünwald   ⬜//// *Campo San Moisè, San Marco 1459, 30124* ☎ *5207022* ⊠ *410075* • AE DC MC V. Large, luxurious but somewhat anonymous, on the Grand Canal. Good views from the roof garden.
La Fenice et des Artistes   ⬜//
Campiello Fenice, San Marco 1936, 30124 ☎ *5232333* ⊠ *411150 fax 5203721* • V. Charming and reasonably priced; popular with artists from the nearby Fenice theatre.
Metropole   ⬜/// *Riva degli Schiavoni 4149, Castello 4149, 30122* ☎ *5205044* ⊠ *410340 fax 5223679* • AE DC MC V. Stately building with comfortable rooms on the main waterfront.
Pullman Park   ⬜// *Giardino Papadopoli, Castello 30135* ☎ *5285394* ⊠ *410310* • AE DC MC V. The most comfortable hotel in the station/ Piazzale Roma area, used by business guests who want quick access in and out of the city.
Saturnia e International   ⬜//// *Via XXII Marzo, San Marco 2398, 30124* ☎ *5208377* ⊠ *410355* • AE DC MC V. Gothic palace converted into efficiently run, comfortable hotel near San Marco; two good restaurants (see *Restaurants*).

Out of town

On the Lido (10–20mins by boat from Venice) the *Grand Hotel des Bains*, Lungomare Marconi 17 ☎ 765921, setting for *Death in Venice*, has a sedate charm; the luxury, modern CIGA *Excelsior*, Lungomare Marconi 41 ☎ 5260201, is much used for conferences by banks, insurance companies and IBM for example. The tiny *Locanda Cipriani* at Torcello has four delightful rooms where you can stay after dinner (see *Restaurants*).

If you have appointments on the mainland there are three modern hotels in Mestre with business facilities. Two are well-equipped for conferences: the *Michelangelo*, Via Forte Marghera 69, 30173 ☎ 986600, which has a garden, and the *Ramada*, Via Orlanda 4, 30173 ☎ 5310500, which is 10mins by minibus from Venice and has a covered pool. The *Ambasciatori*, Corso del Popolo 221, 30172 ☎ 5310699, on a busy Mestre road, is a 4-star business hotel.

Only 16km/10 miles from Mestre is the *Villa Condulmer*, Mogliano Veneto ☎ 457100 (see *Other cities*).

> **Small hotels of character**
> If your visit is for pleasure rather than business or you want to combine the two, the following is a selection of the city's most appealing small hotels near the main sights. The old-fashioned and charming *Accademia*, Fondamenta Bollani, Dorsoduro 1058, 30123 ☎ 5237846, is a perennial favourite of the British. *Do Pozzi*, Via XXII Marzo, San Marco 2373, 30124 ☎ 5207855, ⊠ 420042, is spruce, with neat modern bedrooms. *Flora*, Via XXII Marzo, San Marco 2283a, 30124 ☎ 5205844, is close to San Marco and has a delightful garden. *Giorgione*, Santi Apostoli, Cannaregio 4587, 30121 ☎ 5289332, is quiet and comfortable. The popular *San Cassiano*, Calle della Rosa, Santa Croce 2232, 30135 ☎ 5241733, is a small *palazzo*. The *Seguso*, Zattere 779, Dorsoduro 30123 ☎ 5222340, is an old-fashioned *pensione* where you have to take half board.

Restaurants

Venice has never been noted for gastronomy. The range of food tends to be limited, fish seems ubiquitous, the service can be surly and the prices are way above those of other Northern Italian cities in terms of value for money. For business purposes the most reliable restaurants are those in the top hotels where the service is professional and seldom rushed. Reservations are always advisable.

Antico Martini [L]////
Campo San Fantin 1983 ☎ *5224121 •*
closed Tue, Wed L and Dec–Mar • AE
DC MC V
An old Venetian establishment whose superb cooking and perfect setting draw the fashionable and the rich. The lengthy menu has mainly classic Italian (and Venetian) dishes, with a few concessions to international tastes. The favourite desserts are *crêpes* and *tiramisu*, the feather-light chocolate gateau soaked in liqueur. In good weather you can dine outdoors in a

pretty courtyard. From 10pm it turns into a nightclub with dancing.

La Caravella [L]////
Saturnia e International Hotel
☎ *5208901 •* closed Wed • AE DC MC V
• jacket and tie • no smoking •
reservations essential
Undeniably one of the better restaurants in town, but essentially geared towards moneyed tourists staying near San Marco. The small dining room is decorated like an old Venetian sailing ship. A long and

ambitious menu offers a choice of Venetian, national and international dishes. The other restaurant in the Saturnia e International is the simpler but more spacious Cortile, with a summer courtyard.

Da Fiore   *L|*
Calle del Scaleter ☎ *721308 • closed Sun, Mon, 2 weeks Aug • AE DC V*
The hidden location of this excellent fish restaurant eludes most tourists and diners are almost exclusively Venetian. It is well worth seeking out for hot and cold seafood antipasti, risottos and fish pastas, fresh fish main courses and (unlike most places in Venice) imaginative use of vegetables and herbs. The atmosphere is friendly and relaxed.

Do Leoni   *L|||||*
Londra Palace Hotel ☎ *5200533 • closed Tue off season • AE DC MC V*
This civilized, club-like hotel dining room provides a central setting for business discussions. Standards of food and service are high thanks to the female team of Mirella Battio, a local chef who produces some exquisite Venetian *cucina nuova*, and Baroness Sylvia von Block, an elegant American of central European origin, who manages the dining room. The hotel lies right on the lagoon front close to San Marco and the tables on the open-air terrace are snapped up in summer.

Harry's Bar   *L|||||*
Calle Vallaresso 1323 ☎ *5286931 • closed Mon and Jan–Mar • AE DC MC V*
The original Harry's Bar, frequented by Hemingway for *carpaccio* after hunting wild duck in the lagoon. A few celebrities still drop in, along with star-spotting tourists (mainly American) and chic Venetians. The exterior is inconspicuous, the inside austere and the prices exorbitant but the quality of cuisine (especially soups and pastas) is hard to beat.

Harry's Dolci   *L|*
Giudecca 773 (near Sant'Eufemia landing stage) ☎ *5224844 • closed Sun D, Mon and 5 weeks Jan–Feb • AE V*
For kudos, Harry's Dolci can't match Harry's Bar but the food here is made by the same chefs, the restaurant is more spacious and prices less than half those of the parent establishment. Fashionable Venetians and tourists alike come to eat al fresco beside the Giudecca canal. The menu is short and simple with emphasis on Venetian and regional dishes, served with delicious pastry-like bread. Mouthwatering cakes and desserts are served in the afternoons. Involves a 5min waterbus trip from San Marco.

Poste Vecie   *L|||*
Mercato del Pesce di Rialto, San Polo 1608 ☎ *721822 (913951 for reservations before 6.30) • closed Tue exc Jul–Sep • AE DC MC V*
This rustic trattoria gets its high-quality ingredients from the nearby fish market close to the Rialto. The interior, where log fires burn and paintings clutter the walls, is warm and inviting (helped by the complimentary cocktails). Typical dishes are the seafood antipasti, the creamy fish risotto and the fresh fish. Good value in comparison with restaurants closer to San Marco.

Terrazzo del Doge   *L|||||*
Gritti Palace Hotel ☎ *5226044 • AE DC MC V • reservations essential*
The sophisticated cuisine and quiet atmosphere of this hotel restaurant are well suited to the most important entertaining occasions. The choice is a table outside on the Grand Canal terrace or the beautifully furnished interior restaurant. The menu offers the best of Venetian cuisine (baby soles from the Adriatic, fish risottos and thick soups) along with international *haute cuisine*.

OTHER RESTAURANTS
Antica Besseta, Calle Salvio, off Campo San Giacomo dell'Orio ☎ 721687, serves some of the best fish in town. Close to San Marco, *La Colomba*, Piscina Frezzeria, San

Marco 1675 ☏ 5221175, is known for Venetian dishes and has a pleasant terrace and several indoor dining areas with modern art. *Corte Sconta*, Calle del Pestrin, Castello 3886 ☏ 5227024 (tucked away not far from the Arsenale), serves excellent fish and antipasta and is patronized by smart Venetians. *Da Arturo*, Calle dei Assassini, San Marco 3656 ☏ 5286974, is tiny, with imaginative salads, pasta and meat dishes. More expensive and upmarket are the *Taverna La Fenice*, Campiello La Fenice, San Marco 1938 ☏ 5223856 (close to the Fenice theatre), favoured for its discreet atmosphere by business clients, and *Trattoria Do Forni*, Calle dei Specchieri 457–468 ☏ 5237729, just north of Piazza San Marco, which serves beautifully prepared fish in two rooms, one with Orient-Express decor. The rooftop restaurant of the *Danieli Hotel* (see *Hotels*) ☏ 5226480, has an outdoor terrace overlooking San Giorgio Maggiore shimmering in the distance.

Out of town

Restaurants in Mestre are far better value than those in the city itself. Best of all (and considered by some to be superior to any in Venice) is *Dall'Amelia*, Via Miranese 113 ☏ 913951, spacious, efficiently run and popular with business visitors who come for the superb selection of fresh fish. For a small, welcoming family-run restaurant near the station, try *Valeriano*, Via Col di Lana 18 ☏ 926474.

On the island of Torcello, 45mins by waterbus No. 12 from the Fondamenta Nuove on the north shore, leaving every hour or so, the *Locanda Cipriani* ☏ 730757 is yet another offspring of Harry's Bar, with similar food and prices but a rural and romantic setting. The waterbus service is irregular after 8pm and a watertaxi costs L120,000 each way.

Bars and cafés

Venice has some of the most stylish rendezvous in Europe including the expensive cafés in Piazza San Marco. The oldest and most elegant are *Florian* and *Quadri*, where Venetian society has been meeting since the 1700s. *Harry's Bar*, Calle Vallaresso 1323, is still in vogue for cocktails (try their speciality, *bellini* – sparkling white wine with peach juice). For business over a drink, only the bars of the top hotels – particularly the *Gritti* and the *Danieli* – are suitable.

Entertainment

Venice is a place for *il dolce farniente* – doing sweet nothing, sauntering along mysterious alleyways, being surprised by a palace or church, or just observing the pigeons and people in Piazza San Marco. Cultural activities other than concerts are limited. The Biennale art exhibition is held in even years Jun–Oct in the public gardens of the Arsenale. *Un Ospite di Venezia* details events and times.

Theatre, opera and music The ravishing little *Fenice* theatre, Campo San Fantin ☏ 5210161, is the venue for opera Dec–May and chamber music recitals, symphony and jazz concerts and occasional dramas the rest of the year. The two other main theatres are the *Ridotto*, Calle Vallaresso 1332, San Marco ☏ 5222939, and *Teatro Goldoni*, Calle Goldoni ☏ 5207583. In summer, open-air concerts take place at churches.

Cinema The few cinemas rarely show films in English. The late summer International Film Festival at the Palazzo del Cinema, Lido, is virtually barred to those without the right contacts to get tickets.

Nightclubs The smart *Martini Scala*, Campo San Fantin ☏ 5224121, has live music and a good restaurant, Antico Martini (see *Restaurants*).

Casino From April to September the casino (open 3pm–3am) is on the Lido at 4 Lungomare G. Marconi, from October to May in the Palazzo Vendramin Calergi on the Grand Canal, 2040 Cannaregio. Both are glamorous, with nightclub and restaurant.

163

Shopping

Venice shop fronts are enticing and it is especially worth browsing around in the *calle* near the Fenice theatre.
Fashion Chic boutiques with top designer names are scattered around the San Marco area, notably in Frezzeria, Mercerie and Via XXII Marzo. Leather shoes and handbags are along the Mercerie.
Food Stalls at the Rialto market are overflowing with exotic fruit and vegetables; nearby the colonnaded 14thC fish market exhibits an amazing selection.
Glass The best names are *Pauly* in Piazza San Marco and Ponte dei Consorzi and, for contemporary glass, *L'Isola*, Campo San Moisè 1468. Elsewhere, much of the glass on sale is kitsch. Glass shops on Murano are no cheaper than those in the city.
Lace Beware imitations from the Far East. Watch the genuine product being made at the lace school, Scuola dei Merietti, San Marco 95–96, close to the piazza. Good buys are available in Burano.
Masks A huge variety of masks in anything from papier mâché to top-quality leather can be bought in Venice. For traditional hand-crafted masks, try *San Provolo* Castello 4719/a.
Paper The best paper shop for gifts is *Piazzesi*, Campiello della Feltrina, near Santa Maria del Giglio.

Sightseeing

The whole of Venice is a work of art, bathed in watery light that flickers over marble palaces and tiny bridges. Spending time in museums is second only to passing slowly by resplendent *palazzi* and worn church façades. Take the No. 1 *vaporetto* down the Grand Canal to start your visit. For lovers of art the museums, churches and *scuole* (lay confraternities now containing important works of art) are essential sightseeing. The top attractions – the basilica of San Marco, the Doges' Palace and the Accademia gallery – are less crowded in winter. Ask for a current list of

opening times from the central tourist office; and arrive early.
Accademia The richest collection of Venetian art in existence. Very crowded rooms, particularly No. 5 with Giorgione's enigmatic *Tempest*. *Campo della Carità, Dorsoduro. Open Tue–Sat, 9–2; Sun, 9–1.*
Basilica of San Marco Byzantine church, built in the 11th century to enshrine the body of St Mark. Exterior of domes and dazzling mosaics (often under scaffolding); dark interior with hundreds more mosaics, golden altarpiece, treasury and Roman bronze horses stolen from Constantinople (those outside are replicas). *Piazza San Marco. Open daily, 9.30–5.30.*
Ca' d'Oro Palace on the Grand Canal, once overlaid in gold leaf. Rooms with a fine collection of modern and oriental art were recently reopened. *Grand Canal, Cannaregio. Open Mon–Sat, 9–1.30; Sun, 9–12.30.*
Ca' Rezzonico Handsome baroque palace on the Grand Canal, containing furniture and paintings of 18thC Venice. *Grand Canal, Dorsoduro. Open Mon–Thu, Sat, 10–4; Sun, 9–noon.*
Correr Museum Historical collection and picture gallery. *Piazza San Marco. Open Mon, Wed–Sat, 10–4; Sun, 9–12.30.*
Doges' Palace Residence of the doges and seat of government from the 9th century to the fall of the republic in 1797. A magnificent façade overlooks the lagoon and inside grand rooms contain colossal canvases, arms and armoury, prison cells; outside is the famous Bridge of Sighs. *Piazzetta San Marco. Open Apr–mid-Oct daily, 8.30–6; mid-Oct–Mar, 8.30–4.*
Guggenheim Collection Modern art on the Grand Canal; works by Picasso, Mondrian, Magritte, Bacon, Moore. *Palazzo Venier dei Leoni, Dorsoduro. Open Apr–Oct, Wed–Mon, 2–6; closed winter.*
San Giorgio Maggiore Palladian island church with works by Tintoretto. Superb views from the top of the *campanile. Isola di San Giorgio. Open daily, 9–12.30, 2–7.*

Santa Maria della Salute Magnificent white 17thC church at the entrance of the Grand Canal with paintings by Titian and Tintoretto. *Campo della Salute, Dorsoduro. Open daily, 8–noon, 3–6.*

Santa Maria Gloriosa dei Frari Huge brick Gothic church housing Titian's *Assumption* and other paintings by Titian and Giovanni Bellini. *Campo dei Frari, San Polo. Open Mon–Sat, 9.30–noon, 2.30–6; Sun, 2.30–6.*

Scuola di San Giorgio degli Schiavoni Paintings by Carpaccio of early 16thC Venetian life. *Calle Furlani, Castello. Open Tue–Sat, 10–12.30, 3.30–6; Sun, 10.30–12.30.*

Scuola Grande di San Rocco Dramatic canvases by Tintoretto. *Campo San Rocco, San Polo. Open Mon–Fri, 10–1; Sat, Sun, 10–1, 3–6.*

Scuola Grande dei Carmini Upstairs ceiling with frescoes by Tiepolo. *Campo dei Carmini, Dorsoduro. Open Mon–Sat, 9–noon, 3–6.*

Guided tours
City sightseeing tours, 2hrs on foot, operate all year round. From mid-March to October there are guided tours by private motorboat, excursions to the lagoon islands and gondola cruises.

Out of town
Day trips down the Brenta canal (Apr–Oct, L70,000) include visits to Palladio's Villa Foscarini (La Malcontenta) and Villa Pisani at Stra.

Spectator sports
Lack of space precludes most spectator sports. Rowing regattas are popular and held throughout the year. The most famous event is the *La Vogalonga*, a 32km/20-mile regatta around the lagoon on Ascension Sunday, in May.

Keeping fit
Most sports take place on the Lido, accessible by waterbus from both ends of the Grand Canal. The only Venice hotel with facilities is the *Cipriani*, but guests at CIGA hotels can use the Lido

Venice Club (golf, sailing, tennis, board sailing, aerobics and riding). Nonresidents can buy daily or seasonal tickets.

Golf 18-hole course at *Golf Lido di Venezia*, Alberoni ☎ 731015, open to members of other clubs.

Horseriding Circolo Ippico, Ca' Bianca on the Lido ☎ 765162.

Sailing Excelsior hotel yacht club, 52 Lungomare G. Marconi, Lido.

Swimming The hotels *Cipriani*, *Excelsior* and *Des Bains* have pools open in summer for guests of CIGA hotels.

Tennis Lido Tennis Club, Via Sandro Gallo 163 ☎ 5260954, and courts at the *Des Bains* and *Excelsior* hotels.

Watersports Board sailing and sailing at the Lido beach from the end of May to September.

Local resources
Business services
Executive Service, Rampa Cavalcavia 28, Mestre ☎ 936444, provides offices.

Photocopying Micoud Centro Fotocopie ☎ 5289275.

Printing Gianola ☎ 5226832.

Secretarial and translation Endar ☎ 5238440 provides secretarial and translation services and organizes conferences.

Communications
Local delivery City Express ☎ 936355.

Long-distance delivery Traco ☎ 937600, DHL ☎ 5312488.

Post office Main office: Fondaco dei Tedeschi 80100 ☎ 5286212 and 5204143 (near the Rialto), open 8.30–7.

Telex and fax At main post office.

Conference/exhibition centres
Many conferences and exhibitions are held in the larger hotels; the *Excelsior* on the Lido and other CIGA hotels are frequently used. The main organizers are *Endar*, Fondamenta Osmarin Castello 4966 ☎ 5238440, and *Radiovision*, Fondamenta Osmarin 4975, Castello ☎ 52877557. For

cultural or scientific conferences or exhibitions, the most prestigious centre is in a converted monastery, the *Cini Foundation*, Isola di San Giorgio ☎ 5289900.

Bureaus de change The *Banco Nazionale delle Comunicazioni* at the railway station is open daily 8–7 (usually very busy). Central bureaus de change are open in normal shopping hours. *Thomas Cook*, San Marco 289–305 (in the Piazza) is open Mon–Sat, 8.45–7 in summer, 9.30–6 off-season; and at Rialto 5126 Mon–Sat, 9–6.30 in summer, 9–6 off-season ☎ 5289228.
Hospitals 24hr emergency departments: *Ospedale Civile*, Campo dei SS. Giovanni e Paolo ☎ 5294111 in Mestre, with emergency dental treatment; *Ospedale al Mare*, Lungomare d'Annunzio, Lido ☎ 5294111.
Pharmacies A late-night rota is posted at each pharmacy. See also local newspapers and *Un Ospite di Venezia*.
Police *Questura*: Fondamenta San Lorenzo, Castello 5053 ☎ 5203222.

Business information The *Commercio Estero* department of the Camera di Commercio is at San Marco 2032/2034 ☎ 786111. Their Export/import catalogue (in English) gives useful economic information and lists the main companies.
Local media There are two daily newspapers: the traditional *Gazettina* and the more left-wing *Nuova Venezia*.
Tourist information Calle Ascensione 71c, just off Piazza San Marco ☎ 5226356 (open Mon–Sat, 8.30–7.30, closed Sun) and at the station ☎ 715016 (open daily, 8–8.30), where you can reserve hotel rooms.
In summer there are tourist offices in Piazzale Roma ☎ 5227402 (hotel reservations only) and on the Lido at Gran Viale 6 ☎ 765721, both open daily, 9–9.30.

Chocolates *Andrea Rosa Salva*, Campo S. Luca 4589 ☎ 5225385.
Florists *Fantin*, Salizzada S. Salvador, San Marco 4805 ☎ 5226808. All the main credit cards are accepted.

OTHER CITIES

PADUA (PADOVA)
codes zip 35100 ☎ 049
An important commercial centre, with an ancient university and about 226,000 inhabitants. The postwar business and shopping district is to the north of the historic centre, and trade fairs are held at the Fiera, near the station. The industrial zone – engineering, chemicals, textiles, construction – is concentrated at Camin, and there are shoe factories along the Brenta canal.

There are several 4-star hotels in the Ponte di Brenta area, 5km/3 miles northeast of the centre, near the industrial zone; best equipped, with pools, tennis court and meeting room is *Le Padovanelle* ☎ 625622. At Camin (6km/3.75 miles to the east)

there is the new hotel, the *Admiral* ☎ 760544. At the Padova Est motorway exit (a 10min drive from Mestre) is the *Sheraton Padova* ☎ 8070399, with a modern conference centre (capacity up to 700). The best central hotel is the *Plaza*, Corso Milano 40 ☎ 656822.
In the centre the best restaurants for business entertaining are *El Toulà*, Via Belle Parti 11 ☎ 8751822, and the *Antico Brolo*, Vicolo Cigolo 14 (Prato della Valle) ☎ 664555. The famous neo-classical *Caffè Pedrocchi*, Via 8 Febbraio, is often used as a business rendezvous.
At Abano Terme (12km/7.5 miles to the southwest) the *Grand Orologio* ☎ 669111 is the smartest among scores of hotels with pools but is closed in winter. The Centro Congressi delle Venezie, for

conferences, is in the annexe of the *Terme Alexander* ☎ 668 300.

Relaxation
The sights of Padua include the *Scrovegni chapel*, with frescoes by Giotto, the *Basilica of Sant'Antonio*, the statue of *Gattamelata* by Donatello (outside the Basilica) and the picturesque piazzas (*Piazza dei Signori, Piazza della Frutta, Piazza delle Erbe*).

Boat trips to Venice on the *Brenta* canal, visiting the famous villas, are popular (see *Venice*).

Information sources
Associazione degli Industriali della Provincia di Padova, Via Anghinoni 3 ☎ 664499; *Camera di Commercio*, Via E. Filiberto 34 ☎ 8208111; *Fiera*, Via N. Tommaseo 59, 35131 ☎ 840111. *Executive Service*, Via Savonarola 217 ☎ 654211 (provides office services). *Tourist information*, Riviera Mugnai 8 ☎ 8750655, and at the station ☎ 8752077.

PORDENONE *codes* zip 33170 ☎ 0434
The most industrialized town of Friuli province, with a population of over 52,000. Light engineering predominates but Pordenone is also important for textiles, paper and furniture manufacture and for the food industry. Zanussi (white goods controlled by the Swedish company Electrolux, with over 10% of the European market) is based here and the factory at Porcia employs 3,350. There are also Grandi Impianti factories at Valle Noncella and Villotta.

Hotels and restaurants
Villa Ottoboni, Via 30 Aprile ☎ 21967, is the best-known hotel here; it is owned by Zanussi. *Noncello*, Vle Marconi 34 ☎ 523014, is a smart restaurant with good local cooking.

Relaxation
The old centre was damaged in the 1976 earthquake, but see the *Duomo*

and *Museo Civico*, in the 17thC Palazzo Ricchieri, for paintings by the native artist Pordenone.

Information sources
Camera di Commercio, Corso Vittorio Emanuele 47 ☎ 3811. *Tourist information*, Pza della Motta 13 ☎ 521218.

TREVISO *codes* zip 31100 ☎ 0422
Furniture, domestic appliances and foodstuffs are produced in this area. Zanussi's second biggest plant, employing some 3,000 people, is at Susegana, near Conegliano. The head offices of Zanussi Grandi Impianti (catering and refrigeration equipment) are at Treviso. Textiles are also important; the flourishing Benetton and Stefanel franchizing chains are run from Palladian villas near Treviso, with factories in the province (Benetton's newest is at Castrette). Asolo is known for handspun silk. Treviso's population is over 85,000.

Hotels and restaurants
There are no top-flight hotels in Treviso; the *Continental*, Via Roma 16 ☎ 543774, is an adequate commercial hotel. But celebrated *El Toulà da Alfredo*, Via Collalto 26 ☎ 540275, is undoubtedly the most prestigious restaurant in town.

At Paderno Ponzano (8km/5 miles) *Relais el Toulà*, Via Postumia 63 ☎ (0422) 969023, is a refined rural hotel with restaurant. At Zerman (7km/4.75 miles) is the grand and comfortable 18thC *Villa Condulmer* ☎ (041) 457100, with pool, tennis and golf (but the hotel is closed in winter). Another luxuriously converted country house is the *Villa Corner della Regina* ☎ (0423) 481481 at Cavasagra di Vedelago (18km/10 miles east).

At Asolo (35km/21.75 miles northwest) is the charming, luxurious *Villa Cipriani* ☎ (0423) 55444.

Relaxation
The medieval centre of Treviso is attractive, with some interesting churches. *Villa Barbaro* at Maser

(29km/18 miles to the northwest), with frescoes by Veronese, is worth a visit.

Information sources
Camera di Commercio, Pza della Borsa
☎ 540801.
Tourist information, Via Toniolo 41, Palazzo Scotti ☎ 547632, open Mon–Fri, 9–12.30, 3–6; Sat, 9–12.30.

TRIESTE *codes* zip 34100 ☎ 040
Trieste, with a population of nearly 240,000, is the main port for Austria and an international entrepôt. Enjoying free port status since Habsburg times, its traditional activities are associated with trade and the sea: shipbuilding (Fincantieri, with its diesel engine subsidiary Grande Motori), insurance (Lloyd Triestino and Assicurazioni Generali, the biggest insurance company in Italy and one of the top five in Europe) and oil (with a pipeline to central Europe). Sectors of the free port are devoted to timber and coffee. More coffee is traded and handled here than anywhere else in the Mediterranean; leading firms are Illy, Hausbrandt and Eisner. The port, which is expanding its container facilities, is returning to profit after a prolonged recession.

Many companies including Stock (brandies, liqueurs), have plants in the industrial zone immediately to the south of the city. Other activities include cast iron production and metalworking, paper manufacture, medical instruments and pharmaceuticals. There are also many import-export companies.

A science park, offering companies and institutions inducements for applied research (Area di Ricerca, Padriciano 99, Trieste 34012 ☎ 226011) is growing up behind Trieste, around the European headquarters of the International Centre for Genetic Engineering and Biotechnology and a projected synchroton radiation research laboratory. The International Center for Theoretical Physics at Miramare (6km/4 miles to the northwest) brings

together scientists for courses and seminars.

Monfalcone, 30km/20 miles north, has Italy's largest shipyard: Fincantieri employs 3,000 people.

Hotels and restaurants
The *Duchi d'Aosta*, Pza Unità d'Italia 2, 34121 ☎ 62081, with Harry's Bar and Harry's Grill, is the most central and most luxurious hotel. On the seafront opposite the *Palazzo dei Congressi* is the *Savoia Excelsior Palace*, Riva del Mandracchio 4, 34124 ☎ 7690.

Alla Cantina, Riva Grumula 2 ☎ 305029, *Al Granzo*, Pza Venezia 7 ☎ 306788, *Al Bragozzo*, Riva Sauro 22 ☎ 303001 and *Nastro Azzurro*, Riva Nazario Sauro 12 ☎ 305789, are all good for seafood lunches. In the suburb of San Giovanni *Antica Trattoria Suban*, Via Comici 2 ☎ 54368, has an attractive terrace and good local cooking.

Degli Specchi (once patronized by James Joyce) and *Tommaseo* are among several historic cafés in Trieste.

Relaxation
The *Teatro Comunale Giuseppe Verdi*, Pza Verdi 1, is the main opera house. In July and August an operetta season is staged at the *Politeama Rossetti*, Vle XX Settembre 45. *Son-et-Lumière* performances are held at *Miramare* castle in summer.

The main sights are the cathedral of *San Giusto*, handsome buildings of the Habsburg era, especially in Piazza dell'Unità, and the turreted *Miramare* castle and garden, built by the Emperor Maximilian of Mexico.

Information sources
Camera di Commercio, Pza della Borsa 14 ☎ 67011; *Ente per la Zona Industriale di Trieste*, Via Caboto 14 ☎ 826824 (promotes industry and infrastructure in the industrial zone); *Federazione Regionale degli Industriali del Friuli-Venezia Giulia*, Pza Scorcola 1, Palazzo Ralli ☎ 68826 or 364524.
Tourist information, Pza della Cattedrale 3 ☎ 750002 or 309242 (in the Castello di San Giusto), open

Mon–Fri, 8.30–2, 4–6; Sat, 8.30–1, and at the main railway station/air terminal ☎ 420182, open Mon–Fri, 9–1, 3–7.

UDINE *codes* zip 33100 ☎ 0432
A key town for freight distribution, with good rail and road links to Austria and Yugoslavia (via Gorizia). The expanding industrial sector includes steel, engineering, textiles, paper, food and breweries (notably Moretti).

At Zugliano, on the outskirts of Udine, Cogolo is possibly the biggest leather tanning factory in Europe. Danieli, a major world supplier of machinery for steel mills, now with factories in the USSR, is at nearby Buttrio. Around Manzano is the "chair triangle" where nearly 800 companies produce three-quarters of Italy's chairs (Tonon and Potocco are the largest manufacturers, with 120 employees each). To the north of Udine are Gemona (textile manufacture) and Osoppo, where major companies are Pittini (steel) and Fantoni (furniture and components). The province is also known for wines, especially Tocai, Pinot and Picolit, a dessert wine, and for the famous ham of San Daniele. The population of Udine is over 100,000.

Hotels and restaurants
Ambassador Palace, Via Carducci 46 ☎ 503777, and *Astoria Italia*, Pza XX Settembre 25 ☎ 505091, are the best hotels, both central. Food at the Astoria is very good.

At Tricesimo (12km/7.5 miles to the north) the *Boschetti* ☎ 851230 is a small hotel with a highly-regarded restaurant.

Relaxation
See *Piazza della Libertà* (Venetian Gothic buildings), the paintings by Tiepolo in the *Duomo* and the *Palazzo Arcivescovile*, the archbishop's palace.

Information sources
Associazione degli Industriali della Provincia di Udine, Via dei Torriani 2

☎ 2761; *Camera di Commercio*, Via Morpurgo 4 ☎ 504541.
Tourist information, Via Piave 27 ☎ 295972, open Mon–Fri, 9–12.30, 2.30–6; Sat, 9–12.

VERONA *codes* zip 37100 ☎ 045
An important commercial crossroads for freight distribution to central Europe, at the junction of the Po valley and Brenner Pass, with a population of about 260,000. Industry is mainly in engineering, chemicals and paper (Cartiere Fedrigoni), and in agricultural products such as wine distribution (Bertani, Bolla) and foodstuffs (Hero jams, Bauli cakes). Italy's main international agricultural fair is held in Verona in March, and there are several other specialized fairs, including VinItaly (April). Mondadori's main printing plant is here. Companies with headquarters in the city include Abital (menswear) and several car import-export companies (BMW, Volkswagen, Audi and Porsche). The industrial zone is southwest of the city. It comprises the Quadrante Europa and Centro Intermodale, highly specialized modern complexes for freight storage and distribution, with research laboratories, customs facilities, offices, residential areas, banks and insurance.

In the province, Parona, Bussolengo and Peschiera del Garda are industrialized extensions of Verona; Franke and MAN are at Peschiera. Soave, Valpolicella and Bardolino wines come from near Verona and are even more extensively exported than Chianti. The province of Verona also accounts for one tenth of Italy's shoe production, with factory-outlets all along the route to Lake Garda. The road to Legnago is lined with reproduction antique furniture factories and showrooms.

Hotels and restaurants
Hotel rooms should be reserved well ahead during the main Fairs (Mar–May) and the opera season (Jul, Aug). *Due Torri*, Pza Sant'Anastasia 4 ☎ 595044, is a famous hotel with

top-class comforts and service;
Colomba d'Oro, Via C. Cattaneo 10
☎ 595300, is comfortable and
convenient and the *Accademia*, Via
Scala 12 ☎ 596222, is reliable.

There are several outstanding
restaurants: *Le Arche*, Via Arche
Scaligere 6 ☎ 8007415; *Il Desco*, Via
Dietro San Sebastiano 7 ☎ 595358; *I
Dodici Apostoli*, Corticella San Marco 3
☎ 596999, and *Nuovo Marconi*, Via
Fogge 4 ☎ 595295. At Valeggio sul
Mincio (25km/25miles southwest) the
Antica Locanda ☎ 7950059 is a
riverside inn. *Villa Cortine* ☎ (030)
916021 at Sirmione (40km/25miles
west) is also popular.

The opera season at the *Arena* takes
place in July and August (the
programme is published in January):
information from Ente Arena,
Pza Bra 28, 37121 ☎ 590109 or
590726 ⓉⓍ 480869; tickets from
Servizio Biglietteria, Arcovolo 6
dell'Arena ☎ 596517.

Sights include the *Roman Arena*,
the church of *San Zeno Maggiore*
(romanesque, with an altarpiece by
Mantegna), the *Castelvecchio Museum*
and *Juliet's balcony*. The *Piazza delle
Erbe* and *Piazza dei Signori* are
unspoilt medieval squares.

Information sources
*Associazione degli Industriali della
Provincia di Verona*, Pza Cittadella 12
☎ 8099411; *Camera di Commercio*,
Corso Porta Nuova 96 ☎ 591077;
*Consorzio ZAI (Zona Agricola
Industriale)*, Corso Porta Nuova 4
☎ 596577; *Executive Service*, Via
Fratta 14 ☎ 8000050, for offices, staff
and equipment.
Tourist information, Pza Erbe 38
☎ 30086, and Via Anfiteatro 6b
☎ 592828, open Mon–Fri, 9–12.30,
3.30–6.

VICENZA *codes* zip 36100 ☎ 0444
The Vicenza area is known for the
production of textiles and clothing,
and is one of three centres of
goldsmith craftsmanship in the
country. There are woollen mills at
Schio and Valdagno, where Lanerossi
and Marzotto are the biggest names.
The Fiera trade complex, venue for
international jewellery trade fairs, and
the main industrial zone are about
1.5km/1mile southwest. The city has
a population of about 111,000.

Bassano del Grappa is known for
ceramics and grappa (Nardini). The
family-run Balestra, 1882, is a large
gold jewellery manufacturer.

Hotels and restaurants
Campo Marzio, Vle Roma 21
☎ 545700, is the best hotel in the
town centre. *The Europa*, Vle San
Lazzaro ☎ 564111, is a sound modern
choice, just out of the centre. Near
the Fiera and industrial zone is the
Alfa, Via dell'Oreficeria 52
☎ 565455. To the south of Vicenza,
at Arcugnano, is the appealing *Villa
Michelangelo* ☎ 550300, with a pool
and elegant restaurant overlooking the
park. *Cinzia e Valerio*, Via Porta
Padova 65-67 ☎ 505213, is probably
Vicenza's best restaurant, known for
fish. In Vicenza, *Scudo di Francia*,
Contrà Piancoli 4 ☎ 228655, in an
attractive *palazzo*, and *Tre Visi*,
Contrà Porti 6 ☎ 238677, an old
trattoria, are also recommended.

Relaxation
Vicenza is the birthplace of Palladio
and has some fine examples of his
architecture: palaces in the main street
(Corso Palladio), the *Basilica* in Piazza
dei Signori and the *Teatro Olimpico*.
The local museum is housed in his
Palazzo Chiericati. The famous *Villa
Rotonda* is to the southeast of the
town. Nearby (3km/1.75 miles south
of Vicenza) is the *Villa Valmarana*
with frescoes by Giambattista Tiepolo
and his son, Domenico.

Information sources
Camera di Commercio, Corso
Fogazzaro 37 ☎ 994811; *Fiera*, Vle
dell'Oreficeria ☎ 369111.
Tourist information, Pza Duomo 5
☎ 544122, open Mon–Fri, 9–12.30;
also here is *Vicenza Congressi*.

EMILIA-ROMAGNA

This large region links central Italy with the North and derives its name from the ancient Via Emilia, a Roman trading route which bisects the region from Piacenza to Rimini; Romagna is the part to the south and west of Bologna. The river Po forms much of the region's northern boundary while to the south are the Apennines. On the Adriatic coast the numerous resorts support the local economy and the tiny, touristy republic of San Marino is within day-trip distance of Rimini, the chief resort. The Comacchio lagoons are important for eel fishing.

The whole plain is intensively cultivated for wheat, barley and beet and for fruit and vegetables. Vines produce nearly 1bn litres of wine annually (Lambrusco, especially, being exported in large quantities to the USA). The region to the east of Ferrara, in the river plain, is devoted to rice-growing. Cattle and pig farming is widespread and efficiently organized, with the district around Reggio alone accounting for 10% of national pig production. Throughout the region the cooperative system flourishes. Flat land and efficient farming make for a rather monotonous landscape.

Inevitably many factories specialize in the processing and packaging of agricultural produce: making types of salami, sausages and cheese, bottling wines, canning tomatoes and drying *funghi porcini*. Other small and medium-sized firms produce farm machinery and racing cars, shoes and clothes, furniture and ceramics. Crafts also flourish in the area: beaten and chased metalwork, decorated pottery (notably from Faenza), mosaics (from Ravenna), carved wood, musical instruments (from Mondaino in the province of Forlì, and from Modena), embroidered and woven items.

Bologna is the natural centre of the region, with more than twice as many inhabitants as any of the other provincial capitals. There are international airports at Bologna, Rimini and Forlì.

BOLOGNA
City codes zip 40100 ☎ 051

Bologna, site of one of the oldest universities in Europe and capital of Emilia-Romagna, has developed from a thriving agricultural market town into the fifth most important industrial complex in Italy with a population of nearly 500,000. Its position has always been important and it commands a network of trade routes from the Northern plain, from Ravenna and from the South.

The prosperity of the city and its environs is based on Bologna's role as a focus for the distribution of goods in central Italy, on trade in the rich produce of the Po valley, notably in grain and fruit, and on industry including food processing, especially pasta and chocolates, furniture making, electronics, the manufacture of automobile components, electrical equipment, steel and chemicals; the electro-mechanical sector employs 50% of the work force. Technical expertise and flexibility have been key elements in companies that have responded swiftly to competition; GD, for example, which started as a manufacturer of motorcycles, has become a world leader in making machinery for the packaging of confectionery, soaps and cigarettes. Most industrial concerns are medium to small and many, including some of the larger ones, are family enterprises. Only five companies employ more than 500 people, headed by Marposs, which produces precision instruments, most of which are exported.

Economic growth in the last 20 years has been stimulated by the construction of the increasingly important Fiera exhibition and fair ground; it hosts about 30 fairs a year, 16 of which are of international importance including the fashion, shoe, and children's book fairs. In 1987 its visitors numbered 700,000, of whom 60,000 were foreigners.

The left has been politically dominant in Bologna since World War II, despite the city's bourgeois values, and cooperatives, which have sprouted throughout the region, have collaborated successfully with private enterprise.

The city's economy is flourishing, yet life seems to proceed at a pleasantly leisured pace. The Bolognese like to work hard, and are polite, patient and courteous. It is not for nothing that the city is known as *Bologna la Grassa* ("the Fat"). It has an abundance of good restaurants and long and leisurely meals are a business tradition.

Arriving

Bologna is not well served by regular international flights but is a vital road and rail junction, linking major Northern Italian cities with the centre and South. Autostrada routes radiate to Venice, Milan, Florence, Rome and the Adriatic coast. The city is on the main Milan/Florence/Rome railway line, and there are direct services to Venice, the Adriatic coast (all the way to the far South), Verona and the Brenner Pass. It is also the centre for an efficient long-distance bus network linking major towns and cities in Emilia-Romagna as well as rural regions.

Guglielmo Marconi airport

By 1990, when Italy hosts the soccer World Cup, Bologna's small airport will have grown considerably. Prior to its enlargement facilities were limited to a café, a snack bar, banking and exchange facilities (open weekdays, 8.20–1.20, 2.30–5; Sat and Sun, 10.45–1.20, 2.30–5), a self-service restaurant (in a separate building), and a VIP lounge. Flights connect daily with Paris, Frankfurt and London and six days a week with Munich as well as Milan, Rome, Naples, Alghero and Palermo. Summer charter flights bound for the Adriatic cause congestion. Airport information and freight inquiries ☎ 311578 or 312259.

City link The city centre is 8km/5 miles to the southeast.

Taxi It is best to take a cab and you rarely have to wait long for one; the journey to the centre takes 15–20mins, fare L15,000.

Car rental Europcar, Hertz and Avis have desks at the airport. A car is a liability unless you are travelling outside the city.

Railway station

Bologna's busy and often crowded central station, north of the city centre, handles numerous domestic and international trains. Florence is just 70mins away and a project is under way to speed up links to Milan and Rome (currently 2hrs 30mins away). The journey time to Venice is 2hrs.

A large section of the station has been rebuilt since the right-wing

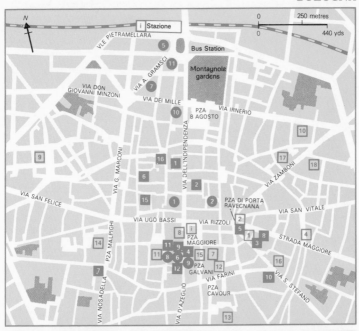

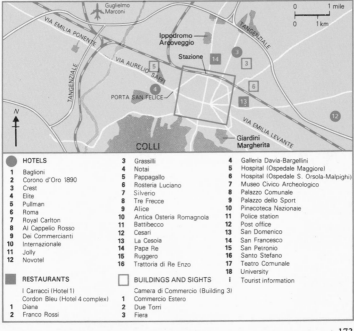

HOTELS		
1	Baglioni	
2	Corono d'Oro 1890	
3	Crest	
4	Elite	
5	Pullman	
6	Roma	
7	Royal Carlton	
8	Al Cappelio Rosso	
9	Dei Commercianti	
10	Internazionale	
11	Jolly	
12	Novotel	

RESTAURANTS

I Caracci (Hotel 1)
Cordon Bleu (Hotel 4 complex)
1 Diana
2 Franco Rossi

3 Grassilli
4 Notai
5 Pappagallo
6 Rosteria Luciano
7 Silverio
8 Tre Frecce
9 Alice
10 Antica Osteria Romagnola
11 Battibecco
12 Cesari
13 La Cesoia
14 Papa Re
15 Ruggero
16 Trattoria di Re Enzo

BUILDINGS AND SIGHTS

Camera di Commercio (Building 3)
1 Commercio Estero
2 Due Torri
3 Fiera

4 Galleria Davia-Bargellini
5 Hospital (Ospedale Maggiore)
6 Hospital (Ospedale S. Orsola-Malpighi)
7 Museo Civico Archeologico
8 Palazzo Comunale
9 Palazzo dello Sport
10 Pinacoteca Nazionale
11 Police station
12 Post office
13 San Domenico
14 San Francesco
15 San Petronio
16 Santo Stefano
17 Teatro Comunale
18 University
i Tourist information

173

extremists' attack in 1980 which killed 85 people (a hole in the wall of one waiting room is a grim reminder). Facilities include self-service cafeteria, 24hr currency exchange, information office (open 7–10), SIAT tourist office, 24hr telegram office, hairdresser and showers. The station is about a 15min walk from the centre. There is a regular bus service to all parts of the city, including the Fiera site. Getting a taxi from the rank outside the station is usually easy. Railway inquiries ☎ 246490.

Getting around

The centre is quite compact and the most sensible way to get around the city is on foot, with 35km/21 miles of arcades for shelter from rain and excessive heat. Taxis are the easiest alternative but there is also a fast, cheap bus network. Plans for an underground railway and a new ring road are constantly under discussion.
Taxis *Radio Taxis* ☎ 372727 or 534141 provide a reliable service; otherwise there are ranks in Piazza Re Enzo, Piazza Galvani and Via Rizzoli. You can hail them in the street, but they are hard to find during the big fairs.
Limousines *Baratta* ☎ 522763, CAB ☎ 553415.
Driving A car is a positive drawback unless you are visiting sites outside the city. The centre (which is a maze of one-way streets) is closed to traffic during the weekends and parking in central streets is not permitted.
Walking Orientation is easy and walking safe except in deserted areas at night. Watch out for bag-snatchers at all hours.
Bus The bus network is useful for places outside walking distance, especially the Fiera, but the system can be confusing in the evenings when lines shorten or change routes and at weekends when the centre is closed to most buses.

Area by area

The main streets of Bologna radiate from Piazza Maggiore towards the city gates and the *viali*, the circle of avenues which follows the ancient walls. Despite the intrusion of postwar architecture in the northeast, the core remains medieval in character: red-brick *palazzi* and mansions and arcades flank many streets.

The indisputable heart of the city has always been the Piazza Maggiore and the adjoining Piazza del Nettuno. This magnificent square, bordered by grand *palazzi* and the huge church of San Petronio, was (and to a certain extent still is) the place where Bolognese gathered for speeches, ceremonies, meetings and protests. But the long-standing symbol of the city is the Piazza di Porta Ravegnana and its two acutely leaning medieval towers (*Due torri*). The university area, with its graffiti-streaked walls and socialist posters, lies northeast along the Via Zamboni.

Business development has largely been outside the *viali* ring road. The Fiera site north of the old city is an avant-garde complex of exhibition pavilions, a business centre and soaring towers with offices, agencies, banks and shops. Close by is the Palazzo dei Congressi conference centre. Farther north, Castel Maggiore is another important commercial quarter, whose Centergross is a large wholesale depot.
The suburbs The most desirable residential quarters are the quiet wooded hills (the Colli district) to the south of the city, where top business executives own luxury villas. The industrial suburbs to the north and east, between the city centre and the *tangenziale* (outer ring road), are less prestigious. In the southwest, Casalecchio di Reno, another industrial and commercial centre, is now almost a part of Bologna.

Hotels

Some new hotels have been built on the outskirts of Bologna, but the demand for accommodation still exceeds the supply. During trade fairs and conventions every room is taken and those who have not made reservations in advance may find themselves staying in hotels as far away as Ferrara (47km/29 miles) or Modena (39km/24 miles). Prices, already high by national standards, rise by 15–20% during these periods. The top hotel is undeniably the Baglioni, with the Royal Carlton coming a close second. The choice otherwise is between large modern blocks on the periphery or smaller less impersonal central hotels with few or no business facilities.

All hotels listed have IDD telephones, room service (not 24hr unless stated), currency exchange and parking arrangements. If you arrive without a reservation, staff at the SIAT offices at the railway station or in Piazza Maggiore may help, but don't count on it during major fairs.

Baglioni [L]////
Via dell'Indipendenza 8, 40121
☎ *225445* ☒ *510242 fax 234840* •
Palace • *AE DC MC V* • *117 rooms,*
8 suites, 1 restaurant (separate
management), 1 bar
Bologna's grandest hotel, which reopened only in 1987 after a closure of ten years, is in the city centre. Today it is a regular rendezvous for the most affluent Bolognese, many of whom come to dine in the very expensive I Carracci (see *Restaurants*). The public rooms have been restored to their former splendour with frescoed walls, moulded ceilings and grand chandeliers. Bedrooms combine classical charm and modern luxury although some are small. The palatial suites are furnished with antiques and include marble bathrooms with jacuzzis. Parking arrangements are cumbersome. 24hr room service, hairdresser • 5 meeting rooms (capacity up to 75).

Corona d'Oro 1890 [L]/
Via Oberdan 12, 40124 ☎ *236458*
☒ *224657 fax 262679* • *AE DC MC V* •
34 rooms, 1 suite, 1 bar
A pleasing small hotel, the Corona d'Oro dates back to the 14th century and is said to have housed Italy's first printing works. The Renaissance portico and 16thC coffered ceilings have been preserved, and the former winter garden transformed into an elegant Art Nouveau entrance hall. On a cobbled, traffic-free street close to the famous leaning towers, the hotel is popular with academics, actors and artists and well suited to business visitors who are happy with a central base offering personal service but limited working facilities. 1 meeting room (capacity up to 45).

Crest [L]//
Pza della Costituzione 1, 40128
☎ *372172* ☒ *510676 fax 357662* •
AE DC MC V • *164 rooms, 1 suite,*
1 restaurant, 1 bar
The Crest is adjacent to the exhibition and trade centres and is a good option as a hotel for a working lunch and for those attending the Fiera. It has an unprepossessing exterior but is welcoming and well-equipped, one of the few hotels in the city with a garden and a pool. Executive rooms are larger and better-equipped than standard rooms, others are kept for nonsmokers and some are decorated and furnished in attractive floral fabrics. It can be difficult to get a taxi into the city centre. 24hr room service • pool • 7 meeting rooms (capacity up to 350).

Elite [L]//
Via Aurelio Saffi 36, 40131 ☎ *437417*
☒ *510067* • *AE DC MC V* • *60 rooms,*
20 suites, 1 restaurant (separate
management) 1 bar
Modern, comfortable and well-appointed, the Elite is just outside the *viali* to the west, a 10min taxi ride from the city centre and not far from the airport. It attracts a mainly business clientele. The suites are large

(some have self-catering facilities) and the restaurant, the Cordon Bleu (see *Restaurants*), is superb. There is also a nightclub. Closed late Jul–late Aug. 3 meeting rooms (capacity up to 150).

Pullman *□/*
Vle Pietramellara 59, 40121 ☎ *248248*
214822 fax 249421 • *Pullman* • *AE DC MC V* • *240 rooms, 1 restaurant, 1 bar*
A large and sober 19thC building facing the station, the Pullman is surprisingly modern and light inside with stylish public rooms and a comfortable bar for meeting business contacts; it was completely rebuilt in the early 1980s. The bedrooms have adequate working space, are well-planned and furnished with pretty, modern fabrics, reproduction antiques and attractive lighting. The quietest rooms are at the back, overlooking an attractive garden (not part of the hotel). 3 meeting rooms (capacity up to 90).

Roma *□*
Via d'Azeglio 9, 40123 ☎ *274400*
583270 • *AE DC MC V* • *87 rooms, 3 suites, 1 restaurant, 1 bar*
Low prices and a civilized atmosphere have made the Roma one of the most sought-after hotels in Bologna, attracting actors, discerning tourists and business travellers who appreciate charm, character and personal service. Another bonus is the quiet position on a smart traffic-free shopping street, just a few steps from the Piazza Maggiore. Public rooms are furnished with antiques and chintz, guest rooms individually decorated with light floral patterns. Advance reservations essential. 1 meeting room (capacity up to 30).

Royal Carlton *□///*
Via Montebello 8, 40121 ☎ *249361*
510356 fax 249724 • *Gamma* • *AE DC MC V* • *250 rooms, 20 suites, 1 restaurant, 1 bar*
The Royal Carlton is a large, luxury hotel standing in its own garden not far from the station. Inside, the emphasis is on space, modern comforts and cool efficiency. The lobby is furnished in brown and beige with mock-leather seating, the large bedrooms are stylish and the suites are luxurious. The bar is the best business rendezvous in Bologna. 24hr room service, hairdresser, secure underground parking • conference centre with 10 meeting rooms (capacity up to 1,000).

OTHER HOTELS
Al Cappello Rosso *□// Via de'Fusari 9, 40123* ☎ *261891* *583304* • *AE DC MC V*. Central, quiet old *palazzo* with ultra-modern rooms.
Dei Commercianti *□ Via de'Pignattari 11, 40124* ☎ *233052* *224657 fax 224733* • *AE DC MC V*. Small, refurbished hotel with limited facilities on quiet, central street.
Internazionale *□// Via dell'Indipendenza 60, 40121* ☎ *254454* *511038* • *Gamma* • *AE DC MC V*. Central with comfortable modern bedrooms, but somewhat gloomy lobby. Rooms at the back are quieter.
Jolly *□/ Pza XX Settembre 2, 40121* ☎ *248921* *510076 fax 249764* • *AE DC MC V*. Big, ugly hotel near the station. Dull public areas in 1950s style; functional modern rooms.
Novotel *□// Via Villanova 31, 40055* ☎ *781414* *213412* • *AE DC MC V*. Huge modern complex 8km/5 miles east with pool, 4 tennis courts, conference and meeting rooms.

Restaurants
It is said that the Emilians eat in a day what the Romans eat in a week. A slight exaggeration perhaps, but the Bolognese love their food and their city is rightly regarded as a mecca of Italian gastronomy. Few other towns can rival the number of top restaurants or the standards of cuisine, but for special business entertaining go to the San Domenico at Imola.

The best known local dishes are *tortellini* and *tagliatelle*, hams, sausages (especially mortadella) and a variety of salami. Unless otherwise stated restaurants offer *à la carte* menus only. Reservations are essential during trade fairs.

I Carracci 🎫////
Baglioni Hotel ☎ *270815 • closed Sun, 4 weeks Jul–Aug • AE DC MC V • reservations essential • jacket preferred*
A 16thC room with a beautifully frescoed ceiling is the setting for this sophisticated restaurant which serves rich regional dishes. It occupies part of the Baglioni Hotel and, though under separate management, is a favourite among the upper strata of the business community, particularly for lunch.

Cordon Bleu 🎫////
Via Aurelio Saffi 38 ☎ *437417 • closed Mon L, Sun, 4 weeks Jul–Aug • AE DC MC V • jacket preferred*
This long-established restaurant continues to produce what many consider the best food in town. A particularly popular lunchtime rendezvous for the business community, it lies just outside the Porta San Felice, in the same complex as the Elite Hotel but under separate management. Pierantonio Zarotti has a bold approach when it comes to introducing new dishes to the Bolognese scene: some are modern adaptions of the classics, others are imported from central and Southern Italy, and a few are entirely his own invention. The choice of fish is excellent and there is a very well stocked cellar.

Diana 🎫/
Via dell'Indipendenza 24 ☎ *231302 • closed Mon, Jan 1–12, most of Aug • AE DC V*
Diana opened at the beginning of the century and still serves authentic Bolognese cooking at reasonable prices.In one of the main shopping streets of the centre, it is a cheerful restaurant with big mirrors and bright chandeliers. A good choice for truffle-lovers and for informal meals, but

usually too busy for discreet conversation.

Franco Rossi 🎫//
Via Goito 3 ☎ *279959 • closed Sun, May–Aug; Tues, Sep–Apr, July • AE DC V • jacket and tie*
One of the most appealing restaurants in the city, for both ambience and cuisine, this smart, family-run establishment offers carefully prepared, imaginative dishes suitable for both business or social occasions. Tables are prettily laid, always with fresh flowers and homemade bread; the menu changes frequently and for those in a hurry at lunch time there is the option of a *piatto del giorno*. A private room for 10 is available for business meetings.

Grassilli 🎫//
Via dal Luzzo 3 ☎ *222961 • closed Wed, mid-Jul–mid-Aug • AE DC V*
A charming setting and a club-like atmosphere – photographs on the walls of artists and intellectuals give the place a slightly arty character – combine to make this tiny restaurant very popular among professionals. It is tucked away in a small street in a very old part of the city. Traditional Italian cuisine features strongly on the menu, as well as international dishes such as fillet steaks prepared in different ways.

Notai 🎫//
Via de'Pignattari 1 ☎ *228694 • closed Sun (except during fairs) • AE DC MC V*
Some of the Bolognese argue that the Notai is not what it was, that standards in food and service have dropped and prices are too steep. However it is still high on the list among foreign visitors, thanks perhaps to its position opposite San Petronio, the Art Nouveau decor and well spaced tables. Food is regional

and there is a 6-course *menu degustazione*. A piano provides background music.

Pappagallo *□///*
Pza della Mercanzia 3c ☎ *232807* • *closed Sun D, Mon, Aug* • *AE DC V*
Opinions are divided about this well-known establishment, one-time symbol of Bolognese gastronomy. It is appreciated for its sophistication, its attentive service and its setting in an old *palazzo* near the two leaning towers, but the Art Nouveau decor is a touch garish and the quality of the food these days is variable and seldom matches that of Gianluigi Morini's other restaurant, the San Domenico at Imola. The cooking is a blend of *nuova* and traditional Bolognese cuisines, and the wines classic Italian. Set menus are available at lunch time.

Rosteria Luciano *□/*
Via Nazario Sauro 19 ☎ *231249* • *closed Tue D, Wed, Aug* • *AE DC MC V*
A small restaurant with excellent regional dishes, the Luciano is central and nearly always packed. Even so it provides an ideal background for discussions of a general nature over lunch. The exterior is unprepossessing but inside the restaurant is smart and modern. Good wine list.

Silverio *□///*
Via Nosadella 37a ☎ *330604* • *closed Mon, Aug* • *AE V*
Silverio's is the place nowadays in Bologna to see and be seen. In company with the fashionable, the beautiful and the intellectual, you can be sure that even the most elaborate dishes will retain the virtues of their natural ingredients. The conversation tends to dwell less on business than on the creativity of the cuisine or on the exhibitions of modern art that grace the walls.

Tre Frecce *□///*
Strada Maggiore 19 ☎ *231200* • *closed Sun D, Mon, Aug* • *AE DC V*
The wooden-columned portico and ancient arches of an old town mansion form the entrance to this small, attractive restaurant which is popular with business people for both lunch and dinner. In one of the oldest parts of the city, it consists of a main dining area decorated with old paintings, and a gallery above reached by a wooden staircase. The food is Bolognese but light, with an imaginative use of vegetables. The *tortelloni* with ricotta and walnut sauce is an established favourite.

OTHER RESTAURANTS
There are many less expensive and more informal restaurants. *Alice*, Via d'Azeglio 65b ☎ 583359, is small, serves superb food, and is always lively with a cosmopolitan crowd of diners from soccer to movie stars. *Antica Osteria Romagnola*, Via Rialto 13 ☎ 263699, specializes in Neapolitan food (reservations are recommended) and *Battibecco*, Via Battibecco 4 ☎ 275845, is animated and known for its fish. *Cesari*, Via de'Carbonesi 8 ☎ 237710, is highly regarded for its authentic Bolognese fare. *La Cesoia*, Via Massarenti 90 ☎ 342854, is excellent value and popular. For a reliable haven from the Fiera at lunch time try *Papa Re*, Pza dell'Unità 6 ☎ 366980. *Ruggero*, Via degli Usberti 6 ☎ 236056, a perennial favourite with locals, serves excellent fresh fish cooked on embers on Thursday and Friday. *Trattoria di Re Enzo*, Via Riva di Reno 79 ☎ 234803, is small but has well-spaced tables; reservations essential.

Out of town
At Casteldebole, 7km/4.5 miles west of central Bologna, the *Antica Trattoria del Cacciatore* ☎ 564203 serves traditional Bolognese cuisine at high prices in an attractive rustic setting and decor. At Imola, 32km/20 miles southeast of Bologna, the *San Domenico* ☎ (0542) 29000, in a 16thC Dominican convent, is the regional temple of gastronomy; its cuisine ranks among the best in Europe. Space is limited; reservations well in advance are essential.

Bars and cafés

The more exclusive hotel bars, particularly the *Royal Carlton* and the cocktail bar of the *Baglioni*, are best for serious discussions. For an informal chat over coffee or Fortnum & Mason tea and cakes, go to *Zanarini* in Piazza Galvani. The most sophisticated bar for a drink and pasta is *Zelig*, Via Porta Nuova 9, which serves good wine and beer. However, the authentic Bolognese meeting places are the *osterie*, long-established venues for social encounters or cultural activities. Many offer full meals and/or provide entertainment such as cabaret, jazz or films. Most are open until after midnight.

Entertainment

Bologna has a long cultural tradition and is proud of its music.
Theatre Small theatres perform comedies and high-quality avant-garde drama from October to early May but there is no permanent civic theatre.
Music The most important venue is the *Teatro Comunale*, Largo Respighi, with an elaborate 18thC auditorium. Symphony concerts and opera take place Sep–Jun; reservations ☎ 529999. Concerts are also organized in other city theatres, in churches and at the *Conservatorio Giambattista Martini*, Pza Rossini 2 ☎ 221483; information ☎ 236346. Jazz has been thriving since the arrival of American troops at the end of World War II, and can be heard in many *osterie* throughout the city, notably at *Dell'Orsa*, Via Mentana 1 ☎ 270744, which attracts big names.
Cinema *Adriano*, Via San Felice 52 ☎ 555127, shows original language films every Monday, Oct–May.
Nightclubs Among the more fashionable clubs are the *Black Shadow Club*, Vicolo Broglio 1 ☎ 229704, with disco, orchestra and cabaret, and *La Fontanina*, a short drive out of town at Via Roncrio 10 ☎ 581070, with dinner and show.

Shopping

The shops of Bologna have all the elegance of a prosperous city.
Fashion The Galleria Cavour (access by Via Foscherai or Via Farini) boasts some of the biggest names in Italian design, but there are boutiques throughout the historic centre, many in beautifully restored old buildings. The Bolognese shoe designer Bruno Magli has shops at Piazza Mercanzia 1 and Via Ugo Bassi 5.
Food is taken very seriously in Bologna and the city's food shops are a treat. The biggest market for fresh produce is the *Mercato delle Erbe*, Via Ugo Bassi 25 (open Mon–Wed, Fri, 7.15–1, 5–7; Sat, 7.15–1). Also worth exploring is the area of Via Pescherie Vecchie (off Piazza Maggiore) and Via Drapperie for food stalls, specialist and delicatessen shops and a covered market with enticing arrangements of vegetables, meat and cheese.

Sightseeing

The charm of Bologna can only be appreciated by walking unhurriedly through the old city and in the university district. The free leaflet/map *Bologna 3 Days* (from the tourist office) gives opening times and brief descriptions of all sights, which include a rich variety of medieval monuments, museums and Gothic churches.
Galleria Davia-Bargellini Intriguing collection of 15th–19thC paintings and applied arts displayed in a splendid *palazzo*. *Strada Maggiore 44. Open Tue–Sat, 9–2; Sun, 9–12.30.*
Museo Civico Archeologico Ancient Egyptian, Etruscan, Greek and Roman finds. *Via dell'Archiginnasio 2. Open Tue–Sat, 9–2; Sun, 9–12.30.*
Palazzo Comunale, Collezioni Comunali d'Arte Bolognese paintings (the *trecento* to late baroque) in impressive ex-papal *palazzo*. *Pza Maggiore. Open Mon, Wed–Sat, 9–2; Sun, 9–12.30.*
Pinacoteca Nazionale Mainly Bolognese art from Gothic to baroque. Important works by Vitale da Bologna, Giotto and Raphael. Rooms devoted to works by the Carracci family, Guercino and Guido Reni. *Via*

Belle Arti 56. Open Tue–Sat, 9–2; Sun and hols, 9–1.

San Domenico Huge 13thC Dominican basilica, reconstructed in the 18th century. Contains Nicola Pisano's vividly carved marble tomb (Arca di San Domenico). *Pza San Domenico.*

San Francesco Imposing 13thC Franciscan church with flying buttresses and chapels radiating from the main altar. *Pza San Francesco.*

San Petronio Massive basilica, whose unfinished Gothic brick façade dominates the main piazza. Finely carved reliefs on the central portal by 15thC Sienese Jacopo della Quercia, and other 15thC works of art inside. *Pza Maggiore.*

Santo Stefano Picturesque group of 8th–13thC sanctuaries, cloisters and crypts, on a square of old houses and *palazzi*. Tiny museum and a shop selling honey and liqueurs made by the monks. *Via Santo Stefano 24.*

University museums There are 24 university museums, containing rare scientific teaching materials from the 16th century on. Guided tours only; ☎ 512151 for information. Most fascinating is the *Museo Ostetrico Givan Antonio Galli* (obstetrics museum) containing life-size terracotta, wax and glass babies used to train midwives (Via Zamboni 33; open Mon–Fri, 9–4; Sat; 9–1). The *Museo Anatomia Umana Normale* (museum of human anatomy) has wax models of the human muscular system (many life size), as used by 18thC students (Via Irnerio 48; open Mon–Fri, 9–1).

Spectator sports

Basketball The most popular sport in the city. Both Bologna's two professional teams (Virtus and Fortitudo) play at the *Palazzo dello Sport*, Pza Azzarita 8 ☎ 557283; tickets are hard to get.

Soccer The local team is in the second division.

Horseracing Popular trotting races take place at the *Ippodromo Arcoveggio* Sep–May. Information ☎ 371505.

Keeping fit

Fitness centres Bologna offers little scope to visitors wishing to work off the effects of all that good food. Of the recommended hotels, only the *Crest* and the *Novotel* have sports facilities, and most good private clubs require membership of at least one month. *Villa Ghigi Club*, Via Mezzacosta 1 ☎ 331701, accepts nonmembers.

Golf The *Golf Club Bologna*, Monte San Pietro, Via Sabattini 69 ☎ 969100, is the most exclusive and requires membership of another club.

Jogging The Bologna marathon is held in May. The best park for jogging is Giardini Margherita.

Squash Muncipal *Squash Center*, Via Amendola 8 ☎ 553528, is open to nonmembers.

Tennis Municipal sports centres run public courts; call *Federazione Tennis*, Via Martelli 31 ☎ 530348.

Local resources

Business services

Hotels can usually arrange secretarial and other services. *Executive Service*, Via A. Saffi 15 ☎ 522578, provides in-house staff, equipment and offices.

Photocopying and printing *Emiliana Macchine Ufficio* ☎ 522370 or 522366; *Gestetner* ☎ 392872 or 399731.

Secretarial and translation *Palazzo dei Congressi 5c* ☎ 6435111.

Communications

Local delivery *Radio Taxis* ☎ 372727 or 534141, *Pony Express* ☎ 222888, *Mini Tras* ☎ 323032.

Long-distance delivery *Express* ☎ 373878 and *Nircoop* ☎ 503107 deliver to major Italian cities, *DHL* ☎ 578927 internationally.

Post office *Posta Centrale*, Pza Minghetti 1 ☎ 223598 (open Mon–Fri, 8.15–6.30 for letters; Sat, 8.15–2), and at the station and the Fiera. Afternoon parcel post from the office at Via Ugo Bassi 2 only. Other city post offices shut at 2pm.

Telex and fax *Errepi*, Via S. Donato 66-13 ☎ 514001 or 501616.

Conference/exhibition centres
The large modern exhibition and trade fair site, the Fiera (Ente Antonomo Fiere di Bologna, Pza Costituzione 6, 40128 ☎ 282111 ☒ 511248), hosts about 20 fairs (including international exhibitions of children's books, footwear and leather, agricultural machinery, technology and equipment for the building trade) and provides 85,000 sq metres of covered exhibition area. The Centro Servizi provides banks, computer terminals, meeting rooms and press room. The nearby Palazzo dei Congressi has an auditorium seating 1,400 and many smaller rooms. The *Palazzo Albergati*, Via Masini 46, Zola Predosa ☎ 750247, a stately home just outside Bologna, can be rented for meetings, conventions and shows, capacity up to 2,000.

Emergencies
Bureaus de change There are 24hr exchange facilities at the railway station exchange offices open 7am–7.30pm and 7.30pm–7am at the ticket office opposite (Eurocheques not accepted).
Hospitals 24hr emergency at *Ospedale Maggiore*, Largo Nigrisoli 2 ☎ 382984, and *Ospedale S. Orsola-Malpighi*, Via Massarenti 9 ☎ 6363111. Doctor and ambulance ☎ 333333. The Maggiore also provides an emergency dental service.
Pharmacies Details of a Sunday and overnight rotating service are available at closed pharmacies, in local newspapers or by ☎ 192.
Police *Questura*: Pza Galileo Galilei ☎ 337111.

Information sources
Business information The *Commercio Estero*, part of the *Camera di Commercio*, Palazzo degli Affari, Pza della Costituzione ☎ 515131, in the Fiera complex, gives advice on economic activity in the province and on setting up a business. The headquarters of the *Commercio Estero* are at Palazzo della Mercanzia, 40125.
Local media The daily *Il Resto del Carlino* has poor business coverage. The *Bologna Economica* is a monthly business paper, published by the chamber of commerce.
Tourist information, Pza Maggiore 6 ☎ 239660, at the railway station ☎ 246541, both open Mon–Sat, 9–7, Sun, 9–1, and at the Fiera (during fairs). Listings can be found in *Pubblifiera* or *Un Ospite di Bologna* (both in English).

Thank-yous
Confectionery The most famous confectioner is *Confetteria Majani*, Via Carbonesi 5 ☎ 234302, the original manufacturer of the Fiat chocolates.
Florists *Romano*, Logge del Pavaglione 4 ☎ 221820, or Via Rizzoli 9 ☎ 222523, will take telephone credit card orders (over L50,000).

OTHER CITIES
FERRARA *codes* zip 44100 ☎ 0532
An important market town for local fruit-growing with about 144,000 inhabitants. There is also some industry, mainly in food (pasta, flour mills, sugar), agricultural machinery and chemicals. Companies of note are Berco (engineering), VM Motori (diesel engines), Colombani (fruit canning) and Coop Costruttori (construction).

Hotels and restaurants
Astra, Vle Cavour 55 ☎ 26234, is a modern hotel with a good restaurant; *Ripagrande*, Via Ripagrande 21 ☎ 34733, is a comfortably converted Renaissance *palazzo* with modern bedrooms.

Relaxation
The *castle* of the d'Este family, and several of their palaces (*Palazzo dei Diamanti, Palazzo di Ludovico il Moro, Palazzo Schifanoia*) should be seen. The *Duomo* contains some fine works of art.

Information sources
Camera di Commercio, Largo Costello 10 ☎ 33371.
Tourist information, Pzta Municipale 19 ☎ 35017, open Mon–Sat, 9–1, 2.30–7; Sun, 9–1.

FORLÌ *codes* zip 47100 ☎ 0543
Agriculture and local food processing constitute the main activities at Forlì (population over 110,000). There are also enterprises producing textiles and chemicals, and Bartoletti makes trailers. At nearby Cesena there is light engineering and the Gruppo Trevisiani.

The successful Gilmar clothing company is at San Giovanni in Marignano. Rimini, Riccione, Cattolica and Cesenatico are popular tourist resorts; international trade fairs are held at Rimini.

Hotels and restaurants
Della Città, Via Fortis 8 ☎ 28297, is the best hotel in Forlì, with a good restaurant (or try *Vecchia Forlì*, Via Maroncelli 4 ☎ 26104). *La Frasca* ☎ 767471 at Castrocaro Terme (11km/6.75 miles) is worth a gastronomic detour.

Relaxation
The main sights are the church of *San Mercuriale* and the art gallery, the *Pinacoteca Comunale*.

Information sources
Camera di Commercio, Corso della Repubblica 5 ☎ 31402.
Tourist information, Via Filopanti 4 ☎ 25532 and Corso della Repubblica 23 ☎ 25026, open Mon–Fri, 9.30–12.30, 4–6.30.

MODENA *codes* zip 41100 ☎ 059
Modena, Bologna's traditional rival, is an important commercial centre on the ancient Via Emilia (also the main shopping street). Apart from a compact historic centre around Piazza Grande, most of the city is postwar. The population is nearly 180,000.

Much of Modena's prosperity is due to the League of Cooperatives, which works in the service sector as well as in agro-industry. The main food cooperative, CIAM, processes vast quantities of pork and beef, for hams, salami and *zamponi* (stuffed pigs' trotters, a local dish). Food processing companies include Inarca (which owns the fast-food chain "Burghy") and Fini (which owns a local hotel and restaurant). The province's sparkling red Lambrusco wine is distributed by CIV & CIV. Modena is famous for racing cars: Ferrari (at Maranello), Maserati and De Tomaso. Also important is agricultural machinery (Italtractor, FiatGeotech), and Sitma leads the world in making machinery to wrap and seal mail packets.

Sassuolo is home of the famous Marazzi tile-making company (also Ceramiche, Ragno and others). Carpi is a footwear and textiles centre, especially important for knitwear. It is also the main base of the CMB construction company, active in many projects abroad as well as in Italy.

Hotels and restaurants
Canalgrande, Corso Canal Grande 6 ☎ 217160, is a comfortable, central hotel with gracious 18thC salons and a very good restaurant, the Secchia Rapita. The *Fini*, Via Emilia Est ☎ 238091, is a good modern hotel on the Bologna road; in the town centre is the *Fini* restaurant, Largo San Francesco ☎ 223324, with a huge variety of local dishes. The *Borso d'Este*, Pza Roma 5 ☎ 214114, is also very good.

Relaxation
The *Duomo* is one of the finest romanesque churches in Italy. In the Palazzo dei Musei, the *Galleria Estense* contains the picture collection of the d'Este dukes.

Information sources
Camera di Commercio, Via Ganaceto 134 ☎ 222529.
Tourist information, Corso Canal Grande 3 ☎ 220136 and Via Scuderi 30 ☎ 222482, open Mon–Fri, 9.45–12.30, 3.30–6.30.

PARMA *codes* zip 43100 ☎ 0521
Parma is a pleasant city, with around
176,000 people, on the banks of a
tributary of the Po. It is an important
food production centre, famous for
Parma ham and Parmesan cheese and
also known for pasta (Barilla,
Braibanti). The Parma ham
processing factories are situated to the
south of the town. Parmalat is at
Collecchio. International food fairs –
Cibus in early May and
Technoconserve in October – are held
at the Fiera trade grounds to the
northwest of the city, near the Parco
Ducale.

Apart from the specialized food
industry, there is building (Incisa,
Pizzarotti and Ceci for prefabricated
housing), publishing, chemicals,
glassware (Bormioli has an enormous
factory here), footwear (Alexander
Nicolet) and clothing.

Fidenza is also an agricultural and
industrial (glass) centre on the Via
Emilia. Langhirano is famous for
hams.

Hotels and restaurants
Palace Maria Luigia, Vle Mentana 140
☎ 281032, is a modern hotel with a
good restaurant, Maxim's.

There are some excellent
restaurants: elegant *La Filoma*, Via
XX Marzo 15 ☎ 34269, and bustling
Parizzi, Strada della Repubblica 71
☎ 285952, are classic, and central.
Parma Rotta, Via Langhirano 158
☎ 581323, is more informal and
rustic with al fresco summer dining.
There are also some very good
restaurants at Collecchio (11km/6.75
miles): *Il Baule* ☎ 804110, with
summer dining outside, and *Ceci*
☎ 805489, in a picturesque old villa.

Relaxation
Parma is known for the *Teatro Regio*
(opera house), for the romanesque
Duomo and *Battistero* and for the
paintings of the native artist Correggio
(1489/94–1534) in the *Duomo* and in
the *Palazzo della Pilotta* (*Galleria
Nazionale*). Most of the sights are on
the east bank of the Parma river.

Information sources
Camera di Commercio, Via Verdi 2a
☎ 45641. *Fiera*, Via F. Rizzi 3,
43031, Baganzola ☎ 9961.
Tourist information, Pza Duomo 5
☎ 34735, open Mon–Fri, 9–12.30,
3–6; Sat, 9–12.30.

PIACENZA *codes* zip 29100 ☎ 0523
Piacenza is an important commercial
centre, with a population of about
106,000, on the Lombardy border just
60km/37 miles south of Milan, at the
junction of the Via Emilia and the
river Po. Apart from industry
connected with the agriculture of the
surrounding plains (tinned foods and
sugar refineries among others), there
are textile, construction, paper,
engineering and chemical plants.
Important companies are Astra (Fiat
group vehicles), Mazzoni (freight
forwarders), Jobs (industrial robots)
and Camillo Corvi (pharmaceuticals).
Mandelli is a world leader in the
building of sophisticated robotic
machine tools; it will have a new fully
automatic factory by the 1990s.

Hotels and restaurants
The *Grande Albergo Roma*, Via
Cittadella 14 ☎ 23201, is the best
hotel, with good views from the
restaurant. The *Antica Osteria del
Teatro*, Via Verdi 16 ☎ 23777, is
generally acclaimed for excellent
service and food.

Relaxation
See the *Piazza dei Cavalli* (equestrian
statues of the Farnese dukes and
Palazzo del Comune, called Il Gotico).
Other sights include the *Duomo* and
Museo Civico (in the Palazzo Farnese)
and the *Galleria dell'Arte Moderna
Ricci Oddi* and *Galleria Alberoni* (at
San Lazzaro).

Information sources
Camera di Commercio, Pza Cavalli 35
☎ 22241.
Tourist information, Via San Siro 17
☎ 34347, and Pza dei Mercanti
☎ 29324, open Mon–Sat, 9.30–12.30;
Mon–Wed, Fri, Sat, 4.30–6.30.

RAVENNA *codes* zip 48100 ☎ 0544
Once capital of the Western Roman
Empire, Ravenna has been developed
as a port with oil refineries and
petrochemical plants (Enichem) since
natural gas was discovered north of
the town in the 1950s. It is also the
headquarters of Ferruzzi (Europe's
largest agro-industrial multinational
and the second largest private sector
group in Italy after Fiat) and of CMC
(infrastructure, civil works), the
largest cooperative in Europe. The
centre of Ravenna, now 12km/7.5
miles from the sea, is sleepy. The
population is about 136,000.

Faenza, famous for the production
of ceramics (also important for
livestock and distilleries), is in the
province 31km/19 miles southwest
(but closer to Forlí). At Alfonsine
Marini produces industrial machinery.

Hotels and restaurants
In the centre, the *Jolly*, Pza Mameli 1
☎ 35762, or the *Bisanzio*, Via Salara 30
☎ 27111, provide the best business
accommodation; *Centrale Byron*, Via
IV Novembre 14 ☎ 22225, is
adequate. The *Park*, Vle delle Nazioni
181 ☎ 431743, at Marina di Ravenna,
13km/8 miles to the north, is a
comfortable resort hotel with pools,
2 tennis courts and conference halls
(capacity up to 500). About 30km/
18.5 miles west from Ravenna, near
Lugo, is the elegantly restored *Villa
Bolis*, Via Corriera 5, Barbiano di
Cotignola ☎ (0545) 78347, a popular
hotel with visitors in the fruit trade.

Tre Spade, Via Rasponi 37
☎ 32382, is the smartest restaurant
with modern cooking and decor; *Bella
Venezia*, Via IV Novembre 16
☎ 22746, is also good, as is the new *Il
Brini*, Vle Po 69 ☎ 67498, about
1km/0.6 miles south of the centre.

Relaxation
The visitor to Ravenna should find
time to see some of the marvellous
Byzantine mosaics, notably in the
Basilica Sant'Apollinare Nuovo,
Basilica di San Vitale and adjacent
Mausoleum of Galla Placida.

Information sources
Camera di Commercio, Vle L.C. Farini
14 ☎ 30387.
Tourist information, Via Salara 8–12
☎ 35404, open daily, 8–1.

REGGIO EMILIA
codes zip 42100 ☎ 0522
A commercial and industrial centre,
with about 130,000 inhabitants,
involved principally in agriculture
(Parmigiano-Reggiano cheese, pig
breeding, Lambrusco wines) and
related activities such as canning,
packaging and the manufacture of
agricultural and processing
equipment. Reggio Emilia was a
traditional centre for silk making and
is still important in clothing
manufacture; Max Mara, the fashion
company, is based in the town and
employs more than 500 people. The
building, furniture and household
appliances sectors are well developed:
SMEG (kitchen and laboratory
equipment) at Guastalla and Tecnogas
(appliances) at Gualtieri. Cavriago is
important for hosiery, Scandiano for
making ties.

Hotels and restaurants
The *Grand Astoria*, Vle Nobili 2
☎ 35245, has a dining room (Il
Girarrosto ☎ 37671) with a splendid
view and excellent food and wines.
More traditional is *La Posta*, Pza
Cesare Battisti 4 ☎ 32944. *Lo Scudo
d'Italia*, Via Vescovado 5 ☎ 34345,
serves excellent local cooking. In
Cavriago try *Picci* ☎ 57201 (famous
for game and mushrooms).

Relaxation
The *Galleria Parmeggiani* contains
Flemish and Spanish art, as well as
Italian paintings. Opera is performed
at the *Teatro Municipale*.

Information sources
Camera di Commercio, Pza della
Vittoria 1 ☎ 33841.
Tourist information, Via Guido da
Castello 7 ☎ 31953, and Pza
Prampolini ☎ 43370, open Mon–Sat,
9–1; Mon–Fri, 3–6.

TUSCANY (Toscana) AND UMBRIA

The harmonious and timeless landscape of Tuscany has undergone many changes since the postwar years; not only has there been a boom in manufacturing but agriculture is becoming more intensive and specialized, particularly in the north. Here, in the fertile basin of the river Arno, traditional agriculture has declined sharply in favour of cash crops like cereals and tobacco. Towns like Prato, Pistoia and Florence have enjoyed considerable economic expansion. Industry along the Arno valley between Pisa and Florence is mainly in crafts, especially leather, and textiles in and around Prato. On the coast, Carrara, Massa and Pietrasanta are important for marble-quarrying and Fiat and Olivetti have factories at Massa. The so-called Riviera della Versilia is important for growing vegetables and flowers as well as supporting several resorts of which Viareggio is the largest. Lucca has two major olive oil exporters (Filippo Berio, Callisto Francesconi) and is a centre for paper making.

The central heartland of Tuscany, around the Chianti hills, preserves the traditional landscape of cypress trees, vines and olives, but is less economically developed than the Arno valley. Since peasant farmers were "encouraged" in the 1960s to move to the towns for employment, many picturesque old farmhouses have been left derelict or bought by foreigners. While the olive oil trade has suffered from a devastating frost in 1984-5, and from competition with other EC countries, the Chianti wine trade flourishes, with more emphasis on regulated (DOC and DOCG) quality. Several zones on the fringes of the Chianti Classico area are also entitled to use the term Chianti. The famous Brunello di Montalcino and Vino Nobile di Montepulciano, farther south, produce over 5m litres a year. West of Siena are the copper-bearing Colline Metallifere. To the south is the Maremma, an area of partly reclaimed marshland used for the cultivation of cereals and vegetables, with a fine national park; Grosseto is the main town and provincial capital. The Val di Chiana is a beef-raising area close to the borders with Umbria where there has been development in mechanical engineering and clothing manufacture. Places on the tourist itinerary less famous than Florence and Siena include Pienza, San Gimignano, Spello and Volterra.

Umbria, promoted by the regional tourist board as the Green Heart of Italy, is a more remote, landlocked region with fewer than 1m people. Over 10% of the population is still employed in agriculture. There are hundreds of small import-export companies for the main sectors: food (oils, wines, confectionery, pasta and truffles), clothing, furniture, mechanical and agricultural machinery. Ceramic production (from Città di Castello, Deruta, Gualdo Tadino, Gubbio and Orvieto) is the main local craft. Orvieto is also known for its wine. In the province of Terni there are hydroelectric power plants, giant steelworks and important chemical industries as well as some production of paper, food, chemicals, textiles and food processing. Assisi, Perugia, Orvieto and Spoleto remain important art centres.

There are airports at Pisa and Perugia.

FLORENCE (Firenze)

City codes zip 50100 ☎ 055

Since Etruscan times, Florence has achieved an unparalleled standard of artistic design which has been combined with an acute business sense. In the 13th century Dante composed poetry and Florence became a centre of international banking and trade. Cosimo de' Medici, progenitor of the great dynasty, secured the status of his family and his city by his financial acumen and established the artistic patronage which made Florence the frontrunner of the Italian Renaissance.

The tourists who flock to see the treasures ensure an income for the 650,000 inhabitants. But there has been technical development also. Engineering has flourished and in the suburbs and farther afield larger industrial enterprises now include metallurgy (Metalli and La Magona), precision engineering (Nuovo Pignone), telecommuncations and electronics (Officine Galileo and Siette), batteries (Superpila), pharmaceuticals (Manetti, Roberts), rubber goods (Gover) and packaging. Prato, the textile town just to the west of Florence, is also the site of engineering concerns, such as Magni, makers of precision machinery and rolling stock.

The Communist town council struggles to run Florence efficiently but, as elsewhere, corruption and crime are still endemic, and the time taken to refurbish monuments or excavate ancient sites such as the Piazza della Signoria is preposterous.

All Florentines are passionately attached to their city but over the centuries they have become pragmatic. The land legislation of the 1960s drastically reduced the incomes of many great families so they have taken to business. Although Florentines tend to have very definite views, many are willing to consider new ideas.

Arriving

Pisa, 85km/53 miles from Florence, is the main international airport which handles scheduled flights from Frankfurt, London and Paris. Florence has first-class rail connections with the major Italian cities and there are services from Paris, London, Munich and Basel. Autostrada routes run north to Bologna and southeast to Rome; west to Pistoia, Lucca and Pisa (and thence to Genoa) and the route south to Siena is being extended to Rome.

Galileo Galilei airport, Pisa
City link Incoming daytime scheduled flights are served by direct trains (which run hourly and take 1hr but can be crowded) to Florence. Taxis are always available at the rank in front of the terminal but the cost of the journey to Florence is about

L80,000. A branch of the Florence–Viareggio autostrada which will give easy access to Pisa airport is under construction. Information ☎ (050) 28088.

There is a check-in for Pisa airport at Florence station.

Peretola airport
This very small airport, 4km/2.5 miles northwest of Florence, handles daily flights from Paris, Munich, Barcelona, Milan, Naples and Rome. Inquiries ☎ 373498.

Railway station
Santa Maria Novella is overcrowded; a long wait at the ticket windows and information desk is normal. Inter City trains run between Florence and Bologna, Milan, Rome and Naples, and the services to regional centres are frequent. Facilities include a hotel

reservations desk and tourist office, currency exchange (open daily, 7–1, 2–8), a bank (open Mon–Sat, 8.20–6.20), computerized train information system (in English), large cafeteria and a gloomy *albergo diurno*. Long lines often wait for taxis outside, but the major hotels operate shuttle buses. Inquiries ☏ 278785.

Getting around
Finding a taxi can be difficult but the city is compact and most of it can be covered on foot.

Identifying street numbers in Florence is a problem. Main entrances to *palazzi* and houses are numbered in black and marked with an N (for *nero*). Numbers for shops, restaurants and other commercial premises within blocks are coloured red with an R above the number. An address can have two numbers, a red for the shop below and a black for apartments above, but the system is not consistently applied.

Taxis Getting a cab can be a problem, even at the ranks at main intersections. Radio taxis ☏ 4390 or 4798.

Driving The centre is closed to most private cars. Residents can obtain a permit for the zone they live in but, because of the restrictions, many Florentines get about by bike or motor-scooter. Hotel guests can drive into their hotel zone and credentials like business cards usually get you past the traffic police. Parking is difficult although there are normally places under the Mercato Centrale. Parking is easier outside the centre, for example at the Lungarno Guicciardini and near the station at Fortezza da Basso (expensive); from the latter there is a free bus service into the city.

Walking Beware of pickpockets and bag-snatchers and avoid deserted areas after dark; however, the city centre is usually crowded until the early hours. Unaccompanied women should be particularly wary at night.

Bus The network is extensive and efficient, but complicated by one-way

systems. Buses displaying a hand holding a coin accept exact change; for others, single or multiple journey tickets, or tickets permitting free transfers to other buses within 70mins, must be purchased from *ATAF* bus offices or at newsstands, tobacconists and some bars.

Area by area
Historic Florence, north of the Arno, is bounded by tree-lined avenues, the *viali*. Built in the 19th century to replace the old walls, these now form a busy ring road around most of the city. The Viali dei Colli, the equivalent roads south of the Arno, wind through rural hillsides and afford views of the city still framed by wooded hills and dominated by the huge red dome of its cathedral.

The heart of Florence consists of three great piazzas and a dense network of narrow medieval streets flanked by imposing *palazzi*. The Piazza della Signoria (undergoing disruptive excavations) is dominated by the Palazzo Vecchio (town hall). The Piazza del Duomo, where pedestrians can now safely approach the magnificent green, white and pink Duomo and Baptistery, is an important crossroads. The third main square is the Piazza della Repubblica, a 19thC intrusion into old Florence.

Northwest of the Duomo is San Lorenzo where Florentines sell their fresh produce in a covered market and their handicrafts from stalls in the nearby streets. Beyond, the station area is strictly functional: fast-food cafés, cheap hotels and conference and trade venues. The Fortezza da Basso, the main site for trade fairs, is one of the few remaining medieval fortresses along the *viali*. The area between Via Tornabuoni and the station around Ognissanti is quiet, has hotels of all categories and some of the best antique shops. Cascine, the large park on both sides of the river, has two racecourses and sports facilities; it is a haunt of prostitutes and transvestites at night. Just east of the centre, Santa Croce is traditionally a working-class

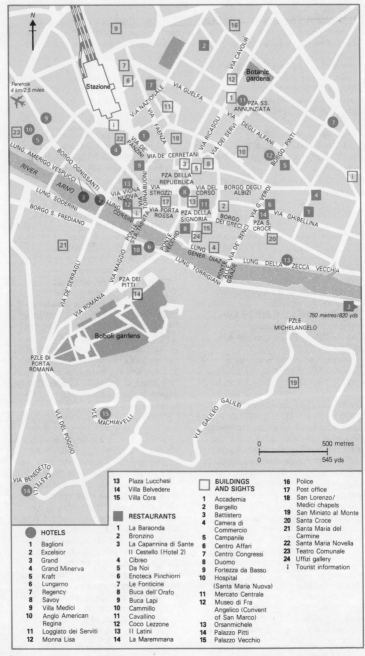

N

Peretola
4 km/2.5 miles

Stazione

750 metres/820 yds

PZLE
MICHELANGELO

Botanic
gardens

Boboli gardens

PZLE DI
PORTA
ROMANA

| 0 | | 500 metres |
| 0 | | 545 yds |

HOTELS

1 Baglioni
2 Excelsior
3 Grand
4 Grand Minerva
5 Kraft
6 Lungarno
7 Regency
8 Savoy
9 Villa Medici
10 Anglo American
   Regina
11 Loggiato dei Serviti
12 Monna Lisa

13 Plaza Lucchesi
14 Villa Belvedere
15 Villa Cora

RESTAURANTS

1 La Baraonda
2 Bronzino
3 La Capannina di Sante
   Il Cestello (Hotel 2)
4 Cibreo
5 Da Noi
6 Enoteca Pinchiorri
7 Le Fonticine
8 Buca dell'Orafo
9 Buca Lapi
10 Cammillo
11 Cavallino
12 Coco Lezzone
13 Il Latini
14 La Maremmana

**BUILDINGS
AND SIGHTS**

1 Accademia
2 Bargello
3 Battistero
4 Camera di
   Commercio
5 Campanile
6 Centro Affari
7 Centro Congressi
8 Duomo
9 Fortezza da Basso
10 Hospital
   (Santa Maria Nuova)
11 Mercato Centrale
12 Museo di Fra
   Angelico (Convent
   of San Marco)
13 Orsanmichele
14 Palazzo Pitti
15 Palazzo Vecchio

16 Police
17 Post office
18 San Lorenzo/
   Medici chapels
19 San Miniato al Monte
20 Santa Croce
21 Santa Maria del
   Carmine
22 Santa Maria Novella
23 Teatro Comunale
24 Uffizi gallery
i Tourist information

area, famous for its leather workshops.

The muddy Arno is spanned by a series of bridges, most famous of which is the Ponte Vecchio, the territory of goldsmiths and jewellers.

South of the river, Oltrarno is a quarter of street markets, artisan workshops, chiefly making furniture, and antique galleries. Here are the Palazzo Pitti and the Boboli gardens.

The suburbs

The most desirable residences are in the hills, particularly near Piazzale

Michelangelo to the south and the hilltop village of Fiesole to the northeast whose villas, gardens and cypress groves have always made it fashionable. Industry and commerce are outside the *viali* in places such as Isolotto, Scandicci and Sesto Fiorentino. In Novoli, Fiat employs 1,000 in a components plant and has plans to fund civic improvements and build a landscaped suburb to which some of Florence's administrative offices can transfer. At Osmannoro, to the northwest, there is a large centre for wholesale goods.

Hotels

There are plenty of small, charming places to stay but only a few good business hotels; the best are the Excelsior, the Baglioni, near the station, the Villa Medici and the Grand Minerva. Several large chain hotels are planned for the outskirts, including a Sheraton. Noise can be a problem, so opt for a quiet room over a garden or courtyard or for one of the more peaceful hotels outside the centre.

Advance reservations are essential from Easter to October and during the fairs. The hotel reservations office at the station may find rooms in an emergency. All hotels listed with full entries provide supervised parking, but not always free or at the hotel, room service and IDD telephones, TVs and minibars in bedrooms.

Baglioni *L* ||||
Pza dell'Unità Italiana 6, 50123
☎ *218441* ⊤ᵡ *570225 fax 215695* •
Palace Hotels • *AE DC MC V* • *195
rooms, 1 suite, 2 restaurants, 2 bars*
The Baglioni is a large, efficiently run hotel opposite the station. It is classical in style and the decor combines Florentine grandeur with modern comforts. The rooftop restaurant and terrace provide a splendid panorama of the city. Bedrooms, with beamed ceilings and Renaissance prints, vary greatly in size; some have balconies. 8 meeting rooms (capacity up to 350).

Excelsior *L* |||||
Pza Ognissanti 3, 50123 ☎ *264201*
⊤ᵡ *570022 fax 210278* • *CIGA* • *AE DC
MC V* • *205 rooms, 5 suites, 1 restaurant,
1 bar*
Florence's most prestigious hotel, on the banks of the Arno, is a large

luxuriously furnished 19thC *palazzo*. The 1920s grandeur of the public rooms and solid comfort of its large bedrooms appeal to executives, celebrities and the top end of the tourist market. It is a popular rendezvous for business people who come either to the first-class Cestello restaurant, with its superb rooftop setting, in summer (see *Restaurants*), or for a drink in the Donatello bar. 24hr room service, hairdresser • 5 meeting rooms (capacity up to 400).

Grand *L* |||||
Pza Ognissanti 1, 50123 ☎ *6813861*
⊤ᵡ *570055 fax 2174000* • *CIGA* • *AE
DC MC V* • *38 rooms (100 rooms by
1990), 2 suites, 1 bar*
A sister hotel of the Excelsior, the Grand stands just across the square, a 19thC neo-classical building whose guests have included Queen Victoria and other foreign royalty. It was

reopened after complete renovation in 1986, and is now comparable with the Excelsior but smaller and with fewer facilities. However, 60 more bedrooms (the majority overlooking the river), a restaurant and six meeting rooms are planned. Meanwhile, guests can use the Excelsior's amenities.

Grand Minerva *L*////
Pza Santa Maria Novella, 50123
☎ 284555 ⊤ⅹ 570414 fax 268281 • *AE DC V* • *107 rooms, 5 suites, 1 restaurant, 1 bar*
Very near the centre and less than 5mins from the station, the cream-washed Grand Minerva is an oasis of calm and efficiency with modern and comfortable rooms. The decor is attractive if bland, the dining room overlooks a garden and there are plenty of areas for informal meetings. Rooftop pool • 4 meeting rooms (capacity up to 250).

Kraft *L*////
Via Solferino 2, 50123 ☎ 284273 ⊤ⅹ 571523 fax 29867 • *Best Western* • *AE DC MC V* • *70 rooms, 1 restaurant, 1 bar*
A quiet pleasant hotel about a 30min walk from the Duomo, near the Cascine park. Efficiently run and popular with Americans. Bedrooms are traditional or modern in style, and there is a spacious sitting-room/bar with beamed ceiling and leather seats. Roof-top terrace (with a small pool). 24hr room service.

Lungarno *L*///
Borgo San Jacopo 14, 50125 ☎ 264211 ⊤ⅹ 570129 fax 268437 • *Penguin* • *AE DC MC V* • *56 rooms, 10 suites, 1 bar*
The Lungarno is one of the city's most attractive modern hotels. Built partly over the Arno, on the south bank, it has excellent river views from the spacious front rooms, some of which have balconies. Business facilities are limited but the quiet, civilized atmosphere and comfortable rooms, which include some large ones

in the 13thC tower, more than compensate. The decor is a successful blend of chintz, rusticity and modern art. 24hr room service • 1 meeting room (capacity up to 30).

Regency *L*/////
Pza Massimo d'Azeglio 3, 50121
☎ 245247 ⊤ⅹ 571058 fax 2342938 • *Ottaviani* • *AE DC MC V* • *33 rooms, 5 suites, 1 restaurant, 1 bar*
On a tree-lined square, 15mins on foot east of the Duomo, the Regency could be taken for a private club. It is small and exclusive, with prices that put off all but the super-rich or those on generous expense accounts. Public rooms are furnished in sophisticated French style. The elegant dining room overlooks the garden. Bedrooms have modern colour schemes. 24hr room service.

Savoy *L*/////
Pza della Repubblica 7, 50123
☎ 28331 ⊤ⅹ 570220 fax 284840 • *Atahotels* • *AE DC MC V* • *101 rooms, 4 suites, 1 restaurant, 1 bar*
An old-style hotel in a *fin-de-siècle* building, the Savoy is the most central of the Florentine de luxe hotels, though not the most characterful. 24hr room service, hairdresser • 3 meeting rooms (capacity up to 200).

Villa Medici *L*/////
Via Il Prato 42, 50123 ☎ 261331 ⊤ⅹ 570179 fax 261336 • *Sina Hotels* • *AE DC MC V* • *99 rooms, 9 suites, 1 restaurant, 1 bar*
Heads of state stay at the Villa Medici but most guests are business travellers, attracted by the quiet garden setting and the sumptuous rooms. Of the original 18thC villa only the façade remains; the rest was built in 1960. Bedrooms are large and decorated in chintz and dark wood, most with balconies overlooking the garden or pool. It is convenient for the station but a good 15min walk from the centre. No private parking. 24hr room service, beauty salon • pool, sauna • 4 meeting rooms (capacity up to 90).

OTHER HOTELS

Anglo American Regina *⊡//// Via Garibaldi 9, 50123 ☎ 282114* ⊠ *570289 fax 268513 • AE DC MC V.* Traditional, civilized hotel in quiet residential area, a 15min walk from the centre.
Loggiato dei Serviti *⊡ Pza Santissima Annunziata 3, 50129* ☎ *263592* ⊠ *575808 • AE DC MC V.* Peaceful and charming.
Monna Lisa *⊡// Borgo Pinti 27, 50121 ☎ 2479751* ⊠ *573300 • AE DC MC V.* An exceptional small hotel, popular with British and Americans, on two floors of an ancient *palazzo.*
Plaza Lucchesi *⊡//// Lungarno della Zecca Vecchia 38, 50122* ☎ *264141* ⊠ *570302 fax 2480921 • AE DC MC V.* Recently refurbished 4-star hotel on the river.
Villa Belvedere *⊡//// Via Benedetto Castelli 3, 50124 ☎ 222501,* ⊠ *575648 • AE DC V.* Modern, spotlessly clean and friendly hotel 3km/2 miles to the south, with beautiful views. Pool, tennis court.
Villa Cora *⊡//// Vle Machiavelli 18, 50125 ☎ 2298451* ⊠ *570604 fax 229086 • AE DC MC V.* On a hillside 3km/2 miles to the south. Lavishly appointed villa with pool.

There are several attractive hotels on the Arno, including the Berchielli (Lungarno Acciaiuoli 14, Pza del Limbo) 6r ☎ 264061), but rooms overlooking the river can be noisy.

Out of town
The very expensive *Villa San Michele* ☎ 59451 at Fiesole, 8km/5 miles to the northwest, is one of Italy's most exclusive hotels; façade by Michelangelo and stunning views of Florence. At Candeli, 7km/4.5 miles east of the city, *Villa La Massa* ☎ 630051 is a 16thC country villa by the river. For a reasonably priced hotel with a pool, try the *Villa Le Rondini* ☎ 400081, 7km/4.5 miles towards Trespiano to the northeast.

Small hotels of character
For those with a few extra days to spend in Florence, the following can be recommended; all take at least some credit cards. *Annalena*, Via Romana 34, 50125 ☎ 222402, a handsomely furnished *pensione* on the upper floor of a 15thC *palazzo* close to the Boboli gardens. *Hermitage*, Vicolo Marzio 1, Pza del Pesce, 50122 ☎ 287216, is small and overlooks Ponte Vecchio (noisy rooms at the front). *Pitti Palace*, Via Barbadori 2, 50125 ☎ 282257, is a favourite among English and Americans just south of the Ponte Vecchio (some noisy rooms). *Silla*, Via dei Renai 5, 50125 ☎ 2342888, is a simple hotel on the south bank of the Arno (no restaurant). *Tornabuoni-Beacci*, Via Tornabuoni 3, 50123 ☎ 570215, is a comfortable small hotel on the top floor of a 14thC *palazzo* in the city's smartest shopping street. *Villa Carlotta*, Via Michele di Lando 3, 50125 ☎ 220530, is in a quiet residential district to the south.

Restaurants
The city's most prestigious restaurant for entertaining is Enoteca Pinchiorri. But there are plenty of other good places to eat, many serving traditional Tuscan dishes, such as *crostini*, thick soups, Tuscan ham and *bistecca alla fiorentina*, a large juicy T-bone steak sold by the kilo. Some of the most successful new restaurants are out of the centre. For a lively informal evening try a *buca*, or barrel-vaulted cellar, in the centre of town.

La Baraonda *⊡/ Via Ghibellina 67 ☎ 2341171 • D only, closed Sun • AE DC MC V •* *reservations essential* La Baraonda is Florence's latest chic trattoria. After six years in England, the welcoming proprietor, Duccio Magni, can explain every last nuance of the delicious menu and the well-chosen wine list. His wife, Elena, masterminds the food; some of the simple but delectable dishes date back to the Renaissance. Companies such as Cartier and Renault use La Baraonda for special occasions.

Bronzino *L*
Via delle Ruote 27r ☎ *495220 • closed Sun, Aug, hols • AE DC MC V • reservations essential*
Named after the 16thC court painter of the Medici, the Bronzino is a spacious, sophisticated restaurant whose proprietors were previously with Il Cestello and Mamma Gina (before the latter went into decline). A little way out of the centre, it is patronized by discerning Florentines (including ex-President Pertini) and offers a wide choice of Tuscan dishes.

La Capannina di Sante *L*||
Pza Ravenna, angolo Ponte da Verrazzano ☎ *688345 • closed Sun, Mon L, one week Aug, Xmas • AE DC MC V • reservations essential*
Some Florentines insist this is the city's best fish restaurant (there is no meat on the menu). This may be a slight exaggeration but top Florentine business people form the bulk of the clients, attracted by the elegant setting and position as well as the food.

Il Cestello *L*||||
Excelsior Hotel ☎ *264201 • AE DC MC V*
The great attraction here is the breathtaking panorama from the rooftop restaurant. Meals are otherwise taken in the richly appointed downstairs restaurant. The menu is essentially Tuscan with a few concessions to international palates. Pastas are excellent and fresh fish is beautifully prepared. A popular rendezvous for professional people.

Cibreo *L*||
Via dei Macci 118r ☎ *2341100 • closed Sun, Mon, 6 weeks Aug–Sep • AE DC*

MC V • reservations essential
This is one of the most successful of the city's newer restaurants. The cuisine consists mainly of *nuova* variations on traditional Tuscan dishes. Superb vegetable purées and *sformati* (like soufflés) are served instead of pasta. The reliable cooking and the slightly obscure location make this a favourite among Florentines, though it is usually too crowded for important discussions. To eat the same dishes at cheaper prices, sit in the small section at the back.

Da Noi *L*||
Via Fiesolana 46r ☎ *242917 • closed Sun, Mon, Aug • no credit cards • reservations essential*
This tiny, prettily furnished restaurant attracts many foreigners (particularly English textile buyers visiting Prato). The owners, Bruno (Italian) and Sabina (Swedish), used to work at Enoteca Pinchiorri and are well known for their creative blending of Italian and *nouvelle cuisine*. There are no menus; dishes of the day are recited at the table.

Enoteca Pinchiorri *L*||||
Via Ghibellina 87 ☎ *242777 • closed Sun, Mon L, Aug, Xmas • AE • reservations essential*
Occupying a splendid Renaissance palace, this sophisticated restaurant ranks among the elite of Europe. Giorgio Pinchiorri is a connoisseur of fine wines (the restaurant is above the Enoteca Nazionale Pinchiorri, well known for outstanding French and Italian wines) and his French wife is an exponent of highly imaginative *nuova cucina*. To sample a variety of dishes, try the seven-course *menu degustazione*. Prices are lower at lunch; in summer you can dine al fresco.

Le Fonticine *L*||
Via Nazionale 79r ☎ *282106 • closed Sun, Mon • AE V*
One of the few good restaurants near the station and exhibition grounds. In the same family for a quarter of a

century, it combines culinary skills with a friendly atmosphere. The Emilian and Tuscan dishes are based on the freshest of ingredients; excellent home-made pastas.

OTHER RESTAURANTS
Buca dell'Orafo, Via dei Girolami 28 ☎ 25619, is a tiny, cramped cellar restaurant which serves up splendid *bistecce* and a most unusual "grass" (*barba*) salad with fast-moving good humour. *Buca Lapi*, Via del Trebbio 1r ☎ 213768, is a cellar restaurant specializing in *bistecca alla fiorentina*. Bustling and friendly, the *Cammillo*, Borgo San Jacopo 57r ☎ 212427, attracts tourists and local antique dealers. Belying its touristy location, *Cavallino*, Via delle Farine 6 ☎ 215818, is a *restaurant d'habitués*, and a comfortable choice for lunch or dinner. *Coco Lezzone*, Via del Parioncino 26 ☎ 287178, is a crowded, white-tiled trattoria very popular with chic locals and tourists (including, recently, British royals) for the excellence of its Tuscan country cooking. Another spot for an informal gathering, *Il Latini*, Via dei Palchetti 6r ☎ 210916, is a noisy, crowded and friendly cellar restaurant where you can rub shoulders with local Florentines and enjoy big helpings of Tuscan food at reasonable prices. *La Maremmana*, Via Verdi 16 ☎ 244615, is a busy family restaurant which serves wonderful food, notably fish. More sophisticated but usually packed with tourists, though also used for business meetings, is *La Loggia*, Pzle Michelangelo ☎ 2342832.

Out of town
Florentines love to eat al fresco in hillside country restaurants overlooking the city in appealing but quite simple trattorias. Easy to reach by taxi are *Omero* ☎ 220053, 5km/3 miles south at Arcetri, and *Centanni* ☎ 630122, at Bagno a Ripoli, 7km/ 4.5 miles southeast of Florence. *La Biscondola* ☎ 821381, at Mercatale Val di Pesa, is 21km/13 miles to the south.

Bars and cafés

Business tends to be conducted in the bars of the top hotels (especially the *Donatello* in the Excelsior). At *Cantinetta Antinori*, Pza Antinori 3, wines from the Antinori estates are served with snacks or full meals (good for lunch). *Caffè*, Pza Pitti 9, is a chic bar owned by a 1960s pop star and specializing in cocktails. The *Doney*, Pza Strozzi 16–19, is a fashionable and elegant café (and restaurant), once the haunt of the *literati*. Among the smartest open-air cafés are: the *Caffè Strozzi*, Pza Strozzi 16–17, *Rivoire*, Pza della Signoria, and the four cafés in Pza della Repubblica.

Entertainment

With its student population and cultural heritage Florence supports a fair amount of theatre and music of a high standard. *Florence Concierge Information*, free from main hotels and tourist offices, lists events.
Theatre, dance, opera, music The main theatre is the *Teatro della Pergola*, Via della Pergola 18 ☎ 2479651, also used for concerts. The *Maggio Musicale* is a festival held mid-May–Jul in different venues throughout the city, with top names performing in concert, ballet and opera; tickets from the *Teatro Comunale*, Corso Italia 16 ☎ 2779236. Important concerts are held at the *Teatro Comunale* and lesser events during summer in piazzas, cloisters and the Boboli gardens.
Nightclubs The most popular discos are *Space Electronic*, Via Palazzuolo ☎ 293082, and *Yab Yum*, Via Sassetti 5 ☎ 282018.

Shopping

Shopping (or window shopping) is usually a part of any visit to Florence. Good craftsmen working in leather, glass and jewellery still abound.

The covered *Mercato Centrale*, north of Piazza San Lorenzo, has a huge range of cheeses, meats, fish, vegetables, fruit (open Mon–Sat, 7.30–1). In nearby streets, stalls display the Florentine crafts especially

leather, jewellery and knitwear.
Department stores *Principe* at Via
Strozzi 21–29 is an upmarket store
selling clothes for all ages.
Fashion The most exclusive area is in
and around Via Tornabuoni with top
designer names such as *Gucci,
Ferragamo, Valentino, Coveri,
Gianfranco Ferrè* and *Armani*. Other
chic shops (many specializing in
shoes) cluster around the Piazza della
Repubblica (particularly in Via Roma
and Via dei Calzaiuoli), the Duomo
and in Ognissanti. You can find silks
in the market in San Lorenzo.
Ice cream In the Santa Croce area,
Vivoli, Via Isole delle Stinche 7, has
an enormous and delicious range of
flavours.
Jewellery There are about 400
jewellery shops in and around
Florence. The top jewellers and
goldsmiths such as Ugo Piccini and
Torrini show their wares in tiny
medieval-looking shops overhanging
the Ponte Vecchio or near by.
Leather City shopfronts and markets
exhibit leather of varying quality
everywhere. For the best, try *Raspini*
at Via Roma 25-29: superb shoes,
bags, leather coats and clothes for
men and women. For more down-to-
earth prices, the *San Lorenzo* market
has a wide choice of leather
accessories.

Sightseeing

Florence is one of the richest cities in
Europe for art and architecture (51
museums, 24 historic churches and
numerous Renaissance *palazzi*). But
the main museums and galleries are
impossibly crowded at Easter and
from June to September, the opening
hours are short (mostly mornings
only) and sights or parts of them are
often closed for restoration. To enjoy
them at their quietest go early. The
tourist office provides a list of current
opening times and the twice monthly
tourist journal *Firenze Oggi*.
Accademia Small collection of
sculpture, paintings and tapestries
including *David*, Michelangelo's most
famous sculpture. *Via Ricasoli 60.*

Open Tue–Sat, 9–2; Sun, 9–1.
Bargello Outstanding collection of
Renaissance sculpture in medieval
fortress. *Via del Proconsolo 4. Open
Tue–Sat, 9–2; Sun, 9–1.*
Battistero Famous for its gilded
bronze doors with panels by Andrea
Pisano and Lorenzo Ghiberti. *Pza del
Duomo. Open daily, 2.30–5.30.*
Campanile Bell-tower designed by
Giotto. Steep haul up to the top but
worth it for the views. *Pza del Duomo.
Open summer, 9–7; winter, 9–5.*
Duomo Santa Maria del Fiore, with
its monumental dome by
Brunelleschi, stands as the symbol of
Florence. The stark interior contrasts
dramatically with the white, green and
rosy marble of the outside. *Pza del
Duomo. Open daily, 10.30–5.30.* Many
monuments have been moved into the
Museo dell'Opera del Duomo. *Open
summer, 9–8; winter, 9–6.*
**Museo di Fra Angelico (Convent of
San Marco)** Frescoes and most of the
greatest panel paintings of Fra
Angelico. *Pza San Marco 1. Open
Tue–Sat, 9–2; Sun, 9–1.*
Orsanmichele Originally a grain
market and consecrated as a church in
1380. Exterior has important
examples of the work of Renaissance
sculptors. *Via dei Calzaiuoli.*
Palazzo Pitti Huge 15th–16thC grand
ducal palace housing several
museums. Impressive picture galleries
and Medici treasures. *Pza Pitti. Open
Tue–Sat, 9–2; Sun, 9–1.*
Palazzo Vecchio Medieval fortress
built as the town hall. Inside are late
Renaissance and baroque frescoes and
paintings. *Pza della Signoria. Open
Mon–Fri, 9–7; Sun, 8–1.*
Pza della Santissima Annunziata
Serene and harmonious square with
Brunelleschi's famous Ospedale degli
Innocenti (Foundlings' Hospital).
San Lorenzo/Medici chapels
Important Renaissance church
designed by Brunelleschi. Old
Sacristy with decorations by
Donatello; Medici Chapels with
Michelangelo's celebrated Medici
tombs in the New Sacristy. *Pza
Madonna degli Aldobrandini. Medici*

Chapels open Tue–Sat, 9–2; Sun, 9–1.
San Miniato al Monte Charming
11th–13thC church in white and green
marble on a hill overlooking the city.
Vle Galileo.
Santa Croce Eminent Florentines
such as Michelangelo and Dante are
celebrated by tombs or monuments
here. Frescoes by Giotto embellish the
chapels of the Bardi and the Peruzzi,
two of the great banking families.
Adjoining is Brunelleschi's early
Renaissance *Pazzi chapel. Pza Santa
Croce. Open daily, 7.30–12.30,
3–6.30.*
Santa Maria del Carmine Famous
fresco cycle by Masaccio and Filippo
Lippi (Brancacci chapel) but under
restoration indefinitely. *Pza del
Carmine. Open daily, 7–12, 4–6.*
Santa Maria Novella Church with
magnificent black and white marble
façade. Major works by Masaccio,
Domenico Ghirlandaio, Filippino
Lippi, Paolo Uccello in the Chiostro
Verde (recently restored) and the
completely frescoed interior of the
*Spanish chapel. Pza Santa Maria
Novella. Open Mon–Sat, 7–11.30,
3.30–6.*
Uffizi The most famous collection of
Renaissance art in the world, fine
classical sculptures and important
Flemish paintings. Many of the 45
rooms are very crowded in summer.
*Loggiato degli Uffizi. Open Tue–Sat,
9–7; Sun, 9–1.*
Vasari Corridorio Links the Uffizi
with the Pitti Palace across the Ponte
Vecchio. Tickets for private tours
only from the Uffizi.

Guided tours
Travel agencies offer city bus tours,
cultural tours on foot, visits to the
Chianti estates and, from April to
October, excursions to nearby towns
(see *Tuscany*) and to Pisa, Siena and
the great Medici villas in the
surrounding hillsides: Villa della
Petraia (3km/2 miles to the north)
with villa, gardens and sculpture; and
Villa di Poggio a Caiano (17km/11
miles northwest), built for Lorenzo
the Magnificent.

Spectator sports
Horseracing *Ippodromo Le Cascine,*
Pzale delle Cascine ☎ 353394;
trotting at the *Ippodromo Le Mulina,*
Vle del Pegaso (Cascine) ☎ 411130.
Soccer First-division, Fiorentina
plays at the *Stadio Comunale.*

Keeping fit
The *Grand Minerva, Villa Medici* and
the *Kraft* hotels have pools.
Fitness centre *Centro Sportivo
Fiorentino*, Via Bardazzi 15 ☎ 430275;
monthly membership. *Tropos*, Via
Orcagna 20/a ☎ 671581, has a
gymnasium, indoor pool and sauna
and is open to visitors.
Golf *Ugolino Impreta* (13km/8 miles
south) ☎ 2051009, is the nearest;
visitors should belong to another club.
Tennis The *Circolo del Tennis*, Vle
Visarno 1, Cascine ☎ 356651;
monthly membership.

Local resources
Business services
The major hotels can organize most of
the services you are likely to need.
Executive Service, Via Ponte Alle
Mosse 61 ☎ 352086, provides staff,
equipment and offices.
Photocopying and printing *Rex-
Rotary* ☎ 287353, *Gestetner*
☎ 670901.
Secretarial and translation *Centro
Conit* ☎ 296272.

Communications
Local delivery *Trane* ☎ 372283,
Cooperativa Taxisti Fiorentini ☎ 4690.
Long-distance delivery *Traco*
☎ 319050, *DHL* ☎ 371907.
Post office Central office: Via
Pellicceria ☎ 216122, open 8.30–7.
Telex and fax At the post office.

Conference/exhibition centres
Conference organizers include *ENIC,*
Via S. Caterina D'Alessandria 12
☎ 496177/78, *OIC (Organizzazione
Internazionale Congressi)* Via G.
Modena 19, 50120 ☎ 577271, and
Public Relations and Meetings, Via
Santa Reparata 40, 50129 ☎ 472585.
The most important trade

exhibition centres are close to the station: *Fortezza da Basso*, is the main venue for fashion fairs (including textiles and raw materials for clothing and furnishing) and the *Centro Affari*, Pza Adua, 50123 ☎ 27731, is an ultra-modern spacious complex. The main conference centre is the *Centro Congressi*, Pza Adua, 50127 ☎ 262241, an old classical-style villa whose main auditorium can accommodate 1,000.

Emergencies
Bureaus de change *American Express*, Via Guicciardini 49r ☎ 278751, open 9–5.30, and at the station.
Hospitals 24hr emergency admissions at *Santa Maria Nuova*, Pza Santa Maria Nuova 1 ☎ 27581, and *Generale di Careggi*, Vle G.B. Morgagni 85 ☎ 43991. *Nuovo S. Giovanni di Dio*, Via Torregalli 3 ☎ 27661 is new but not central. The private *Tourist Medical Service*, Via Lorenzo Il Magnifico 59 ☎ 475411, provides emergency services (including dental treatment).
Pharmacies Late-night rotas are displayed at every pharmacy. There is one open 24 hrs at the station and the booklet *Florence Concierge Information* lists others. *International Pharmacy*, Via Tornabuoni 2r, stocks British and American products.

Police *Questura*: Via Zara 2 ☎ 4977.

Information sources
Business Information *Camera de Commercio* The *Commercio Estero* department of the local chamber of commerce, Pza dei Giudici 3, 50122 ☎ 2795275, advises on local industries and how to do business in the area. Istituto Nazionale per il Commercio Estero (ICE), Via Tornabuoni 3 ☎ 298493.
Local media *La Nazione* is a daily paper which regularly carries local and national business news.
Tourist information Via Tornabuoni 15 ☎ 216544/5, provides maps and leaflets on the city but is only open Mon–Sat, 9–1, closed Sun. The tourist office at the railway station is open daily Apr–Nov, 8.30–9.30; Dec–March, 8.30–9.00 and provides a hotel reservations service. The EPT, Via Manzoni 16 ☎ 2478141, gives information on the province of Florence.

Thank-yous
Confectionery *Robiglio* has branches at Via dei Servi 112r ☎ 214501 and at Via dei Tosinghi 11 ☎ 215013.
Florist *Ditta Leopoldo Mercatelli*, Via Tornabuoni 6 ☎ 214006.
Paper Pineider, Pza della Signoria 14r.

OTHER CITIES

AREZZO *codes* zip 52100 ☎ 0575
A major distribution centre at the heart of the agricultural Val di Chiana with a population of over 90,000. There are more than 400 gold jewellery factories in the area. Uno-A-Erre is a goldsmith giant and the MGZ factory is a world leader in high-tech jewellery-making machinery; both firms are subsidiaries of the Gori & Zucchi group. Terziani is another major group. Agricultural machinery, fabrics and women's fashions are also produced here; Lebole (Marzotto group), Confar and Bianchi are among the important clothing manufacturers.

Buitoni, the famous pasta-making company (now part of Nestlé), was founded at Sansepolcro where there is still a factory. Also at Sansepolcro is Ingram (shirtmakers), now a large group. Metallurgical plants include the Deltasider state steelworks at San Giovanni Val d'Arno.

Hotels and restaurants
Minerva, Via Fiorentina 6 ☎ 27891, is a comfortable hotel on the road from Florence. In the centre the modern *Continental*, Pza Guido Monaco 7 ☎ 20251, also has the best restaurant for business entertaining. Dine at *Le Tastevin*, Via de' Cenci 9 ☎ 28304, to the accompaniment of a piano, or at *Il*

Principe ☎ 362046 at nearby Giovi,
which serves good fish.

Relaxation
The frescoes of Piero della Francesca
in the church of *San Francesco*,
illustrating the Legend of the True
Cross, are the highlight of a visit to
Arezzo. Other churches and the
archeological museum are worth seeing.
There is an antiques fair on the Piazza
Grande on the first Sunday of every
month.

Information sources
Camera di Commercio, Via Giotto 4
☎ 28891.
Tourist information, Pza Risorgimento
116 ☎ 23952, open Mon–Fri, 9–12,
4–6.

LIVORNO *codes* zip 57100 ☎ 0586
This large container port, one of the
most important in the Mediterranean
(and a traditional rival of Pisa), is an
industrial centre for shipbuilding,
chemicals, petrochemicals and
engineering. Important companies are
Whitehead Motofides (Gilardini
Group, making submarines) and SPIGA
(car components). It is also the supply
base for the US troops based here.
The population is over 174,000.

In the province are Piombino, with
important iron and steel works
(Nuova Deltasider/ILVA), and
Rosignano Solvay, with chemical
factories.

Hotels and restaurants
The *Gran Duca*, Pza Micheli 16
☎ 891024, on the port, is a
convenient hotel.

L'Antico Moro, Via Bartelloni 59
☎ 884659, is an excellent fish
restaurant (reservations essential); the
bistro atmosphere is suitable for
dinner. *La Barcarola*, Vle Carducci 63
☎ 402367, is more formal, but can be
noisy. At Ardenza, just south of
Livorno, try *Oscar*, Via O. Franchini 78
☎ (0586) 501258, for a business lunch.

Relaxation
Little remains of the old town. If you
have spare time take a boat trip to
Elba or visit *Pisa*. There is
horseracing at Ardenza on Sundays.

Information sources
Camera di Commercio, Pza Municipio
48 ☎ 37831.
Tourist information, Pza Cavour 6
☎ 57126.

PERUGIA *codes* zip 06100 ☎ 075
In Perugia, which has 146,000
inhabitants, the main activities are in
food and textiles (including knitwear).
Perugina (Baci chocolates) and IBP
(Industria Buitoni Perugia, pasta-
makers) are twin companies owned by
Nestlé. Other famous names are
Spagnoli and Umberto Ginocchietti
(designer clothes), IGI (children's
shoes) and Ellesse (sportswear). Most
industry is concentrated to the west of
the city towards Corciano and Lake
Trasimeno. There is an important
international university here as well as
the ancient University of Perugia.

In the province, important
companies include Petriai Spigadoro
(pasta and animal feed) and Deltafina
(tobacco) at Bastia; EMU (a European
leader in garden furniture) at
Marsciano; ICAP (clothing) at Assisi
and Angela Antoni (vacuum
chambers) at Massa Martana. At
Deruta there is a flourishing industry
in decorated ceramics, with direct-sell
factories.

The airport (Sant'Egidio) is
between Perugia and Assisi. There are
weekday flights to and from Milan.
Information ☎ 6929447.

Hotels and restaurants
The *Brufani*, Pza Italia 12 ☎ 62541, is
the top hotel in Perugia, the *Bella
Vista* ☎ 20741, being the less
expensive part. Almost next door, *La
Rosetta*, Pza Italia 19 ☎ 20841, is a
much cheaper second best, with a
good restaurant often used for
business meals. Other reliable
restaurants include the excellent *Bocca
Mia*, Via Rocchi 36 ☎ 23873, and
Falchetto, Via Bartolo 20 ☎ 61875,
which serves Umbrian cuisine.

Some business visitors may find it convenient to stay outside the centre. *Colle della Trinità*, at Fontana near Corciano ☎ 79548, is a conference hotel in a beautiful hillside position; the functional *Hit Hotel* ☎ 799247, 6km/4 miles from the centre, has a good restaurant. The *Osteria dell'Olmo* at Olmo ☎ 799140 is another popular place to lunch near Corciano. At Torgiano (15km/9 miles), *Le Tre Vaselle* ☎ 982447 is a very comfortable small hotel with a reputation for its excellent food and Lungarotti wines. There is a wine museum and a conference centre used for exhibitions and meetings (capacity up to 200).

Relaxation
The major sights are all close to the main street, Corso Vannucci: the *National Gallery of Umbria* (in the imposing *Priors' Palace*), the *Collegio del Cambio* (with frescoes by Perugino), and the *Duomo* and the great fountain, *Fontana Maggiore*.

Information sources
Camera di Commercio, Via Cacciatori delle Alpi 40 ☎ 2981 (also for Umbria).
Tourist information, Corso Vannucci 94a ☎ 23327, open Mon–Sat, 8.30–1.30, 3.30–6.30.

PISA *codes* zip 56100 ☎ 050
Pisa, with over 100,000 inhabitants, has been a university town since 1338. Employment here is in services, particularly the airport (flights connecting with London, Paris, Geneva and Frankfurt), and in tourism and banking, although there is also some manufacturing industry, notably in glass and, at nearby Cascina, furniture. Pisa is an important freight distribution centre for Tuscany, since the inland port is connected by rail to the airport. There is a fully-equipped conference hall, the *Palazzo dei Congressi* (capacity up to 800 people).
    The province is known for footwear (Castelfranco di Sotto; tanneries at

Santa Croce sul'Arno). Piaggio-Fiat has a factory at Pontedera. Volterra is known for alabaster.

Hotels and restaurants
The *Dei Cavalieri*, Pza della Stazione 2 ☎ 43290, is the best hotel in Pisa and *Sergio*, Lungarno Pacinotti 1 ☎ 48245, the most appropriate place for business entertaining; it has outstanding wines. *Vecchi Macelli*, Via Volturno 49 ☎ 20424, is also excellent. There are some good fish restaurants at Marina di Pisa.

Relaxation
The superb Romanesque *Leaning Tower*, *Cathedral* and *Baptistery* should not, of course, be missed. Visitors should also see the museum housed in the *San Matteo monastery* and Piazza dei Cavalieri. The *Prato degli Escoli* is a famous racecourse (season Jan–Apr), and there is opera at the *Teatro Comunale*. In June there are several local festivals (not all annual, however).

Information sources
Camera di Commercio, Pza V. Emanuele II 5 ☎ 28021 or 501066.
Tourist information, Pza del Duomo ☎ 560464, open Mon–Fri, 9–12.30, 3–5.30, and at the station, open Mon–Fri, 9–12, 3.30–6.30.

PISTOIA *codes* zip 51100 ☎ 0573
Manufacturing activities in Pistoia and the area include transport (Breda Ferroviaria), furniture and shoes (at Monsummano). The nearby spa of Montecatini Terme (15km/9 miles to the southwest) hosts many conferences. The population is over 95,000.

Hotels and restaurants
The *Milano*, Via Pacinotti 12 ☎ 23061, provides adequate accommodation. At Montecatini Terme there are many hotels; the most famous is the *Grand la Pace*, Via della Torretta 1 ☎ (0572) 75801; the *Bellavista*, Via Fedeli 2 ☎ (0572) 78122, is also good.

Pistoia is a pleasant town with
extensive remains of the medieval
walls, Pisan romanesque churches, the
Duomo, a *civic museum* and, on the
façade of the *Ospedale del Ceppo*, a
ceramic frieze by the della Robbias.

Information sources
Camera di Commercio, Corso S. Fedi 78
☏ 20031.
Tourist information, Pza del Duomo
☏ 21622, open Mon–Fri, 9.30–12.30,
3.30–6.30.

PRATO *codes* zip 50047 ☏ 0574
Prato, with 165,000 inhabitants, is
only 19km/11 miles north of Florence.
It is a major European centre for
woollen cloth, regenerated and
"English" textiles. Over 50% of the
world demand for unprocessed wool
comes from here. There are some
15,000 firms with 2,000 small-scale
textile manufacturers, dyers and
finishers. Major companies include
Linea Più, Pecci, Gommatex and
Bellucci. New technology is being
introduced without the loss of
specialized traditional processes.

Hotels and restaurants
The *Palace*, Via Piero della Francesca
71 ☏ 592841, is a modern conference
hotel with a pool just a taxi ride from
the centre, near the *superstrada*. In the
centre, the *Flora*, Via Cairoli 31
☏ 20021, is small and comfortable;
near the station, the *Milano*, Via
Tiziano 15 ☏ 23371, is more basic.
For a business lunch in the centre,
Bruno, Via Verdi 12 ☏ 23810, is
popular and on the southern outskirts.
Il Piraña, Via Tobia Bertini ☏ 25746,
is a good fish restaurant. But *Villa
Santa Cristina*, Via Poggio Secco 58
☏ 595951, an 18thC villa, is the best
place to take important guests.

Relaxation
The impressive *Duomo* (outside,
pulpit; inside, frescoes by Filippo
Lippi) is the chief sight; and the
Pinacoteca and several other churches
are worth seeing.

Information sources
Camera di Commercio, Via Valentini 14
☏ 26061.
Tourist information, Via Luigi Muzzi 51
☏ 35141 and Via Cairoli 48 ☏ 24112,
open Mon–Fri, 8.30–6.30; Sat,
8.30–1.30.

SIENA *codes* zip 53100 ☏ 0577
Siena itself has almost no industry,
but is the regional capital for the
Chianti area with a population of
nearly 60,000. It is an important
sightseeing base, with good hotels.
The world's oldest bank, the Monte
dei Paschi di Siena, was founded here
in 1472 (now with branches in New
York, Singapore and Frankfurt).
    Manufacturing, notably in furniture
and bathroom ceramics, is
concentrated in the Val d'Elsa at busy
Poggibonsi and the modern part of
Colle Val d'Elsa (known for the
manufacture of crystal). There is an
annual Chianti fair at Greve.

Hotels and restaurants
Certosa di Maggiano, Strada de
Certosa 82, 53100 ☏ 288180, is
exquisite and exclusive (in both size
and cost); it is in a converted
monastery in its own grounds with a
pool and tennis court. Also
comfortable are the *Park*, Via di
Marciano 16 ☏ 44803, *Grand Villa
Patrizia*, Via Fiorentina 58 ☏ 50431, .
and *Villa Scacciapensieri*, Via di
Scacciapensieri 10 ☏ 41442, all with
parks and pools. (See also *Country
hotels*.)
    All the best hotels are on the
outskirts; the *Duomo*, Via Stalloreggi 38
☏ 289088, provides simple, central
accommodation.
    Restaurants on the Campo are
touristy and should be avoided. *Le
Logge*, Via del Porrione 33 ☏ 48013,
is a popular trattoria for business
lunches.

Relaxation
Visitors need at least a day to cover
the main sights: the *Palazzo Comunale*
on the *Piazza del Campo*, the
Cathedral (with the Piccolomini

library), the museum (*Museo dell'Opera*) and the art gallery (*Pinacoteca*), with works by masters of the Sienese School. The Corso del Palio, a horserace round the Campo, takes place on 2 July and 16 August.

The *Enoteca Italica Permanente*, in the Fortezza Medicea, is open daily 3pm–midnight for the sampling and purchase of Italian wines. In August and September there is a season of concerts at the prestigious *Accademia Musicale Chigiana*, Palazzo Chigi-Saracini, Via di Città 89 ☎ 46152.

Information sources
Camera di Commercio, Pza Matteotti 30 ☎ 45051; *Enoteca Italica Permanente*, Fortezza Medicea ☎ 288497 (promotes business contacts).
Tourist information, Pza del Campo 56 ☎ 280551, and Via di Città 43 ☎ 42209, open Mon–Fri, 9–12.30, 3.30–7; Sat, 9–12.30.

Tuscan and Umbrian country hotels and restaurants

In the Chianti district are the *Villa le Barone* at Panzano in Chianti ☎ (055) 852215, a charming country house, and the *Tenuta di Ricavo* at Castellina in Chianti ☎ (0577) 740221, a medieval village converted into a luxurious hotel; each has a restaurant and pool. At Gaiole two restaurants offer typical Tuscan food in medieval monastic surroundings: *Castello di Spaltenna* ☎ (0577) 749483 (with simple accommodation) and *Badia a Coltibuono* ☎ (0577) 749424.

The delightful *Locanda dell'Amorosa*, at Sinalunga between Siena, Arezzo and Perugia ☎ (0577) 679497, is a Renaissance villa and farm buildings offering a high standard of cooking and 12 simple, pretty bedrooms (closed mid Jan–end Feb). Also worth a special gastronomic detour (60km/37 miles south of Siena) is *La Chiusa* at Montefollonico ☎ (0577) 669668, another picturesque farmhouse and old out-buildings – offering accommodation – and one of the best restaurants in the whole country.

THE MARCHES (Marche) AND ABRUZZO

With a total population of around 1.5m, less than that of Milan, the Marches are not very significant economically, although there are signs of improvement. In the 1960s traditional agriculture was abandoned for employment in the hotels and restaurants on the coast. But now the region is an up-and-coming location for new businesses, including small craft workshops in the hills. There is some activity in construction, engineering and food manufacture, mostly around Ancona. Trade fairs and exhibitions are held at Civitanova Marche and Pesaro is a centre for the manufacture of mechanical products and kitchens (Scavolini, Febal, Berloni). Poor planning has spoilt much of the coast, and the hinterland has more to offer the visitor; the main art centres are Ascoli Piceno, a well-preserved medieval town, and the Palazzo Ducale at Urbino.

Abruzzo, a rugged mountainous area in the centre of the peninsula, with some agricultural production on the reclaimed Lake Fucino, is in the Mezzogiorno. Local handicrafts (weaving, metal-working, ceramics, marquetry, embroidery and lace-making) employ much of the population of around 1.3m. But modern industries are growing up in the Chietino; Lanciano is a prosperous town. The airport at Pescara is being extended to cater for seasonal international flights.

ANCONA *codes* zip 60100 ☎ 071
The chief administrative centre and
port for the Marches, with a
population of over 106,000.
Shipbuilding (Cantiere Navale),
metallurgy, engineering, chemicals
and food are the main sectors.
Girombelli is one of Italy's leading
clothing manufacturers (making
clothes for the Genny, Biblos,
Complice and Claude Montana labels)
and is now expanding to Japan. Also
important are ICIC (soya, sunflower oil
processing) and ACRAE
(pharmaceuticals).

In the province, Fabriano is known
for the production of paper (since the
14th century) and more recently of
domestic appliances; Merloni is the
third-ranked producer in Europe and
Italy's market leader, producing
Ariston and Indesit models. Jesi is
known for silk and Verdicchio wines,
Castelfidardo for accordions.
Senigallia is the main resort.

The airport at Ancona handles daily
flights to Milan and Rome;
information ☎ 26257. The busy port
serves ferries to and from Greece and
Yugoslavia.

The *Grand Palace*, Lungomare
Vanvitelli 24 ☎ 201813, overlooking
the port, and the quieter *Grand
Passetto*, Via Thaon de Revel 1
☎ 31307, are the best hotels. *Il
Passetto*, Pza IV Novembre 1
☎ 33214, is the most suitable
restaurant for business entertaining.

Janus Fabriano, Pza Matteotti 45
☎ (0732) 4191, is the best hotel in
Fabriano. At Jesi (32km/20 miles
from Ancona) there is the prestigious,
well-equipped new hotel and
convention centre, *Federico II*
☎ (0731) 543631 (eat out at *Galeazzi*
☎ (0731) 57944 or *Hostaria Santa
Lucia* ☎ (0731) 64409).

Sights include the *Duomo*, *Trajan's
arch* and the *Pinacoteca Comunale* (for
paintings by Crivelli, Guercino,
Lorenzo Lotto), but the town shows it

has suffered from war damage, flood
and earthquake. In the province visit
Jesi (*Pinacoteca Civica*) and
Chiaravalle (*Cistercian monastery*).
Fabriano has a *Duomo* and medieval
palazzi.

Camera di Commercio, Pza XXIV
Maggio 1 ☎ 58981; *Associazione degli
Industriali*, Pza della Repubblica 1
☎ 57352.
Tourist information, Via Thaon de
Revel 4 ☎ 33249, and Via Marcello
Marini 14 ☎ 200313, open Tue, Thu,
Sat.

PESCARA *codes* zip 65100 ☎ 085
A modern city, provincial capital, port
and resort, Pescara is the leading
commercial centre of Abruzzo with
131,000 inhabitants. The industrial
zone is around Via Torretta, and
spreads inland towards Chieti (15km/9
miles), also a provincial capital, where
there is a Telettra factory. In the area
Pirelli and Fiat-Sevel (a joint venture
producing light commercial vehicles)
have factories. De Cecco is a leading
pasta manufacturer south of Chieti.
Pescara airport (daily flights to Milan
and Turin) information ☎ 206197.

The renovated, modernized *Carlton*,
Vle Riviera 35 ☎ 373125, is the best
hotel in Pescara. There are a number
of seafood restaurants along the Viale
della Riviera and Lungomare
Matteotti; the best is *Guerino*, Vle
Riviera 4 ☎ 4212065.

Pescara itself has little to offer the
tourist; visit *L'Aquila* (100km/62
miles to the west) if you have a day off
(*Basilica di Santa Maria di
Collemaggio* and *Basilica di San
Bernardino*).

Camera di Commercio, Via Conte di
Ruvo 2 ☎ 6761.
Tourist information, Via Fabrizi 173
☎ 4211707, open Mon–Fri, 8–2.

THE SOUTH

Il Mezzogiorno, the South of Italy, starts just to the south of Rome. As well as Abruzzo (see *The Marches and Abruzzo*) and Molise, it consists of Campania (capital Naples); Apulia (capital Bari); and Calabria and Basilicata, two administrative regions. Potenza, the capital of Basilicata, and Reggio Calabria and Catanzaro, joint capitals of Calabria, are smaller than many minor Northern towns. Throughout history economic development has taken place along the coast, and the ports remain the most important cities, pre-eminently Naples and Bari which now possess large industrial agglomerations. Most of the South is mountainous, with the exception of the rocky but fertile "table" constituting Apulia, and the Southern economy is predominantly agricultural.

The South is famous for its problems – its comparative poverty, backwardness and crime – but the problems take a different form in each of the regions, and it is doubtful whether Apulia is disadvantaged at all. The traditional solution to the problem of poverty has been emigration, to the North or out of the country altogether. Recently there has been some movement back from the North, adding to unemployment problems. Since World War II the central government and the EC have invested money in the South in various ways. But the policy of superimposing heavy industries (such as the Italsider steel works at Taranto or the oil refinery at Gela in Sicily) has not been a success: apart from the effect on tourism, these "cathedrals in the desert" have failed on the whole to generate secondary industry. Besides agriculture, the construction industry is often the only other major employer, and its activities have not improved the landscape, either.

Meanwhile the major sector, agriculture, is in difficulties. In the 1960s, with the benefit of new techniques, Southern agriculture was expanding and finding a ready outlet in Northern Europe; now its prices and its viability are threatened by the same produce in the same markets from Spain, Greece and all over the Mediterranean. It has not responded well to the challenge, and growing new crops can only be a temporary measure.

For the South as a whole a better hope for the future seems to lie in an already perceptible "osmosis" from the North; as communications continue to improve, it may become worthwhile to switch operations towards the South because costs are lower. In 1988 it was announced that a consortium led by Fiat had decided on considerable new investment in the South. Such an osmosis would most favour Campania and Apulia. Campania is now firmly locked into the Northern infrastructure by air at Naples, by rail and by autostrada; Apulia is well connected by land up the Adriatic coast to the Po valley and across to Campania via Benevento, and has airports at Bari and Brindisi. The Autostrada del Sole has rendered the long mountainous peninsula of Calabria more accessible, and there are airports at Lamezia Terme (serving Cosenza and Catanzaro), Crotone and Reggio Calabria, but the main railway line is still single-track for long stretches and Reggio to Rome takes seven hours whereas Milan to Rome, the same distance, takes only four.

Campania

Most of Campania is mountainous or hilly, composed of part of the Apennine chain and, along the coast, a second range of hills designated pre-Apennine. This coastline is volcanic round the bay of Naples and to the north, as are most of the islands off the coast, although not Capri.

Campania is one of the most densely populated regions of Italy (238 per sq km) and the most industrialized in the South, although the capital, Naples, concentrates most of the industry, and the provincial capitals of the hinterland, Avellino, Caserta and Benevento, are largely market towns and centres of not much more than administration. Agriculture is comparatively prosperous, except that the province of Benevento is mountainous and poor, more like neighbouring Basilicata. The area between Naples and Salerno, an important container port, is heavily industrialized, notably around Sarno. However, neither this nor the accompanying commercial activity have been enough to redeem the problems of the region, bedevilled by urban and rural poverty and organized crime and further degraded by the severe earthquake of 1980, signs of which are still clearly visible.

Apulia (Puglia)

Apulia becomes mountainous only in the Monte Gargano peninsula in the north and on the border with Basilicata in the west; the rest is a flat rocky limestone table, producing geological oddities such as the Grotte di Castellana caves and Lecce stone, which can be turned on a lathe. For most of its history Apulia has exported the produce of its rich soil; inadequate rainfall has been supplemented by improved irrigation techniques, deep wells and a new aqueduct, which have made modern systematic farming possible. Its main produce consists of olives (45% of Italy's entire output, and thus about a sixth of the world's), wine (especially table grapes) and green vegetables, but a wide variety of crops can be grown, and there is also good pasture.

The region is divided administratively into five provinces: Foggia, Bari, Taranto, Brindisi and Lecce. Bari is much the most densely populated (1.5m), and the most heavily and variously industrialized. Although industry and commerce is centred in the city of Bari, it has spread up the coast within the province to Trani and Barletta, where there is an oil refinery.

To the North, Foggia supports rich agriculture and more modest industry; it has a relatively unspoilt resort area in the Monte Gargano peninsula and the Tremiti islands, though there is a chemical works at Manfredonia. It is an area of considerable potential, and Foggia is well placed on the road and rail systems. It already has an airport, but only for private planes.

South of Bari communications by rail become noticeably less efficient, though Bari, Taranto, Lecce and Brindisi are linked by routes which are part autostrada and part *superstrada*. The area is more provincial, but prosperous enough; industry is located in pockets. Taranto is entirely dependent on its Italsider steelworks, which is also responsible for most of the tonnage passing through its port, the most active in Apulia. At Brindisi, which has an airport and is the main ferry port for Greece, there are oil refineries and the Montedison petrochemical works. Lecce, at the end of the main railway system (there are some local lines extending farther south), has only light industry. The region taken as a whole exports more than it imports, nationally and internationally.

Basilicata

The mountainous back of Basilicata leaves insufficient space for good agricultural land and was widely and irrecoverably deforested in the last century. Despite gas deposits it has little industry, even round its capital, Potenza. The city of Matera, still famous for its cave homes, is no longer troglodyte but business potential is very limited. Potenza is high on a hill in difficult country, and communications altogether are slow.

Calabria

Mountainous Calabria has a long coastline which means it has more fertile land than Basilicata but it is one of the poorest and least densely inhabited regions of Italy. The main crops are olives, citrus fruit and wine grapes. In what is now a national park, the interior contains beautiful lakes and forests, and its coastline is punctuated by tourist villages. There are a few small-scale industrial enterprises at Cosenza, Catanzaro, Crotone and Reggio, but Cosenza is more of a commercial than an industrial centre.

NAPLES (Napoli)   City codes zip 80100 ☎ 081

Naples, famous for its superb bay and its terrible squalor, its friendly people and its appalling crime, enervating heat and effervescent anarchy, not surprisingly presents some economic paradoxes too. For all the primitive conditions that excite comparison with the Third World, this city has an advanced industrial base, notably in shipbuilding, aerospace (Aeritalia), automobiles (Alfa-Romeo) and telecommunications (Selenia and a small Olivetti plant at Pozzuoli), and has achieved a growth rate (4% in 1987) equal to or better than the rest of Italy. Furthermore, it has seen some dramatic turnabouts, particularly at Alfa-Romeo; bought in ailing condition from the state by Fiat in late 1986, within a year it had become profitable and had re-employed many previously laid off. A colossal further investment in the South by a consortium led by Fiat is promised before 1992 and a new urban centre just north of the station is planned. Naples also has an important light industry sector, especially food processing and dressmaking, gloves and shoes (the fashion king Valentino is a Neapolitan), and is an emporium for the whole of the South. With a population of 1.2m, it lies at the heart of a conurbation of nearly 4m people that stretches northeast to Caserta and south to Salerno. Yet the overall growth of the area according to 1987 figures was only 1.5%, very much down on the national average, and unemployment, a long-time problem, reached twice the Italian average in 1987 and was still climbing.

Naples is the only city in Italy in which tourism has declined since World War II. This is due partly to its infamous street crime and the despoliation of its natural beauties, but more especially to the general switch to air travel; its harbour is no longer the gateway to Italy. Even so, Naples remains the largest port in the South, but is more significant for the metallurgical coal and iron ore it handles than for the cruise liners that dock here; it has container facilities and handles the significant ferry trade to far and near islands in the Mediterranean. Round the bay at Fuorigrotta are the important Mostra d'Oltremare trade fair grounds, and nearby are the RAI radio and television station and a NATO headquarters.

Arriving

Naples is well served with flights from the rest of Italy and Europe. There are fast and frequent trains from and to Rome (2hrs) and the North; the service is not so good in other directions. Autostrada routes provide easy access from neighbouring cities and the national network.

Capodichino airport

This small airport is one of the busiest in Italy. It handles several weekly scheduled flights of British Airways, Air France and Lufthansa, as well as Alitalia, but most of the traffic is within Italy. Facilities include a restaurant, snack bar, post office (open Mon–Sat, 8.30–7.40; Sun, 8–1.30), international telephone office (open 8–9.30pm), bank (open normal bank hours) and small duty-free shop airside. Inquiries ☎ 7805721 (often busy).

City link Naples airport is only 7km/ 4 miles northeast of the centre. A taxi or bus takes 10–15mins.

Taxi Cabs from or to the airport charge double tariff, at least L30,000, and waiting for one is usual.

Car rental Major car rental firms have booths here, but a car is only advisable for trips out of town.

Bus The No. 14 leaves every 20mins (just after the hour from midnight) for the main railway station; buy the L600 ticket at the airport newsstand beforehand

Railway stations

Stazione Centrale at the east of the city is the main station. Underneath it is Stazione Piazza Garibaldi from or through which run two local lines, the Metropolitana and the Circumvesuviana, as well as some mainline trains. A fourth railway system, the Cumana, starts at Stazione Cumana, near Piazza Dante.

Stazione Centrale The concrete umbrella of the Stazione Centrale terminus faces onto Piazza Garibaldi, where there are a bus terminus and plenty of taxis. It has suffered disruption from partial rebuilding and provides few reliable services: the bank has normal banking hours, abnormally bad rates and does not take credit cards; the car-rental booths, tourist office and restaurant may be closed at any time.

Porters do not meet trains but prefer to wait on the main concourse. In order to avoid irritation, be sure to identify the ticket window which serves the function you want before waiting by it. Beware any kindly approach or English-speaker on the station precinct or by the taxis.

Stazione Piazza Garibaldi Finding a departure platform is confusing. Platforms 2 and 3 (signed as "Piazza Garibaldi" on the departures board and often used for the Rome *rapidi*) are below the main concourse of Stazione Centrale and accessible only by an inconvenient and circuitous walk.

Platforms 1 and 4 are for the Metropolitana, which covers the city centre and its western suburbs, and the Circumvesuviana which runs from a different set of platforms again. Mainline inquiries ☎ 5534188.

Other stations North–South mainline *rapidi* often stop at Mergellina, Campi Flegrei and Pozzuoli, stations on the Metropolitana which are convenient for hotels around the bay or for the Mostra d'Oltremare.

Getting around
Naples spreads along the steep shore of its widely curving bay and so some kind of transport is essential. Traffic is clogged in the old city but fairly free otherwise.

Taxis Taxis are numerous and available at ranks throughout the city or by telephone. All have meters, but you may get a driver who will demand more than the registered fare. *Radio Taxi* ☎ 364340 or 364444.

Limousines can be hired through *CIT*, Pza Municipio ☎ 5525426, or other travel agencies.

Driving Neapolitan driving is dangerously frantic. Traffic lights and bus or other lanes are rarely respected; passing is competitive; scooters or motorcycles are everywhere, sometimes with extremely young riders. Outside the centre driving is usually calmer. In

the city, unattended cars are stolen or broken into with notorious frequency.

There are autostrada links with the suburbs and nearby cities, including Salerno, 60km/37 miles to the southeast.

Walking usually involves negotiating crowds, parked cars and rubbish, and risking encounters with pickpockets and bag-snatchers.

Bus The system is not easy to master but buses conveniently go along Corso Umberto and Via Roma, though they are often crowded and robbery is a hazard. Blue SITA buses depart frequently from Piazza Municipio and Piazza Garibaldi for neighbouring towns.

Trains The *Metropolitana*, running from Piazza Garibaldi to the west of the city (Campi Flegrei) and beyond, is useful for longish journeys. Trains average five an hour, 6–midnight.

The *Circumvesuviana* follows the coast east of Naples to Torre del Greco, Ercolano and Pompeii before returning inland to the city. Inquiries ☎ 7792444.

The *Cumana* is the slow commuter service to the western suburbs,

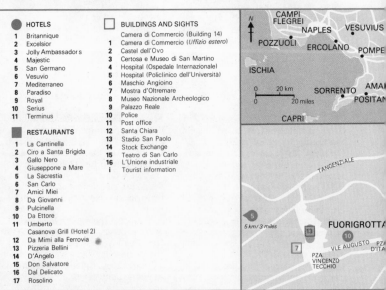

HOTELS
1 Britannique
2 Excelsior
3 Jolly Ambassadors
4 Majestic
5 San Germano
6 Vesuvio
7 Mediterraneo
8 Paradiso
9 Royal
10 Serius
11 Terminus

RESTAURANTS
1 La Cantinella
2 Ciro a Santa Brigida
3 Gallo Nero
4 Giuseppone a Mare
5 La Sacrestia
6 San Carlo
7 Amici Miei
8 Da Giovanni
9 Pulcinella
10 Da Ettore
11 Umberto
Casanova Grill (Hotel 2)
12 Da Mimi alla Ferrovia
13 Pizzeria Bellini
14 D'Angelo
15 Don Salvatore
16 Dal Delicato
17 Rosolino

BUILDINGS AND SIGHTS
Camera di Commercio (Building 14)
1 Camera di Commercio (*Uffizio estero*)
2 Castel dell'Ovo
3 Certosa e Museo di San Martino
4 Hospital (Ospedale Internazionale)
5 Hospital (Policlinico dell'Università)
6 Maschio Angioino
7 Mostra d'Oltremare
8 Museo Nazionale Archeologico
9 Palazzo Reale
10 Police
11 Post office
12 Santa Chiara
13 Stadio San Paolo
14 Stock Exchange
15 Teatro di San Carlo
16 L'Unione industriale
i Tourist information

Pozzuoli and beyond. Stazione Cumana, Via Montesanto, is also on the Metropolitana. Inquiries ☎ 5513328.

Funiculars Three funiculars link the the city centre with the Vomero: the Centrale and Montesanto from stations near both ends of Via Roma and the Chiaia from near Piazza Amedeo. The Funicolare Mergellina rises not far from Porto Sannazzaro marina to the heights of Posillipo. Operational daily, 7–10.

Area by area

Central Naples is set on the two arcs which compose the great bay of Naples. The arcs meet at the horn of Pizzofalcone, off which squats the Castel dell'Ovo, once the citadel. Here now are Via Partenope, the Hotel Excelsior, several other first-class hotels and restaurants and a yacht marina. Behind, more or less at the root of the horn, the Piazza del Plebiscito constitutes one end of Via Roma (or Via Toledo), also known as "Spaccanapoli" ("Divide-Naples"), the city's main thoroughfare. It runs north eventually up to the heights of

Capodimonte. "Spaccanapoli" divides Naples into east and west: to the east is the district also known as Spaccanapoli, a poorer area of narrow streets, and the commercial quarter centred round Piazza Bovio, more commonly known as Piazza della Borsa (Stock Exchange). Between the Piazza del Plebiscito and Piazza della Borsa are the present town hall and the old royal residences, the Bourbon Palazzo Reale and the earlier castle called the Maschio Angioino. From Piazza della Borsa, Corso Umberto leads up to Piazza Garibaldi and the Stazione Centrale. Farther east is an industrial area connected to the port. There are plans to develop a 270-acre site north of the station as part of a revitalized infrastructure (including a subway) and hub for commercial and administrative activities.

Except for an area at the south end of Via Roma, the western side is smarter and more residential. It extends round the bay to Mergellina and beyond, but is most elegant near the sea around the Piazza dei Martiri and up on the Vomero heights.

Farther west is the hilltop, sea-view

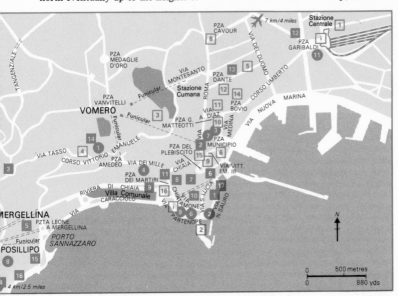

207

residential quarter of Posillipo, in the suburb of Fuorigrotta. The wide boulevard of Viale Augusto leads into the trade fair (Mostra d'Oltremare) and the stadium (Stadio San Paolo); beyond is the racecourse and the Campi Flegrei. The coast is built up around the headland to Bagnoli (where the steelworks, an important employer, is threatened with closure) and on to Pozzuoli.

Capri and Ischia are off the eastern and western headlands of the gulf respectively. To the east of Naples are Vesuvius with its famous victims Ercolano (Herculaneum) and Pompeii and the beautiful, though not unspoilt, coastline round to Sorrento.

Hotels

All the grand hotels in Naples serve the business traveller, including the Excelsior and the Vesuvio, but they were built 100 years or more ago, and generally standards are lower than in Milan, Rome and Turin. Most of the city's hotels are old stock and have been renovated but not many very recently. Several were built in the 1960s and 1970s.

Early reservation is essential, especially during major shows at the Mostra d'Oltremare. Specify if you want a room overlooking the sea. All the hotels listed have air conditioning, IDD telephones in rooms and a garage, but not 24hr room service; and the large ones are well geared-up for conventions and conferences.

Britannique _▢//_
Corso Vittorio Emanuele 133, 80121
☏ _660933_ ▢ _722281 • AE DC MC V •_
80 rooms, 4 suites, 1 restaurant, 1 bar
The Britannique was renovated in 1984 and offers attractive rooms overlooking the sea, a garden (which is a great rarity) and a small roof terrace. Set in the hilly suburbs, it is a tranquil haven from the toil of the city, 3km/2 miles distant. 2 meeting rooms (capacity up to 100).

Excelsior _▢///_
Via Partenope 48, 80121 ☏ _417111_
▢ _710043 • CIGA • AE DC MC V • 124 rooms, 12 suites, 1 restaurant, 1 bar_
The Excelsior was built in 1907 in a style designed to emulate the Ritz, a venture financed from Switzerland. Both before and after World War I it welcomed royalty, film stars and many other folk heroes and heroines into its columned halls. The CIGA stamp is instantly recognizable today from the tailcoated uniforms and the high standard of service. Though the building has undergone major modification, its neo-Empire style has been maintained. Business travellers now constitute a major part of its clientele. Its restaurant, the Casanova Grill, is highly regarded (see _Restaurants_). Rooftop solarium • in-house secretarial services, 1 meeting room (capacity up to 350).

Jolly Ambassador's _▢//_
Via Medina 70, 80133 ☏ _416000_
▢ _720335 • AE DC MC V • 278 rooms, 1 restaurant, 1 bar_
This is a cut above the usual Jolly hotel. It is well placed for the Piazza della Borsa, a short walk up the road. A skyscraper built in 1960, it was modernized in 1980. The lobby is welcoming and always busy. The rooms and the rooftop restaurant, for clients and their guests only, enjoy fine views over the bay and the city, and the hotel caters for large parties. 8 meeting rooms (capacity up to 280).

Majestic _▢/_
Largo Vasto a Chiaia 68, 80121
☏ _416500_ ▢ _720408 fax 422484 •_
AE DC MC V • 125 rooms, 6 suites, 1 restaurant, 1 bar
Near elegant Piazza dei Martiri, the building is late 1950s, but the decor is

1987, and successfully blends relaxed serenity with businesslike efficiency. The lobby contains plush sofas and desks with telephones. The rooms are not soundproofed, but noise is only a problem at weekends. Restaurant open in the evenings only. Variable-partition meeting rooms (capacity up to 150).

San Germano *[L]|*
Via Beccadelli 41, 80125 ☎ *7605422*
⊠ *720080 fax 7601546 • Marco Polo*
• AE DC MC V • 105 rooms,
2 restaurants, 1 bar
The San Germano is a newly modernized hotel, but it is on the other side of the Mostra d'Oltremare, more than 10km/6.5 miles from the city. However, it is ideal for trade fairs, for the NATO headquarters, for RAI and for the various sports arenas here. Its clientele includes jockeys and footballers, but they make little impact on the quiet atmosphere. Pool, other sports at the nearby Agnano Terme club • office for use of guests, 8 meeting rooms (capacity up to 500).

Vesuvio *[L]||*
Via Partenope 45, 80121 ☎ *417044*
⊠ *710127 fax 417044 • Steigenberger •*
AE DC MC V • 150 rooms, 10 suites,
1 restaurant, 1 bar
Built 20 years earlier than its upstaging neighbour the Excelsior, the Vesuvio has suffered the further indignity of losing its fifth star since World War II. It remains

unmistakably a *grand hotel de luxe*, fallen equally unmistakably on hard times; but restructuring is due to be completed in 1990. The service, however, is still good, it is central and its rooftop restaurant and many rooms have good views of the bay. 3 meeting rooms (capacity up to 350).

OTHER HOTELS
Mediterraneo *[L]|| Via Nuova*
Ponte di Tappia 25, 80133 ☎ *5512240*
⊠ *721615 fax 5518989 • Quality • AE*
DC MC V. Near the commercial centre. Few single rooms, limited public areas but 4 meeting rooms (capacity up to 150).
Paradiso *[L]| Via Catullo 11,*
80122 ☎ *660233* ⊠ *722049 • Marco*
Polo/Best Western • AE DC MC V. A busy hotel in Posillipo, with facilities of variable quality, catering for business visitors.
Royal *[L]||| Via Partenope 38,*
80121 ☎ *400244* ⊠ *710167 fax*
411561 • Quality • AE DC MC V. Not top-class but good facilities and rooftop pool (open irregularly).
Serius *[L] Vle Augusto 74, 80125*
☎ *614844 • EC only.* This smallish and particularly pleasant hotel is well sited for the Mostra d'Oltremare, but 8km/5 miles from the city centre. Make early reservations.
Terminus *[L] Pza Garibaldi 91,*
80142 ☎ *286011* ⊠ *722270 • AE DC*
MC V. Beside the main station; exceptionally well-equipped office facilities available to nonresidents.

Restaurants

Naples's leading restaurants are old established and in classic style but the cuisine is not up to the standard of the best in the larger Northern cities. For a serious discussion, to show respect or to celebrate a successful deal, Neapolitans go to exclusive places like the Sacrestia or Cantinella in which the food is excellent and being known is important. These restaurants are mostly in the chic suburbs; reservations are advisable.

At the other end of the scale are the *pizzerie*, the best of which are to be found in the less smart quarters, especially off Corso Umberto and Via Roma. In between, there are numerous typical trattorias. In general, if you eat badly in Naples you have been unlucky. Fish is ubiquitous, but shellfish should be eaten only in recommended restaurants; and be warned, the local wine takes its flavour from the sulphur-rich soil.

La Cantinella *L*∥

Via Cuma 42 ☎ 404884 • closed Sun •
AE DC MC V • reservations essential
Though the Cantinella, on the
seafront around the corner from Via
Partenope, specializes in seafood, it
has a large menu and aims to provide
whatever guests may fancy. Similarly,
the wine list carries more than 1,000
names. The impression fostered is
that this is the haunt of the great and
powerful. You have to ring at the
side-door in Via Cuma to get in, but
this procedure is fairly common in
Italy. The Cantinella is famous for
having a telephone on every table, and
some come simply to dine on the
phone.

Ciro a Santa Brigida *L*

Via Santa Brigida 71 ☎ 5524072 •
closed Sun, Aug • AE DC V
This restaurant has remained
consistently popular with business
people over the years and enjoys a
high reputation. It has a pleasantly
busy atmosphere (seating 250), its
prices have remained reasonable and it
is as Neapolitan as is Naples.

Gallo Nero *L*∥

Via Tasso 466 ☎ 643012 • closed Sun
D, Mon L, Aug • AE V • jacket and tie
The setting is an 18th-century villa
towards Mergellina, where a refined
atmosphere is carefully cultivated.
The sunset terrace for summer dining
has recently been extended. Its
traditional Neapolitan cuisine is
notable not only for fish and pasta but
also for meat dishes. Accepts limited
parties of business guests for
cocktails, lunches and suppers.

Giuseppone a Mare *L*∥

Via F. Russo 3 ☎ 7696002 • closed
Sun, Xmas, New Year • AE DC V
Also at Posillipo, and with fine views
over the sea, this large restaurant
specializes in fish – its reputation
based as much on the quality of the
catch as on the cooking of it.
Although the food and service are
variable, it remains a great favourite
with Neapolitans.

La Sacrestia *L*∥∥

Via Orazio 116 ☎ 664186 • closed
Wed (Sun in Jul), Aug • AE MC V
This is the most famous and most
highly regarded restaurant in Naples,
its long-held preeminence seemingly
unassailable. The luxurious setting
and tableware are complemented by a
panoramic view, for the restaurant is
up on the hills of Posillipo; in summer
you can eat in the garden. Not only
the seafood but also the pasta are to
be savoured. Service is impeccable.

San Carlo *L*∥

Via Cesario Console 18 ☎ 417206 •
closed Sun, Aug • AE DC V •
reservations essential
A small, busy restaurant which is
known primarily but not exclusively
for seafood, and the pasta is excellent.
Diners include those who have
business with government, lawyers or
colleagues nearby. The atmosphere is
a little less formal than at the
neighbouring Cantinella.

OTHER RESTAURANTS

Several central restaurants, though
not regarded as fashionable, serve
Neapolitan fare of good quality. These
include *Amici Miei*, Via Monte di Dio 78
☎ 405727; *Da Giovanni*, Via D.
Morelli 14 ☎ 416849; and *Pulcinella*,
Vico Ischitella 4 ☎ 42249. For a
change in gastronomy, *Da Ettore*, Via
Santa Lucia 56 ☎ 421498, produces
interesting "peasant" dishes; and
Umberto, Via Alabardieri 30
☎ 418555, is one of the best
restaurants with pizza on the menu. If
good food alone were enough, the
Casanova Grill, in the Hotel Excelsior
☎ 417111, would be more popular
but it is simply not "Neapolitan."

Farther east, there are restaurants
for relaxed occasions and authentic
pizzerie, off Corso Umberto. Near the
station and a flourishing street
market, *Da Mimi alla Ferrovia*, Via
Alfonso d'Aragona 21 ☎ 15538525,
offers good food in a dubious area.

Around Piazza Dante, the
restaurants are not high-tone, but
many are enjoyably Neapolitan. The

Pizzeria Bellini, Via Santa Maria di Constantinopoli 80 ☎ 459774, is a venerable institution. On the Vomero probably the best is *D'Angelo*, Via A. Falcone 203 ☎ 5789077.

Posillipo's superb position has attracted some of the best and most fashionable restaurants in Naples; in particular, try *Don Salvatore*, Via Mergellina 5 ☎ 660788, and *Dal Delicato*, Largo Sermonetta 34 ☎ 667047.

Bars and cafés

Via Roma's plentiful bars include some famous ones, such as *Caflisch* and *Gambrinus* towards the sea end. The *Galleria Umberto* near the Piazza del Plebiscito, once a busy rendezvous, is nowadays seedy. Instead the *Cafeteria* in Piazza dei Martiri, in a privileged little corner of the city, would be a better meeting place.

Entertainment

Opera and music The opera season is December to June, when visiting companies of international repute perform at the 250-year old *Teatro di San Carlo*, Via San Carlo ☎ 7972370 or 7972412 ✆ 721606 fax 7972306.
Out-of-season concerts are also held there.

Nightclubs are not really Neapolitan fare, though they exist. The *Shaker Club*, Via N. Sauro 24 ☎ 416775, is smart, and in the same district is a piano bar, *Gabbiano*, Via Partenope 27 ☎ 411666. *Rosolino*, Via N. Sauro 5-7 ☎ 415873 or 403513, is a versatile institution. Named after its proprietor, Giorgio Rosolino, who also owns La Cantinella close by (see *Restaurants*), it is piano bar and excellent restaurant, top nightclub (presenting musicians, shows or speeches) and meeting room, particularly for evening sessions (capacity up to 350).

Shopping

Naples is not regarded as a fashionable shopping centre. The smartest shops are around Piazza dei

Martiri and down Via Roma and Via dei Mille. Clothes and shoes are good value but not cheap.

The traditional local pottery is distinctive. Off Via Roma and north of Piazza Garibaldi are bargain shops, and colourful Neapolitan street-life as it is lived; everywhere you will be importuned by hawkers.

Sightseeing

Strolling round Naples, however picturesque parts of it may seem, is not generally enjoyable. It is noisy and chaotic, its architecture is grim and repetitive and, following the 1980 earthquake, many monuments are shabby or under scaffolding, notably the triumphal arch at the entrance to the Castel Nuovo (or Maschio Angioino) and some of the more interesting churches. However, money is being invested in restoration as part of a deliberate policy of improvement. There are three major museums, a baroque palace and one church worth seeing and not under repair.

Certosa e Museo di San Martino Contains important paintings by the city's flourishing baroque school, the elaborate cribs (*presepi*) for which Naples is famous and a historical collection. Do not expect everything to be open, here in particular. *Largo San Martino 5. Open Tue–Sat, 9–2; Sun, 9–1.*

Museo di Capodimonte Notable collections of late medieval, Renaissance and 19thC works of art, including several major masterpieces. *Via Capodimonte. Open Tue–Sat, 9–2; Sun, 9–1.*

Museo Nazionale Archeologico Most of the best works of art unearthed in Pompeii and Herculaneum are displayed here. *Pza Museo 35. Open Tue–Sat, 9–2; Sun, 9–1.*

Palazzo Reale Paintings and tapestries in a 17thC palace. *Pza del Plebiscito 1. Open Tue-Sat, 9–2; Sun, 9–1.*

Santa Chiara Gothic church with tiled pillars supporting the cloister roof. *Strada S. Chiara. Cloister open daily, 8–1, 4–7.*

Out of town

The sweep of the bay of Naples, with its capes, islands and mountains, has been praised since Roman days but time and development have affected its charms. The hilltop drive to *Sorrento*, *Positano* and *Amalfi* is still beautiful, and there are some fine hotels set on the cliffs, but the public places are tawdry.

Boats to *Capri* and *Ischia* leave the quay (Molo) at Piazza Municipio five or six times a day, run by *Carimartel* ☎ 5513882. Alternatively, there is an hourly service from Via Caracciolo, Mergellina, run by *Alilauro* ☎ 7611004 or SNAV ☎ 7612348 (also to Sorrento). The appeal of both islands is real enough – and hackneyed. But there are good restaurants and resort hotels (Ischia is a popular spa) with seaside sports facilities.

The crater of *Vesuvius* is most easily accessible from Ercolano, Torre del Greco or Boscotrecase. A new funicular is to be in operation by 1990.

Pompeii (24km/15 miles) and *Herculaneum* (11km/7 miles) are two very different sites. Herculaneum is small (most of it is still under the modern town of Ercolano) and nearly all its interesting objects are in the archeological museum in Naples. Pompeii is vast, and much is still *in situ*, including, just outside the town, the orgiastic wall-paintings of the Villa dei Misteri. For 2 or 3hr guided tours around Pompeii, contact the tourist office there ☎ 8610913.

Pompeii and Herculaneum are not the only ancient sites in the area. Around the bay to the west of Pozzuoli, *Bacoli* and *Baia* have significant Roman ruins, and *Cuma* (19km/11.5 miles) is an ancient site. Farther down the coast, 100km/62 miles to the southeast, are the Greek temples of *Paestum*.

Spectator sports

Inquire at your hotel or the tourist office what may be on at the Ippodromo at Agnano ☎ 7601660,

the Palazzetto dello Sport (basketball) ☎ 7609573 or the Stadio San Paolo (soccer) ☎ 615623, all over at Fuorigrotta.

Keeping fit

It is not part of the Neapolitan lifestyle generally to participate in sports, and the only sport a visitor can pursue easily is tennis, at the *Tennis Club Napoli*, Vle Dohrn ☎ 667678. The *Federazione Italiana Tennis* ☎ 7608154 will provide information about courts. No city hotel has a pool (except for the Royal, open sometimes); several hotels on Ischia and Capri and at Sorrento have pools and other sports facilities. But only 10km/6.5 miles west of Naples, the San Germano Hotel has a pool and access to other sports.

Local resources

Business services

The international *Executive Service*, Via Gianturco 5a ☎ 205444 ☒ 722039 fax 268720, will provide secretarial and translation services, an office and the latest equipment. Offices, services and equipment can be hired temporarily at the Terminus Hotel (see *Hotels*).
Photocopying Hotels will arrange for photocopying and other kinds of reproduction.

Communications

Local delivery CREC ☎ 418766 or 421904.
International delivery F. Cianciarosa, at the airport ☎ 7805522 and in town at 22 Piazza Bovio ☎ 5523961 or 5523111. DHL, Via Argine 491 ☎ 7520688.
Post offices Central post office: Pza Matteotti (open Mon–Fri, 8.30–2; Sat, 9–12). The post office at the airport has longer hours.
Telex and fax At the central post office.

Conference/exhibition centres

The *Mostra d'Oltremare*, Pzle Tecchnio 25, 80125 ☒ 722244 fax 7258336, holds about 20 events a year (including exhibitions of fashion and leather goods), the most important being the Fiera della Casa at the end of June. It has 24,000 sq metres of exhibition space with back-up facilities. Inquiries ☎ 7258111. The large hotels host conferences all year round.

Bureaus de change The bank at the station is not often open outside normal hours and does not accept credit cards.
Hospitals Ospedale Internazionale, Via Tasso 38 ☎ 7612060. Policlinico dell'Università, Pza Miraglia 192 ☎ 455005.
Pharmacies Those open late are listed every day in Il Mattino.
Police Vigili urbani ☎ 7513177. Questura: Via Medina 75 ☎ 7941111.

Business information Camera di Commercio has a main office, with the Uffizio Studi for general inquiries, in the Stock Exchange (Borsa), Via Sant'Aspreno 2 ☎ 285322; the Uffizio Estero, for foreign trade, is at Corso Meridionale 60 ☎ 5545013. L'Unione industriale della Provincia di Napoli is in Piazza dei Martiri 58 ☎ 406522.
Local media Naples's newspaper is Il Mattino, with occasional business supplements.
Tourist information Main office, Via Partenope 10a ☎ 406289 (open Mon–Fri, 9–1; Sat, 8–12); at the station (open in theory Mon–Fri, 8–8; Sun, 8–2); and at the airport (open Mon–Sat, 2–8).

Confectionery De Luca, Via Roma 45 ☎ 5520263 or ☎ 5514582.
Florists Gae Odin, Via Roma (Toledo) 291 ☎ 5513491, Via Chiaia 237 (Vomero) ☎ 422824 and elsewhere.

BARI

City codes zip 70100 ☎ 080

The people of Bari (capital of Apulia) like to think of their city as the Milan of the South, a claim which is partly true, except that it is so much smaller and much more provincial. Despite phenomenal growth since World War II, the population is under 400,000 and, if anything, is now diminishing. Nevertheless some of its industries compare in kind if not in size with those of the North, particularly electronics, machine tools and vehicle parts; trucks built by Officina Calabrese come from Bari. Household names with factories here include Firestone, Philips, Osram and Fiat (making agricultural equipment). Chimica D'Agostino produces detergents, MECA, electric cables, and the publishing house of Laterza is also here. At Valenzano, just south of the city, a new "Technopolis" concentrates on new technology.

Milan has lakes, but Bari has the sea. Its port, however, is comparatively minor, overshadowed by Brindisi and even more by Taranto, and it is just the largest of several cities along this stretch of coast. Fishing, however, is still important and its fish market is famous. The province of Bari has 1.5m inhabitants, mostly on the coast and many working in industry, though the agricultural hinterland is intensively farmed. The capital brings together the lion's share of the service, administrative and commercial activities of Apulia; and its September trade fair, the Fiera del Levante, which is one of the most important commercial fairs in Europe, convulses the city.

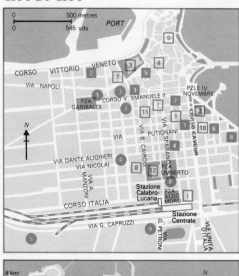

HOTELS
1 Executive Business
2 Grand Ambasciatori
3 Palace
4 Victor
5 Villa Romanazzi-Carducci
6 La Baia
7 Boston
8 Grand Hotel Leon d'Oro
9 Jolly

RESTAURANTS
1 Ai Due Ghiottoni
2 Le Maschere
3 La Panca
4 Alla Vecchia Bari
5 Al Pescatore
6 Al Sorso Preferito
7 La Pignata
8 Taverna Verde

BUILDINGS AND SIGHTS
1 Alitalia terminal
2 Camera di Commercio
3 Castello
4 Cattedrale
5 Fiera di Levante
6 Hospital (Policlinico)
7 Police
8 Post office
9 San Nicola
10 Teatro Petruzzelli
11 Teatro Piccinni
12 University
i Tourist information

Arriving

Bari is easily reached by road, rail and
air from Rome or Milan. Autostrada
routes link the city northwest and
southeast along the Adriatic coast and
inland to Benevento and so to Naples.
There are good roads to neighbouring
cities, although off the autostrada the
coast is congested with traffic. Fairly
frequent *rapidi* trains go north up the
coast and across to Caserta and Rome,
but the service elsewhere is limited.

Palese airport

The city's small airport has scheduled
daily connections with Rome and
Milan. Charters arrive here from
European capitals, the USA and Far
East. Facilities are limited; there is no
duty-free shop airside, but a bank is

open daily, 8–12, 2.20–8. Inquiries
☎ 370299.
Nearby hotels Hotels on the coast
road between the airport and the city
include *La Baia* (see *Hotels*),
Palumbo, Via Vittorio Veneto 31,
Bari-Palese (3km/1.75 miles from the
airport) ☎ 322779.
City link The airport is 12km/7.5
miles west of the city centre. Hertz,
Maggiore and Europcar have offices
here. A taxi to the centre costs about
L25,000. Alitalia operates a bus
service connecting with its incoming
flights and leaving its terminal at Via
Calefati 37 an hour before departure;
inquiries ☎ 369288.

Railway stations

Bari Centrale is at the edge of the

modern city centre, at the south end of Via Sparano. There are two platform sequences: those with numbers only are for through lines, and those with the word "Ovest" (west) after the number are for services starting from Bari; these are reached by walking down platform 1. Inquiries ☎ 216801.

Calabro-Lucane is adjacent to Bari Centrale on Piazza Aldo Moro. It serves the slow branch lines into the hinterland.

Getting around

Central Bari is a compact square that takes no more than 30mins to cross on foot. However, the city has extensive suburbs that can only be reached by taxi, bus or car. Parking is seldom a problem, and the hotels have garages, so a car is a good option.

Taxis There is no radio taxi service. Cabs are obtained at or by calling the nearest stand: at the station ☎ 210600; off the Corso Vittorio Emanuele II (Via Andrea da Bari) ☎ 5210500; off Corso Cavour by the Teatro Petruzzelli ☎ 210800. The station is the best bet at night. Fares are metered and very reasonable.

Driving Europcar ☎ 213936 or at the airport ☎ 371092 for car hire; limousines are also available.

Walking In the modern city centre walking is a convenient way of getting around. But beware of robbery in the old town, especially after dark.

Bus Yellow buses run through the city

and out to the suburbs; blue buses connect with nearby towns or villages. The free tourist publication *Eccobari* (in English) gives details.

Area by area

Bari conforms to a standard pattern in Apulia: the old city huddles around the port and its fortress, the modern city extends behind in grid plan. In Bari the Corso Vittorio Emanuele II ("the Corso") constitutes the border between the two. The old city is largely a slum. The modern city, though laid out at the beginning of the 19th century, was bombed in World War II, and few postwar buildings are made of materials other than concrete. Its central area is bounded by the Corso to the north, the station and railway lines to the south, with the main shopping street, Via Sparano, running between.

On the east, the Corso Cavour leads from the end of the Corso to a bridge over the railway, giving access to characterless residential blocks and then to villas, punctuated by institutions such as the Policlinico (general hospital) and the university. To the east, across the Corso Cavour, is quite a fashionable area close to the sea.

The city stretches north of the central grid to the sea and west of it to the industrial zone inland. The Fiera del Levante complex is along the coast to the northwest, about 2.5km/2 miles from the old city.

Hotels

Bari's hotels rely almost entirely on business travellers as tourism is insignificant. They vary considerably from the soulless to the designer chic to the new up-to-the-minute Executive Business. During the big September Fiera accommodation is very hard to find, except perhaps at the top of the market.

All hotels listed have IDD telephones and air conditioning in rooms, and garages.

Executive Business 〔L〕/
Corso Vittorio Emanuele II 201, 70122
☎ *216810* ⊠ *810208 fax 216810* • *AE DC MC V* • *21 rooms, 1 bar*

This small hotel has several outstanding features. Built in 1984, it is luxuriously equipped. Double rooms were designed to convert into offices: the second bed can fold into the wall to give more space, each room is furnished with an office-type, high-backed chair and ample worktop, and there is a video-answer-phone down to the lobby. An oddity of each room is a ceiling plaque indicating the direction of Mecca because the owner, though Italian, is Muslim. There is no restaurant. 2 meeting rooms (capacity up to 160).

Grand Ambasciatori *[L]//*
Via Omodeo 51, 70125 ☎ *410077*
TX *810405 fax 410077 • AE DC MC V •*
163 rooms, 14 suites, 1 restaurant, 2 bars
Built out in the suburbs in 1976, the Ambasciatori benefits from spacious surroundings and has wide views from its external elevator, rooftop restaurant and pool. It runs a shuttle to the airport, the Fiera complex and the centre. It is a "grand" hotel, with well-appointed bedrooms and ample public areas. Half the guests at any one time will be attending events in the conference rooms. Rooftop heliport • heated pool, gym • in-house business facilities, 15 meeting rooms (capacity up to 500).

Palace *[L]//*
Via Lombardi 13, 70122 ☎ *216551*
TX *810111 fax 5211499 • AE DC MC V*
• 210 rooms, 7 suites, 1 restaurant, 1 bar
This is the only *hotel grand de luxe* in the city centre. Built in 1956 on the Corso, it was extended in 1965 and succeeds in being a traditional hotel in furnishing, service and atmosphere. It is efficiently run and aware of business needs, and nearly half its trade derives from hosting conventions. 24hr room service, hairdresser • 16 meeting and banqueting rooms (capacity up to 850).

Victor *[L]/*
Via Nicolai 71, 70122 ☎ *216600*
TX *812272 fax 216600 • AE DC MC V •*
77 rooms, 4 suites, 1 bar
Although only 13 years old, this

popular central hotel was redecorated in 1987 by Missoni (the designer more famous for knitwear than for interiors). He created unusual open-plan public spaces with an overall colour-scheme of swimming-pool blue, and with an island reception and a waterfall in the lobby. The bedrooms are less startling. Accommodation should be reserved well in advance. No restaurant. 2 meeting rooms (capacity up to 60).

Villa Romanazzi-Carducci *[L]///*
Via G. Capruzzi 326, 70124 ☎ *227400*
TX *812292 fax 227400 • AE DC MC V •*
89 rooms, 1 restaurant, 1 bar
Although located just behind the station, the Romanazzi-Carducci was a 19thC villa set in its own park. It was converted into a hotel in 1980. Accommodation is in well-appointed apartments comprising either two or three rooms. The restaurant is open only during conferences. Pool, gym, sauna, other sports by arrangement • 9 meeting rooms in a special centre (capacity up to 130).

OTHER HOTELS

La Baia *[L]* *Via Vittorio Veneto 29a, Palese* ☎ *320264 or 320288 fax 320288 • AE DC MC V.* On the coast, between the city (10km/6 miles) and the airport (2km/1.5 miles) and well-placed for the Fiera; high standard of service and pleasant rooms.
Boston *[L]* *Via Piccinni 155, 70122* ☎ *216633 • Best Western • AE DC MC V.* Good service in this central 1960s hotel but the rooms are noisy and need refurbishing.
Grand Leon d'Oro *[L] Piazza A. Moro 4, 70122* ☎ *235040* TX *810311 fax 5211555 • AE V.* Despite perfunctory service in the hotel, the bar and restaurant are popular meeting places.
Jolly *[L]/ Via Giulio Petroni 15, 70124* ☎ *364366* TX *810274 fax 365219 • AE DC MC V.* A standard Jolly hotel with extensive conference facilities. On the other side of the railway tracks, so a taxi ride from the town centre.

BARI

Restaurants

Entertaining business contacts in small groups is sometimes regarded here as a foreign custom although in the South of Italy it is very common to dine in large parties whatever the occasion. Visitors may have the privilege of being invited to join business guests dining privately at the Circolo della Vela (yacht club). Among restaurants Ai Due Ghiottoni is clear favourite. Hotel restaurants, notably in the Palace, Grand Leon d'Oro and Grand Ambasciatori, are much frequented for discussions over a meal.

Few menus give more than the traditional local fare, in which fish or shellfish and *orecchiette* (ear-shaped pasta shells, typically with a broccoli sauce) predominate. Reservation is always advisable.

Ai Due Ghiottoni [L]/
Via Putignani 11b ☎ *232240* • *closed Sun* • *AE DC MC V* • *reservations essential*
This popular restaurant presents the best of local produce – wine, mozzarella and fish – all of which are served rather as if they were prize exhibits. Though they taste as good as they look, quantities are over generous (*ghiottone* means glutton). Tables set into niches allow private discussion.

Le Maschere [L]/
Via Bonazzi 66 ☎ *216186* • *closed Wed, 2 weeks Aug* • *MC V*
This new restaurant and piano bar (music every night) has yet to establish itself, but seems to have a successful formula: it is small, has smart tableware and classic, rather pale decor, attentive service and comparatively high prices. The cuisine is local.

La Panca [L]/
Pza Massari 8 ☎ *216096* • *closed Wed* • *AE V* • *reservations essential*
Situated just off the Corso, La Panca is much favoured for large gatherings as well as by individual diners. The decor of its several rooms is rustic: no tablecloths, plain wood and pots hanging from the ceiling. The food is varied, fresh and unpretentious.

Alla Vecchia Bari [L]/
Via Dante Alighieri 47 ☎ *216496* • *closed Fri, mid-Aug* • *AE DC MC V* • *reservations essential*
Probably the first choice after Ai Due Ghiottoni, on culinary grounds at least. The setting is comfortable, there are photographs on the walls, stacked wine racks and tunnel-vaulted ceilings. Well-spaced tables, mostly in niches, permit private conversation.

OTHER RESTAURANTS
Also recommended are:
Al Pescatore, Pza Federico di Svevia 8 ☎ 237039, known for its fish, is near the sea in the old city. *Al Sorso Preferito*, Via V. N. De Nicolò 46 ☎ 235747, is closed Sun. *La Pignata*, Via Melo 9 ☎ 232481, closes Wed and Aug. *Taverna Verde*, Largo Adua 19 ☎ 540309, is closed Mon.

Bars and cafés
Several modern bars are to be found along the Corso, notably the refurbished *Sai Café* and, at the corner with Piazzale IV Novembre, *Motta* offers cakes and a "tea-room." For business purposes, however, a rendezvous in a hotel bar is customary.

Entertainment
Bari has two main theatres, which put on opera and concerts as well as plays: *Teatro Piccinni*, Corso Vittorio Emanuele II ☎ 213717, and *Teatro Petruzzelli*, Corso Cavour ☎ 5241761, where high-quality opera is performed during Jan–Mar.
The *Ideal Club*, Via Bovio 13 (intersection with Via Giusso) ☎ 483434, is a well-known discotheque and piano bar.

Shopping

The main street in Bari, which contains some smart shops, is the traffic-free Via Sparano; Italian and some internationally known designers have outlets here. It is worth investigating the shops in the cross streets as well but really distinctive local merchandise is not easy to find. Cheaper and bargain shops line the Corso Cavour. There is a small food market at the east end of the Corso.

Sightseeing

In the old town are the 13thC *Castello* erected by Frederick II (open Tue–Sat, 9–1, 4–7) and two outstanding romanesque churches, the *Cattedrale* and *San Nicola* (important sculpture of 11thC bishop's chair). Visits to the old town should be made only in daylight.

The *Museo Archeologico* contains important pre-Greek, Greek and Roman finds.

Out of town

In the hinterland and along the coast there are several spectacularly sited medieval buildings. Most extraordinary is Emperor Frederick II's octagonal castle or hunting lodge, *Castel del Monte*, isolated on a hill top 50km/31 miles inland (open Tue–Sun, 9–1). Beside it is an excellent restaurant, Ostello di Federico ☎(0883) 83043.

Several coastal towns west of Bari have fine romanesque cathedrals richly decorated with sculpture, but none in such a splendid setting as that of *Trani*, on the edge of the sea. In the town there are several good fish restaurants.

Discovered in 1938, the *Grotte di Castellana*, 40km/25 miles to the southeast, are the largest series of caverns in Italy, famous for their light effects, stalagmites and stalactites (open daily, 8.30–12.30, 3–6.30).

Not far from Castellana is a region distinguished by its strange buildings called *trulli*, circular houses built of stone with conical roofs. *Alberobello*, 73km/45 miles southeast of Bari, is its

capital and a tourist trap; but *Locorotondo*, where they make the wine, is charming, and so is *Martina Franca*, where there is a music festival, end Jul–early Aug.

Sports and keeping fit

The possibilities are fairly limited, and of the hotels listed only the Grand Ambasciatori and the Villa Romanazzi-Carducci have any sporting facilities. Riding, tennis and sailing are popular, but there is no nearby golf course. The public pool, Pza Stadio della Vittoria ☎ 441766, also has a gymnasium.

Sailing Try the *Circolo della Vela*, Lungomare Sauro ☎ 5212002, if you can find a member to invite you, or the *Circolo Barion*, Molo San Nicola ☎ 219558.

Tennis Renna, on the road to Renna, at Palese ☎ 320128 (open to nonmembers); *Country*, Via Santa Caterina 18g ☎ 451284 (temporary membership available).

Local resources

Business services

Centro Internazionale di Congressi, Vle Papa Pio XII 18 ☎ 5510558 or 517299, provides all kinds of assistance from secretarial and translation services to modern equipment and office rental.

Photocopying and printing Bari has few quick-print shops. Hotels always have a photocopier; otherwise use *Centro Internazionale di Congressi*.

Communications

Local delivery Pony Express, Via Giovene ☎ 5041049.

Long-distance delivery Morfini & Co, at the airport ☎ 371756.

Post office Palazzo delle Poste, Via Cairoli at the intersection with Via Nicolai ☎ 5212250, open daily, 8.30am–1.30pm.

Telex and fax At the central post office.

Conference/exhibition centres

Fiera del Levante, Lungomare Starita, an important site for a whole range of trade fairs, has 25,000 sq metres of exhibition space. The September Fiera del Levante (the second largest trade fair in Europe) is an international exhibition of a wide variety of products – agricultural, industrial and consumer goods. The next largest event is the Expolevante in March covering camping, leisure, sports and holidays. Information ☎ 206111.

The *Baricentro*, 18km/12 miles outside Bari, has 900,000 sq metres, mostly used for warehousing, but including banks, post office, restaurants and conference rooms (capacity up to 750); a hotel is under construction and when complete Baricentro will be able to cater for a maximum of 5,000 people. Inquiries Via Sparano 115 ☎ 5212058.

Emergencies

Bureaus de change The *cambio* window at the station is open Sat and Sun.
Hospitals *Policlinico*, Pza Giulio Cesare ☎ 271111 (just south of the railway line); emergencies ☎ 365400.
Pharmacies *Logacono*, Corso Cavour 47 ☎ 512615 is open at night. *Calabrese*,

Via Salandra 23b ☎ 221714.
Police *Vigili urbani* ☎ 5210344.
Questura: Via Murat 4 ☎ 291111.

Information sources

Business information *Camera di Commercio*, Corso Cavour 2 ☎ 274111 ☒ 810399 fax 274228. The information office at the Fiera ☎ 206111 can also be helpful.
Local media Apulia's newspaper is the *Gazzetta del Mezzogiorno*, published in Bari.
Tourist information Pza Moro 33 ☎ 5242361, or the Azienda di Turismo, Corso Vittorio Emanuele 68 ☎ 219951. Open only in the mornings, if then. The free tourist publication *Eccobari* gives information on local matters such as events and transport.

Thank-yous

Confectionery and cakes *Motta*, corner of Corso Vittorio Emanuele and Corso Cavour ☎ 216038. *Sai Café*, Corso Cavour 119 ☎ 521068 or 5210667.
Florists *Astra-Flora*, Corso B. Croce ☎ 360364. *Florate*, Corso B. Croce 141a ☎ 226075.

OTHER CITIES

BRINDISI *codes* zip 72100 ☎ 0831
Brindisi has been a ferry port for Greece since Roman times; it is now also a naval base and an industrial port serving the considerable Montedison petrochemical works. The present population is under 100,000.

Hotels and restaurants

The best hotel is the *Majestic*, Corso Umberto I 151 ☎ 222941. The best restaurant is *La Lanterna*, Via Tarantini 14–18 ☎ 224026 or 24950.

Relaxation

The modern-looking city has few signs of its Roman and Crusader past. Outside town it is worth driving to attractive places such as *Martina Franca* in the *trulli* district (see *Bari*, 60km/37 miles to the west), or *Ostuni*

(25km/15 miles northwest), with its cathedral, or to beach resorts along the coast.

Information sources

Camera di Commercio, Via Bastioni Carlo V 4 ☎ 222010.
Tourist information, Pza Dionisi ☎ 21944, open daily, 8.30–1, 4–7.

COSENZA *codes* zip 87100 ☎ 0984
While the old town sleeps more or less untouched by progress, new town Cosenza is active chiefly in commerce. There is no significant industry; the population is over 106,000. The airport is at Lamezia Terme (44km/27 miles, near the west coast), which has flight connections with Rome, Milan and Bologna. There is a small industrial zone here.

Hotels and restaurants

San Francesco is outside town at Rende di Cosenza, Via Ungaretti ☎ 861721, with a restaurant, pool and meeting rooms (capacity up to 110).

Relaxation

Parts of the nearby *Sila Grande* remain wild, and the mountains are spectacular, especially at *Lake Arvo*, part of the Calabria national park. There are many seaside resorts along the coast.

Information sources

The Fiera grounds are at Via Pasquale Rossi ☎ 34993, and the biggest general trade fair is in May.
Camera di Commercio, Via Calabria 33 ☎ 28859, or Via Alimena 33 ☎ 22588.
Tourist information, Via P. Rossi ☎ 39095.

FOGGIA *codes* zip 71100 ☎ 0881
Frederick II, Holy Roman Emperor, made Foggia a centre of activity, but it now presides over no more than a rich agricultural province, exporting chiefly table grapes and green vegetables. Its mills have to import grain from the USA to supply not just pasta to Italy but *couscous* to Algeria. It has a population of 160,000, and in its industrial zone are factories producing textiles (Lanerossi), chemicals, plastics and bricks. The chief employer is Sofim, a Fiat subsidiary, employing 1,000 people. Well connected by rail north and south and across to Benevento and Naples, and on the autostrada, Foggia has the second largest international agricultural fair in Italy.

Hotels and restaurants

The *White House*, Via Sabotino 24 ☎ 21644, decorated in sumptuous classic style, opened in 1987.
Cicolella, Vle XXIV Maggio 60 ☎ 3890, is older and plainer but larger and held to be the leading hotel. An alternative out of the centre is the *President*, Via degli Aviatori 80 ☎ 20139.

Though in the suburbs, *Pietra di Francia*, Vle I Maggio 2 ☎ 34880 (closed Tue), is now regarded as the best restaurant in town. But the old favourite is the well-known *Cicolella* in the Cicolella hotel; there is another *Cicolella in Fiera*, Via Bari, corner of Vle Fortore ☎ 32166, in the trade fair complex.

Relaxation

The *Monte Gargano* peninsula, with mountains, valleys and plateaus, cliffs, clear sea and clean beaches, is easily accessible by road about 50km/ 30 miles northeast. The coastal centres are Vieste and Peschici, where you can rent a boat.

From the airport you can take a helicopter (☎ 71236) out to the idyllic *Isole Tremiti*; or take a boat from Manfredonia. In the massif there is an 8thC Lombardic shrine at *Monte Sant'Angelo* that is still a pilgrimage centre (avoid weekends), and two fine isolated romanesque churches on the road from Foggia at Siponto.

Inland, other fine examples of medieval architecture include *Troia* cathedral with its bronze doors (17km/10 miles southwest of Foggia), and *Lucera* (18km/11 miles to the west), with its enormous castle dominating a rolling vista and its Roman amphitheatre. *Castel del Monte* is not far to the south (see *Bari*).

Information sources

At the *Ente Fiera Foggia*, 71100 ☎ 39021 ▭ 812091 fax 637104, there are conference facilities available during or outside fair times and 230,000 sq metres of exhibition space. The biggest fair is the international agricultural fair, end Apr–beg May.
Camera di Commercio, Via Dante Alighieri 27 ☎ 23204 ▭ 810112.
Tourist information, Via Senatore Emilio Perrone 17 ☎ 23141 or 23650, open Mon–Fri, 9–1; Tue, 8–7.

REGGIO CALABRIA

codes zip 89100 ☎ 0965
Reggio is the traditional capital of Calabria but since 1970 has shared the

honour with Catanzaro. With a population of about 180,000, it has little industry, but railway carriages (OMECA) and steel armatures for concrete are made here. The agriculture of the surrounding district is devoted primarily to olives, vines and citrus fruits, including 80% of the world's bergamot (a citrus fruit) for the perfume industry. There is an airport 4km/2.5 miles south of the town (scheduled flights to Milan and Rome). The main ferry service across the strait to Sicily leaves from Villa San Giovanni, 15km/9 miles to the north, though *aliscafi* (hydrofoils) run regularly and frequently across to Messina.

Hotels and restaurants
The two major hotels are the *Grand Excelsior*, Via Vittorio Veneto 66 ☎ 25801, at the museum end of the Corso Garibaldi, and the *Ascioti*, Via San Francesco da Paola 79 ☎ 97041 TX 912565, at the other end, by the station. But there are two good hotels in Messina, and the *aliscafo* takes 15mins from the Reggio Stazione Marittima; SNAV ☎ 29568.

The *Buonaccorso*, Via C. Battisti 8 ☎ 96048, is the best restaurant, though not as good as the best in Messina.

Relaxation
Reggio is a quiet town; Messina across the strait is livelier. Reggio's most exciting possessions are the Riace bronzes, 5thC BC lifesize Greek statues recently retrieved from the sea and now in the *Museo Nazionale*, Pza de Nava (open Tue–Sat, 9–1.30; Sun, 9–1). On the coast are many resorts.

Information sources
Fiera di Reggio Calabria, Parco Pentimele, 89100 ☎ 43044. The international handicrafts exhibition and citrus fruits fair are held here.
Camera di Commercio, Via Campanella 12 ☎ 24401.
Tourist information, Corso Garibaldi 329e ☎ 92012, open Mon–Fri, 8–1.30, 4.30–8.

SALERNO *codes* zip 84100 ☎ 089
Though it has its own gulf and its own port, Salerno is virtually a suburb of Naples, 60km/37 miles away to the west across the neck of the Sorrento peninsula, and forms the southern end of the industrialized belt stretching east from Naples. Industries include chemicals, metallurgy, packaging (Medac), food processing and textiles. Population 155,000.

Hotels and restaurants
Lloyd's Baia, Vietri sul Mare, 84019 ☎ 210145, is the only first-class hotel. It has three restaurants, private beach and business facilites, including secretarial services and 7 meeting rooms (capacity up to 250). Down on the port is the *Jolly*, Lungomare Trieste 1 ☎ 225222, and by the station the *Plaza*, Pza Ferrovia o Vittorio Veneto ☎ 224477. There is no outstanding restaurant: *La Brace*, Lungomare Trieste 11 ☎ 225159, is the best.

Relaxation
Salerno's major monument is the *Duomo*, founded by the Normans in the late 11th century. Out of town 25km/15.5 miles to the west are picturesque *Amalfi*, with its cathedral and cloisters, the panoramas of the *Sorrento peninsula* and the bay of Naples and *Naples* itself. *Paestum*, with its famous Greek temples (open daily, 8–2) and a long beach, is 50km/31 miles to the southeast.

Information sources
Camera di Commercio, Via Roma 29 ☎ 224777; *Associazione Industriale*, Via Madonna di Fatima 194 ☎ 711501.
Tourist information, Pza Ferrovia o Vittorio Veneto ☎ 231432, Pza Amendola 8 ☎ 224744, open daily, 8.30–8.

TARANTO *codes* zip 74100 ☎ 099
Taranto has a superb natural harbour and has been a leading port since ancient Greek times. It is also an important naval dockyard, but both

town and port depend on its enormous Italsider steelworks, and the related chemicals, cement and mechanical engineering concerns. The total population is around 245,000.

Hotels and restaurants

Taranto's leading hotels are together along Viale Virgilio overlooking the sea. The best is *Grand Delfino*, Vle Virgilio 66 ☎ 3205, which has convenient business facilities including meeting rooms (capacity up to 300), and a pool. Alternatively, try *Park Mar Grande*, Vle Virgilio 90 ☎ 330861. Near the administrative centre is the *Plaza*, Via D'Aquino 46 ☎ 91925. Outside town, 16km/10 miles north on *statale* 7 at Massafra, the new *Appia Palace* ☎ 881505 offers tennis, gym, private beach and golf nearby; it has 3 meeting rooms (capacity up to 300).

The best business restaurants are *Il Caffè*, Via D'Aquino 8 ☎ 25097, *La Nuova Lampara*, Vle Jonio 198 ☎ 531051, on the road east towards Brindisi, and still farther out the refurbished *Mandragora* at San Francesco degli Aranci ☎ 514093.

Relaxation

Taranto has an important archeological museum, *Museo Nazionale* (open Tue–Sat, 9–2; Sun, 9–1), with notable Greek sculpture and pottery. The old island city has an early though remodelled *Duomo* and the new town a cathedral built in 1971. Out of town there are seaside sports, riding and golf; or visit some pretty, out-of-the-way places such as *Ostuni* (98km/60 miles northeast), *Martina Franca* (see *Bari*) or the larger city of *Lecce*, with its remarkable baroque churches, 86km/53 miles east.

Information sources

Camera di Commercio, Vle Virgilio 19 ☎ 94402 ⊠ 860231.
Tourist information, Corso Umberto 113 ☎ 21233, open Mon–Fri, 9–1, 4.30–6.30.

SICILY

Sicily shares the same type of terrain, climate and demography and most of the problems of the South of Italy. Compared with the North its industrial and entrepreneurial development is backward, it is excessively dependent on agriculture – still engaging nearly 40% of the work force in 1987 – which can no longer command economic prices in flooded markets, and it has serious unemployment; meanwhile a combination of factors including Mafia-organized crime hinders amelioration.

As in the mainland South, population and activity are concentrated on the coast, which is also more fertile than the mountainous interior. Inland Sicily produces mostly wheat but on the coastal plains conditions are suitable for citrus fruits and vines. The two largest of the nine provinces into which the island is divided are Palermo and Catania. Palermo in the west has been the capital since the 10th century, when, under Arab rule, it was one of the largest cities in Europe, but the eastern part of the island has been more dynamic during the 20th century. Catania is the commercial capital, and most of the island's industry is on the east. Five large refineries produce nearly one-third of the total oil refined in Italy. Petrochemical plants exploit the nearby oil deposits at Syracuse and Ragusa. There has been some recent investment in industry in the island from Northern Italy and by local concerns. After Palermo and Catania, Syracuse with the port at Augusta nearby, Ragusa and Messina are the most important cities in the economy, and Gela is a significant oil port.

PALERMO

City codes zip 90100 ☎ 091

A port and the administrative and tourist capital of Sicily, Palermo has a history stretching back to the Phoenicians and a population (724,000) nearly twice that of Catania, its traditional rival.

The largest industrial sectors are construction, equipment for the building industry, chemicals and food processing. Fiat also employs a sizeable work force, and work has started on an industrial port at Carini. The agricultural products of the area, especially citrus fruits, are of outstanding quality, but increased competition here has caused difficulties. A more longstanding and seemingly intractable problem for Palermo is the Mafia, with ramifications in all areas of activity.

Arriving

There are scheduled flights from major European and some non-European cities. The new autostrada network enables Sicily to be crossed by car in three hours and all the main cities are within easy reach. Except for a few *rapidi*, rail travel is generally slow. Overnight ferries connect with Naples.

Punta Raisi airport

Several flights a day arrive from Rome and Milan, there are daily services from Bologna, Genoa, Naples, Pisa, Turin and Venice, and flights from some cities within and outside Europe, including New York. However, it is hemmed in by sea and mountains, so landing is tricky, and it is more liable to close than many airports. There are few facilities (no restaurant; no duty-free shop airside), but work has started on substantial improvements promised for completion by April 1990. Inquiries ☎ 591698.

City link The airport is 32km/20 miles northwest of the city. Taxis are available, but cost at least L50,000 (the asking price may be L100,000; the driver may not use the meter). Blue buses (not air conditioned) meet Alitalia flights but waiting around is normal. They run every 1–2 hrs to and from the Alitalia terminal at Via della Libertà 29, near the Politeama (cost L3,400); timetable inquiries ☎ 580457. Cars can be rented at the airport from Hertz and Rentacar.

Railway station

The main station is at the south end of Via Roma. There are fast services to Messina and Catania but other routes are slow. Inquiries ☎ 6166000.

Getting around

You should either have a car or use taxis. Palermo is extensive and even getting around the centre on foot takes time.

Taxis Taxis wait at central intersections like the Politeama ☎ 588133 and by the station ☎ 6162001 but calling a cab is simple. *Radio-taxi* ☎ 513374.

Limousines Labisi, Via Sandron 11 ☎ 341418.

Driving Not infrequently city traffic can come to a standstill, especially round the Quattro Canti, and locals are impatient and impetuous. There is a dearth of traffic lights and the right of way is often not clear. Parking restrictions are limited to the main roads. Theft is always a danger.

Walking It is safe and pleasant to walk short distances around the Politeama. Elsewhere your shoes and clothes will get dirty; Palermo is extremely grimy. In tourist areas portables of any kind are commonly snatched, sometimes with force.

Bus Buses along the main thoroughfares are convenient for short distances. For out-of-town journeys the blue SAIS buses, leaving from the station area, can be more reliable and quicker than the train; inquiries ☎ 6166027.

HOTELS
1 Astoria Palace
2 Politeama Palace
3 Villa Igiea
4 Grande Albergo e delle Palme
5 Jolly
6 President

RESTAURANTS
1 Charleston
2 Gourmand's
3 Harry's Bar
4 Chamade
5 La Scuderia
6 Friend's Bar
  Villa Igiea (Hotel 3)
  Astoria Palace (Hotel 1)
7 Renato L'Approdó
8 Trattoria al Trittico

BUILDINGS AND SIGHTS
1 Camera di Commercio
2 Cattedrale
3 Chiesa della Martorana
4 Galleria Nazionale
5 Hospital
6 Museo Archeologico
7 Palazzo dei Normanni
8 Police
9 Politeama
10 Post office
11 San Giovanni degli Eremiti
i Tourist information

Area by area

The main axis of historic and commercial Palermo is Via Maqueda, becoming as it extends northwards Via Ruggero Settimo and then Via Libertà, built at the turn of the century. For much of its course it is one-way (running south), and is supplemented by the parallel Via Roma flowing the other way. Via Maqueda links the city's two major landmarks, the Quattro Canti, the centrepiece of the city in the Bourbon era, and the Politeama, a 19thC monument and the node of the present business and administrative quarter. Here the broad straight streets are on a grid. Old Palermo, composed of short, narrow, winding streets, is still desolate after heavy bombing in World War II; whole streets are walled off, there are vast razed spaces, and baroque palaces near the Quattro Canti are still floorless. Only in 1988, with the promise of EC funds, was there a change of policy: to rehouse and rebuild in the centre rather than to contribute to the concrete sprawl that now disfigures the Conca d'Oro, the fertile valley running inland from Palermo to Monreale.

Down by the old port, now used only by fishing boats, is the Kalsa. From here, the inconveniently narrow Corso Vittorio Emanuele runs straight across Via Roma and Via Maqueda to the Palazzo dei Normanni, becoming Corso Calatafimi, then to the town and monastery of Monreale.

Suburbs extend all around the city, between the hills and the sea. The smarter ones are to the north: along Via Libertà, and Viale Strasburgo, where most of the building is prewar; at Monte Pellegrino and Mondello beach; and along the airport road. The less affluent and more extensive development has mostly been southwest towards Monreale.

Hotels

Until the opening of the modern Astoria Palace in 1988, visitors to Palermo had little choice at the top end of the market: of the city's old hotels, only the Villa Igiea had kept up its standards. All hotels listed have air conditioning, IDD telephones and private parking.

Astoria Palace 　*L|*
Via Montepellegrino 62, 90142
☎ *6371820* ⊠ *911045 fax 6372178* •
AE MC V • *296 rooms, 16 suites,*
4 restaurants, 2 bars
Opened in 1988 and provided with the latest available comforts and gadgets, from built-in hairdryers to electronic-code keys, the Astoria Palace is in a class of its own. It was designed for business visitors, especially those attending the conventions held in its versatile conference spaces, and translation and other business services are on hand. Public areas are numerous and spacious. The restaurant is excellent with a wide choice. Convenient for the Fiera. Shuttle to and from Politeama • 6 meeting rooms (capacity up to 1,000).

Politeama Palace 　*L|*
Pza Ruggero Settimo 15, 90139
☎ *322777* ⊠ *911053* • *AE DC MC V* •
102 rooms, 1 restaurant, 1 bar
A modern, well-equipped hotel conveniently located in the shadow of the Politeama, and correspondingly busy. Though the restaurant is not first rate and the service is poor, the staff in the rest of the hotel are helpful. The rooms are spacious and light and windows double-glazed.

Villa Igiea 　*L|||*
Via Belmonte 43, 90142 ☎ *543744*
⊠ *910092* • *AE DC MC V* • *117 rooms,*
5 suites, 1 restaurant, 2 bars
Even though Wagner chose to stay in the Grande Albergo e delle Palme, the Villa Igiea was the usual choice for crowned and other glittering heads before World War I. Out of town overlooking the sea, the Villa retains its gardens and grandeur, its seclusion and its standards of service. Its terrace restaurant and its *cassate* are also famous. Mainly a tourist hotel. Pool, private beach, tennis court •
1 meeting room (capacity up to 400).

OTHER HOTELS

Grande Albergo e delle Palme 　*L|* 　*Via Roma 396, 90139*
☎ *583933* ⊠ *911082 fax 331545* •
AE DC MC V. Old and prestigious but predominantly for tourists. Good summer restaurant beside the roof garden.
Jolly 　*L|* 　*Foro Italico 22, 90133*
☎ *6165090* ⊠ *910076 fax 6161441* •
AE DC MC V. The usual Jolly service on the edge of the Kalsa.
President 　*L|* 　*Via F. Crispi 230, 90133* ☎ *580733* ⊠ *910359* • *AE DC MC V*. An adequate hotel reasonably close to the Politeama.

Restaurants

Palermo is the capital of Sicily when it comes to food and wine, and contains numerous good restaurants. The first three listed are the ones to be seen in.

Palermo cuisine is seldom subtle: meat dishes are rich and juicy, sweet dishes are very sweet. However, excellent fish can be found everywhere.

Charleston 　*L|||*
Pzale Ungheria 30 ☎ *321366 (Nov–Jun)* • *Mondello, Viale Regina Elena*
☎ *450171 (end Jun–Oct)* • *closed Sun*
• *AE DC MC V*
The Charleston is *the* establishment

restaurant in Palermo: situated in the banking quarter, with the kind of ambience and service called *accurato* – attended to, and got right. It has food and wine to match. The meal will probably be a little heavy as well as exquisite, for the pasta and antipasta, the fish and the *pasticceria* have all to be enjoyed.

In summer the Charleston at Mondello, out on a pier, is even more popular and more fashionable.

Gourmand's *L*||
Via Libertà 37e ☎ *323431 or 329464 • closed Sun, Feb–Oct • AE DC MC V*
This is now preferred by many to the Charleston, which is too much of an institution. The setting of Gourmand's is modern, with a little more space. The restaurant is most famous for its smoked swordfish (*spada*), but also has delicious pasta and desserts.

Harry's Bar *L*||
Via Ruggero Settimo 74 ☎ *586517 • closed Sun • AE DC MC V • reservations essential*
This is a small place discreetly off Via Ruggero Settimo near the Politeama, offering privacy and intimacy behind locked doors. There is no real connection with the original in Venice, but the service and food are comparably excellent.

OTHER RESTAURANTS
None of the following, for all their qualities, have the cachet of the three above. The *Chamade*, Via Torrearsa 22 ☎ 322204, moves to Mondello Jun–Sep (Vle Regina Elena 43 ☎ 450407), but even there plays second fiddle to the Charleston. Farther out, *La Scuderia*, Vle del Fante 9 ☎ 520323, is in the Favorita park by the racecourse, a fashionable area; *Friend's Bar*, Via Brunelleschi 138 ☎ 201401, is to the west; and the restaurant of the *Villa Igiea* (see *Hotels*) is famous. The good food and ambience in the restaurant of the *Astoria Palace* make it a suitable place for business entertaining. On the road south out of town by the sea, past the Kalsa, is *Renato L'Approdo*, Via Messina Marine 224 ☎ 470103. Beyond the Palazzo dei Normanni, in the direction of the Policlinico, is *Trattoria al Trittico*, Largo Montalto 7

☎ 345035. Little restaurants now opening in the Kalsa offer good food.

Bars and cafés
Bars and cafés are stand-up affairs, but the bars of the Astoria Palace and the Villa Igiea hotels are useful meeting places.

Sports
The *VIP Club*, Via Granbretagna 3 ☎ 510001, has a gymnasium and a sauna but invitation from a member is required. The *Circolo del Tennis Palermo*, Vle del Fante 3 ☎ 362552, is the town tennis club. There is horseracing at the race course ☎ 510462. You can swim at beaches near Palermo or even Cefalù, although the water is not very clean unless you go to Trapani, 104km/64 miles west.

Entertainment
The arts and music feature only occasionally in Palermo life. Out at Mondello, during the spring and into the late summer, there are several fashionable nightspots, such as *Waakiki*, Vle Galatea 670 ☎ 454196.

Shopping
The smartest shops, notably for clothes, are along Via Libertà north from Piazza Ruggero Settimo. Stalls offering regional delicacies line the coast road out towards Cefalù.

Sightseeing
Palermo has several remarkable medieval monuments created by its Norman kings in the 12th century. These include the Palatine Chapel in the *Palazzo dei Normanni*, Porto Nuova (open Mon, Fri, Sat, 9–12), with its carved wooden Moorish ceiling and partly Byzantine mosaics, and the pretty cloister of *San Giovanni degli Eremiti* nearby in Via dei Benedettini (open Tue–Sun, 9–12.30); the Sicilian-Norman *Cattedrale*, Corso Vittorio Emanuele; and close to Quattro Canti in Piazza Bellini the *Chiesa della Martorana*, with its famous portrait of King Roger II and the best preserved mosaics in

the city (open daily, 8.30–1; Mon–Sat, summer, 1.30–7; winter, 1.30–5).
The *Galleria Nazionale* in Palazzo Abatellis, Via Alloro, in the Kalsa is also worth visiting, for it has a few masterpieces and is a fine 15thC building (open Tue–Sat, 9–2; Sun, 9–1). The *Museo Archeologico*, Via Roma 185, contains the most important archeological finds in Sicily (open Tue–Sat, 9–2; Sun, 9–1).

Out of town
The Duomo (and cloister) of *Monreale* (8km/5 miles west), built by King William II in the 12th century, is famous for its mosaic cycle of the Old and New Testaments, its bronze doors and its idyllic cloister with rich carvings. (Duomo: open daily except 12.30–2.30; cloisters: open summer, Tue–Sun, 9–12.30, Tue–Sat, 4–7; winter Tue–Sat, 9–2.30.)
Round the bay at *Cefalù* (70km/ 43.5 miles) is an earlier church (now a cathedral) founded by King Roger II, again with magnificent mosaics.
Ancient Greek sites accessible from Palermo include *Segesta* (75km/46.5 miles), with its classical temple of the same date as the Parthenon and a theatre in a splendid setting; *Selinunte* (115km/71.5 miles), with several temples by the sea; *Agrigento* (130km/ 87.5 miles), with its "Valley of Temples," among them an unusually intact Temple of Concord. *Piazza Armerina* (160km/100 miles) is a late Roman villa furnished with superb floor mosaics.
Also worth visiting are the hilltop town of *Erice* (96km/60 miles) with its stunning views – the Hotel Moderno, Via Vittorio Emanuele 63 ☎ (0923) 869300, can provide an excellent lunch – together with *Trapani* (104km/64 miles) beneath it and, farther down the coast, *Marsala*. In the interior there is scenic country, notably round another hilltop town, *Enna* (133km/82.5 miles).
Guided tours Labisi, Via Sandron 11 ☎ 341418; *CIT*, Via Libertà 12 ☎ 586782; *Ruggeri Giovanni & Figli*, Via Amari 40 ☎ 587144.

Local resources
Business services
Inquire at the Fiera del Mediterraneo ☎ 6209122. Hotels will photocopy.

Communications
Local delivery Moto-taxi ☎ 6511265.
Long-distance delivery DHL ☎ 582311 or 582346.
Post office Palazzo delle Poste, Via Roma ☎ 589068, open Mon–Sat, 8–1.40.
Telex and fax At the central post office ☎ 581419.

Conference/exhibition halls
Fiera del Mediterraneo, Pza Generale Cascino, 90142 ☎ 543755 ☒ 911174 fax 6209170, had over 1m visitors in 1988 to its biggest fair, Fiera Campionaria in May–Jun, an annual international event covering a wide range of products. More specialized fairs include furniture, food and building.

Emergencies
Bureaus de change At the station but not open at weekends or evenings.
Hospitals Ospedale Civico Regionale, Via Lazzaro ☎ 592122.
Pharmacies Night pharmacies are listed each day in the local paper.
Police Questura: Pza della Vittoria ☎ 210111.

Information resources
Business information Camera di Commercio, Via Amari 11 ☎ 589922.
Local media The local daily paper covering national and international news is *Il Giornale di Sicilia*.
Tourist information, Pza Castelnuovo 34 ☎ 583847; at the station ☎ 6165914; at the airport ☎ 591698.

Thank-yous
Confectionery The best *pasticcerie* are *Mazzara*, Via Generale Magliocco 15 ☎ 321366, and *Caflisch*, Via Libertà 35 ☎ 320107.
Florist Cascino, Via Maqueda 128 ☎ 331144; Vle Emilia 10 ☎ 518344.

CATANIA

City codes zip 95100 ☏ 095

Since World War II Catania has emerged as the unchallenged commercial and industrial capital of Sicily, although Palermo is the administrative capital. Commercial activity is still rapidly accelerating, stimulated by strengthening links with companies based in the North, its airport is expanding and its hotels are filled with visitors selling goods and services. There is a NATO base near the airport.

Catania's industrial sector is the most advanced on the island though, relative to the North of Italy, it is on a comparatively small scale: most significant are pharmaceutical products (SIFI) and agro-chemical companies (Cyanamid which employs 800 people), and AID (Agriculture Industrial Development) which, though employing only 200 here, has a base in the USA and is in the forefront of research. The micro-electronics group SGS has a plant here employing 2,500. Textiles, clothing and the processing of citrus fruits also contribute to the local economy.

But these larger businesses are the exceptions; most enterprises are semi- or fully artisan concerns. And for all Catania's thriving commerce, unemployment in the province is high, about 15% of the work force. Agriculture there remains pre-eminent, above all citrus fruits, almonds and figs, but inadequate response to competition in the 1980s, particularly in the German market, has created problems.

Arriving

Catania airport handles scheduled national and charter international flights. Flying is by far the most convenient way to arrive although the airport suffers from strikes; the journey by car or train from Rome takes not much less than 10 hours. There are good autostrada connections and adequate rail links with other cities on the island, including Palermo (under 3hrs). Regular ferry services connect the port with Reggio Calabria (several times a week), Naples and Syracuse.

Catania-Fontanarossa airport

This airport presently serves five flights a day from Milan and eight from Rome as well as daily services from other Italian cities. Charters connect with London, Paris, Frankfurt and Düsseldorf as well as cities in the Americas and the Far East.

Airport facilities are minimal: a bar, a self-service restaurant, a lounge; no duty-free shop airside. The bank has ordinary banking hours. The tourist office, open daily, 8–8, can help you find a hotel. Airport inquiries ☏ 341615.

City link The airport is only 7km/4 miles south of the city, a 15min drive. Taxis, though usually available, charge double tariff to and from the airport, a minimum of L25,000 (make sure the meter is turned on at the start of the journey). City bus No. 24 runs about every 20mins during the day. The major car rental firms have booths at the airport.

Railway station

The station is near the sea at the eastern edge of the city centre. There are trains regularly to Messina, Syracuse and Palermo, and buses and taxis into town. Inquiries ☏ 532226.

Getting around

Catania is too large to cover comfortably on foot, and many hotels, offices and restaurants are on the periphery. Buses cross the city and taxis can be summoned without difficulty, but visitors are expected to have the use of a car.

Taxis There is no radio taxi service. Taxis wait at – or must be summoned by telephone from – stands in Piazza Duomo ☎ 341087, Piazza Cavour ☎ 341087, or out along the northern coast road past Ognina at Via Scogliera Baia Verde ☎ 494757. Night service ☎ 346366.
Driving Neither driving nor parking (except on the city's main thoroughfares which can be badly congested) present difficulties apart from the danger of theft. *Hertz* ☎ 322560.
Walking You can normally walk in the streets unmolested during the day but bag-snatching does occur and foreigners should be aware of the dangers from street crime.
Bus Many of the numerous AST bus routes pass through Piazza Duomo and connect the centre with the suburbs; inquiries ☎ 348083. Blue SAIS buses depart to other cities in Sicily and to the mainland from Piazza Bellini, not far from the south end of Via Etnea; inquiries ☎ 316942.

Area by area
Catania's layout is simple but it has no heart. Its spine is a single street, the Via Etnea, which runs north from the Piazza Duomo near the port on a steady upward slope that if continued would eventually reach the top of Mount Etna. Southwest of Piazza Duomo is the 13thC Castello Ursino and a largely slum residential area. The administrative and commercial centre is north of Piazza Duomo, but Via Etnea, and the streets on both sides of it, diminish in significance after its junction with Viale XX Settembre. This major boulevard constitutes the second main street, which becomes Corso Italia as it extends eastwards and culminates in Piazza Europa, by the sea. Viale Vittorio Veneto crosses Corso Italia at right angles and runs south, as Viale della Libertà, to the station at Piazza Giovanni XXIII, and Via Vittorio Emanuele II links the station to Piazza Duomo.

Most of the better hotels and restaurants, and the more prosperous villas, are well outside both the inner and outer city, in the higher ground to the north, along the coast at Ognina, with its marina, or still farther to the northeast at Cannizzaro and towards Acireale. The commercial development has been to the north and west.

Hotels
Catania is well equipped with hotels, thanks to its prominence as a commercial centre. Most are along the coast, sited at short intervals all the way north to Taormina. Hotels listed have air conditioning, IDD telephones in rooms and private parking.

Baia Verde *[L]//*
Via Musco 8-10, 95020 ☎ 491522 TX 970285 fax 494464 • AE DC MC V • 122 rooms, 1 restaurant, 2 bars
This is a modern business hotel, though it is located 5km/3 miles northeast of the city and has a private beach (rocks, not sand) and sporting facilities. Its public spaces are light and open, the bedrooms, some of which have balconies, are furnished in clear, plain colours and the service is pleasant and efficient. Pool, tennis court • 2 meeting rooms (capacity up to 350).

Central Palace *[L]//*
Via Etnea 218, 95131 ☎ 325344 TX 911383 • AE DC MC V • 104 rooms, 7 suites, 1 restaurant, 1 bar
The Central Palace, called by its staff "Palacheh," not "Palass," is the best central hotel, set back from Via Etnea and not too noisy; but ask for an inside room nevertheless. Many of the bedrooms, which are modern in style, overlook the hanging gardens. The clientele is mainly Italian and German and its restaurant is popular with business guests for both lunch and dinner.

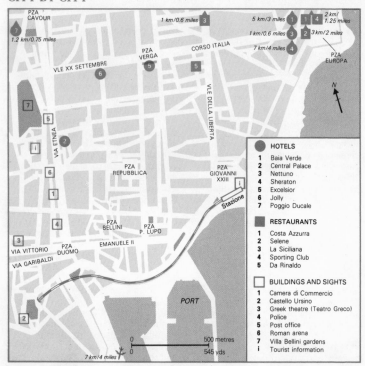

PZA
CAVOUR
1 km/0.6 miles 3
5 km/3 miles 1 1 4 2 km/
1.25 miles
7 1 km/0.6 miles 3 2 3 km/2 miles
1.2 km/0.75 miles
PZA
VERGA
CORSO ITALIA
7 km/4 miles 4
PZA
EUROPA
VLE XX SETTEMBRE
6 5
N
7
5
VLE DELLA LIBERTA
VIA ETNEA
i 2
6 PZA
REPUBBLICA
PZA
GIOVANNI
XXIII
1 i
Stazione
4 PZA
BELLINI
PZA
P. LUPO
3 PZA
DUOMO
EMANUELE II
VIA VITTORIO
VIA GARIBALDI
2
PORT
0 500 metres
0 545 yds
7 km/4 miles

HOTELS
1 Baia Verde
2 Central Palace
3 Nettuno
4 Sheraton
5 Excelsior
6 Jolly
7 Poggio Ducale

RESTAURANTS
1 Costa Azzurra
2 Selene
3 La Siciliana
4 Sporting Club
5 Da Rinaldo

BUILDINGS AND SIGHTS
1 Camera di Commercio
2 Castello Ursino
3 Greek theatre (Teatro Greco)
4 Police
5 Post office
6 Roman arena
7 Villa Bellini gardens
i Tourist information

Nettuno *L*
Vle Ruggero di Lauria 121, 95127
☎ *493533* ▥ *911451* • *AE DC MC V* •
83 rooms, 1 restaurant, 1 bar
The Nettuno is a popular and well-known hotel with friendly service, but it is not in the top category. It is strictly for business, though it is on the sea to the northeast of town. Pool.

Sheraton *L*
Via Antonello da Messina 45,
Cannizzaro 95020 ☎ *271557*
▥ *971438* • *AE DC MC V* • *167 rooms,*
2 suites, 1 restaurant, 2 bars
Although the Sheraton is primarily a business hotel 7km/4 miles northeast of the town centre, and conferences make up a significant portion of its trade, it has a private beach, and the accent is on what the Italians call "relax." Shops • pool, tennis • 8 meeting rooms (capacity up to 900).

OTHER HOTELS
Excelsior *L* / *Pza Verga 39, 95129*
☎ *325733* ▥ *972250 fax 321540* •
Atahotels • *AE DC MC V*. Grand hotel services and an imposing central setting. This large modern establishment has comfortable bedrooms but is not oriented to business needs although it caters for parties, conventions and group tours.
Jolly *L* / *Pza Trento 13, 95129*
☎ *316933* ▥ *970080* • *AE DC MC V*.
Central, modernized in 1979, efficient and a typical Jolly hotel, with 6 meeting rooms (capacity up to 70).
Poggio Ducale *L* / *Via Paolo Gaifami 5* ☎ *330016* • *AE DC MC V*.
Just off the northern *tangenziale*, Viale Oderico da Pordenone, the hotel's surroundings are not impressive, but it has a restaurant (closed Sun D and Mon L) which is favoured by business people.

Restaurants

The best restaurants offer *gastronomia marinara*, not just seafood but dishes based on it. There is more variety, and more unusual items are included, than the designation seafood may imply, and the food in Catania is generally good. All the leading restaurants have a predominantly business clientele. Reservation is always advisable.

Costa Azzurra [L]
Via De Cristofaro 4 ☎ *494920 • closed Mon, Aug • AE DC V*
Generally judged to be the leading restaurant in town, the Costa Azzurra offers not only excellent *gastronomia marinara* and a pleasant setting above the marina at Ognina but, more importantly, a certain sense of familiarity with those in power. Good local wine.

Selene [L]
Via Mollica 24–26, Cannizzaro ☎ *494444 • closed Tue, Aug • AE DC V*
The Selene is regarded as coming a close second to the Costa Azzurra. The ambience is lively with much animated discussion, especially in the evenings. The highlight of the menu is the restaurant's *gastronomia marinara*.

La Siciliana [L]
Vle Marco Polo 52a ☎ *376400 or 370003 • closed Sun D, Mon, 2 weeks end Jul • AE DC MC V*
This is an old-established restaurant still held in high regard. Its bamboo interior is somewhat dated, and it has fans instead of air conditioning. The area is rather grim, but the right people come here and the three brothers who own and run it uphold high standards. The cuisine is local, seasonal and varied.

Sporting Club [L]
Vle Alagona 4 ☎ *491117 • closed Wed, end Aug • AE DC MC V*
The *gastronomia marinara*, the setting and the service are all very good here, though among the local Catanesi the restaurant ranks behind the Costa Azzurra opposite, across the marina, and is usually not so full. Pianist three nights a week.

OTHER RESTAURANTS
The unpretentious trattoria *Da Rinaldo*, Via Simili 59 ☎ 532312, provides an excellent meal at modest prices.

Bars and cafés

The traditional place for a business rendezvous is in a hotel, but there are some pleasant bars such as the *Caprice* and the *Charmant*, at the south end of Via Etnea. Along Viale XX Settembre and Corso Italia there are more modern, slicker bars.

Entertainment

Theatre, music and opera are rare. The town has two discotheques, *McIntosh*, Via Principe Nicola 43h ☎ 371767, and *Club Medea 5*, Via Medea 5 ☎ 492286.

Shopping

The smartest streets are Viale XX Settembre, the lower stretch of Via Etnea and Corso Italia (particularly for clothes). A market offering all the variety of Sicily's marvellous produce operates just south of Piazza Duomo. *Savia*, Via Etnea 302 ☎ 22335, sells superb *pasticcerie*.

Sightseeing

The imposing and grim 13thC *Castello Ursino*, built by Frederick II, houses the Museo Civico, which is not expected to reopen until at least 1990. *Piazza del Duomo* is the town centre, with an assembly of baroque *palaces*, the *cathedral*, and the elephant fountain, emblem of Catania. Near Via Etnea are a *Greek theatre* and *Roman arena*.

At 3,340 metres/10,955ft Etna is the largest active volcano in Europe. Oranges, lemons, olives and figs grow on the lower slopes; there is snow for skiing in winter on the desolate upper lava stretches. From Catania to Rifugio Sapienza on the south side is 30km/18.5 miles (☎ 914141). Make sure before you leave that the funicular which ends near the summit is working. Take windcheating clothing and lava-beating footwear. All visitors should check that the summit is accessible and make the excursion only with an authorized guide. A bus leaves Catania station for the Rifugio every morning.

Out of town
Up the coast (52km/32 miles) is the famous and still pretty resort of *Taormina*, with its well-preserved ancient theatre, picturesque bay and several first-class hotels. Most of the rest of Sicily is within reach by car: *Syracuse*, the Greek and Roman capital, is 60km/37 miles to the south; and the 4thC villa at *Piazza Armerina*, with an extraordinary series of floor mosaics, is 85km/53 miles inland.

Sports and keeping fit
Swimming from private hotel beaches, particularly the Baia Verde, is good; the Nettuno and Sheraton (see *Hotels*) have pools and can usually arrange other sports facilities.

Local resources
Business services
Executive Service, Corso Italia 85 ☎ 375990 or 375855, fax 375855 (day), 375170 (evening), arranges temporary secretarial and translation services, and the hire of office equipment as well as providing photocopying and printing services.

Communications
Local delivery Use taxis (see *Getting around*).
Long-distance delivery DHL, Via S. Giuseppe Larena 87 ☎ 346224.
Post office Via Etnea, near Villa Bellini ☎ 312658, open 8.30–10.
Telex and fax At the post office.

Conference/exhibition centres
The main general fair is held in the spring at the Ente Fiera alla Plaia ☎ 349514. One of several convention centres in Taormina is *Centro Studi Congressi* ☎ (0942) 23836.

Emergencies
Bureaus de change At the airport and station. *Agenzia Cambio*, Via Santa Maria del Rosario 2 ☎ 317732.
Hospitals Ospedale Garibaldi, Pza Santa Maria di Gesù ☎ 254111.
Pharmacies Croce Rossa, Via Etnea 274 ☎ 317053.
Police Questura: Pza San Nicoletta 8 ☎ 317733.

Information sources
Business information Camera di Commercio, Via Cappuccini 2 ☎ 321155.
Local media La Sicilia has national, international and local news.
Tourist information Largo Paisello 5 ☎ 312124; tourist offices at the station ☎ 531802 and the airport ☎ 341900, open daily, 8–8.

Thank-yous
Confectionery Cavierzel, Via Etnea 196 ☎ 3267922.
Florist Saro, Via Gabriele D'Annunzio 47 ☎ 444546 or 444547.

OTHER CITIES
MESSINA *codes* zip 98100 ☎ 090
Messina, with a population of 270,000, is a product of its position facing the mainland across the straits, and its port, a commercial and transit centre. It has an oil refinery and there is another, and an industrial zone, on the north coast at Milazzo.

Hotels and restaurants
Messina's two main hotels are the central *Royal Palace*, Via Cannizzaro is. 224 ☎ 2921161, and the *Jolly*, Via Garibaldi 126 ☎ 43401, on the port near the *aliscafo* (hydrofoil) terminal for Reggio on Via Vittorio Emanuele II; SNAV information ☎ 364044.

The city has three excellent restaurants. *Alberto*, Via Ghibellina 95 ☎ 710711 (closed Sun), has private rooms, classic decor, attentive service and exceptional cuisine; it is known as one of the best in Sicily. Close by is *Belle Epoque*, Via T. Cannizzaro 155 ☎ 718040 (closed Sun, Aug), comprising several rooms, with Art Nouveau decor. The third is also in the centre, *Pippo Nunnari*, Via Ugo Bassi is. 157 ☎ 2938584 (closed Mon, early July).

Relaxation
The town has suffered much from earthquakes and from bombing in World War II, but is a relatively pleasant place to walk around. The *Museo Nazionale*, past the port along Viale della Libertà, has important paintings, notably by Caravaggio.

Out of town, *Taormina* (see also *Catania*) is only 50km/31 miles south; the equally scenic but less well-known ruins of Greek and Roman *Tindari* are the same distance away on the northern coast. From the port, *aliscafi* leave about twice an hour (7am–10.30pm) to Reggio. There is one boat each day to the volcanic Isole Lipari or Eolie where you can arrange to stay overnight (but not on the most famous island of Stromboli); SNAV ☎ 364044.

Information sources
E.A. Fiera Campionaria di Messina, Vle della Libertà, 98100 ☎ 54451 TX 890142, organizes the main international exhibition (Internazionale di Messina), a general fair of interest to businesses and consumers held in August.
Camera di Commercio, Pza Cavallotti 3 ☎ 7772 TX 980149.
Tourist information, Pza Stazione ☎ 7770731, open Mon–Sat, 9–12.30.

SYRACUSE (Siracusa)
codes zip 96100 ☎ 0931
At Siracusa there is a Montedison chemical plant, and 30km/18 miles to the north Augusta has an important port (ferries to Naples, Reggio Calabria and Catania), petrochemical plant and oil refinery. Other industries include papermaking and construction materials (Sicilmontaggi). The town has a population of over 120,000 and is on the Sicilian tourist itinerary.

Hotels and restaurants
The *Jolly*, Via Gelone 45 ☎ 64744, is the only reasonable hotel. The *Grand Villa Politi*, Via Politi Laudien 2 ☎ 32100 is, or still shows that it once was, grand but has not been modernized and is sadly dusty, creaky and faded. The restaurants with the highest local reputations are *Arlecchino*, Via dei Tolomei 5 ☎ 66386, and the *Ionico*, Riviera Dionisio il Grande ☎ 65540, which overlooks the sea.

Relaxation
Syracuse is an appealing town, both in its old island quarter and in its new well laid-out avenues and piazzas. The remarkable *Duomo*, with baroque façade, incorporates an ancient Greek temple. The *Zona Archeologica*, off Vle P. Orsi (open Tue–Sun, 9–1hr before sunset), contains the remains of a well-preserved theatre and the infamous quarries where Athenian prisoners of war perished in the 5th century BC.

Out of town, *Avola* (11km/7 miles) and *Noto* (32km/20 miles) to the south, *Ragusa* (79km/49 miles west), and *Augusta* were all rebuilt after the earthquake of 1693 in an exuberant and charming baroque style.

Information sources
Camera di Commercio, Via Duca Abruzzi 4 ☎ 60774 or 67744.
Tourist information, Via San Sebastiano 43 ☎ 67710 or at the station ☎ 67964, open Mon–Fri, 8–6.

Planning and Reference

Entry details

Visitors to Italy are required to register with the police within three days of arrival. Your hotel will request a passport or other formal identification with a photograph (*documenti*) and attend to formalities.

Documentation

Visas Visas are not required for visits of up to three months by visitors from many countries including Australia, Canada, Japan, New Zealand, the USA and EC countries. Other nationals may need entry or transit visas, and should check with the Italian consulate.

Passports or national identity cards A passport, valid for at least three months, is required. Nationals from all the EC countries may use identity cards, excursion passes or visitors' passports.

Work permits are required by non-EC nationals.

Driving licence Any EC country driving licence (with an official translation obtainable from motoring organizations or the Italian Tourist board), or the new EC licence, is valid in Italy. Drivers from other countries should have international driving licences. Motorists must carry an international green card (strongly advised) or evidence of third party insurance and their vehicle registration document (if not in their own name, with written permission from the owner to drive the vehicle).

Customs regulations

Most personal possessions and professional equipment can be imported duty-free for personal use, provided that you do not sell or give them away.

Goods bought in Italy up to a maximum total of L525,000 can be exported duty-free; for goods exceeding this value an application to export must be presented, through a bank or forwarding agent, to the customs authorities. Controls on the export of antiquities, antiques and modern works of art are strict: an application must be presented to the Export Department of the Italian Ministry of Education (Ministero della Pubblica Istruzione), and procedures are very slow.

Group A Goods bought duty-free *Group B* Goods bought within the EC		
	Group A	Group B
cigarettes	200	300
or cigarillos	100	150
or cigars	50	75
or tobacco	250g	400g
wine	2l	4l
and either:		
drinks over 38.8°	1l	1.5l
or drinks 38.8°		
or under	2l	3l
perfume	50g	75g
toilet water	250ml	375ml

The maximum amount of money you can import into Italy is L400,000 although legislation is under revision. Those intending to re-export more than L1m of other currencies should complete Form V2 at the customs on entry.

Climate

The Italian climate is more varied than its sunny reputation suggests. Generally, while the South and coastal areas enjoy a Mediterranean climate, with mild, wet winters, the North and mountainous areas are continental with hot, stormy summers and cold winters. Everywhere precipitation is high although rainfall is more evenly distributed throughout the year in the North.

The Po valley is notorious for damp, foggy winters (and often humid summers) and visitors to Milan or Turin will need some warm clothing until April or May. Foggy weather often adversely affects autumn and winter flights, especially to Milan's Linate airport. Venice can be colder than London in winter and the Trieste area is sometimes affected by the cool *bora* wind. On the other hand the Italian Riviera, protected by the Apennines, enjoys a relatively mild and sunny climate all year round; Genoa's minimum average temperature is 8°C/46°F, though winter rainfall is high, particularly in November.

Central Italy is hot and usually dry in summer (Florence and Bologna are as hot as Rome or Palermo); spring and autumn are variable (often windy) but only December, January and February are really cold and snow is a rarity except in the mountains.

Holidays

In mid-July there is a mass exodus from the cities to the countryside or coast and Italy all but grinds to a halt until after the holiday of *Ferragosto* (Aug 15). Most factories and some shops and restaurants are closed for the whole of August. School holidays are from the second week in June until mid-September and at Christmas (two weeks) and Easter (five days).

Listed below are the main national public and religious holidays, when offices, banks and shops are shut. Public offices may be closed on the eve of some holidays.

Jan 1 New Year's Day (Capodanno)
Jan 6 Epiphany (Epifania)
Late Mar/Apr Easter Monday (Sant'Angelo/Lunedì di Pasqua)
Apr 25 Liberation Day (Giorno della Liberazione)
May 1 Labour Day (Festa del Lavoro)
Aug 15 Assumption of the Blessed Virgin Mary (Ferragosto)
Nov 1 All Saints' Day (Ognissanti)
Dec 8 Immaculate Conception (Immacolata Concezione)
Dec 25 Christmas Day (Natale)
Dec 26 St Stephen's Day (Santo Stefano)

Every town is closed for the local saint's day. Traditional *feste* can also affect business appointments, although many historic events are celebrated at weekends. Some important dates to avoid for business are:
Feb Venice carnival (week before Lent)
Apr 25 Venice, Festa di San Marco
May 7–8 Bari, Sagra di San Nicola
Jun 16–17 Pisa, regatta
Jun 24 Florence, Genoa, Turin, Festa di San Giovanni
Jun 29 Rome, Festa di San Pietro e San Paolo
Jul 15 Palermo, Sta Rosalia
Sep 1–10 Naples, Piedigrotta
Sep 19 Naples, San Gennaro
Oct 4 Bologna, San Petronio
Nov 21 Venice, Festa della Salute
Dec 7 Milan, Sant'Ambrogio

Money

Local currency
The currency is the *lira* (L) although this scarcely exists as a unit. There are plans to introduce the heavy lira in the future. Denominations of banknotes are issued for 100,000, 50,000, 20,000, 10,000, 5,000 and 1,000 *lire*. There is always a danger of confusing L100,000 and L10,000 notes. Coins are mostly 500, 200, 100 or 50 *lire*; although smaller denominations (5, 10, 20) exist they are practically worthless (and even correctly counted would not be appreciated by shopkeepers). You may be given small change in *gettoni* (telephone tokens worth L200). Public telephones take L100, L200 and (newer machines) L500 coins. L (for lire) is sometimes written like the sterling £ sign, or as *lit.*

Credit and charge cards are accepted in the smarter hotels, restaurants and shops, but seldom at filling stations or smaller family-run trattorias or stores. All car rental firms and some taxis will take major credit cards. Many railway stations also accept credit card payment for tickets. But as yet it is unwise to rely solely on this method of payment, especially in the South.

Changing money

Banks usually offer the best rates of exchange but these vary slightly from bank to bank, as do commission rates which may be charged on a percentage basis or per transaction. Branches at airports and railway stations are open outside normal hours.

Exchange procedures at banks are often slow and you will usually be required to show your passport, even when this is not legally necessary (for instance with a Eurocheque card). You may have to join a line at the *cambio* counter and again at the *cassa* to collect the money. Banks are also usually slow over the transfer of funds.

Banking hours are complicated, with opening and closing times often not exactly on the hour or half-hour. There are regional variations but generally banks are open Mon–Fri, 8.20 or 8.30 to 1.20 or 1.30 or 2; many are also open for an hour in the afternoon, usually 2.45 or 3 to 3.45 or 4. In Rome and some other cities there are one or two banks offering evening (usually Thursday), Saturday and even Sunday opening.

The largest banks are Banco Nazionale del Lavoro, Banca Commerciale Italiana, Credito Italiano and Banco di Roma. Most foreign banks are based in Milan or Rome. **Other options** When banks are closed, money can be exchanged at a bureau de change (*cambio*) or travel agent (both open during shop hours). American Express cardholders can cash personal cheques at their offices. Automatic cash dispensers for use with American Express and Visa cards are appearing at airports and banks. Hotels usually offer the worst rates of exchange.

Tipping

Hotels Service is included but it is usual to tip porters; L2,000 per bag is reasonable.
Restaurants and bars A service charge is usually added by the restaurant but it is normal to round up the figure or leave about 5% for

good service. Waiters at bars should be left cash tips.
Taxis It is normal although not obligatory to tip taxis (the Milanese often do not). If in doubt, round up the fare or give a minimum of L500, maximum L3,000.
Other Car park attendants and hairdressers should be tipped. Cloakroom attendants expect about L200. Garage attendants who wash your windscreen do not solicit tips but accept them graciously. There is usually a fixed rate for porterage at railway stations and airports.

Small favours can be obtained by tipping the right person: for instance a museum attendant may show you a room that is normally closed and a train guard may be able to find you a sleeper, if you have not reserved one, or guarantee a single sleeping compartment in second class.

Getting there

Business visitors normally fly to Italy, although rail communications to the North – especially Milan – are good, frequent and convenient (with customs formalities on board). Road connections with the rest of Europe are also good but frontier tunnels (Mont Blanc and Frejus from France, Gran San Bernardo from Switzerland) are time-consuming and tolls expensive.

Gateway airports

Alitalia, the national airline, provides a service from and to 95 countries in the world, including direct flights from major cities in the USA, the Far East and Australia. About 80 other major international airlines fly in and out of Italy, mainly to Milan and/or Rome. There are 25 main airports in Italy.

Major train services

There are Euro City services from Dortmund (via Munich), Geneva, Hamburg, Lausanne, Paris and Stuttgart to Milan and from Nuremberg (via Munich), Paris and Vienna to Rome. There is a service from Paris to Venice and Florence and from Geneva to Venice. Seats must be reserved in advance on some services. There are sleepers on longer routes. A TEE (Trans Europe Express) train runs from Zürich to Milan (reservations compulsory), the luxury Orient Express from London to Venice.

Getting around

Business executives are wary of air strikes and will travel by train for quite long distances. Overnight sleepers are popular for journeys of over 500km/310 miles between, for instance, Rome and Genoa or Venice. The twice daily high-speed train from Rome to Milan (4hrs) provides hot competition for the airlines.

Air

The Alitalia domestic network (including its subsidiary, Aero Trasporti Italiani) covers 21 mainland and Sicilian airports (plus several on other islands). Airlines offering useful domestic flights to the minor airports are Aliblu (to Foggia), Alinord (Rome to Bergamo and Parma, Milan to Perugia), Avianova (Rome to Forlì) and Transavio (Rome and Milan to Siena). Rome is within 70mins flying time of all other Italian airports; from Milan to Palermo takes 1hr 35mins.
Fares There are discounts of 30% for returns from one weekend to the next and 50% for day return flights on Sundays, and reductions of 50% or more for immediate family (minimum three passengers) travelling with you.
Reservations Alitalia has over 200 ticket offices in Italy and many abroad.

Train

The extensive rail network, run by *Ferrovie dello Stato*, a commercial state-owned corporation, provides a convenient and very cheap way of getting around Italy. It is invariably worth going first class. Trains are comfortable and usually punctual but can be very crowded, especially

around the *Ferragosto* holiday and Christmas. Sleepers and couchettes can be reserved on many services. Telephones are available on some fast trains.

There are information offices, travel agents, currency exchange facilities, photocopying machines, bars, restaurants and *alberghi diurni* (day hotels) at major stations.

There are several classes of train.
Euro City A high-speed train linking important European cities; 1st and 2nd class.
Inter City A fast (*super rapido*) train running between the major Italian cities. Most trains are first class only. The most useful service to business visitors is the high-speed Milan–Rome ETR 450 *Pendolino*, with refreshment service, newspapers and magazines. An even faster version, the ETR 500 (to be inaugurated in 1990), will have telephones, telex and fax.
Rapido A fast train running between major towns and cities, now mainly superseded by the *Inter City* service. Some consist only of first-class coaches.
Espresso A slower train stopping at major stations. Trains marked *diretto* or *locale* are very slow, with frequent stops at minor stations.

Restaurants operate on most international and long-distance trains; otherwise luncheon trays, snacks and drinks are usually available. On all fast trains internal telegrams can be sent (ask the guard for a special form).

Average times are: Rome–Milan 4hrs (Pendolino), Milan–Genoa 1hr 30mins, Milan–Turin 1hr 35mins, Milan–Florence 3hrs, Rome–Palermo 11hrs 12mins, Rome–Bologna 3hrs 26mins (all *Inter City*).
Fares Fares are based on the distance travelled. *Euro City*, *Inter City* and *Rapido* trains carry a supplement of 30% on the normal fare.
Reservations should be made 24hrs in advance through travel agents or at the station and are obligatory for most fast trains. There is a surcharge of 20% for tickets bought on the train.

Car

The autostrada system, covering over 6,000km/3,700 miles, is one of the best in the world and links all major cities and towns. Signs are green and routes are indicated with an "A" for autostrada (blue indicates a *superstrada*). Tolls, payable on most stretches of autostrada but not in parts of the South, are expensive; the journey from Milan to Rome costs over L40,000. Fuel is also expensive by European standards and the complex coupon packages (including motorway toll vouchers and free ACI breakdown service) offer scant savings. These packages are only available to foreign-registered cars and must be purchased before departure from national motoring organizations. Traffic builds up at the main city toll stations and borders, especially on busy summer weekends.

Ordinary roads are satisfactory but can be very slow through built-up town outskirts (the autostrada is often more scenic). All roads are patrolled by the *polizia stradale*.

In cities on-street parking is limited, garage parking is expensive, and motorcycles and trams can be additional hazards.

Italians tend to drive fast and may overtake illegally on the inside on the autostrada. Especially in the South, drivers use their horns a great deal (although this is prohibited in larger towns); any driver hooting and waving a white handkerchief is indicating an emergency and should be given priority. From Rome southwards the red traffic light is not universally respected.

Car rental A car is useful for visiting out-of-town factories or several provincial towns. Both self-drive and chauffeured cars are available and cars can be rented in conjunction with an Alitalia flight. All the top firms take major credit cards. You must hold a valid international driving licence, a new EC licence or a licence from an EC country, with translation. Most car rental firms require drivers to be over 25. Avis, Budget, Europcar, Hertz and InterRent plus the Italian firms Maggiore and Tirreno are widely represented, with branches at airports and railway stations. It is cheapest to reserve a car through one of the major international firms before leaving home.

Filling stations On the autostrada there are 24hr filling stations every few kilometres, usually with good refreshments, sometimes with excellent restaurants. Other filling stations are usually closed at lunch time (until 3pm) and after 7pm but at some there are automatic, self-service pumps which accept L10,000 banknotes.

Legal requirements Seat belts are now compulsory. Speed limits are to be reduced and while legislation is in progress the limits are as follows: on autostrada routes 130kph/80mph Mon–Fri and 110kph/68mph Sat–Sun; on other roads 90kph/56mph and in built-up areas 50kph/31mph. There are hefty on-the-spot fines for speeding; you may also pay by post.

All cars must carry warning triangles which can be rented from the Italian Automobile Club (ACI) offices at the frontier. Cars drive on the right and give priority to traffic coming from the right.

Emergencies In an emergency telephone 113 (ambulance, police). If you have a breakdown telephone 116 (ACI 24hr emergency), giving the operator your location and car type and registration number. There are telephones 2kms apart on the autostrada. Red warning triangles should be placed 45 metres/50yds behind any obstructing vehicle. For 24hr advice, contact the head office of ACI (Automobile Club Italiano) in Rome ☎ (06) 4212. Local ACI offices can supply names of spare part stockists. Garages are generally not expensive and mechanics usually obliging.

Ferry and hydrofoil

Italian State Railways run ferry services to Sicily. Aliscafi SNAV operates hydrofoils between Palermo

and Naples and between Reggio
Calabria and Messina.

Bus

It is invariably quicker to rent a car
than to travel by bus. There is no
national bus company with a
comprehensive network; local
companies vary widely in services
offered and are generally most useful
in the South. In cities the bus can be
convenient. Tickets are bought from
tobacconists and stamped on entry to
the bus by the rear door. Weekly
tourist tickets can be bought in some
cities.

Taxi

Taxi ranks are located on the main
streets and intersections of towns and
at stations and airports. They do not
cruise for custom (although in some
places they may stop if hailed); it is
better to ask your hotel to call a cab.

In Milan, Rome and several other
cities, official taxis are yellow;
everywhere they should have a taxi
sign on the roof and a meter. Fares
and the fixed starting price vary.
There are extra charges for night
service, Sundays, public holidays and
baggage. Some journeys outside the
town (to the airport, for instance) are
subject to a fixed fare.

Taxi drivers will provide receipts
for journeys: ask for a *ricevuta*.

Hotels

The very finest Italian hotels cater for
the richer tourist and the international
executive, with high standards of
service and often a splendid location,
perhaps in a converted *palazzo* or
villa. In the major cities, there are
some grand old 19thC hotels, with
traditional decor, period furnishings
and formal service. The best (several
run by the CIGA chain) are ideal for a
senior business clientele, but many
have come down in the world. There
are some luxurious resort hotels, often
equipped for conferences or incentive
weekends, on the Ligurian and
Tuscan coasts and the Northern
Lakes.

As yet there are few hotels with
modern "business centres." The best-
equipped hotels tend to be the
international chains, usually modern
blocks quite far from city centres. In
the middle range the Jolly chain
provides reliable business
accommodation in all major cities.

The typical Italian hotel, especially
in provincial towns and in the cities of
the South, provides functional, fairly
modern accommodation for local
business people and travelling sales
representatives. Most will have private
washing facilities, but often only a
shower. Larger hotels exist mainly for
trade fair or conference clientele, and
will also take busloads of tourists. All
can be very dull and soulless. It is
more enjoyable to seek out a small
family-run hotel with some character
and charm or a luxurious country
restaurant with rooms. Do not expect
Teutonic efficiency or Scandinavian
standards of cleanliness.

Categories and grading Hotels are
officially graded from five stars down
to one according to their facilities.
Provincial tourist boards have some
autonomy and standards and
requirements vary, so official hotel
lists (which are often a year out of
date) should be used only as a general
indication of quality and cost.

Pensioni, separately graded, are no
longer required to provide meals, and
some are quite smart small bed-and-
breakfast hotels (these will be in the
top three-star category).

Facilities Most of the better hotels are
geared to the needs of the business
traveller. There is usually access to
the hotel's own telex, photocopier or
fax machine and additional services
can be arranged with local secretarial
companies. Milanese hotel staff are
the most efficient in this respect.

Business class hotels normally have
bedrooms with international direct
dial telephones (IDD), colour TVs and
minibars (but almost never tea-
making facilities). Some bathrooms,
especially with single bedrooms, have
showers only. In older hotels rooms
vary considerably in size, comfort and

price. Singles are often poky back rooms; those with a small double bed (*letto francese*) are sometimes more spacious. Even in luxury hotels, bedrooms can be very small and it is advisable to ask to see the room before accepting it. Newly fitted bathrooms in smarter hotels usually have hairdryers. Trouser-presses are rare, but the better hotels have laundry or valeting services. Room service is usually available until 11pm or midnight; 24hr service is rare. Most major hotels are fully air conditioned, although in some old-fashioned establishments it can be a noisy extra (minibars, too, sometimes shudder irritatingly). Double glazing (for soundproofing as well as temperature control) is also common, but not a guarantee of a peaceful night. A few city hotels have pools, but none in Milan. Some hotels have garages, others offer parking with a local garage.

Many hotels have rooms for meetings or conferences invariably equipped with projectors, audiovisual systems and microphones; closed-circuit television and simultaneous translation are sometimes offered.
Prices Italian hotels are very expensive by most standards; the luxury-class hotels, especially in Venice, are among the most expensive in the world. Milan prices are 15% above the national average. Room prices are officially limited according to the category of the establishment and should be displayed. However, prices listed, or quoted, may or may not include breakfast, which is usually an overpriced affair of coffee and rolls. Service and IVA (service tax, 10%) are usually included in the room rate except in luxury hotels where IVA is 19% and sometimes added to the account. The small daily city tax or *imposta di soggiorno* is usually included in prices.

Resort hotels and those in major tourist cities can offer seasonal rates. Few hotels offer cheaper corporate rates or weekend discounts for business guests, except for conferences.
Day hotels (*alberghi diurni*) are establishments with bathrooms, a barber, cleaning services, rest and reading rooms, usually in or near main railway stations.

Making reservations

Advance reservations are always advisable and essential for visits coinciding with major trade fairs or tourist seasons (for instance, Rome at Easter). Reservations must be made by telephone, telex or fax, or through a reservations office in your own country. A toll-free number (*linea verde*) is available for some major groups. If a deposit (*caparra* or *versamento*) is requested, send it by express mail and confirm that you have done so by telex or fax. You may be asked what time you will arrive and rooms may be given away if you do not "show" at the appointed hour.

If you want a bath it is important to specify *con la vasca* (*con bagno* is ambiguous). Confusion can also arise over breakfast; find out whether it is included in the price and specify at the time of reservation whether or not you wish to have it at the hotel.

Hotel groups

Modern chain hotels are frequently outside the city centres, but often convenient for the airport, exhibition halls (Fiere) or other business areas. The main international chains are represented: Hilton, Holiday Inns, Ibis, Intercontinental, Novotel and Trust House Forte all have one or more hotels in Italy. Motelagip is the Italian motel chain; many have good restaurants.
Atahotels ☎ (02) 8467541 or 8490058 (Milan). Both well-equipped modern and grand traditional hotels. Strong presence in Sicily.
CIGA ☎ (02) 62661 or 626622 ℡ 314547 (Milan) or (06) 4758420 ℡ 613320 (Rome). This Aga Khan-owned luxury chain promises and delivers a happy blend of "classic tradition and modern efficiency" in a score of hotels, mostly in Northern

Italy, especially Venice. Most de luxe rooms have recently been refurbished in standardized Empire style. Nearly all have smart restaurants and bars; country and resort hotels have sporting or health club facilities. Service is impeccable (sometimes 24hr). Facilities include executive jet rentals, voucher "welcome" schemes with discounts of up to 40% and combination programmes (for example, for skiing weekends at Cortina).

Crest ☎ (051) 372172 (Bologna). This UK-based chain has two reliable modern hotels (Bologna, Florence) with well-equipped bedrooms (including nonsmoking and ladies' rooms), several meeting rooms and outdoor pools. Crest Business Club offers corporate benefits.

Interhotel ☎ (02) 8490058 (Milan) or (06) 493807 (Rome). Vast modern hotels and convention centres with leisure facilities.

Italhotels ☎ (1678) 01004, toll free in Italy. Group of some 40 individual hotels, mainly in the North. Management and service are professional, but style and decor vary.

Jolly ☎ (02) 7703 ⊺ 331582 (Milan) or (06) 4940541 ⊺ 612682 (Rome). Well-distributed business chain with 30 hotels (including 6 in Sicily, and 6 in Milan's centre and suburbs). The standard Jolly is functional, modern and impersonal, but some hotels are more luxurious. They are useful in the South, where reliable accommodation is sparse. All are air-conditioned, most have parking facilities, a few have pools.

Ottaviani (no central reservations number). Four hotels (two luxury) in Rome and Florence. The emphasis is on a calm atmosphere, uninstitutional decor and faultless service.

Star Hotels (no central reservations number). Well-equipped but dull business hotels in seven main cities.

Associations
Many individually owned and managed hotels belong to organizations for joint marketing and

reservations. These include:

Best Western Italia ☎ (1678) 20080, toll free in Italy. Over 50 city and resort hotels, mostly well suited to business travellers.

Cityhotels ☎ (0165) 765333, toll free in Italy. A consortium of 3- and 4-star hotels of variable quality, mostly in Northern and central Italy. Weekend discounts.

Relais et Châteaux (no central reservations number). Independently owned luxury hotels, mostly in country villas.

Space Hotels ☎ (06) 4940346 (Rome). Wide range of over 50 hotels, mostly good of their kind. Reservations offices in major cities.

Our recommended hotels
The hotels given full entries in this guide are those most suited to the international business traveller. These are the most comfortable and well-run hotels in the area, and include luxury hotels also used by tourists. More functional ones convenient for people visiting trade fairs or non-central business districts, and the best hotels geared specifically to conferences, are also given entries.

Listed under "Other hotels" are cheaper, less prestigious, but convenient and reasonably comfortable hotels. In provincial towns these may include fairly basic accommodation, always the most comfortable available.

The "Out of town" section lists useful suburban accommodation and some luxurious country and resort hotels, used for conferences, for holiday weekends or in certain cases for "commuting."

The price symbols have the following meanings:

⊥	up to L90,000
⊥/	90,000–130,000
⊥//	130,000–170,000
⊥///	170,000–220,000
⊥////	220,000–300,000
⊥/////	over L300,000

These reflect the cost in lire at the time of going to press for one person occupying a typical/standard room.

241

Restaurants

Eating out has always been a way of life in Italy, although the midday meal has traditionally been a home-based family affair, and in some places the habit dies hard. Most entertaining of business guests is done in restaurants, usually over lunch at around 1.30. In the South, lunch may be followed by a siesta. Dinner is at 8.30 or 9, although smart dinners in Rome are often later (9.15 or 9.30).

Restaurants are closed (for the *chiusura* or *turno settimanale*) one day a week (often Sunday or Monday), sometimes for one other meal and many in August.

Types of restaurant

It is important to gauge the occasion and company carefully when choosing where to eat. Italians often enjoy a jolly trattoria more than a smart restaurant, but for business entertaining a serious restaurant may be more suitable (even if the food is blander) as tables tend to be better spaced and service more professional.

Unless it has a really exceptional reputation for food (or perhaps views), do not invite Italian guests to dine at your hotel; it implies a lack of interest in or knowledge of the local restaurant scene. There are exceptions to this general rule, particularly in Rome where the finest food and most luxurious surroundings are found in the top hotels.

In theory the *ristorante* is a smarter, more formal establishment than a *trattoria*, which is usually cavernous with rustic seating and a bustling atmosphere. An *osteria* or *hostaria* (typically Roman) is basic although there are a few with this title which are extremely grand. Cheap meals or snacks are found at a *pizzeria*, *rosticceria* (grill) or *tavola calda* (self-service buffet, common in Florence). Quite often an establishment will call itself *Ristorante-trattoria-tavola calda*, so distinctions can only be general. Only in Milan have plastic burger bars really proliferated. For quick lunches, Italians order a snack at a bar and eat it there, and in Milan there are quite a few US-style sandwich bars or *paninoteche*.

In a *ristorante* it is not usually "done" to eat just a first course, the *primi piatti*, although these are usually filling and nourishing. Italians often request a small portion (*mezza porzione*) of the pasta course if they do not want a heavy meal. Note that "main" dishes (*secondi*) may be less substantial than the pasta course, and are not usually automatically accompanied by vegetables (*contorni*). **Menus** are displayed outside restaurants, and are usually *à la carte*; some restaurants also offer a fixed-price menu. In addition there may be a *piatto del giorno* or a section entitled *oggi lo chef consiglia*: the dish of the day or the chef's recommendations (these usually arrive quickly). Any set menu for tourists (*menu turistico*) is to be avoided (usually cheap, but poor value) and restaurants offering this are often suspect anyway. On the other hand a fixed-price *menu gastronomico* or *menu degustazione* (small portions of the chef's best dishes) in a very prestigious restaurant is a fair choice if your guest or host opts for it too. In many restaurants, as well as in the small family-run country trattorias, the menu will often be recited at your table.

The wine list is usually, but not invariably, separate in the smarter restaurants. Offer your guest a *spumantino* or an aperitif. It is, of course, good manners to order an Italian wine, and a wine of the region if it is a matter of local pride. However, the more prestigious restaurants usually have a good selection of French wines. Water is invariably offered.

Payment A compulsory cover charge (*coperto*) of up to L10,000 per person will be levied. Service (12–15%) is usually included or added. Visa and American Express are the most widely accepted credit cards. A tax receipt (*ricevuta fiscale*) will be issued and, in theory, you may be asked to show it on leaving the restaurant.

Reservations

It is always safer to make reservations a day or two in advance, but a morning telephone call will often secure a table for lunch or dinner that day. For very smart or very small restaurants, and for specific requirements like a table outside or a private room, it is sensible to reserve a few days in advance. This also applies to Friday and Saturday nights and during holidays. At the quietest times (Sunday evenings, August) you may have difficulty finding a good restaurant.

Rules and customs

There are seldom hard-and-fast rules about dress, although many restaurants prefer men to wear jackets and ties. In any case, Italians generally take care to look their best in public. Guests are rarely asked to refrain from smoking and few restaurants have nonsmoking tables.

Southerners are not used to women dining out alone; Sicilian restaurants are usually full of men, except on obviously family occasions, such as Sunday lunch.

Our recommended restaurants

The restaurants given full entries have been selected for their proven reputation in business circles. All are suitable for entertaining local guests or colleagues. While the quality of food and wine offered has been taken into account, atmosphere, service, clientele and location are given greater priority than in most gastronomic guides. Many classic restaurants featured in food guides will of course be found here too.

Under "Other restaurants" are more informal places, suitable for an evening off and including some with a good gastronomic reputation but perhaps an inconvenient location, erratic service, very spartan decor or cramped tables. The majority listed here are cheaper, but several may be quite luxurious restaurants more suitable for a romantic dinner than for a business meeting. A few are open only in the evenings. In larger cities the section on "Other restaurants" ensures a reasonable coverage of all areas of the city.

Some of the classiest establishments, as well as some of the "fun" places, may be "Out of town" and popular at weekends. This section also includes places highly regarded by gourmets which may merit a gastronomic pilgrimage.

The price symbols used in the guide have the following meanings:

▯	up to L30,000
▯/	30–50,000
▯//	50–70,000
▯///	70–90,000
▯////	90–110,000
▯/////	over L110,000

These reflect the price at the time of going to press of a typical meal including half a bottle of house or modestly priced wine, coffee and service.

La cucina italiana

Italy's cuisine is still based on rural, regional tradition and the local market (any frozen produce must by law be indicated as such on the menu). There are a few broad generalizations (rice and butter in the North, pasta and oil in the South, fish on the coast) but every region or city has its own special dishes and you will be popular with your host if you find out about, and order, these. Italians are very conservative about their food: regional recipes are usually sacrosanct – only a few new-wave chefs add non-traditional ingredients or more than a generous pinch of imagination – and fussy presentation is not appreciated. But heavier Northern recipes are sometimes adapted to suit the current fashion for lighter meals, especially in more sophisticated and cosmopolitan cities. Special diets are not often catered for (a vegetarian is considered eccentric) but requests can usually be satisfied. Few restaurants specialize in the cooking of other nations, except in large cities. Foreign restaurants should be avoided unless strongly recommended.

243

Regional cuisines

Abruzzo *Brodetto*; *maccheroni alla chitarra* (macaroni with tomato and bacon); *cassata abruzzese* (dessert).

Emilia-Romagna Parma ham and various pastas; *bollito misto* (mixed boiled meats, served with a *salsa verde*, green sauce); *zampone* (stuffed pigs' trotters, from Modena); *bomba di riso* (pigeon dish with rice, from Parma); Parmesan cheese.

Friuli-Venezia Giulia Prosciutto di San Daniele (ham from north of Udine); *La Jota* (bean soup); fish and shellfish.

Liguria *Burrida*, *zimino* and *zuppa di datteri* (fish/shellfish soups); *pansoti* (ravioli). From Genoa: *trenette al pesto* (pasta with basil and Parmesan sauce); *cima* (veal roll).

Lombardy Bresaola della Valtellina (smoked beef); *polenta* (maize); fish from the Lakes. From Milan: *risotto alla milanese* (saffron rice); *costoletta milanese*, *ossobuco*.

The Marches *Brodetto* (fish soup); *garagoli in porchetta* (shellfish); *vincisgrassi* (lasagne dish). Lamb and rabbit. Pastries.

Piedmont Truffles (in *agnolotti* or *finanziera*); *pollo alla marenga* (chicken dish); *vitello tonnato* (veal in tunny sauce); *brasato al Barolo* (beef in red wine); *zabaglione*.

Sicily *Caponata* (marinaded eggplant); *pasta con le sarde* (with sardines) or *alla norma* (with eggplant); *pescespada* (swordfish).

The South Fish and shellfish; *vitello alla pizzaiola* or *alla napoletana* (with tomatoes and garlic). From Bari: *gnummerieddi* (lamb sausages) and *tortiera alla Barese* (savoury pie with mussels).

Tuscany *Crostini* (croutons with wild boar pâté); *cinghiale* (wild boar) and *lepre* (hare); beef from the Val di Chiana; *baccalà livornese* (cod with tomatoes) and *cacciucco* (fish soup), both from Livorno. From Florence: *bistecca alla fiorentina*.

Umbria Spit-roasted meat and game, including *beccacce* (woodcock), *palombacci* (pigeons) and *quaglie* (quails); truffles from Norcia, trout from Lake Trasimeno.

The Veneto Poultry and game including *sopa coada* (pigeon soup), *pollo alla padovana* (chicken fricassée). Fish including *Baccala vicentina* (salt cod from Vicenza). *Tiramisu* (sponge and liqueur dessert). From Venice: *fegato alla veneziana* (liver with onions).

Italian wine

Italy leads the world in volume and variety of wines, but the scope is not so daunting in the top bracket, where bottles are usually within reach of a travel budget. Italy's elite red wines can approach ranked French *crus* in class if rarely in price. Then again, it is not always clear which belong to the elite. Classification is no guarantee; over 10% of the total – 220 wines in all – are classed as *denominazione di origine controllata* (DOC) or *garantita* (DOCG) – while some of Italy's finest wines are unclassified *vini da tavola*.

By now most good urban *ristoranti* have a decent wine list and, with luck, even a trained sommelier to explain it. But a little basic knowledge can enable one to choose rather than have bottles imposed. The following wines offer undisputed quality with wide availability.

Red wines First on the list come the traditional DOCG aged reds for which Italy is most noted. Piedmont has two: *Barolo* and *Barbaresco*. Ceretto and Bruno Giacosa excel with both, as do the larger houses of Pio Cesare, Alfredo Prunotto and Fontanafredda. In Barolo look for Aldo Conterno, Vietti and Guiseppe Mascarello. In Barbaresco the leader is Gaja, though Marchesi di Gresy and Castello di Neive are also widely admired.

Tuscany has three vaunted DOCGs: *Brunello di Montalcino*, *Vino Nobile di Montepulciano* and *Chianti*. In Brunello, Biondi Santi upholds status and price, though Villa Banfi, Il Poggione and Tenuta Caparzo can compete in quality. Avignonesi may be the noblest of Vino Nobile. Chianti Classico is led by the large Antinori firm with Villa Antinori and Peppoli, followed by Riserva Ducale from Ruffino and Castello di Brolio from Ricasoli. Prestigious estates include Castello di Ama, Badia a Coltibuono, San Felice, Fontodi, Castello di Volpaia and Castello dei Rampolla. Frescobaldi's Castello di Nipozzano and Montesodi exemplify Chianti outside Classico. Some of Tuscany's best reds are unclassified; the list now runs into the dozens, preceded by Antinori's *Tignanello* and Incisa della Rocchetta's *Sassicaia*.

Neighbouring Umbria offers the aristocratic *Torgiano Rubesco Riserva* from Lungarotti. No serious list could be without the pride of Verona, the rich *Amarone* from Valpolicella, as made by Masi, Allegrini, Quintarelli, Tedeschi and Seregho Alighieri. Fine reds are made elsewhere, North and South; a highly recommended local wine is always worth a try.

White wines The quality of dry white and Champagne-method sparkling wines has improved dramatically in recent times. Remember, though, that the Italian preference is for fresh, clean varietal whites of northern Friuli and Alto Adige, rather than the woody and complex. Among Italian whites there is much to recommend, but wines that are as reliable as they are available include *Villa Antinori Bianco*, Anselmi's *Soave*, *Corvo Bianco* and Mastroberardino's *Greco di Tufo*.

For whites with Burgundy-style complexity, look for the *Chardonnay* from Ca' del Bosco or Gaja's *Gaia & Rei*, the Umbrian *Cervaro della Sala* from Antinori and the *Vernaccia di San Gimignano* from Teruzzi & Puthod known as Terra di Tufo.

Vintages Fine vintages for Barolo and Barbaresco were the *grandioso* 85, as well as 82, 79 and 78. Passable vintages in 84 and 83 are nearing primes, and most of the weak 81 and 80 wines are now exhausted. Moving backward, wines from the superb 71 and 64 vintages may still be impressive.

In Tuscany, 85 was also the best vintage in recent times, though 88, 86

and 82 had much to commend them. With few exceptions, 87 and 84 are best avoided, though some good wines remain from 81, 79 and 78. Reserve *Brunello* can go back much farther, to the great vintages of 75, 71, 64 and, in the case of Biondi Santi's, to 1891 and 1888.

Bars and cafés

There is a vast number of bars in almost every town in Italy, and, apart from a few smart establishments in major cities, they vary little in character. Trendy winebars or cocktail bars are rare (except in Milan), but there are some elegant middle-European style 19thC cafés in the cities of the North.

A typical bar has a zinc counter and rather functional decor, often with more appealing café tables outside in summer. The various types of coffee served are: very concentrated, black (*ristretto*); concentrated, black (*espresso*); less concentrated, black (*lungo*); concentrated with a little cold milk (*macchiato*), and a larger cup of coffee with hot, frothy milk (*cappuccino*). All can be made with decaffeinated coffee (ask for Caffè Hag). Other drinks include fruit juices, wine by the glass or carafe, local aperitifs and liqueurs. Non-alcoholic drinks (*analcolici*) are becoming more popular. Most bars have Italian and foreign beers and spirits. Home-made ice creams and simple snacks (sweet pastries at breakfast time, sandwiches and rolls – *tramezzini* and *panini* – at lunch) are often provided. In addition to confectionery and cigarettes (look for the "T" sign), some bars sell stamps and bus tickets and many have public telephones (yellow dial sign). Drinks served by waiters at tables are double the price of drinks taken standing at the bar (in larger bars and on the autostrada you usually pay at the till first and then present the receipt to the barman). Bars are open until around midnight.

Bars are widely used by locals and tourists as meeting places, usually for a quick drink, seldom for prolonged drinking sessions except in remoter rural areas. Even here chat, male companionship, a game of cards and watching the world go by (or television) are usually more important than drinking. Women in bars alone in the evenings are inviting male attention. In the South women tend to stay at home more and so those on their own attract more interest.

For an important business discussion, a hotel bar would be more appropriate. If meeting for a meal, the bar of the restaurant may be suitable. The smarter cafés of Turin or Milan are also civilized venues; in other cities they may be overrun with tourists.

Shopping

Shops are usually open from 8.30 or 9 until 1 or 1.30 and from 3.30 or 4 to 7, 7.30 or 8 in the evening on weekdays. Hours tend to be later in summer (when most shops close on Saturday afternoons) than in winter (when they close on Monday mornings instead). Wednesday or Thursday is usually early closing (1.30) for food shops. Some shops especially in the North no longer close for lunch (*orario continuo*). These include some department stores. Many shops are closed in August (after sales in July), except in Venice when they often shut in December or January instead.

Italians normally shop for food early in the morning (especially at the regular local markets or small *alimentari*, more common than supermarkets). Other shopping is done in the late afternoon or evening.

The main department stores are *La Rinascente* (branches in Milan and Rome, open all day) and the more popular *Coin*. *Standa* and *Upim* are cheap chain stores. But in all except the remotest provincial towns, the department stores pale beside the competition of smaller shops, especially on the fashion front.
Tax IVA can be reclaimed on substantial purchases (over L525,000)

by nationals of non-EC countries, but the procedure is tiresome. Usually only larger shops catering to tourists offer the discount and they should display a "Tax Free System" sign. You pay the full amount at the time of purchase and then present the invoice to the customs officer at the airport on departure. In Rome cash reimbursements can be collected from the Banco di Santo Spirito at Fiumicino airport. Otherwise mail the stamped invoice to the shop (stamped addressed envelope provided), for a credit to your account or a cash refund through the mail.

Sights and entertainment

Opening hours of museums and galleries vary considerably and it is advisable to get a current list from the local tourist office. State museums are normally open 9–2 (9–1 on Sundays) and most museums close on Mondays. Archeological sites are usually open until dusk. Most sights, including churches, are closed for lunch and may not reopen until late in the afternoon.

Some bigger cities have a cinema showing foreign-language films. Many city-centre cinemas show dubious programmes.

Information sources

In your own country
The overseas division of your country's trade ministry should be able to provide information and advice on doing business in Italy. The Italian Embassy may have a commercial section and there may be a branch of the Italian Chamber of Commerce which will supply details of trade fairs in Italy. The *Italian Institute for Foreign Trade* (ICE, see below), with 75 offices abroad, promotes Italian exports (mainly foodstuffs, especially fruit and vegetables for which it is responsible for quality control) and provides market information and advice to importers.

For general information contact the *Italian State Tourist Office* (ENIT) which has offices in 20 countries.

In Italy
Chambers of Commerce There are
94 provincial chambers of commerce.
The most important for foreign trade
is in Milan: *Camera di Commercio,
Industria, Artigianato e Agricoltura*, Via
Meravigli 9b, 20123 Milan ☎ (02)
85151. There are also 20 chambers of
commerce for the regions, based in
the regional capitals; some have a
separate *centro estero* which promotes
export trade. The *Unione Italiana delle
Camere di Commercio*, Pza Sallustio 21,
00187 Rome ☎ (06) 479961, makes
representations on behalf of business
and industry to the government.
There are also many foreign chambers
of commerce (or trade institutes,
centres or councils), nearly all in
Milan, which promote trade with Italy
and may assist business visitors of
their own nationality. For addresses
contact the *Unione delle Camere di
Commercio Estere ed Italo-Estere in
Italia*, Via Ludovico da Viadana 2,
20122 Milan ☎ (02) 873000.
Other organizations *Confcommercio
(Confederazione Generale Italiana del
Commercio)*, Pza G.G. Belli 2, Rome
☎ (06) 58661.
*Confindustria (Confederazione Generale
dell'Industria Italiana)*, Vle
dell'Astronomia 39, 00144 Rome-EUR
☎ (06) 59031.
*ICE (Istituto Nazionale per il Commercio
Estero)*, Via Liszt 21, 00144 Rome
☎ (06) 59921 or 5992504 ⊠ 610160,
is the government agency for the
promotion of foreign trade,
responsible to the Ministry; it
provides market information to
foreign companies and helps with
participation at international trade
fairs, and it has 38 offices in Italy,
many in regional capitals.
ISTAT (Istituto Centrale di Statistica),
Via Balbo 16, 00184 Rome ☎ (06)
4673 and Via della Repubblica, 20124
Milan ☎ (02) 6595133, compiles
official statistics.
ITC (International Trade Center), Via
Galvani 12, 20124 Milan ☎ (02)
6081079, provides general commercial
and industrial assistance.
  The local trade fair and exhibition

centre (Fiera), Stock Market (*Borsa
Merci*) or import-export consortium
may also be helpful.
Tourist information At frontiers and
airports there are branches of ENIT
(*Ente National per il Turismo*), the
Italian State Tourist Office. Each of
the 20 regions has its own Tourist
Board in the regional capital. All the
95 provincial capitals have a
Provincial Tourist Board (*EPT: Ente
Provinciale Turismo* or *APT: Azienda
Provinciale Turismo*). These promote
tourism in the area and publish
brochures, maps and hotel lists. They
also have information offices, where
English is normally spoken, many
with branches at airports, railway
stations and ports and on the
autostrada. There are also over 400
local tourist boards, some with
separate information offices (often
seasonal in resorts) providing
information for the town or resort
only.
  Town directories (*Tuttocittà*) are a
useful source of general information,
with maps. The Yellow Pages
directory is called *Pagine Gialle*.

Crime
Beware of bag-snatchers and
pickpockets, especially in Rome and
Naples; leave valuables in the hotel
safe. It is unwise to wear conspicuous
jewellery. In Rome and the South,
begging gypsy children may be
pickpockets working in pairs; be alert
for attempts to distract your attention.
  Always lock your car and never
leave possessions in it; car thieves are
particularly active in Milan, Rome
and in the South (locals have
detachable radios). Foreign number
plates attract attention. Visitors to
Sicily are usually warned about car
theft. Beware motorcycle riders
who may smash car windows at traffic
lights; in rough areas lock doors and
do not leave valuables within reach.
  Milan, Turin, Florence, Rome,
Naples and Palermo are the worst
cities for drug addiction and,
therefore, for drug-related crime.
  In the event of a theft or other

crime you should report to the nearest police station (*Polizia* or *Carabinieri*) and give a statement (*dichiarazione*). If you need an official copy the report should be on official, stamped paper (*carta bollata*) bought from a tobacconist. The *Questura* has a Foreigners' Office, with English-speaking staff.

Police There are several types of police in Italy, with different but sometimes overlapping roles. All are responsible for upholding the law. The *Carabinieri* have wide-ranging duties and in wartime become a fighting force. Responsibility for public order, however, lies mainly with the *Polizia di Stato*, state police, under the Interior Ministry; the *Polizia stradale* patrol the autostrada and other roads. The *Guardia di Finanza* act as customs officers at ports and borders. The *Vigili urbani*, or city police, are responsible for regulating traffic, enforcing local laws (including parking) and giving information. The *Metronotte* (private security guards) check banks and shops at night.

If you are arrested If you are taken into custody or charged with a serious offence insist on your consulate being informed. They can provide a list of English-speaking lawyers and demand that you are treated as well as an Italian national.

Embassies

All are in Rome; many also have consulates in Milan and other major cities.

Australia Via Alessandria 215 ☎ (06) 832721
Austria Via Pergolesi 3 ☎ (06) 868241
Belgium Via dei Monti Parioli 49 ☎ (06) 3609441
Canada Via G.B. de Rossi 27 ☎ (06) 855341
Denmark Via dei Monti Parioli 50 ☎ (06) 3600441
Finland Via Lisbona 3 ☎ (06) 858329
France Pza Farnese 67 ☎ (06) 6565241
Germany (Federal Republic) Via di Trasone 56–58 ☎ (06) 8390045

Greece Via S. Mercadente 36 ☎ (06) 859630
Ireland Largo del Nazareno 3 ☎ (06) 6782541
Japan Via Quintino Sella 58–60 ☎ (06) 4817151
Netherlands Via Michel Mercati 8 ☎ (06) 873141
New Zealand Via Zara 28 ☎ (06) 851225
Norway Via delle Terme Deciane 7 ☎ (06) 5755833
Portugal Via G. Pezzana 9 ☎ (06) 873801
Spain Palazzo Borghese, Largo Fontanella Borghese 19 ☎ (06) 6878172
Sweden Pza Rio de Janeiro 3 ☎ (06) 860441
Switzerland Via Barnaba Oriani 61 ☎ (06) 803641
UK Via XX Settembre 80a ☎ (06) 4755441
USA Via Vittorio Veneto 119a ☎ (06) 4674
Yugoslavia Via dei Monti Parioli 20 ☎ (06) 3600796

Health care

The Italian health service is state-run on the British National Health model, with even worse problems. You will invariably have to wait at emergency departments (*pronto soccorso*) in public hospitals. But there are many private hospitals (*case di cura cliniche*), and private practice flourishes. Hospitals in the North, especially university teaching hospitals, are usually better than those in the South. In general standards of health care are not as high as in Britain or the United States, and in some hospitals much nursing is left to families. Insurance must cover emergency repatriation.

There are US military hospitals at bases in Vicenza, Livorno and Naples. There are specialized anti-poisoning centres at hospitals in Rome, Milan, Turin, Genoa, La Spezia and Cesena, with English-speaking personnel.

Alternative therapies Italians are conservative in their attitudes to health, although homeopathy is widely practised. Keeping fit is becoming a preoccupation and most cities, especially in the North, have health clubs; but few hotels have fitness facilities.

If you fall ill

The local *Guardia medica* will send a doctor round if you are ill. Visitors taking prescribed medication should carry stocks or clear prescriptions. Anyone with a chronic medical complaint, allergy or unusual blood type should bring a letter from a doctor translated into Italian.

Pharmacies, identified by a red cross, are usually open 8.30–1 and 4–8, with local variations. All towns have at least one pharmacy open 24hrs, listed in the telephone directory or newspaper. Each pharmacy should display a list of those open at night and on Sundays as well as the nearest 24hr pharmacy. The pharmacist can prescribe some medicines such as antibiotics for which a doctor's prescription may be needed in your own country. By Italian law, pharmacies cannot stock foreign products. It is advisable to know the chemical composition of any medication being taken so that an equivalent can be supplied.

Seeing a doctor Doctors often speak some English. Your hotel or, in major cities, consulate should be able to recommend a doctor. The title "Dottore" does not necessarily indicate a doctor of medicine; for a medical doctor request *un medico*.

Emergency treatment For an ambulance telephone ☎ 113. Local ambulance services are listed in newspapers and telephone directories and taxi drivers should know the nearest hospital (*ospedale*, indicated by the letter H on a blue sign).

There are first aid (*pronto soccorso*) services, with a doctor, at airports and railway stations.

Dental treatment Consulates and hotels will advise on the best local dentist.

Paying for treatment

It is wise to take out adequate insurance. Nationals of EC countries can claim the same free or reduced-cost emergency health services available to Italians on presentation of form E111 (obtainable before leaving home), but the process is cumbersome.

Communications

The chronic inefficiency of the Italian postal service means that businesses are making increasing use of fax machines and private couriers. The quickest way to send an urgent document is to use courier services based at airports; other national courier services normally take 24hrs. Procedures at post offices (often crowded) are slow.

Telephones

The Società Italiana per l'Esercizio Telefonico pA (SIP) runs the service and has offices where you can make long-distance and international calls.

The dialling tone is regular alternating short and long tones; the busy line tone is a quick series of staccato notes. International connections will often be better than internal trunk calls although the intercity network is now fully automatic.

Calls are cheapest between 8pm and 8am, and at weekends and on holidays. Telephoning long-distance from your hotel room is considerably more convenient than any other method, but is expensive.

Public telephones (payphones), are operated with coins and *gettoni* (tokens, value L200). Magnetic phone cards are sold at SIP offices and some newsstands and tobacconists but may be hard to get. There are also public telephones at some bars (indicated by a yellow dial); in remote country towns a telephone on the counter, or a *gettone*-operated payphone, may be the only public telephone.

Long-distance calls can be dialled direct from public booths; or you can telephone from the nearest SIP office, which will have telephone directories for the whole country. Tell the desk which town (and country) you want, saying if you wish to make more than one call; you will be allotted a booth. At busy times you may have to wait for "your" town to be called. Calls are metered and payment is made at the desk. Local calls are not allowed in the booths and there are usually some public phones for these.

Most SIP offices are open 7am–10pm (some 24hrs) but are often busy in the evening when soldiers on national service like to ring home.

The Italians cite telephone numbers in pairs. If spelling out a name over the telephone, they invariably use city names to avoid confusion between like-sounding letters.

Emergency services Ambulance, fire, police ☎ 113.

Operator Europe ☎ 15, outside Europe ☎ 170.

Inquiries Local ☎ 12, long distance ☎ 176.

Telegrams *Italcable* operates services abroad. Telegrams may be dictated ☎ 186.

Telex and fax
There are facilities at major post offices. For local postal information telephone ☎ 160 (8am–8pm; English- and French-speaking personnel).

Mail
Letters can take up to two weeks from city to city. Italian businesses send mail by express delivery (supplement L3,000) and use fax machines. An international courier service, CAI-post, is available at main city post offices. Delivery to EC countries should be within 48hrs but it is often quicker to use a private courier service.

Stamps are sold by some tobacconists as well as at post offices. Main central post offices of big cities are usually open until 8 or 9 at night and until noon or 2pm on Saturdays. Others are closed in the afternoons.

Some international dialling codes
Before dialling the country's code, dial 00. In the following list, the figures in brackets indicate how many hours the country is ahead or behind Central European Time (one hour ahead of Greenwich Mean Time). From the last weekend in March to the last weekend in September, clocks are put forward one hour.

Australia	61 (+7–9hrs)
Austria	43
Belgium	32
Canada	1 (-4hrs 30mins–9hrs)
Denmark	45
France	33
Germany West	49
Greece	30 (+1hr)
Hong Kong	852 (+7hrs)
India	91 (+4hrs 30mins)
Ireland	353 (-1hr)
Israel	972 (+1hr)
Japan	81 (+8hrs)
Netherlands	31
New Zealand	64 (+11hrs)
Norway	47
Pakistan	92 (+4hrs)
Portugal	351 (-1hr)
Singapore	65 (+7hrs)
Spain	34
Sweden	46
Switzerland	41
UK	44 (-1hr)
USA	1 (-6hrs–11hrs)

Conversion charts
Italy uses the metric system of measurement.

Length			**Mass (weight)**		
centimetres (cm)	cm or in	inches (in)	kilograms (kg)	kg or lb	pounds (lb)
2.54	= in 1 cm =	0.394	0.454	= lb 1 kg =	2.205
5.08	2	0.787	0.907	2	4.409
7.62	3	1.181	1.361	3	6.614
10.16	4	1.575	1.814	4	8.819
12.70	5	1.969	2.268	5	11.023
15.24	6	2.362	2.722	6	13.228
17.70	7	2.756	3.175	7	15.432
20.32	8	3.150	3.629	8	17.637
22.86	9	3.543	4.082	9	19.842
25.40	10	3.937	4.536	10	22.046
50.80	20	7.874	9.072	20	44.092
76.20	30	11.811	13.608	30	66.139
101.60	40	15.748	18.144	40	88.185
127.00	50	19.685	22.680	50	110.231

Distance			**Volume**		
kilometres (km)	km or miles	miles	litres	litres or UK galls	UK galls
1.609	= m 1 km =	0.621	4.546	= l 1 gall =	0.220
3.219	2	1.243	9.092	2	0.440
4.828	3	1.864	13.638	3	0.660
6.437	4	2.485	18.184	4	0.880
8.047	5	3.107	22.730	5	1.100
9.656	6	3.728	27.276	6	1.320
11.265	7	4.350	31.822	7	1.540
12.875	8	4.971	36.368	8	1.760
14.484	9	5.592	40.914	9	1.980
16.093	10	6.214	45.460	10	2.200
32.187	20	12.427	90.919	20	4.399
48.280	30	18.641	136.379	30	6.599
64.374	40	24.855	181.839	40	8.799
80.467	50	31.069	227.298	50	10.998

Temperature

32	40	50	60	70	75	85	95	105	140	175	212	°F
0	5	10	15	20	25	30	35	40	60	80	100	°C

Index